STUDY GUIDE TO ACCOMPANY McCONNELL
ECONOMICS

STUDY GUIDE TO ACCOMPANY McCONNELL
ECONOMICS
SIXTH EDITION

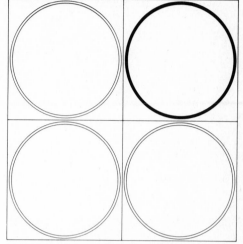

ROBERT C. BINGHAM

Professor of Economics
Kent State University

McGRAW-HILL BOOK COMPANY

New York   St. Louis   San Francisco   Auckland   Düsseldorf   Johannesburg   Kuala Lumpur   London
Mexico   Montreal   New Delhi   Panama   Paris   São Paulo   Singapore   Sydney   Tokyo   Toronto

This book was set in News Gothic by Monotype Composition Company, Inc.
The editors were J. S. Dietrich, Michael Elia, and Edwin Hanson;
the designer was J. E. O'Connor;
the production supervisor was Leroy A. Young.
George Banta Company, Inc., was printer and binder.

STUDY GUIDE TO ACCOMPANY McCONNELL
ECONOMICS

ISBN 0-07-005294-8

567890 BABA 79876

TO PQK

CONTENTS

HOW TO USE
THE STUDY GUIDE
IN ORDER TO
LEARN ECONOMICS

This *Study Guide* was designed to help you read and understand Campbell R. McConnell's textbook, *Economics: Principles, Problems, and Policies*, Sixth Edition. If used properly, a guide can be a great aid to you in what is probably your first course in economics.

No one pretends that the study of economics is easy, but it can be made easier. Of course a study guide will not do your work for you, and its use is no substitute for reading the text. You must be willing to read the text, spend time on the subject, and work at learning if you wish to understand economics.

Many students do read their text and work hard on their economics course and still fail to learn the subject. This is because principles of economics is a new subject for them, and they have had no previous experience in learning economics. They want to learn but do not know just how to go about it. Here is where the *Study Guide* can come to their assistance. Let us first see what the *Study Guide* contains and then how to use it.

■ WHAT THE STUDY GUIDE IS

The *Study Guide* contains forty-five chapters —one for each chapter in the text—and an ANSWER SECTION. Each of the chapters has seven parts:

1. An *introduction* explains what is in the chapter of the text and how its subject matter is related to material in earlier and later chapters. It points out topics to which you should give special attention, and reemphasizes difficult or important principles and facts.

2. A *chapter outline* shows how the chapter is organized and summarizes briefly the essential points made in the chapter.

3. A list of the *important terms and concepts* found in the chapter points out what you must be able to define in order to understand the material in the chapter.

4. *Fill-in questions* (short-answer and list questions) help you to learn and remember the crucial and important generalizations and facts in the chapter.

5. *Problems and projects* assist you in learning and understanding economic relationships and get you to think about certain economic problems.

6. *Objective questions* (true-false and multiple-choice) can be used to test yourself on the material in the chapter.

7. *Discussion questions* can be used to test yourself, to identify important questions in the chapter, and to prepare for examinations.

■ HOW TO STUDY AND LEARN WITH THE HELP OF THE STUDY GUIDE

For best results, quickly read the introduction, outline, and list of terms and concepts in the *Study Guide* before you read the chapter in the text. Then read the chapter in the text slowly, keeping one eye on the outline and the list of terms and concepts. Always read with pencil in hand and use your textbook as if you expected to sell it for wastepaper at the end of the year. The outline in the *Study Guide* contains only the major points in the chapter. Outline the chapter as you read it by identifying the major *and the minor* points and by placing appropriate numbers or letters (such as I or A or 1 or a) in the margins. It is also wise to underline the major and minor points in the chapter and to circle important terms and concepts. When you have completed the chapter, you will have the chapter outlined and your underlining will give you a set of notes on the chapter. It is not necessary to keep a separate notebook for textbook notes or outlines. Be careful to underline only the really important or summary statements.

After you have read the chapter in the text through once, turn again to the introduction, outline, and list of terms and concepts in the *Study Guide*. Reread the introduction and outline. Does everything there make sense? If not, return to the text and reread the topics that you do not remember well or that still confuse you. Look at the outline. Try to recall each of the minor topics or points that were contained in the text under each of the major points in the outline. When you come to the list of terms and concepts, go over them one by one. Define or explain each to yourself and then look it up in the text chapter. Check your own definition or explanation with that in the text. Make any correction or change in your own definition or explanation that is necessary. It is a good idea to put the page number or numbers on which the term or concept is discussed in the text after each term and concept on the list.

When you have done all this, you will have a pretty fair general idea of what is in the text chapter. Now take a look at the short-answer questions, the problems and projects, and the objective questions. Tackle each of these three sections one at a time, using the following procedure. (1) Answer as many questions as you can without looking in the text or in the answer section. (2) Check the text for whatever help you need. It is a good idea to do more than merely look for answers in the text; reread any section for which you were not able to answer questions. (3) Then consult the answer section for the correct answers and

reread any section of the text for which you missed questions.

The questions in these three sections are not all of equal difficulty. Do not expect to get them all right the first time. Some are designed to pinpoint things of importance which you will probably miss the first time you read the text and to get you to read about them again. None of the questions is unimportant. Even those that have no definite answers will bring you to grips with many important economic questions and increase your understanding of economic principles and problems.

In answering the discussion questions—for which no answers are given—it is not necessary to write out answers. All you need to do is mentally outline your answer. For the more difficult discussion questions you may want to write out a brief outline of the answer or a full answer. Do not avoid the difficult questions just because they are more work. Answering these questions is often the most valuable work a student can do toward acquiring an understanding of economic relationships and principles.

■ SOME FINAL WORDS

Perhaps the method of using the *Study Guide* outlined above seems like a lot of work. It is. Study and learning necessarily entail work on your part. This is a fact you should willingly accept.

After you have used the *Study Guide* to study three or four chapters, you will find that some sections are of more value to you than others. Let your own experience determine how you will use it. But do not discontinue use of the *Study Guide* after three or four chapters merely because you are not sure whether it is helping you. Stick with it.

In addition to the material in the *Study Guide*, there are questions at the end of each chapter in the text. Some of these questions are similar to questions in the *Study Guide*, but none is identical. It will be worthwhile for you to examine all the questions at the end of each chapter and to work out or outline answers for them. The student who has trouble with the problems in the *Study Guide* will find the end-of-chapter problems useful in determining whether he has actually mastered his difficulties. All students will find many of

HOW TO USE THE STUDY GUIDE IN ORDER TO LEARN ECONOMICS xi

the end-of-chapter questions more thought-provoking than the discussion questions in the *Study Guide*.

For students who either have trouble with or wish to learn more rapidly the sections of the text containing explanations of economic theory (or principles), let me recommend my *Economic Concepts: A Programmed Approach*. A programmed book is a learning device which speeds and increases comprehension. Its use will greatly expand the student's understanding of economics.

Robert C. Bingham

STUDY GUIDE TO ACCOMPANY McCONNELL
ECONOMICS

THE NATURE AND METHOD
OF ECONOMICS

Chapter 1 introduces the reader to the study of economics. Its aim is to explain the subject matter of economics and the methods economists employ in the study of this subject matter.

While this chapter attempts to indicate the value to be derived from the study of economics and the importance of economic questions and problems to every individual, the heart of the chapter is the discussion of economic principles. Economic principles are generalizations based on facts; but, because the subject matter of economics is human behavior and because the economist cannot employ laboratory experiments to test his generalizations, these principles are always imprecise and subject to numerous exceptions. Economics is a science but it is not an exact science.

If the study of economics is to be of any worth to a student, it is necessary to understand from the very beginning that economic principles are simplifications—approximations —of a very complex real world and that both the formulation and application of these principles present many opportunities for the making of serious mistakes. Economic principles are not the answers to economic questions but are tools—intellectual tools—for analyzing economic problems and finding pol-

icies to solve these problems. Selection of the economic policies to follow depends not only upon economic principles but also upon the value judgments of society—that is, upon the goals of the economy.

Pages 12 to 13 of the textbook outline a few of the almost innumerable errors of commission and omission of which the beginner in economics ought to beware. The study of economics is difficult enough without compounding the difficulty with emotional, logical, and semantical errors.

■ CHAPTER OUTLINE

1. Citizens in a democracy must understand elementary economics in order to understand the present-day problems of their society and to make intelligent decisions when they vote. Economics is an academic rather than a vocational subject, but a knowledge of it is valuable to businessmen, consumers, and workers.

2. Economists gather relevant facts to obtain economic principles that may be used to formulate policies which will solve economic problems.

a. Descriptive economics is the gathering of relevant facts about the production, exchange, and consumption of goods and services.

1

b. Economic theory is the analysis of the facts and the derivation of economic principles. These principles are generalizations and abstractions (or approximations) of reality.

c. Policy economics is the combination of economic principles and economic values (or goals) to control economic events.

3. Economists in recent decades have rapidly expanded our economic knowledge; but a number of people have, for a variety of reasons, criticized economics.

4. Straight thinking in the study and use of economic principles requires strict application of the rules of logic—rules in which personal emotions are irrelevant, if not detrimental. There are at least nine pitfalls encountered in studying and applying economic principles.

■ IMPORTANT TERMS

Descriptive economics	**Mutually exclusive goals**
Economic principle (law)	**Complementary goals**
Economic theory (analysis)	**Emotionally loaded terminology**
Generalization	**Dual terminology**
Economic model	**Social point of view**
Abstraction	**Fallacy of composition**
"Other things equal" assumption	**Macroeconomics**
Directly related	**Microeconomics**
Inversely related	***Post hoc, ergo propter hoc* fallacy**
Applied (policy) economics	**Intentions vs. realizations**
Economy policy	**Expectations (anticipations)**
Value judgment	

■ FILL-IN QUESTIONS

1. The study of economics is the study of the _____,

_____,

and _____
of goods and services.

2. Economic laws are _____
concerning man's economic behavior and as

such necessarily involve _____
from reality.

3. Economic laws are imprecise and subject to exceptions because _____

_____

4. Economic principles enable the economist to predict the result of a certain economic act or of certain economic behavior; this ability to predict is valuable because it makes it possible to _____

5. Six widely accepted economic goals in the United States are _____,

_____, _____,

_____, _____,

and _____

6. The three steps involved in the formulation of economic policy are:

a. _____

b. _____

c. _____

7. What three dangers are inherent in the construction and application of economic models?

a. _____

b. _____

c. _____

8. The correct economic policy to employ today to achieve a given end may be inappropriate for the achievement of the same end tomorrow because _____

_____

9. Economists often use "dual terminology." This means that they _____

10. Macroeconomics is concerned with the

_____

output of the economy and the _____
level of prices, while microeconomics is concerned with output in a(n) _____

_____

and the price of a(n) _____

_____

■ PROBLEMS AND PROJECTS

1. "In 1973 the demand for wheat in the United States increased and caused the price of wheat throughout the United States to rise." This is a *specific* instance of a more *general* economic principle. Of which economic *generalization* is this a particular

example? _____

_____

_____

2. Following is a list of factors—economic and noneconomic—which may or may not be related to the number of automobiles produced in the United States in a year and the average price at which the automobiles are sold. In the space to the right of each factor indicate whether you think the factor is relevant (R) or irrelevant (I) and whether in your opinion the factor is economic (E) or noneconomic (N).

a. The cost of living in Detroit _____
b. The price of the rotary engine Mazda

_____

c. The attitude of the oil-producing nations toward the foreign policies of the United

States _____
d. The average price of stocks on the New

York Stock Exchange _____
e. The rate at which corporation profits are

taxed _____
f. The extent to which automation has been introduced into the production of automobiles

_____

g. The price of gasoline in the United States

_____

h. The size of the budget deficit of the

United States government _____
i. The percentage of the United States pop-

ulation living in rural areas _____

j. Bus fares in Hoboken, New Jersey _____

k. The provisions of the Federal laws requiring the installation of antipollution and

safety devices in new cars _____
l. The star of a television program spon-

sored by the Ford Motor Company _____
m. The chief of the Antitrust Division of the

U.S. Department of Justice _____
n. The price of wheat in Kansas City, Mis-

souri _____

3. Below are several current economic questions or problems. Indicate in a few words what you believe the answer to the question is or what should be done to solve the problem. You are not really expected to have, at this point in your study of economics, well-thought-out and/or correct answers, but you probably have some opinions or ideas on these questions and problems.

a. How to prevent inflation. _____

_____

b. How to prevent unemployment. _____

_____

c. Whether to impose a ceiling on the price

of gasoline in the United States. _____

_____

d. How to reduce poverty in the United

States. _____
e. How to help underdeveloped and backward nations to raise their standards of living.

_____

f. Whether the public (national) debt is too

large. _____

4. Examine your answers to question 3, using the following criteria.

a. Is your solution or answer based on what others have told you the solution or answer

should be? _____
b. Is your solution or answer practical? Is

it politically feasible? _____
c. Are you employing a theory to arrive at

a solution or answer? _____
d. Do you need more facts to answer the

question? If so, what kind of facts? _____

_____

e. Are you guilty of being an "economic quack," or biased? Have you based your answer on some preconceived notions which might be completely wrong? _____

5. Below are four statements. Each of them is an example of one of the pitfalls frequently encountered in the study of economics. Indicate in the space following each statement the type of pitfall involved.

a. "Thrift (or saving) promotes the welfare of the economy." _____

b. "An unemployed worker can find a job if he looks diligently and conscientiously for employment; therefore, all unemployed workers can find employment if they are diligent and conscientious in looking for a job." _____

_____

c. Jones: "Underdeveloped nations are unable to increase their standards of living because they are unable to accumulate capital." *Smith:* "This is not correct. They are unable to increase their standards of living because they are consuming all they produce." _____

d. "The stock market crash of 1929 was followed by and resulted in 10 years of depression." _____

6. Below are two exercises in making graphs. On the graphs plot the economic relationships contained in each exercise. Be sure to label each axis of the graph and to indicate the unit of measurement and scale used on each axis.

a.

National income, billions of dollars	Consumption expenditures, billions of dollars
$100	$100
150	145
200	185
250	220
300	250
350	275
400	300

Graph national income on the horizontal axis and consumption expenditures on the vertical axis; connect the seven points and label the curve "Consumption Schedule."

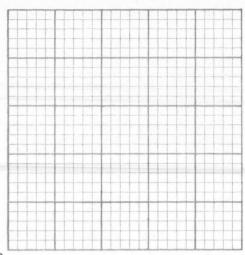

0

b.

Rate of interest, %	Investment expenditures, billions of dollars
8	$15
7	17
6	20
5	24
4	29
3	35
2	42

Graph investment expenditures on the horizontal axis and the rate of interest on the vertical axis; connect the seven points and label the curve "Investment Schedule."

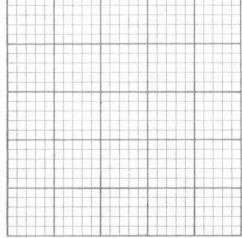

0

c. The relationship between national income and consumption expenditures is a(n) _____ one and the Consumption Schedule a(n) _____ sloping curve.

d. The relationship between the rate of interest and investment expenditures is a(n)

_____ one and the Investment Schedule is a(n) _____ sloping curve.

■ SELF-TEST

Circle the T if the statement is true, the F if it is false.

1. Economics is academic and of little value because it does not teach the student how to earn a living.   **T   F**

2. Economic principles are derived from the facts of economic behavior.   **T   F**

3. Economics deals with the activities by which man earns a living and improves his standard of living.   **T   F**

4. The ability to predict the economic consequences of various acts is important because it enables both businessmen and government officials to formulate policies that will tend to bring about the results they desire.   **T   F**

5. The first step in the formulation of an economic policy, the statement of the goal or desired result, may be an occasion for disagreement because different people may have different and conflicting goals.   **T   F**

6. Once a single goal or end has been determined as the sole objective of economic policy, there is seldom any question of which policy to adopt to achieve that goal.   **T   F**

7. If you speak of "capital" to the average person, he understands you to be referring to money. The economist, therefore, is obligated to use the term "capital" to mean money.
                                             T   F

8. "Business expects to be able to sell 10,000 pairs of shoes this year and so produces 10,000 pairs. They actually sell 12,000 pairs." This illustrates the difference between macroeconomics and microeconomics.   **T   F**

9. It is relatively easy to distinguish propositions involving economic quackery from those based on scientific economic principles by a careful examination of economic statistics and by testing the propositions in the harsh light of economic reality.   **T   F**

10. The Law of Demand is an example of an economic policy.   **T   F**

Underscore the letter that corresponds to the best answer.

1. Economics is a practical field of study in several ways. Which one of the following is *not* an element of its practicality? *(a)* every person affects and is affected by the operation of the economy; *(b)* every person has to earn a living in some manner, and economics develops skills and trains the student in the art of making a living; *(c)* every person in a democracy is confronted with its political problems, many of which are economic in nature; *(d)* every person who understands the overall operation of the economy is in a better position to solve his personal economic problems.

2. One economic principle states that the lower the price of a commodity, the greater will be the quantity of the commodity which consumers will wish to purchase. On the basis of this principle *alone*, it can be concluded that *(a)* if the price of mink coats falls, more mink coats will be purchased by consumers; *(b)* if the price of mink coats falls, Mrs. James will purchase two instead of one; *(c)* if the price of mink coats falls and there are no important changes in the other factors affecting their demand, the public will probably purchase a greater quantity of mink coats than it did at the higher price; *(d)* if more mink coats are purchased this month than last month, it is because the price of mink coats has fallen.

3. Knowing that as the price of a commodity rises the quantity of the commodity sold decreases and that the imposition of a tax on a commodity increases its price, the economist concludes that if the government taxes cigarettes, fewer cigarettes will be sold. This is an example of: *(a)* prediction; *(b)* control; *(c)* policy; *(d)* the fallacy of composition.

4. An economic model is *not*: *(a)* an ideal type of economy or an economic policy for which we ought to work; (b) a tool which the economist employs to enable him to predict; (c) one or a collection of economic principles; (d) an explanation of how the economy or a part of the economy functions in its essential details.

5. Which of the following is *not* a danger to be encountered in the construction or application of economic models? (a) it may contain irrelevant facts and omit more relevant data; (b) it may come to be accepted as "what ought to be" rather than as "what is"; (c) it may be overly simplified and so be a very poor approximation of the reality it explains; (d) it may result in a conclusion that is unacceptable to the citizens or the government of a nation.

6. Which of the following economic goals is subject to reasonably accurate measurement? (a) economic security; (b) full employment; (c) economic freedom; (d) an equitable distribution of income.

7. To say that two economic goals are mutually exclusive means that: (a) it is not possible to achieve both goals; (b) these goals are not accepted as goals in the U.S.S.R. (c) the achievement of one of the goals results in the achievement of the other; (d) it is possible to quantify both goals.

8. During World War II the United States employed price controls to prevent inflation; this was referred to as "a fascist and arbitrary restriction of economic freedom" by some and as "a necessary and democratic means of preventing ruinous inflation" by others. Both labels are examples of: (a) economic quackery; (b) the fallacy of composition; (c) the misuse of commonsense definitions; (d) emotionally loaded terminology.

9. The government increases its expenditures for road-construction equipment and the average price of this equipment falls. To reason that the lower price was due to the increase in government expenditures may be an example of: (a) the *post hoc, ergo propter hoc* fallacy; (b) the fallacy of composition; (c) a generalization that is true during a depression but untrue during prosperity; (d) using dual terminology.

10. If an individual determines to save a larger percentage of his income, he will no doubt be able to save more money. To reason, therefore, that if all individuals determine to save a larger percentage of their incomes they will all be able to save more money is an example of: (a) the *post hoc, ergo propter hoc* fallacy; (b) the fallacy of composition; (c) a generalization that is true during a depression but untrue during prosperity; (d) using dual terminology.

■ DISCUSSION QUESTIONS

1. What are the principal reasons for studying economics?

2. What is the relationship between facts and theory? Can a theory be *proved?* Can a theory be *disproved?*

3. Define and explain the relationships between descriptive economics, economic theory, and applied economics.

4. What is a "laboratory experiment under controlled conditions"? Does the science of economies have any kind of laboratory? Why do economists employ the "other things equal" assumption?

5. What is meant by an "economic model"? Can you think of any models employed in the other courses you are taking (or have taken)? (Omit from your consideration courses in the Art Department.)

6. Why are economic principles and models necessarily abstract and generalized?

7. In what ways are the construction and application of economic models dangerous?

8. What procedure should be followed in formulating sound economic policies?

9. "Good economic policy depends upon the development of good economic theories." Is this true? Are good economic theories all that is necessary to bring about improved economic conditions?

10. Of the six economic goals of American capitalism listed in the text, which one would you *rank* first, second, third, etc.? Would you add any other goals to this list? If economic goals 2 and 3 were mutually exclusive, which goal would you prefer? Why? If goals 1 and 4

were mutually exclusive, which would you prefer? Why?

11. What evidence is there "that economics has achieved rapid and significant progress in recent decades"? Despite this progress economics has been the subject of a good deal of criticism. Why?

12. Explain briefly the difference between macroeconomics and microeconomics.

AN INTRODUCTION
TO THE ECONOMIZING PROBLEM

The aim of Chapter 2 is to explain the central problem of economics and the Five Fundamental Questions into which this central problem can be divided.

The central problem of economics is that resources—the ultimate means of satisfying material wants—are scarce *relative* to the insatiable wants of society. Economics as a science is concerned with the study of the various aspects of the behavior of society in its effort to allocate the scarce resources—land, labor, capital, and entrepreneurial ability—in order to satisfy as best it can its unlimited desire for consumption. This basic problem becomes, in reality, five problems: what to produce, how to produce it, for whom to produce it, the achievement of full employment of resources, and the maintenance of economic flexibility.

The production possibilities table and curve are used in this chapter to illustrate the meaning of the scarcity of resources and of increasing costs. It is only an illustrative device, but it should help the student to understand the nature of several economic concepts and problems.

Every economy is faced with the problem of scarce resources and has to find answers to the Five Fundamental Questions. But no economy arrives at solutions to its fundamental economic problems in the same way that another economy does. Between the extremes of pure laissez faire capitalism and communism lie various economic systems; all systems are simply different devices—different methods of organization—for finding answers or systems which are employed to find economic answers; Chapters 3 to 8 explain in greater detail how the American economy is built and operates.

Throughout Chapter 2 of the textbook there are numerous economic definitions and classifications. It would be well for the student to learn these definitions and classifications *now*. They will be used later on and it will be necessary for the student to know and understand them if he is to understand what follows.

■ CHAPTER OUTLINE

1. The bases upon which the study of economics rests are two facts.
   a. Society's material wants are unlimited.
   b. The economic resources which are the ultimate means of satisfying these wants are scarce in relation to the wants.

2. Economics, then, is the study of how society's scarce resources are used (administered) to obtain the greatest satisfaction of its material wants.

a. To be efficient in the use of its resources an economy must achieve both full employment and full production.

b. The production possibilities table indicates the alternative combinations of goods and services an economy is capable of producing when it has achieved full employment and full production.

c. The data contained in the production possibilities table can be plotted on a graph to obtain a production possibilities curve.

d. Which of these alternative combinations society chooses—which product-mix it selects—depends upon the preferences of that society; and preferences are subjective and nonscientific.

e. Because resources are not completely adaptable to alternative uses, the production of any product is subject to the law of increasing costs.

3. The following modifications make the production possibilities concept more realistic.

a. The failure to achieve full employment and full production reduces the output of the economy.

b. Improvements in technology and increased amounts of resources expand the output the economy is capable of producing.

c. The combination of goods and services an economy chooses to produce now helps to determine its production possibilities in the future.

4. Faced with unlimited wants and scarce resources, every economy must find answers for the Five Fundamental Economic Questions: what goods and services to produce, how to produce them, how to divide the total output among the members of society, how to bring about the full employment of its resources, and how to assure a flexible economic system.

5. Different economic systems—capitalism, socialism, and communism—are based on different philosophies and institutions and employ different methods to obtain answers to these Five Fundamental Questions.

■ IMPORTANT TERMS

The economizing problem

Unlimited wants

Scarce resources

Land, capital, labor, and entrepreneurial ability

Real capital

Money (financial) capital

Rental income, interest income, wages, and profit

Factors of production

Economics

Full employment

Full production

Unemployment

Disguised unemployment

Consumer goods

Capital goods

Economic efficiency

Production possibilities table

Production possibilities curve

Law of increasing costs

Five Fundamental Economic Questions

Economic flexibility

Laissez faire capitalism

Liberal or democratic socialism

Communism or authoritarian socialism

Opportunity cost

Economic growth

■ FILL-IN QUESTIONS

1. The two fundamental facts which provide the foundations of economics are:

a. _____

b. _____

2. Complete the following classification of resources:

a. _____

(1) _____

(2) _____

b. _____

(1) _____

(2) _____

3. The incomes of individuals are received from supplying resources. Four types of incomes are _____, _____, _____, and _____

4. Economics can be defined as _____ _____

5. When a production possibilities table or curve is constructed, three assumptions are made. These assumptions are:

a. _____

b. _____

c. _____

6. Both consumer goods and capital goods satisfy material wants. However, consumer goods satisfy human wants _____ while capital goods satisfy human wants ____

_____

7. Below is a production possibilities curve for tractors and suits of clothing.

Tractors

0   Suits of clothing

a. If the economy moves from point A to point B it will produce (more, fewer) _____ _____ tractors and (more, fewer) _____ suits of clothing.
b. If the economy is producing at point X, some of the resources of the economy are either _____ or _____
c. If the economy moves from point X to point B (more, fewer) _____ tractors and (more, fewer) _____ suits will be produced.
d. If the economy is to produce at point Y, it must either _____
or _____

8. The more an economy consumes of its current production, the (more, less) _____ it will be capable of producing in future years, other things being equal.

9. The cost of producing a commodity tends to increase as more of the commodity is produced because _____

_____

10. Four functions which the entrepreneur performs are:

a. _____

b. _____

c. _____

d. _____

11. List the Five Fundamental Questions which every economy must attempt to answer.

a. _____

b. _____

c. _____

d. _____

e. _____

12. The quantity of other goods and services an economy must go without in order to produce low-cost housing is the _____ of producing low-cost housing.

13. Unemployment can take two forms: ____

_____

unemployment and _____ unemployment.

14. Economic efficiency requires that there be both _____ of resources and _____

15. The extent to which resources are used in an economy depends upon the degree to which the economy is _____ to use its resources and the extent to which it is _____ to use its resources.

16. An economy needs flexibility because

_____,

_____,

and _____ are constantly changing.

17. All the combinations of products shown in the production possibilities table (or on the curve) can be achieved only if there are both full employment and full production in the economy; the best combination of products

depends upon the _____

of that society and is a _____
matter.

18. Different societies have different output

_____ and employ different economic

_____ and _____
to achieve them. The two extreme systems of economic organization in the modern, industrially advanced nations are _____

_____ and _____

■ PROBLEMS AND PROJECTS

1. Below is a list of resources. Indicate in the space to the right of each whether the resource is land, capital (C), labor, entrepre-

neurial ability (EA), or some combinations of these.

a. Fishing grounds in the North Atlantic

_____

b. A cash register in a retail store _____

c. Uranium deposits in South Africa _____

d. An irrigation ditch in Nebraska _____

e. The work performed by the late Henry Ford _____

f. The oxygen breathed by human beings

_____

g. The U.S. Steel plant in Gary, Indiana

_____

h. The goods on the shelf of a retail store

_____

i. The work done by a laborer on an assembly line _____

j. The tasks accomplished in perfecting color television for commercial sales _____

2. A production possibilities table for two commodities, wheat and automobiles, follows.

0

The table is constructed employing the usual three assumptions. Wheat is measured in units of 100,000 bushels and automobiles in units of 100,000.

Combination	Wheat	Automobiles
A	0	7
B	7	6
C	13	5
D	18	4
E	22	3
F	25	2
G	27	1
H	28	0

a. Following the general rules for making graphs (Chapter 1), plot the data in the table on the graph (page 11) to obtain a production possibilities curve. Place wheat on the vertical axis and automobiles on the horizontal axis.

b. Fill in the table below showing the *opportunity cost per unit* of producing the 1st through the 7th automobile.

Automobiles	Cost of production
1st	————
2d	————
3d	————
4th	————
5th	————
6th	————
7th	————

3. Below is a production possibilities curve. Draw on this graph:

a. A production possibilities curve which indicates greater efficiency in the production of good A.

b. A production possibilities curve which indicates greater efficiency in the production of good B.

c. A production possibilities curve which indicates an increase in the resources available to the economy.

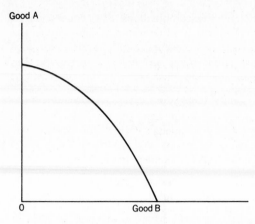

Good A

Good B

0

4. Below is a list of economic goods. Indicate in the space to the right of each whether the good is a consumer good (CON), a capital good (CAP), or whether the answer depends (DEP) upon who is using it and for what purpose.

a. An automobile ———

b. A tractor ———

c. A taxicab ———

d. A house ———

e. A factory building ———

f. An office building ———

g. An ironing board ———

h. An icebox ———

i. A telephone ———

j. A quart of Scotch whisky ———

k. A cash register ———

l. A screwdriver ———

■ SELF-TEST
Circle the T if the statement is true, the F if it is false.

1. The wants with which economics is concerned include only those wants which can be satisfied by goods and services.   **T   F**

2. Resources are scarce because society's material wants are unlimited.   **T   F**

3. Money is a resource and is classified as "capital."   **T   F**

4. It is not possible for an economy capable

of producing just two goods to increase its production of both. **T F**

5. The cost of producing a good tends to increase as more of it is produced because resources less suitable to its production must be employed. **T F**

6. At full employment and full production, the more capital goods an economy produces today, the smaller the amount of consumer goods it will be able to produce today. **T F**

7. If an economy increases the percentage of the current output it consumes, its production possibilities curve will move to the left. **T F**

8. The more capital goods an economy produces today, the greater will be the total output of all goods it can produce in the future, other things being equal. **T F**

9. The opportunity cost of producing antipollution devices is the other goods and services the economy is unable to produce because it has decided to produce these devices. **T F**

10. It is economically desirable to have unemployed resources at the outbreak of a war because resources need not be shifted from consumer-good production in order to produce military goods. **T F**

Underscore the letter that corresponds to the best answer.

1. An "innovator" is defined as an entrepreneur who: *(a)* makes basic policy decisions in a business firm; *(b)* combines factors of production to produce a good or service; *(c)* invents a new product or process for producing a product; *(d)* introduces new products on the market or employs a new method to produce a product.

2. A farmer who produces his crops by inefficient methods is: *(a)* an unemployed worker; *(b)* an underemployed worker; *(c)* a fully employed worker; *(d)* an apparently unemployed worker.

3. At point A on the production possibilities curve in the next illustration: *(a)* more wheat than tractors is being produced; *(b)* more tractors than wheat are being produced; *(c)* the economy is employing all its resources; *(d)* the economy is not employing all its resources.

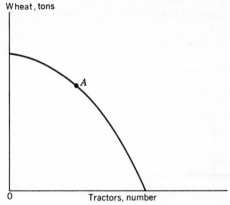

Wheat, tons

Tractors, number

4. If the production possibilities curve on the graph below moves from position A to position B, then: *(a)* the economy has increased the efficiency with which it produces wheat; *(b)* the economy has increased the efficiency with which it produces tractors; *(c)* the economy has put to work previously idle resources; *(d)* the economy has gone from a full-employment situation to a less-than-full-employment situation.

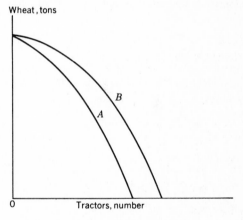

Wheat, tons

Tractors, number

5. If there is an increase in the resources available within the economy: *(a)* more goods and services will be produced in the economy; *(b)* the economy will be capable of producing more goods and services; *(c)* the standard of living in the economy will rise; *(d)* the technological efficiency of the economy will improve.

6. Which one of the following is *not* one of the Five Fundamental Economic Questions which every economy must answer? *(a)* determining what is to be produced; *(b)* deciding the level of resource use; (c) distributing output; (d) enforcing the law of increasing costs.

7. During the Middle Ages the feudal society found answers to the Fundamental Economic Questions through a system of: (a) custom and tradition; (b) laissez faire capitalism; (c) democratic socialism; (d) communism.

8. If the economic system of a nation is liberal or democratic socialism, there is: (a) public ownership and control of the bulk of industry and agriculture; (b) virtually no government planning or control; (c) a mixture of public and private ownership and decision making; (d) reliance on the price system only as a means of implementing central planning.

9. The combination of products in a society's production possibilities table which is its optimum product-mix depends upon that society's: (a) resources; (b) technology; (c) level of employment; (d) values or priorities.

10. An economy is efficient when it has achieved: (a) full employment; (b) full production; (c) either full employment or full production; (d) both full employment and full production.

■ DISCUSSION QUESTIONS

1. Explain what is meant by the "economizing problem." Why are resources scarce?

2. In what sense are wants satiable and in what sense are they insatiable?

3. What are the four economic resources? How is each of these resources defined? What is the income earned by each of them called?

4. Every individual has his own personal economic problem—just as every economy has its economic problem. How would you state this individual economic problem?

5. When is a society economically efficient?

What is meant by "full production" and how does it differ from "full employment"?

6. Why cannot an economist determine which of the combinations in the production possibilities table is "best"? What determines the optimum product-mix? How and why do the product-mixes of the U.S. and the U.S.S.R. differ?

7. Explain the difference between a "good" and a "service."

8. Why is the production possibilities curve "concave" to the origin? What would such a curve show if it were convex to the origin or a straight line connecting the two axes?

9. What three assumptions are made in drawing a production possibilities curve or schedule? How do technological advance and an increased supply of resources in the economy affect the curve or schedule?

10. What is the important relationship between the *composition* of the economy's current output and the *location* of future production possibilities curves?

11. Many people do not spend all their income on goods and services but rather save some of it. Does this indicate to you that their desires for goods and services have been fully satisfied, or does it indicate that money saved satisfies some other human desire?

12. What is opportunity cost? What is the law of increasing cost? Why do costs increase?

13. What are the Five Fundamental Economic Questions and how are they related to the economizing problem?

14. Laissez faire capitalism, democratic socialism, and communism differ in their underlying assumptions, institutions, and methods for solving their fundamental economic problems. Contrast these economic systems.

PURE CAPITALISM
AND THE CIRCULAR FLOW

Chapter 3 has three principal aims: to outline the six ideological and institutional characteristics of pure capitalism, to explain three practices found in all modern economics, and to sketch in extremely simple terms the fundamental operation of a capitalistic economy. A more detailed explanation of the institutions, practices, and behavior of the American economy—which is not *purely* capitalistic—is found in the chapters that follow. If the aims of this chapter are accomplished, the student can begin to understand the system and methods employed by our economy to find answers to the Five Fundamental Economic Questions discussed in Chapter 2.

The resources of the American economy are owned by its citizens, who are free to use them as they wish in their own self-interest; prices and markets serve to express the self-interests of resource owners, consumers, and business firms; and competition serves to regulate self-interest—to prevent the self-interest of any person or any group from working to the disadvantage of the economy as a whole and to make self-interest work for the benefit of the entire economy.

Based on comparative advantage and specialization, trade is made more convenient by the use of money as a medium of exchange. Trade increases the production possible in an economy with a given quantity of resources.

Trade also increases the interdependence of the members of the economy. The principle of comparative advantage is the basis for all trade between individuals, firms, regions, and nations; and the student ought to be sure to understand what is meant by comparative advantage, how specialization is determined on the basis of comparative advantage, and why trade and specialization tend to increase the total production of the economy.

The circular-flow-of-income model (or diagram) is a device which illustrates for a capitalistic economy the relation between households and businesses, the flow of money and economic goods and services between households and businesses, their dual role as buyers and sellers, and the two basic types of markets essential to the capitalistic process.

Understand these essentials of the economic skeleton first; then a little flesh—a little more reality, a little more detail—can be added to the bones. Understanding the skeleton makes it much easier to understand the whole body and its functioning.

■ CHAPTER OUTLINE

1. The American economy is not pure capitalism, but it is a close approximation of pure capitalism. Pure capitalism has six important

peculiarities that distinguish it from other economic systems.

2. In common with all other advanced economies of the world, the American economy has three major characteristics.
 a. It employs complicated and advanced methods of production and vast amounts of capital equipment to produce goods and services.
 b. It is a highly specialized economy; specialization is based on the principle of comparative advantage and increases the productive efficiency of the economy.
 c. It also uses money extensively to facilitate trade and specialization.

3. The circular flow model is a device used to clarify the relationships between households and business firms in a purely capitalistic system, the part that each of them plays in the economy, and their respective roles in the resource and product markets.

■ IMPORTANT TERMS

Private property	Terms of trade
Self-interest	Money
Competition	Medium of exchange
Freedom of choice	Barter
Freedom of enterprise	Coincidence of wants
Roundabout production	Circular flow of income
Specialization	Household
Division of labor	Resource market
Comparative cost	Product market
Comparative advantage	

■ FILL-IN QUESTIONS

1. The institution of _____ entails the ownership of the means of production by private individuals and institutions.

2. Two basic freedoms encountered in a capitalistic economy are the freedoms of _____

_____

and _____

3. Self-interest means that each economic

unit _____

_____;
this self-interest might work to the disadvantage of the economy as a whole if it were not

regulated and constrained by _____

4. According to the economist, competition is present if two conditions prevail; these two conditions are:

 a. _____

 b. _____

5. If the number of buyers and sellers in a market is large, no single buyer or seller is

able to _____

6. In a capitalistic economy no one individual determines the answers to the fundamental questions of what and how to produce and how the product will be distributed. These decisions are made by many individuals and

are made effective through a _____

_____

system in a _____
type of economy.

7. In a capitalistic economy new products and more efficient methods of production are

introduced by _____

_____

motivated by the desire for _____

_____

8. The three practices or institutions common to all modern economies are _____

_____,

_____,

and _____

9. If an economy engages in extensive specialization the individuals living in the economy are extremely _____;

and _____
among the individuals is necessary if they are to enjoy the benefits of specialization.

10. In modern economies money functions

chiefly as a _____

11. Barter between two individuals will take place only if there is a _____

12. In the circular flow model, households are buyers and businesses sellers in the _____

_____

market; and businesses are buyers and households sellers in the _____

market.

13. For an item to be "money," it must be

_____

14. The income of any household depends

upon two things: _____

and _____ ;
the income of any business also depends upon

two things: _____

and _____

_____

■ PROBLEMS AND PROJECTS

1. The countries of Lilliput and Brobdingnag have the production possibilities tables for apples and bananas shown below.

LILLIPUT PRODUCTION POSSIBILITIES TABLE

Product (lbs.)	Production alternatives					
	A	B	C	D	E	F
Apples	40	32	24	16	8	0
Bananas	0	4	8	12	16	20

BROBDINGNAG PRODUCTION POSSIBILITIES TABLE

Product (lbs.)	Production alternatives					
	A	B	C	D	E	F
Apples	75	60	45	30	15	0
Bananas	0	5	10	15	20	25

Note that the costs of producing apples and bananas are constant in both countries.
  a. In Lilliput the cost of producing:

  (1) 8 apples is _____ bananas

  (2) 1 apple is _____ bananas
  b. In Brobdingnag the cost of producing:

  (1) 15 apples is _____ bananas

  (2) 1 apple is _____ bananas
  c. In Lilliput the cost of producing:

  (1) 4 bananas is _____ apples

  (2) 1 banana is _____ apples
  d. In Brobdingnag the cost of producing:

  (1) 5 bananas is _____ apples

  (2) 1 banana is _____ apples
  e. The cost of producing 1 apple is **lower**

in the country of _____
and the cost of producing 1 banana is lower

in the country of _____
  f. Lilliput has a comparative advantage in

the production of _____
and Brobdingnag has a comparative advantage

in the production of _____
  g. The information in this problem is not sufficient to determine the exact terms of trade; but the terms of trade will be *greater*

than _____ apples for 1 banana and *less* than

_____ apples for 1 banana. Put another way,

the terms of trade will be between _____

bananas for 1 apple and _____ bananas for 1 apple.
  h. If neither nation could specialize, each would produce production alternative C. The combined production of apples in the two

countries would be _____ apples and the com-

bined production of bananas would be _____ bananas.
  (1) If each nation specializes in producing the fruit for which it has a comparative advantage, their combined production will be

_____ apples and _____ bananas.
  (2) Their gain from specialization will be

_____ apples and _____ bananas.

2. Here is another problem to help you understand the principle of comparative advantage and the benefits of specialization. A tailor named Hart has the production possibilities table for trousers and jackets given below. He chooses production alternative D.

HART'S PRODUCTION POSSIBILITIES TABLE

Product	Production alternatives					
	A	B	C	D	E	F
Trousers	75	60	45	30	15	0
Jackets	0	10	20	30	40	50

Another tailor, Schaffner, has the production possibilities table below and produces production alternative E.

SCHAFFNER'S PRODUCTION POSSIBILITIES TABLE

Product	Production alternatives						
	A	B	C	D	E	F	G
Trousers	60	50	40	30	20	10	0
Jackets	0	5	10	15	20	25	30

a. To Hart

(1) the cost of one pair of trousers is _____ jackets

(2) the cost of one jacket is _____ pairs of trousers

b. To Schaffner

(1) the cost of one pair of trousers is _____ jackets

(2) the cost of one jacket is _____ pairs of trousers

c. If Hart and Schaffner were to form a partnership to make suits

(1) _____ should specialize in the making of trousers because he can make a pair of trousers at the cost of _____ of a jacket while it costs his partner _____ of a jacket to make a pair of trousers.

(2) _____ should specialize in the making of jackets because he can make a jacket at the cost of _____ pairs of trousers while it costs his partner _____ pairs of trousers to make a jacket.

d. Without specialization and between them Hart and Schaffner were able to make 50 pairs of trousers and 50 jackets. If each specializes completely in the item in the production of which he has a comparative advantage, their combined production will be _____ pairs

of trousers and _____ jackets. Thus the gain from specialization is _____
_____

e. When Hart and Schaffner come to divide the income of the partnership between them, the manufacture of a pair of trousers should be treated as the equivalent of from _____ to _____ jackets (or a jacket should be treated as the equivalent of from _____ to _____ pairs of trousers).

3. In the circular flow diagram below, the upper pair of flows (a and b) represent the product market and the lower pair (c and d) the resource market.

Supply labels or explanations for each of the four flows:

a. _____

b. _____

c. _____

d. _____

Circle the T if the statement is true, the F if it is false.

1. The American economy can correctly be called "pure capitalism."   **T   F**

2. There are definite legal limits to the right of private property.   **T   F**

3. The consumer is sovereign in a capitalistic economy because it is he who ultimately determines what the economy will produce.
   T   F

4. Businessmen and resource owners always act only to further their own self-interest.
   T   F

5. If a person, firm, or region does not have a comparative advantage in the production of a particular commodity, it should not specialize in the production of that commodity.   **T   F**

6. Money is a device for facilitating the exchange of goods.   **T   F**

7. "Coincidence of wants" means that two persons desire to acquire the same good or service.   **T   F**

8. Cigarettes may serve as money if buyers and sellers are generally willing to accept them as money.   **T   F**

9. In the circular flow of income, the household functions on the demand side of the resource and product markets.   **T   F**

10. The price system is not employed in communistic and socialistic economies.   **T   F**

Underscore the letter that corresponds to the best answer.

1. Two regions, Slobovia and Utopia, have the production possibilities tables below.

SLOBOVIA PRODUCTION POSSIBILITIES TABLE

Product	Production alternatives					
	A	B	C	D	E	F
Cams	1,500	1,200	900	600	300	0
Widgets	0	100	200	300	400	500

UTOPIA PRODUCTION POSSIBILITIES TABLE

Product	Production alternatives				
	A	B	C	D	E
Cams	4,000	3,000	2,000	1,000	0
Widgets	0	200	400	600	800

In Slobovia the comparative cost: *(a)* of 1 cam is 3 widgets; *(b)* of 1 widget is ⅓ cam; *(c)* of 1 cam is ⅓ widget; *(d)* of 3 widgets is 1 cam.

2. Using the production possibilities tables in the question above, which of the following statements is *not* true? *(a)* Slobovia should specialize in the production of widgets; *(b)* Slobovia has a comparative advantage in the production of widgets; *(c)* Utopia should specialize in the production of widgets; *(d)* Utopia

has a comparative advantage in the production of cams.

3. Employing the same information contained in question 1, the terms of trade will be: *(a)* greater than 7 cams for 1 widget; *(b)* between 7 cams for 1 widget and 5 cams for 1 widget; *(c)* between 5 cams for 1 widget and 3 cams for 1 widget; *(d)* less than 3 cams for 1 widget.

4. Still using the schedules in question 1, assume that if Slobovia did not specialize it would produce alternative C and that if Utopia did not specialize it would select alternative B. The gains from specialization are: *(a)* 100 cams and 100 widgets; *(b)* 200 cams and 200 widgets; *(c)* 400 cams and 500 widgets; *(d)* 500 cams and 400 widgets.

5. Which of the following is *not* a necessary consequence of specialization? *(a)* people will use money; *(b)* people will engage in trade; *(c)* people will be dependent upon each other; *(d)* people will produce more of some things than they would produce in the absence of specialization.

6. In an economy in which there are full employment, constant amounts of resources, and unchanging technology: *(a)* to increase the production of capital goods requires an increase in the production of consumer goods; *(b)* to decrease the production of capital goods necessitates a decrease in the production of consumer goods; *(c)* to increase the production of capital goods is impossible; *(d)* to increase the production of capital goods a decrease in the production of consumer goods is needed.

7. Which of the following is *not* a characteristic of competition as the economist sees it? *(a)* the widespread diffusion of economic power; *(b)* a large number of buyers in product markets; *(c)* at least several sellers of all products; *(d)* the relatively easy entry to and exit of producers from industries.

■ DISCUSSION QUESTIONS

1. Explain the several elements—institutions and assumptions—embodied in capitalism.

2. What do each of the following seek if they pursue their own self-interest? Consumers, resource owners, and businessmen.

3. Explain what economists mean by competition. Why is it important in an economy whose members are motivated by self-interest?

4. What are the advantages of "indirect" or "roundabout" production?

5. How does an economy benefit from specialization and the division of labor?

6. What disadvantages are there to specialization and the division of labor?

7. Why do specialization and an advanced technology go hand in hand?

8. Explain what is meant by comparative cost and comparative advantage. What determines the terms of trade? What is the gain that results from specialization in the products in the production of which there is a comparative advantage?

9. What are the principal disadvantages of barter?

10. What is money? What important function does it perform? Explain how money performs this function and how it overcomes the disadvantages associated with barter. Why are people willing to accept paper money in exchange for the goods and services which they have to sell?

11. In the circular-flow-of-income model: *(a)* What two markets are involved? *(b)* What role do households play in each of these markets? *(c)* What role do businesses play in each of these markets? *(d)* What two income flows are pictured in money terms? In real terms? *(e)* What two expenditure flows are pictured in money terms? In real terms?

12. What are the five shortcomings of the circular-flow-of-income model?

THE MECHANICS
OF INDIVIDUAL PRICES:
DEMAND AND SUPPLY

Chapter 4 is an introduction to the most fundamental tools of economic analysis: demand and supply. If you are to progress successfully into the later chapters it is essential that you understand what is meant by demand and supply and how to use these powerful tools.

Demand and supply are simply "boxes" or categories into which all the forces and factors that affect the price and the quantity of a good bought and sold in a competitive market can conveniently be placed. It is necessary to see that demand and supply do determine price and quantity exchanged and to see *why* and *how* they do this.

Many students never do understand demand and supply because they never learn to *define* demand and supply *exactly* and because they never learn (1) what is meant by an increase or decrease in demand or supply, (2) the important distinctions between demand and quantity demanded and between supply and quantity supplied, (3) the equally important distinctions between an increase (or decrease) in demand and an increase (or decrease) in quantity demanded and between an increase (or decrease) in supply and an increase (or decrease) in quantity supplied.

Having learned these, however, it is no great trick to comprehend the so-called "law of supply and demand." The equilibrium price—that is, the price which will tend to prevail in the market as long as demand and supply do not change—is simply the price at which quantity demanded and quantity supplied are equal. The quantity bought and sold in the market (the equilibrium quantity) is the quantity demanded and supplied at the equilibrium price. If you can determine the equilibrium price and quantity under one set of demand and supply conditions, you can determine them under any other set and so will be able to analyze for yourself the effect of changes in demand and supply upon equilibrium price and quantity.

In analyzing equilibrium price and quantity, two important assumptions are made. One is that the higher the price of a good, the smaller will be the quantity demanded of the good (and vice versa); this assumption is called the law of demand. The second is that the higher the price of a good, the larger will be the quantity supplied of that good (and vice versa); this second assumption is the law of supply.

The chapter includes a brief examination of the factors that influence demand and supply and of the ways in which changes in these influences will affect and cause changes in demand and supply. A graphic method is employed in this analysis in order to facilitate an understanding of demand and supply, equilibrium price and quantity, changes in demand and supply, and the resulting changes in equilibrium price and quantity. In addition to understanding the definitions of demand and supply *exactly*, it is necessary to understand the two counterparts of demand and supply: the demand *curve* and the supply *curve*. These are simply graphic (or geometric) representations of the same data contained in the schedules of demand and supply—and demand and supply can only be expressed in terms of schedules or these graphic counterparts.

■ CHAPTER OUTLINE

1. Demand is a schedule of prices and the quantities which buyers will purchase at each of these prices during some period of time.

a. As price rises buyers will purchase smaller quantities, and as price falls they will purchase larger quantities; this is the law of demand.

b. The demand curve is a graphic representation of demand and the law of demand.

c. Market (or total) demand for a good is a summation of the demands of all individuals in the market for that good.

d. The demand for a good depends upon the tastes, income, and expectations of buyers; the number of buyers in the market; and the prices of related goods.

e. A change (either an increase or a decrease) in demand is caused by a change in any of the factors (in *d*) which determine demand, and means that the demand schedule and demand curve have changed.

(1) If an increase in the income of a consumer increases his demand for a good, the good is a normal one; if it decreases his demand, the good is an inferior one.

(2) If an increase (decrease) in the price of one good causes the demand for another good to increase (decrease), the two goods are substitute goods; if it causes the demand for the other good to decrease (increase), the two goods are complementary; and if it causes no

change, the two goods are independent goods.

f. A change in demand and a change in the quantity demanded are *not* the same thing.

2. Supply is a schedule of prices and the quantities which sellers will sell at each of these prices during a given period of time.

a. The law of supply indicates that as the price of the good rises larger quantities will be offered for sale, and that as the price of the good falls smaller quantities will be offered for sale.

b. The supply curve is a graphic representation of supply and the law of supply; the market supply of a good is the sum of the supplies of all sellers of the good.

c. The supply of a good depends upon the prices of the resources used to produce it, the prices of other goods which might be produced, the techniques which are used to produce it, price expectations, the number of sellers of the product, and the extent to which the good is taxed or subsidized.

d. Supply will change when any of the determinants of supply changes; a change in supply is a change in the entire supply schedule or curve.

e. A change in supply must be distinguished from a change in quantity supplied.

3. The market or equilibrium price of a commodity is that price at which quantity demanded and quantity supplied are equal; and the quantity exchanged in the market (the equilibrium quantity) is equal to either the quantity demanded or the quantity supplied.

a. The rationing function of prices is the elimination of either a shortage or surplus of the commodity.

b. A change in demand, supply, or both affects both the equilibrium price and quantity in definite ways.

c. In resource markets suppliers are households and demanders are business firms, and in product markets suppliers are business firms and demanders are households; supply and demand are useful in the analysis of prices and quantities exchanged in both these markets.

d. When demand and supply schedules (or curves) are drawn up it is assumed that all the nonprice determinants of demand and supply remain unchanged.

■ IMPORTANT TERMS

Demand schedule

Law of demand

Demand curve

Individual demand

Total or market
demand

Increase (or decrease)
in demand

Normal (superior)
good

Inferior good

Substitute (com-
peting) good

Complementary good

Independent good

Quantity demanded

Supply schedule

Law of supply

Supply curve

Increase (or decrease)
in supply

Quantity supplied

Equilibrium price

Equilibrium quantity

Rationing function
of prices

Price-increasing
effect

Price-decreasing
effect

Quantity-increasing
effect

Quantity decreasing
effect

■ FILL-IN QUESTIONS

1. In resource markets prices are determined

by the demand decisions of _____

and the supply decisions of _____ ;
in product markets they are determined by

_____

and _____

2. When demand is graphed, price is placed

on the _____

axis and quantity on the _____
axis.

3. The relationship between price and quan-

tity in the demand schedule is a(n) _____

_____

relationship; in the supply schedule the rela-

tionship is a(n) _____
one.

4. When a consumer demand schedule or
curve is drawn up, it is assumed that five
factors that determine demand are fixed and
constant. These five determinants of consumer demand are:

a. _____

b. _____

c. _____

d. _____

e. _____

5. A decrease in demand means that consumers will buy (larger, smaller) _____
quantities at every price or will pay (more,

less) _____
for the same quantities.

6. If a consumer's demand for a product decreases when his income increases, the prod-

uct is a(n) _____
good; if his demand for it increases when his

income increases, the product is a(n) _____

_____
good.

7. If a consumer's demand for a product decreases when the price of another product

increases, the two products are _____
goods; if a consumer's demand for a product
increases when the price of another product

increases, the two products are _____

_____
goods.

8. A change in income or in the price of another product will result in a change in the

(demand for, quantity demanded of) _____

_____

the given product, while a change in the price

of the given product will result in _____

_____

9. The fundamental factors which determine
the supply of any commodity in the product
market are:

a. _____

b. _____

c. _____

d. _____

e. _____

f. _____

10. An improvement in the technology of producing a product is apt to _____ _____ the supply of that product; a(n) (increase, decrease) _____ in the prices of resources used to produce the product will have the same effect.

11. The equilibrium price of a commodity is the price at which _____

_____

12. If quantity demanded exceeds quantity supplied, price is (greater, less) _____ than the equilibrium price.

13. In the spaces below each of the following, indicate the effect [*increase* (+), *decrease* (−), *no change* (0), or *indeterminate* (?)] upon equilibrium price and equilibrium quantity of each of these changes in demand and/or supply.

a. Increase in demand, supply constant

____ ____

b. Increase in supply, demand constant

____ ____

c. Decrease in demand, supply constant

____ ____

d. Decrease in supply, demand constant

____ ____

e. Increase in demand, increase in supply

____ ____

f. Increase in demand, decrease in supply

____ ____

g. Decrease in demand, decrease in supply

____ ____

h. Decrease in demand, increase in supply

____ ____

14. If supply and demand establish a price for a good such that there is no shortage or surplus of the good, then price is successfully performing its _____ function.

15. To assume that all the nonprice determinants of demand and supply do not change is to employ the _____ assumption.

■ PROBLEMS AND PROJECTS

1. Using the demand schedule below, plot the demand curve on the graph (page 25). Label the axes and indicate for each axis the units being used to measure price and quantity.

Price	Quantity demanded, 1,000 bushels of soybeans
$6.20	10
6.00	15
5.80	20
5.60	25
5.40	30
5.20	35

2. The demand schedules of three individuals (Roberts, Charles, and Lynn) for loaves of bread are shown below. Assuming there are only three buyers of bread, draw up the total or market demand schedule for bread.

Price	Quantity demanded, loaves of bread			Total
	Roberts	Charles	Lynn	
$.40	1	4	0	____
.36	3	5	1	____
.32	6	6	5	____
.28	10	7	10	____
.24	15	8	16	____

3. Below is a demand schedule for bushels of apples. In columns 3 and 4 supply *any* new figures for quantity which represent in column 3 an increase in demand and in column 4 a decrease in demand.

(1) Price	(2) Quantity demanded	(3) Demand increases	(4) Demand decreases
$6.00	400	____	____
5.90	500	____	____
5.80	600	____	____
5.70	700	____	____
5.60	800	____	____
5.50	900	____	____

0

4. Assume that O'Rourke has, when his income is $100 a week, the demand schedule for good A shown in columns 1 and 2 of the table below and the demand schedule for good B shown in columns 4 and 5. Assume that the prices of A and B are $.80 and $5, respectively.

a. How much A will O'Rourke buy? _____

How much B? _____
b. Suppose that, as a consequence of a $10 increase in O'Rourke's weekly income, the quantities demanded of A become those shown in column 3 and the quantities demanded of B become those shown in column 6.

(1) How much A will he now buy? _____

How much B? _____

(2) What type of good is A? _____

(3) What type of good is B? _____

5. The market demand for good X is shown

Demand for A (per week)			Demand for B (per week)		
(1)	(2)	(3)	(4)	(5)	(6)
	Quantity	Quantity		Quantity	Quantity
Price	demanded	demanded	Price	demanded	demanded
$.90	10	0	$5.00	4	7
.85	20	10	4.50	5	8
.80	30	20	4.00	6	9
.75	40	30	3.50	7	10
.70	50	40	3.00	8	11
.65	60	50	2.50	9	12
.60	70	60	2.00	10	13

in columns 1 and 2 of the table below. Assume the price of X to be $2 and constant.

(1) Price	(2) Quantity demanded	(3) Quantity demanded	(4) Quantity demanded
$2.40	1,600	1,500	1,700
2.30	1,650	1,550	1,750
2.20	1,750	1,650	1,850
2.10	1,900	1,800	2,000
2.00	2,100	2,000	2,200
1.90	2,350	2,250	2,450
1.80	2,650	2,550	2,750

a. If as the price of good Y rises from $1.25 to $1.35 the quantities demanded of good X become those shown in column 3, it can be concluded that X and Y are _____ goods.

b. If as the price of good Y rises from $1.25 to $1.35 the quantities demanded of good X become those shown in column 4, it can be concluded that X and Y are _____ goods.

6. Plot the supply schedule which follows on the same graph on which you plotted demand in problem 1.

Price	Quantity supplied, 1,000 bushels of soybeans
$6.20	40
6.00	35
5.80	30
5.60	25
5.40	20
5.20	15

a. The equilibrium price of soybeans will be

$_____

b. _____
thousand bushels of soybeans will be exchanged at this price.

c. Indicate clearly on the graph the equilibrium price and quantity by drawing lines from the intersection of the supply and demand curves to the price and quantity axes.

7. In a local market for hamburger on a given date, each of 300 sellers of hamburger

has the following supply schedule. In column 3 construct the market supply schedule for hamburger.

(1) Price	(2) Quantity supplied— one seller, lb.	(3) Quantity supplied— all sellers, lb.
$1.65	150	_____
1.60	110	_____
1.55	75	_____
1.50	45	_____
1.45	20	_____
1.40	0	_____

8. Below is the market demand schedule for hamburger on the same date and in the same market as that given in problem 7. The equilibrium price of hamburger will be between

$ _____

and $ _____

the equilibrium quantity will be between _____

_____

and _____
pounds.

Price	Quantity demanded, lb.
$1.65	28,000
1.60	31,000
1.55	36,000
1.50	42,000
1.45	49,000
1.40	57,000

9. Each of the following events would tend to affect (that is, increase or decrease) either the demand for or the supply of television sets, and thus affect the price of television sets. In the first blank indicate the effect upon demand or supply and in the second the effect (increase or decrease) upon price.

a. It becomes known that a local department store is going to have a sale on television sets three months from now _____;

_____

b. The workers who produce the sets go on

strike for over two months. _____;

_____

c. The workers in the industry receive a 90-cent-an-hour wage increase. _____;

_____

d. The average price of movie tickets increases. _____; _____

e. The firms producing the sets undertake to produce a large volume of missile components for the Defense Department. _____;

_____

f. Several large areas in the country, previously without television stations, become regions in which programs can be received. _____

_____; _____

g. Because of the use of mass-production techniques, the amount of labor necessary to produce a set decreases. _____;

_____

h. The price of high-fidelity phonograph sets decreases. _____; _____

i. The average consumer believes that a shortage of sets is developing in the economy. _____; _____

j. The Federal government imposes a $50 per set tax upon the manufacturers of TV sets.

_____; _____

10. Below is the supply schedule for a certain product. In column 3 place any new price figures which indicate an increase in supply; in column 4 put new price figures which indicate a decrease in supply.

(1) Price	(2) Quantity supplied	(3) Supply increase	(4) Supply decrease
$10	950	$_____	$_____
8	900	_____	_____
6	850	_____	_____
4	800	_____	_____
2	750	_____	_____

Circle the T if the statement is true, the F if it is false.

1. Demand is the amount of a commodity or service which a buyer will purchase at a particular price.   T F

2. The law of demand states that as price increases, the quantity of the product demanded increases.   T F

3. In graphing supply and demand schedules, supply is put on the horizontal axis and demand on the vertical axis.   T F

4. If price falls, there will be an increase in demand.   T F

5. If the demand curve moves from D_1 to D_2 in the graph below, demand has increased.   T F

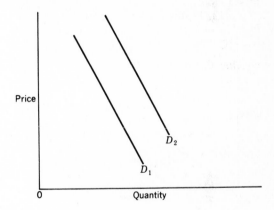

6. A fall in the price of a good will cause the demand for goods which are substitutes for it to increase.   T F

7. If two goods are complementary, an increase in the price of one will cause the demand for the other to increase.   T F

8. If the market price of a commodity is for a time below its equilibrium price, the market price will tend to rise because demand will decrease and supply will increase. T F

Underscore the letter that corresponds to the best answer.

1. Which of the following can cause a decrease in consumer demand for product X? (a) a decrease in consumer income; (b) an increase in the prices of goods which are

good substitutes for product X; *(c)* an increase in the price which consumers expect will prevail for product X in the future; *(d)* a decrease in the supply of product X.

2. If two goods are substitutes for each other, an increase in the price of one will necessarily: *(a)* decrease the demand for other; *(b)* increase the demand for the other; *(c)* decrease the quantity demanded of the other; *(d)* increase the quantity demanded of the other.

3. The income of a consumer decreases and he increases his demand for a particular good. It can be concluded that the good is: *(a)* normal; *(b)* inferior; *(c)* a substitute; *(d)* a complement.

4. If the supply curve moves from S_1 to S_2 on the graph below, there has been: *(a)* an increase in supply; *(b)* a decrease in supply; *(c)* an increase in quantity supplied; *(d)* a decrease in quantity supplied.

5. An increase in demand and a decrease in supply will: *(a)* increase price and increase the quantity exchanged; *(b)* decrease price and decrease the quantity exchanged; *(c)* increase price and the effect upon quantity exchanged will be indeterminate; *(d)* decrease price and the effect upon quantity exchanged will be indeterminate.

6. An increase in supply and an increase in demand will: *(a)* increase price and increase the quantity exchanged; *(b)* decrease price and increase the quantity exchanged; *(c)* affect price in an indeterminate way and decrease the quantity exchanged; *(d)* affect price in an indeterminate way and increase the quantity exchanged.

7. Which of the following could not cause an increase in the supply of cotton? *(a)* an in-

crease in the price of cotton; *(b)* improvements in the art of producing cotton; *(c)* a decrease in the price of the machinery and tools employed in cotton production; *(d)* a decrease in the price of corn.

8. The law of supply states that as price increases: *(a)* supply increases; *(b)* supply decreases; *(c)* quantity supplied increases; *(d)* quantity supplied decreases.

■ DISCUSSION QUESTIONS

1. Explain the difference between an increase in demand and an increase in quantity demanded, and between a decrease in supply and a decrease in quantity supplied.

2. Neither demand nor supply remain constant for long because the factors which determine demand and supply do not long remain constant. What are these factors? How do changes in them affect demand and supply?

3. How are normal, inferior, substitute, complementary, and independent goods defined, and how can these concepts be used to predict the way in which a change in income or in the prices of other goods will affect the demand for a given good?

4. Given the demand for and the supply of a commodity, what price will be the equilibrium price of this commodity? Explain why this price will tend to prevail in the market and why higher (lower) prices, if they do exist temporarily, will tend to fall (rise).

5. Would you define a decrease in supply as a decrease in the amounts that would be supplied at various prices or as an increase in the prices necessary to ensure various amounts of the good being offered for sale? Explain your preference.

6. Analyze the following quotation and explain the fallacies contained in it. "An increase in demand will cause price to rise; with a rise in price, supply will increase and the increase in supply will push price down. Therefore, an increase in demand results in little change in price because supply will increase also."

7. What is meant by the "rationing function of prices"?

8. What is the difference between individual and market demand; and what is the relationship between these two types of demand? Does this distinction and relationship also apply to individual and market supply?

9. Suppose housewives, because of higher meat prices, decide to boycott meat. What effect will the boycott, as long as it lasts, have upon the demand for meat and the price of meat? After the housewives end their boycott what will happen to the demand for and the price of meat?

10. The supply of beef has decreased (because of the increased costs of producing beef) and the price of beef has started to rise toward its new equilibrium price when the Federal government freezes the price of beef at its original equilibrium price. What will be the effects of the beef-price freeze upon cattle ranchers? Upon the housewife?

THE FIVE FUNDAMENTAL
QUESTIONS AND THE
PRICE SYSTEM

In Chapters 2, 3, and 4 we examined the institutions and characteristics of pure capitalism and saw how supply and demand determine equilibrium prices and equilibrium quantities in resource and product markets. Chapter 5 draws these elements together into an explanation of the ways in which the market system finds answers for the first four of the Five Fundamental Economic Questions. This explanation is only an approximation—a simplified version or a model—of the methods actually employed by American capitalism. Yet this simple model, like all good models, contains enough realism to be truthful and is general enough to be understandable.

The model is intentionally and specifically unrealistic because the economic role of government is ignored and because actual competition in American capitalism is probably much less effective than is assumed in Chapter 5. These shortcomings, however, do not invalidate the major points made in the chapter about the functioning of the price-market system; and the shortcomings are corrected in later chapters to make the model more realistic.

The section entitled "Operation of the Price System" (beginning on page 84 of the textbook) is both the most important part of this chapter and the part the student will find most difficult. If the student will try to understand how the American system of prices and markets finds answers for each of the four basic questions by examining them *individually* and in the order in which they are presented, he will understand more easily how the price system as a whole operates. Actually the price system finds answers for all these questions simultaneously, but for purposes of explanation and comprehension it is much simpler to consider them as if they were separate questions.

In addition to explaining how the price system operates, Chapter 5 also takes up the question of how well it operates. Here the student will find the going much easier. It should be particularly noted, however, that the price-market system is a widely accepted method of allocating scarce resources because it is economically quite efficient in the allocation of resources. But even so, it, like every other economic system devised by man, is not as efficient as it might be. The specific criticisms leveled against the price-market system are well worth noting because, as will be seen in Chapter 6, many of government's functions in the economy are directed toward the correction of the system's faults which have been pointed out by its critics; in fact, one of the reasons for ignoring the role of government in

Chapter 5 is to emphasize the shortcomings of pure capitalism in the absence of government.

A few final words of advice to the student. He should be sure he understands the *importance* and *role* of each of the following in the operation of the price-market system: (1) the rationing and directing functions of prices, (2) substitutability between different products and between different resources, (3) the profit motive of business firms, (4) the entry and exodus of firms from industries, (5) competition, and (6) consumer sovereignty.

■ CHAPTER OUTLINE

1. The price system consists of product and resource markets in which prices and quantities exchanged are determined. In the product markets households demand the products supplied by business firms, while in the resource markets businesses demand the resources supplied by households.

2. Households and business firms as demanders and suppliers are faced with the necessity of making choices.

a. Choices are necessary because resources are scarce.

b. Choices are possible only to the extent that there is substitutability between resources and between products.

c. The actual choices made by households and firms depend upon the prices (or scarcity) of products and resources and upon the amount of substitution possible.

3. The system of prices and markets and the choices of households and business firms furnish the economy with answers to the first four Fundamental Economic Questions.

a. The demands of consumers for products and the desire of business firms to maximize their profits determine what and how much of each product is produced and its price.

b. The desire of business firms to maximize profits by keeping their costs of production as low as possible guide them to employ the most efficient techniques of production and determines their demand for and prices of the various resources; competition forces them to use the most efficient techniques and ensures the most efficient will be able to stay in business.

c. With resource prices determined, the money income of each household is determined; and with product prices determined, the quantity of goods and services which these money incomes will buy is determined.

d. The price-market system communicates changes in consumer tastes, the availability of resources, and techniques of production to business firms.

(1) The desire for maximum profits and competition will then result in a new set of answers to the first three Fundamental Economic Questions.

(2) Competition and the desire to increase profits promote both better techniques of production and capital accumulation.

e. Competition in the economy compels firms seeking to promote their own interests to promote (as though led by an "invisible hand") the best interest of society as a whole: an allocation of resources appropriate to consumer wants, production by the most efficient means, and the lowest possible prices.

4. The price system has been praised and damned because it has both merits and faults.

a. The major merits of the system are that it efficiently allocates scarce resources and allows individuals a large amount of personal freedom.

b. The chief faults are the decline in the competitiveness of markets and wasteful and inefficient production.

c. The analysis of the price system found in this chapter is only a rough approximation of how the American economy actually operates because the bigness of some buyers and sellers has often resulted in weak competition and because the economic role of government has been ignored.

■ IMPORTANT TERMS

Substitutability	Economic efficiency
Economic choice	Consumer sovereignty
Normal profit	Directing (guiding) function of prices
Economic cost	
Economic profit	Invisible hand
Prosperous industry	Least-cost technique
Unprosperous industry	Self-limiting adjustment

■ FILL-IN QUESTIONS

1. The competitive price system is a mechanism for both _____
the decisions of producers and households and

_____
these decisions.

2. Given its money income, each household tries to spend its income on that combination of products which _____

_____

_____

3. The economy—producers and households —must make economic choices because ____

_____ ;
choices are only possible because different products and different resources are, to some degree, _____
for each other.

4. A normal profit is an economic cost because _____

_____

5. If firms in an industry are earning economic profits, firms will _____
the industry, the price of the industry's product will _____, and the industry will employ a _____ quantity of resources and produce a _____ quantity of output; the industry's economic profits will _____
to _____

6. In determining the distribution of total output in the economy, the price system is involved in two ways, which are:

a. _____

b. _____

7. In deciding whether an economy is flexible, the two questions which must be answered are:

a. _____

b. _____

8. The *opportunity* for technological advance exists in the capitalistic system because there are no _____
to restrict it.

9. The entrepreneur uses money which he obtains either from _____
or from _____
to acquire capital goods.

10. If the price system is competitive, there is an identity of _____ interests and the _____ interest: firms seem to be guided by an _____
to allocate the economy's resources efficiently.

11. The chief economic advantage of the price system, it is said, is that _____

_____ ;
its chief noneconomic advantage is that ____

_____

_____

12. Critics of the price system argue that:

a. competition tends to _____
because _____
and _____

b. the system is inefficient because

(1) the distribution of income is _____
(2) even competitive markets fail to recognize social _____ and _____
(3) resources are _____
(4) it does not ensure the _____

_____ of resources.

■ PROBLEMS AND PROJECTS

1. Assume that a firm can produce either product A, product B, or product C with the resources it is currently employing. These resources *cost* the firm a total of $50 per week. Assume, for the purposes of the problem, that the firm's employment of resources cannot be changed. The market prices of and the quantities of A, B, and C these resources will produce per week are given below. Compute the firm's profit when it produces A, B, and C; and enter these profits in the table below.

Product	Market price	Output	Economic profit
A	$7.00	8	$_____
B	4.50	10	_____
C	.25	240	_____

a. Which product will the firm produce? ____
b. If the price of A rose to $8, the firm would _____
(*Hint:* You will have to recompute the firm's profit from the production of A.)
c. If the firm were producing A and selling it at a price of $8, what would tend to happen to the number of firms producing A?

2. Suppose that a firm can produce 100 units of product X by combining labor, land, capital, and entrepreneurial ability in four different ways. If it can hire labor at $2 per unit, land at $3 per unit, capital at $5 per unit, and entrepreneurship at $10 per unit; and if the amounts of the resources required by the four methods of producing 100 units of product X are as indicated in the table, answer the questions below.

Resource	Method			
	1	2	3	4
Labor	8	13	10	6
Land	4	3	3	2
Capital	4	2	4	7
Entrepreneurship	1	1	1	1

a. Which method is the least expensive way of producing 100 units of X? _____
b. If X sells for 50 cents per unit, what is the economic profit of the firm? $_____
What is its profit if X sells for 60 cents per unit? $_____
c. If the price of labor should rise from $2 to $3 per unit and if at the same time the price of X should rise from 50 cents to 70 cents per unit,

(1) The firm's use of:

Labor would change from _____ to _____

Land would change from _____ to _____

Capital would change from _____ to _____
Entrepreneurship would not change.
(2) The firm's economic profit would change

from $_____ to _____

3. Assume that the market prices of products A, B, and C are $1, $2, and $3, respectively, and that the market prices of labor, land, capital, and entrepreneurial ability are $2, $4, $6, and $10, respectively. There are four methods of producing A, B, and C *in lots of 100 units;* the quantities of resources needed to produce the products in lots of 100 are shown in the tables below.

Resource	Method			
	1	2	3	4
Product A				
Labor	25	20	15	10
Land	5	6	6	7
Capital	6	6	7	8
Entrepreneurship	1	1	1	1
Product B				
Labor	40	35	30	25
Land	9	13	13	14
Capital	10	11	12	12
Entrepreneurship	1	1	1	1
Product C				
Labor	90	85	80	75
Land	12	13	15	20
Capital	12	14	16	20
Entrepreneurship	1	1	1	1

If these are the only opportunities open to the firm:

a. What product should it produce? _____
b. The firm will wish to hire

(1) _____ units of labor

(2) _____ units of land

(3) _____ units of capital

(4) _____ units of entrepreneurial ability.
c. How much economic profit will the firm

receive? $_____

d. If the price of product C rose from $3 to $4 per unit:

(1) What product would the firm produce?

_____

(2) What would happen to the firm's employment of:

Labor _____

Land _____

Capital _____

Entrepreneurship _____
(3) What would happen to the economic

profit of the firm? _____

▪ SELF-TEST

Circle the T if the statement is true, the F if it is false.

1. Prices are indicators of the relative scarcity of resources and products. **T F**

2. Industries in which economic profits are earned by the firms in the industry will attract the entry of new firms into the industry. **T F**

3. If firms have sufficient time to enter and leave industries, the economic profits of industry will disappear. **T F**

4. Resources will tend to be used in those industries capable of earning normal or economic profits. **T F**

5. If the market price of resource A increases, firms will tend to employ smaller quantities of resource A. **T F**

6. Changes in the tastes of consumers are reflected in changes in consumer demand for products. **T F**

7. The incentive which the price system provides to induce technological improvement is the opportunity for economic profits. **T F**

8. Contraction in the size of an industry is always the consequence of improved methods of production in that industry. **T F**

9. In a capitalistic economy it is from the entrepreneur that the demand for capital goods arises. **T F**

10. An increase in the size of the firms in an industry generally leads to a smaller number of firms in the industry. **T F**

Underscore the letter that corresponds to the best answer.

1. The wants of consumers are expressed on: *(a)* the demand side of the resource market; *(b)* the demand side of the product market; *(c)* the supply side of the resource market; *(d)* the supply side of the product market.

2. Which of the following best defines economic costs? *(a)* total payments made to workers, landowners, suppliers of capital, and entrepreneurs; *(b)* only total payments made to workers, landowners, suppliers of capital, and entrepreneurs which must be paid to obtain the services of their resources; *(c)* total payments made to workers, landowners, suppliers of capital, and entrepreneurs *less* normal profits; *(d)* total payments made to workers, landowners, suppliers of capital, and entrepreneurs *plus* normal profits.

3. If less than normal profits are being earned by the firms in an industry, the consequences will be that: *(a)* lower-priced resources will be drawn into the industry; *(b)* firms will leave the industry, causing the price of the industry's product to fall; *(c)* the price of the industry's product will rise and fewer resources will be employed by the industry; *(d)* the price of the industry's product will fall and thereby cause the demand for the product to increase.

4. Which of the following would *not* necessarily result, sooner or later, from a decrease in consumer demand for a product? *(a)* a decrease in the profits of the industry producing the product; *(b)* a decrease in the output of the industry; *(c)* a decrease in the supply of the product; *(d)* an increase in the prices of resources employed by the firms in the industry.

5. If firm A does not employ the most "efficient" or least costly method of production, which of the following will *not* be a consequence? *(a)* firm A will fail to earn the greatest profit possible; *(b)* other firms in the industry will be able to sell the product at lower prices; *(c)* new firms will enter the industry and sell the product at a lower price than that at which firm A now sells it; *(d)* firm A will be spending less on resources and hiring fewer resources than it otherwise would.

6. Which of the following is *not* a factor in determining the *share* of the total output of the economy received by any household: *(a)* the prices at which the household sells its resources; *(b)* the quantities of resources which the household sells; *(c)* the tastes of the household; *(d)* the prices which the household must pay to buy products.

7. If an increase in the demand for a product and the resulting rise in the price of the product causes the supply of the product, the size of the industry producing the product, and the amounts of resources devoted to its production to expand, price is successfully performing its: *(a)* guiding function; *(b)* rationing function; *(c)* medium-of-exchange function; *(d)* standard-of-value function.

8. In a capitalistic economy characterized by competition, if one firm introduces a new and better method of production, other firms will be forced to adopt the improved technique: *(a)* to avoid less-than-normal profits; *(b)* to obtain economic profits; *(c)* to prevent the price of the product from falling; *(d)* to prevent the price of the product from rising.

9. Which of the following would be an indication that competition does not exist in an industry? *(a)* less-than-normal profits in the industry; *(b)* inability of the firms in the industry to expand; *(c)* inability of firms to enter the industry; *(d)* wages lower than the average wage in the economy paid to workers in the industry.

10. Economic criticism of the price system is widespread and has pointed out many of the failures of the system. However, the chief economic virtue of the system remains that of: *(a)* allowing extensive personal freedom; *(b)* efficiently allocating resources; *(c)* providing an equitable distribution of income; *(d)* eliminating the need for decision making.

■ DISCUSSION QUESTIONS

1. Explain why the substitutability of resources for each other and the substitutability of products for each other is important if an economy is to allocate its resources efficiently and best satisfy human wants.

2. In what way does the desire of entrepreneurs to obtain economic profits and to avoid losses make consumer sovereignty effective?

3. Why is the ability of firms to enter industries which are prosperous important to the effective functioning of competition?

4. Explain *in detail* how an increase in the consumer demand for a product will result in more of the product being produced and in more resources being allocated to its production.

5. Explain the difference between a price system which is adaptable to change and a price system which is conducive to change.

6. To what extent are firms "free" to produce what they wish by methods which they choose? Do resource owners have freedom to use their resources as they wish?

7. What is meant when it is said that competition is the mechanism which "controls" the price-market system? How does competition do this? What do critics of the price system argue tends to happen to this controlling mechanism as time passes, and why do they so argue?

8. What are the two important functions of prices? Explain the difference between these two functions.

9. "An invisible hand operates to identify private and public interests." What are private interests and what is the public interest? What is it that leads the economy to operate as if it were directed by an invisible hand?

10. If the basic economic decisions are not made in a capitalistic economy by a central authority, how are they made?

11. What reasons are advanced to explain why modern technology results in firms which are large both in absolute size and in relation to the size of their markets?

12. What five arguments do critics of the price system advance to refute the contention that the price system allocates resources efficiently?

13. To what extent is this chapter unrealistic?

MIXED CAPITALISM AND
THE ECONOMIC FUNCTIONS
OF GOVERNMENT

Chapter 6 introduces the student to the five basic functions performed by Federal, state, and local governments in America's mixed capitalistic economy. This is an examination of the actual role of government in an economy which is neither a purely planned nor a purely market-type economy. The discussion points out the degree and the ways in which government causes the American economy to differ from a purely market-type economy. The chapter does not attempt to list all the *specific* ways in which government affects the behavior of the economy. Instead it provides a *general* classification of the tasks performed by government.

Following an explanation of each of the five functions of government in the American economy, the chapter attempts to evaluate the economic role of government in the United States. Here it is pointed out that people generally agree that government should perform these functions. But they disagree on how far government should go in performing them and over whether specific government actions and programs are needed for government to perform these functions. Governments today frequently employ benefit-cost analysis to determine whether they should or should not

undertake some specific action—a particular act, project, or program. This kind of analysis forces government to estimate both the costs and the benefits of the project or program; to expand its activities only where the benefits exceed the costs; and to reduce or eliminate programs and projects when the costs exceed the benefits.

The latter part of Chapter 6 examines two important questions which are related to the economic role of government in the American economy. The first question is whether or not too few of the economy's resources are devoted to the production of public (or social) goods and services and too many are used for the production of private goods and services. The question is whether there is social imbalance or social balance; and the author presents the student with the arguments on both sides of the question. The second question is whether an increase in the size of government's role in the economy reduces or expands the freedoms of the individual members of the American society. The author presents the case of those who argue that expanded governmental activity reduces personal freedom and the case of those who contend it may actually lead to greater individual freedom.

■ CHAPTER OUTLINE

1. The American economy is neither a pure market economy nor a purely governmentally directed or planned economy. It is an example of mixed capitalism and is predominantly a market economy with some government direction and planning.

2. Government in the American economy performs five economic functions. The first two of these functions are designed to enable the price system to operate more effectively; and the other three functions are designed to eliminate the major shortcomings of a purely market-type economy.

3. The first of these functions is to provide the legal and social framework that makes the effective operation of the price system possible.

4. The second function is the maintenance of competition and the regulation of monopoly.

5. Government performs its third function when it redistributes income to reduce the extent of income inequality.

6. When government reallocates resources it performs its fourth function.
  a. It reallocates resources to take account of spillover costs and benefits.
  b. It must also reallocate resources to provide society with social goods and services.
  c. Social (or public) goods are not subject to the exclusion principle and are goods which have large spillover benefits for society.
  d. Government reallocates resources from the production of private to the production of social goods by levying taxes and then using the tax revenues to purchase (or produce) the social goods.

7. Its fifth function is stabilization of the price level and the maintenance of full employment.

8. In evaluating government's role in the economy:
  a. It is generally agreed that it is desirable for government to perform these functions.
  b. There is a good deal of controversy concerning how far it should go in performing them.

9. Whether there is social balance (an optimal allocation of resources between the private and public sectors) in the United States today is a debatable issue.
  a. Those who believe that there is a social *imbalance*—too large an output of private and too small an output of public goods—assert that the demand for social goods has increased.
  b. The existence of a number of obstacles, they argue, has prevented the supply of social goods from increasing as rapidly as the demand, and has brought about social imbalance.
  c. Critics of the social imbalance doctrine contend that there is no serious imbalance; and that if it did exist increased public spending would not necessarily help to solve the problem.

10. The nature and amount of government activity and the extent of individual freedom may be related to each other.

■ IMPORTANT TERMS

Market economy	**Private goods**
Planned economy	**Exclusion principle**
Mixed capitalism	**Quasi-public goods**
Monopoly	**Benefit-cost analysis**
Spillover	**Social balance**
Spillover costs	**Social imbalance**
Spillover benefits	**Wagner's Law**
Social (public) goods	**Fallacy of limited decisions**

■ FILL-IN QUESTIONS

1. All actual economies are "mixed" because they combine elements of a _____ economy and a _____ economy.

2. List the five economic functions of government:

  a. _____

  b. _____

  c. _____

  d. _____

  e. _____

3. To control monopoly in the United States government has:

a. created a commission to _____ the prices and the services of the _____ monopolies;

b. taken over at the local level the _____

_____
electric and water companies;

c. enacted _____ laws to maintain competition.

4. The price system, because it is an im-personal mechanism, results in _____ in the distribution of income. To redistribute income from the upper to lower income groups the Federal government has:

a. enacted _____ programs;

b. engaged in _____ intervention;

c. used the _____ tax to raise much of its revenues.

5. In a competitive market for a product:
a. the benefits to consumers from using the product is expressed by the _____ curve for the product;

b. the cost of producing the product is ex-pressed by the _____ curve;

c. in equilibrium the extra or marginal ____ _____ of the last unit of the product consumed is equal to the extra or marginal _____ of producing that last unit.

6. Competitive markets bring about an opti-mum allocation of resources only if there are

no _____

or _____ in the consumption and production of the good or service.

7. There is a spillover whenever some of the costs of producing a product or some of the benefits from consuming it accrue to _____

8. Whenever in a competitive market there are:
a. spillover costs the result is an (over-, under-) _____ allocation of resources

to the product because units of the product whose _____ exceed their _____

_____ are produced;

b. spillover benefits the result is an _____

_____ allocation of resources to the product because units of the product whose

_____ exceed their _____

_____are not produced.

9. What two things can government do to:
a. Make the market reflect spillover costs?

(1) _____

(2) _____

b. Make the market reflect spillover benefits?

(1) _____

(2) _____

10. Public (or social) goods tend to be goods

which are not subject to the _____

principle and which have large _____ benefits.

11. To reallocate resources from the produc-tion of private to the production of social goods government reduces the demand for

private goods by _____ consumers and

firms and then _____ social goods.

12. To stabilize the economy government:

a. _____ aggregate demand by ____

_____ its expenditures for social

goods and services and _____ taxes when there is less than full employ-ment;

b. _____ aggregate demand by ____

_____ its expenditures for social

goods and services and _____ taxes when there are inflationary pressures.

13. Throughout most of its history govern-ment in the United States has performed in some degree each of the five functions except

that of _____

14. In applying benefit-cost analysis, government should employ more resources in the public sector if the benefits from the additional _____ exceed the costs that result from having fewer _____

15. When government employs benefit-cost analysis it often finds that:

a. it is difficult to _____ the benefits and the costs of a program;

b. the program not only reallocates resources but also affects the _____ of the economy and the _____ of income.

16. Despite the recognition of governmental inefficiency, it should be noted that there is also inefficiency in the _____ _____ of the economy.

17. Social imbalance means that too many resources are allocated to the production of _____ and too few to the production of _____

18. Economists who see social imbalance in the contemporary American economy argue that the _____ for social goods and services has increased more rapidly than their _____

a. The former tends to increase as the real per capita income of the economy increases because consumers want relatively more public goods and relatively fewer private goods; this is called _____

b. The latter tends to increase slowly because of the following five obstacles.

(1) _____
(2) _____
(3) _____
(4) _____
(5) _____

19. Critics of the social imbalance doctrine contend that the _____ for social goods in the United States has

increased at a more rapid rate than the _____ _____;

that a number of forces have led to an _____ _____ of resources to the production of social goods and services; and that more _____ spending does not necessarily lead to greater production of high priority and smaller production of low priority goods and services.

20. To reason that increased governmental activity necessarily reduces private economic activity is an example of the fallacy of _____

■ PROBLEMS AND PROJECTS

1. Below is a list of various government activities. Indicate in the space to the right of each into which of the five classes of government functions the activity falls. If the activity falls under more than one of the five functions, indicate this.

a. Maintaining an army _____
b. Providing for a system of unemployment compensation _____
c. Establishment of the Federal Reserve Banks _____
d. Insuring employees of business firms against industrial accidents _____
e. Establishment of an Antitrust Division in the Department of Justice _____
f. Making it a crime to sell stocks and bonds under false pretenses _____
g. Providing low-cost lunches to school children _____
h. Taxation of whiskey and other spirits _____
i. Regulation of organized stock, bond, and commodity markets _____
j. Setting tax *rates* higher for large incomes than for smaller ones _____

2. On the graph are the demand and supply curves for a product bought and sold in a competitive market. Assume that there are no spillover benefits or costs.

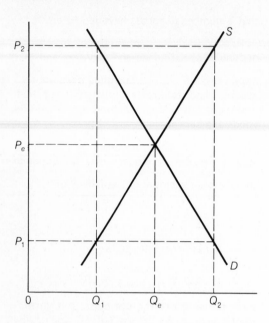

a. Were this market to produce an output of Q_1 there would be an underallocation of resources to the production of this product because at output Q_1 the benefit from the last

unit consumed equals _____ and exceeds the

_____ cost of producing that last unit.

b. Were this market to produce Q_2 there would be an overallocation of resources be-

cause at Q_2 the _____ cost of producing the

last unit exceeds the _____ benefit obtained from consuming that last unit.

c. At the equilibrium output of Q_e there is

an _____ allocation of resources to the production of this product because the cost and the benefit obtained from the last

unit of the product produced both equal _____

3. On two graphs on page 41 are product demand and supply curves that do *not* reflect the spillover costs of producing the product or the spillover benefits obtained from its consumption.

a. On the first graph draw in another curve that reflects the inclusion of spillover *costs*.

(1) The inclusion of spillover costs in the total cost of producing the product (increases,

decreases) _____ the output of the

product and _____ its price.

(2) Were the output Q_e produced there would be an overallocation of resources to this product because at Q_e the extra cost is

_____ than the extra benefit to the economy.

b. On the second graph draw in another curve that reflects the inclusion of spillover *benefits*.

(1) The inclusion of the spillover benefits in the total benefits obtained from consuming

the product (increases, decreases) _____

the output of the product and _____ its price.

(2) Were the output Q_e produced there would be an underallocation of resources to this product because at Q_e the extra cost is

_____ than the extra benefit to the economy.

4. Imagine that a state government is considering the construction of a new highway to link its two largest cities. Its estimate of the total costs and the total benefits of building 2, 4, 6, and 8 lane highways between the two cities are shown in the table on page 41. (All figures are in millions of dollars.)

a. Compute the marginal cost and the marginal benefit of the 2, 4, 6, and 8 lane highways.

b. Will it benefit the state to allocate re-

sources to construct a highway? _____

c. If the state builds a highway:

(1) It should be a _____ lane highway.

(2) The total cost will be $_____

(3) The total benefit will be $_____

(4) The *net* benefit to the state will be $_____

5. Since the following questions have no factual answers there are no answers given in the Answer section at the back of the book.

a. List five specific and most important types of social goods and services which you personally believe should be produced in greater quantities:

(1) _____

(2) _____

(3) _____

(4) _____

(5) _____

b. Now list five specific and most important types of private goods and services which you personally believe should be produced in smaller quantities:

(1) _____

(2) _____

(3) _____

(4) _____

(5) _____

c. What would you estimate would be the extra cost involved if the five items in (a) were increased by the amounts you believe necessary? $_____ How do you propose that governments obtain this extra revenue?

_____

d. How do you propose to induce consumers to want less and the economy to produce fewer of the items you listed in (b)?_____

_____

e. Do you believe that there is an imbalance between the output of social and the output of private goods? _____ Why do you

believe this? _____

f. Ignoring military expenditures, do you believe that governments supply too much of

some social goods and too few of others?____

_____ If your answer is yes, which things would you have government supply less of?

_____

Which more of? _____

g. Do you believe that the private sector of the economy would be better off if it had less of certain private goods and more of some

Project	Total cost	Marginal cost	Total benefit	Marginal benefit
No highway	$ 0		$ 0	
2 lane highway	500	$_____	650	$_____
4 lane highway	680	_____	750	_____
6 lane highway	760	_____	800	_____
8 lane highway	860	_____	825	_____

other private goods? _____ If your answer is yes, which private goods should it have less of and which more of? _____

_____

How would you attempt to achieve the greater and the smaller consumption of these items?

_____

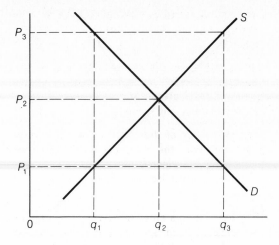

■ SELF-TEST

Circle the T if the statement is true, the F if it is false.

1. The American economy cannot be called "capitalistic" because its operation involves some "planning." **T F**

2. When the Federal government provides for a monetary system, it is functioning to provide the economy with social goods and services. **T F**

3. An economy in which strong and effective competition is maintained will find no need for programs designed to redistribute income. **T F**

4. Competitive product markets ensure an optimal allocation of an economy's resources. **T F**

5. In a competitive product market and in the absence of spillover costs, the supply curve or schedule reflects the marginal cost of producing the product. **T F**

6. If demand and supply reflected all the benefits and costs of a product, the equilibrium output of a competitive market would be identical with its optimum output. **T F**

The graph in the next column should be used to answer true-false question 7 and multiple-choice questions 3 and 4.

7. Assuming there are no spillover costs or benefits, the production of q_1 units of this product would result in an overallocation of resources to the production of the product. **T F**

8. The inclusion of the spillover benefits would increase the demand for a product. **T F**

9. When there are spillover costs involved in the production of a product, more resources are allocated to the production of that product and more of the product is produced than there would be if there were no spillover costs. **T F**

10. Reduced taxation of firms producing goods which provide spillover benefits will usually result in a better allocation of reserves. **T F**

11. If the economic role of government in the United States is evaluated objectively, it becomes clear that the scope of the government's activities is too large and that government's efficiency in performing its role has been inadequate. **T F**

12. In a democracy, government tends generally to perform those tasks which the majority of society demands of it. **T F**

13. Reduced government spending is the same as economy in government. **T F**

14. In practice it is usually quite simple to estimate the costs and the benefits of a project financed by government. **T F**

15. Those who argue that there is social imbalance in the American economy contend that as the economy has developed the production of private goods has been slighted in favor of public goods. **T F**

16. The alleged cause of social imbalance is the failure of the demand for public goods and services to increase as rapidly as the supply of public goods and services. **T F**

17. The benefits of social goods and services tend to be remote and uncertain to the individual taxpayer who is not able to select and pay for only the social goods and services he desires.   **T   F**

18. Inflation, according to those who argue the case of social imbalance, tends to create strong public pressure for reduced government spending and taxes.   **T   F**

19. The critics of the social imbalance thesis point out that the typical individual citizen tends to view an increase in the supply of public goods and services as costless to him.

T   F

20. Both liberals and conservatives agree that the expansion of government's role in the economy has reduced personal freedom in the United States.   **T   F**

Underscore the letter that corresponds to the best answer.

1. Which of the following is *not* one of the methods utilized by government to control monopoly? *(a)* the imposition of special taxes on monopolists; *(b)* government ownership of monopolies; *(c)* government regulation of monopolies; *(d)* antitrust laws.

2. One of the following is *not* employed by government to redistribute income. Which one? *(a)* the negative income tax; *(b)* direct market intervention; *(c)* income taxes which take a larger part of the incomes of the rich than the poor; *(d)* public assistance programs.

Use the graph on page 42 to answer the following two questions.

3. If there are neither spillover costs nor spillover benefits, the output which results in the optimum allocation of resources to the production of this product is *(a)* q_1; *(b)* q_2; *(c)* q_3; *(d)* none of these outputs.

4. If there are no spillover costs or benefits, the marginal benefit (or satisfaction) from producing q_3 units of this product is *(a)* p_1; *(b)* p_2; *(c)* p_3; *(d)* none of these.

5. When the production and consumption of a product entails *both* spillover costs and benefits, a competitive product market results in *(a)* an underallocation of resources to the product; *(b)* an overallocation of resources to

the product; *(c)* an optimum allocation of resources to the product; *(d)* an allocation of resources that may or may not be optimum.

6. Which of the following is the best example of a good or service providing the economy with spillover benefits? *(a)* an automobile; *(b)* a drill press; *(c)* a high school education; *(d)* an operation for appendicitis.

7. In the American economy the reallocation of resources needed to provide for the production of social goods is accomplished mainly by means of: *(a)* government subsidies to the producers of social goods; *(b)* government purchases of social goods from producers; *(c)* direct control of producers of both private and social goods; *(d)* direct control of producers of social goods only.

8. In assessing the desirability of government performing the five basic economic functions in the United States, there seems to be rather general agreement that: *(a)* the functions ought to be increased in number and government's role in the economy expanded; *(b)* the functions ought to be decreased in number and government's role in the economy reduced to a minimum; *(c)* the functions are those which the government ought to perform, but there is no general agreement as to the extent to which government should go in performing them; *(d)* with the exception of stabilizing the economy, these are legitimate tasks for government to perform as long as government, in performing them, does not interfere with the operation of the economy.

9. Which of the following is characteristic of social goods? *(a)* they have large spillover benefits; *(b)* they are sold in competitive markets; *(c)* they are subject to the exclusion principle; *(d)* they can be produced only if large spillover costs are incurred.

10. Which of the following functions of government most affects the area of macroeconomics? *(a)* maintaining competition; *(b)* redistributing income; *(c)* reallocating resources; *(d)* stabilizing the economy.

11. Assume that a government is considering a new antipollution program and has a choice of four different projects. The total cost and the total benefits of each of the four projects is given below.

Project	Total cost	Total benefit
#1	$2 million	$5 million
#2	$5 million	$7 million
#3	$10 million	$10 million
#4	$20 million	$15 million

Which projects should it adopt? *(a)* #1; *(b)* #1 and #2; *(c)* #1, 2, and #3; *(d)* all of the projects.

12. Which of the following is *not* a factor that would prevent the supply of public goods and services from growing as rapidly as the demand for them? *(a)* Wagner's Law; *(b)* the advertising of producers of private goods and services; *(c)* the effects of inflation; *(d)* the need for higher taxes.

■ DISCUSSION QUESTIONS

1. Why is it proper to refer to the United States economy as "mixed capitalism"?

2. What are the five economic functions of government in America's mixed capitalistic economy? Explain what the performance of each of these functions requires government to do.

3. Would you like to live in an economy in which government undertook only the first two functions listed in the text? What would be the advantages and disadvantages of living in such an economy?

4. Why does the market system provide some people with lower incomes than it provides others?

5. Explain why, when there are neither spillover costs nor spillover benefits, competitive product markets bring about an optimum allocation of resources to the production of the goods and services bought and sold in these markets. Why do spillover costs and benefits bring about a less than optimum allocation of resources?

6. What is meant by a spillover, a spillover cost, and a spillover benefit? What specific spillover costs and benefits seem to you to be significant in the American economy? How would the inclusion of spillover costs and the inclusion of spillover benefits affect the allocation of the economy's resources?

7. What methods do governments employ to *(a)* redistribute income; *(b)* reallocate resources to take account of spillover costs; *(c)* reallocate resources to take account of spillover benefits?

8. What is meant by the "exclusion principle"? How is this principle related to the distinction made between private and social goods?

9. What basic method does government employ in the United States to reallocate resources away from the production of private goods and toward the production of social goods?

10. Is there agreement on whether government should perform its five economic functions? Why is there criticism of government activity?

11. Explain what benefit-cost analysis is and how it is used. What is the major problem encountered when benefit-cost analysis is utilized by government?

12. Is government, in your opinion, more or less efficient than the private sector of the economy? Explain the difference between "economy in government" and "reduced government spending."

13. Explain what is meant by social balance and social imbalance. What are the alleged causes of social imbalance in the American economy? In your answer use the concepts of increasing demand and increasing supply of public goods. Explain why the former tends to increase as the economy becomes more affluent and the obstacles to the increase in the latter.

14. Why do some economists argue that there is little or no social imbalance in the United States?

15. Do you think government limits or expands personal freedom by performing its economic functions?

THE FACTS
OF AMERICAN CAPITALISM:
THE PRIVATE SECTOR

The American economy has two major parts or sectors. This chapter is concerned with the private sector: the sixty-two million households and the eleven and one-half million business firms in the economy. The next chapter deals with the public sector of the economy: the more than eighty-one thousand governments found in the United States. These two chapters aim to acquaint the student with a few of the facts relevant to an understanding of American capitalism.

The first third of Chapter 7 examines the households of the economy, the distribution of income in the United States, and the uses to which the households put their incomes. The distribution of income means the way in which the total income which people receive is divided up (or distributed) among them. Two different ways of viewing the distribution of income are stressed: the way in which it is distributed among people according to the function they perform in the economy and the way in which it is distributed among the different income classes in the economy. Attention should be concentrated on the *general* facts of income distribution (not the exact figures), the conclusions which are drawn from these general facts, and the definitions of the new terms employed. In the examination of the different uses households make of

their incomes, several new terms and concepts are introduced; and figures are employed in the discussion. Again, attention should be paid to the generalizations and to the new terms.

The latter two-thirds of the chapter is concerned with the business firms of the United States. It is apparent that what most characterizes American business is the differences existing among firms insofar as their size, legal form, and life-span are concerned, as well as in the products they produce. The student should note the distinction between a proprietorship, a partnership, and a corporation and the advantages and disadvantages of each.

The chapter also contains an introduction to what many economists consider a serious economic and political problem in the United States today: the large size of a relatively few firms. There is an examination of the degree to which "big business" prevails in the economy, of why and how firms get to be giants, and of the question of whether these giants are good or bad for the economy as a whole.

The device employed in the last section of the chapter to explain the receipts and expenditures of business is the income (or profit and loss) statement. This statement simply shows from whom a firm or a group of firms received their income during some period of time—usually a year—and what they did with it after they got it. Special attention should be paid to the item in the income statement that is most difficult for students to understand: *depreciation*. Unlike the other items on the allocations side of the income statement, depreciation represents *not* a cash payment to those who have supplied the firm with resources, but an accounting notation that a part of the firm's income was obtained at the "expense" of the wearing out of some of the firm's equipment and that this expense has to be covered by income before a profit can be shown. If a firm buys equipment which lasts a year or a number of years, the firm's income must in both cases exceed all its expenses, including the cost of the equipment, before the firm can show a profit. Depreciation is merely a bookkeeping device for allocating the cost of equipment which is used more than one year to those years in which it is used, rather than to the year in which it is purchased.

■ CHAPTER OUTLINE

1. Households play a dual role in the economy: They supply the economy with resources, and they purchase the greater share of the goods and services produced by the economy. They obtain their incomes in exchange for the resources they furnish the economy. The way in which the total income of all households is divided among (or shared by) them is called the distribution of income.
a. A functional distribution of income indicates the way in which total income is divided into wages, rent, interest, and profits.
b. A personal distribution of income indicates the way in which total income is divided among households in various income classes and is of particular importance because it affects the total output of the economy and the types of goods and services demanded by consumers.

2. Households use their incomes to purchase consumer goods, to pay taxes, and to accumulate savings.
a. Personal taxes constitute a deduction from a household's total income; what remains after taxes can be either saved or spent.
b. Saving is what a household does not spend of its after-tax income.

c. Households spend for durable goods, nondurable goods, and services.
d. Consumer protection and the improvement of consumer knowledge results in a better allocation of society's resources.

3. The business population of the American economy consists of many imperfectly defined and overlapping industries; business firms which operate one or more plants and produce one or more products are the components of these industries. Firms vary greatly in size and in the length of time they remain in business.

4. The three principal legal forms of organization of firms are the proprietorship, the partnership, and the corporation; each form has special characteristics, advantages, and disadvantages. The form of organization which any business firm should adopt depends primarily upon the amount of money capital it will require to carry on its business. Although the proprietorship is numerically dominant in the United States, the corporation accounts for the major portion of the economy's output.

5. A relatively large percentage of the total output of and employment in the American economy is generated by the relatively small percentage of firms in the manufacturing sector of the economy.

6. Big business is characteristic of the American economy; the economy and many of its industries are dominated by giant firms which produce a relatively large proportion of the total output.
a. While no simple measure exists to calculate the extent of industrial concentration, statistics do reveal that concentration exists in many industries.
b. Business firms have grown large in order to increase their productive efficiency, their power and prestige, their chances of survival, and their profits by the elimination of competition. This growth has resulted both from the internal expansion of firms and from the combination of firms.
c. Whether big firms should be feared depends upon the answer to this question: Do the advantages associated with large-scale production outweigh the disadvantages associated with a decline in competition?

7. Business's dual role in the economy consists of producing and selling goods and services which satisfy human wants *and* employing the economy's resources and thereby creating income for the suppliers of resources.

a. The income statement of an individual firm shows the receipts of a firm (from sales) and the allocation (or use) of these receipts during some period of time.

b. The consolidated income statement for all business firms in the economy shows the receipts of these firms from sales to the three major classes of customers and the allocation of these receipts to suppliers of resources, government, and owners during a given time period.

■ IMPORTANT TERMS

Private sector	Vertical combination
Public sector	Conglomerate combination
Functional distribution of income	Sole proprietorship
Personal distribution of income	Partnership
Personal consumption expenditures	Corporation
	Unlimited liability
Durable good	Limited liability
Nondurable good	Separation ("divorce") of ownership and control
Personal taxes	
Personal saving	Internal growth
Plant	Combination
Firm	Income (profit and loss) statement
Industry	Depreciation
Horizontal combination	

■ FILL-IN QUESTIONS

1. The approximately _____ million households in the United States play a dual role in the economy because they _____ and _____

2. The share of national income going for wages and salaries is about _____%.

3. The personal distribution of income is of

particular importance because it affects the

_____

and the _____ of national income, output, and employment.

4. In a price-market system the money income of a family or person depends roughly upon its _____

5. The total income of households is disposed of in three ways: _____, _____, and _____

6. Households use about _____ percent of their total income to pay personal taxes, the greater part of which goes to the _____ government to pay their personal _____ taxes.

7. Based on their durability, consumer spending is classified as spending for _____, _____, and _____

8. Households save primarily in order to obtain _____ and for purposes of _____

9. There are about _____ business firms in the United States.

10. The liabilities of a sole proprietor and of partners are _____ while the liabilities of stockholders in a corporation are _____

11. Indicate in the spaces to the right of each of the following whether these business characteristics are associated with the proprietorship (PRO), partnership (PART), corporation (CORP), two of these, or all three of these legal forms.

a. Much red tape and legal expense in beginning the firm _____

b. Unlimited liability _____

c. No specialized management _____
d. Has a life independent of its owner(s)

_____

e. Decided tax advantage if its profits are

large _____
f. Greatest ability to acquire funds for the

expansion of the firm _____
g. Permits some but not a great degree of

specialized management _____
h. Possibility of an unresolved disagreement

among owners over courses of action _____
i. Makes it possible for a businessman to

avoid responsibility for illegal actions _____

12. What are the four basic reasons why business firms desire to grow big?

a. _____

b. _____

c. _____

d. _____

13. Small firms become large firms either as

consequence of _____

or _____
or both. Most large firms have depended to a

large degree upon _____

14. The dual role of business in the economy

is _____

and _____

15. An income (or profit and loss) statement

shows _____

and _____

16. Depreciation is an estimate of _____

_____

17. On the receipts side of a consolidated income statement for the business sector of the economy, "sales of output" are subdivided, in the order of their relative importance into

sales to _____,

_____,

and _____

18. A consolidated income statement for the business sector of the economy shows only

those sales to other businesses where _____

_____;
to include *all* sales would *not* result in an accurate measure of _____

_____

because _____

■ **PROBLEMS AND PROJECTS**

1. Below is the functional distribution of income in the United States for the year 1972. In the space at the right, place the figures which indicate the percentage shares of income. (Because of rounding, the sum of the shares may not equal the total.)

	Billions of dollars	Percentage share
Wages and salaries	$707.1	_____
Proprietors' income	74.2	_____
Corporate profits	91.1	_____
Interest	45.2	_____
Rents	24.1	_____
National income	941.8	100.0

2. Indicate to the best of your ability what you would call the industries in which the following firms operate:
a. Sears, Roebuck and Company
b. The General Electric Company
c. A used-car dealer in your town
d. Gimbels department stores
e. Your local gas or electric company
f. A new-car dealer
g. The Mars Candy Company
h. The Aluminum Company of America
i. The Anaconda Copper Company
j. The William Wrigley Chewing Gum Company

3. Below are items taken from the income statement of a single corporation.
Arrange these items in the form used in Table 7–7 of the text on the blank income state-

	Thousands of dollars
Indirect business taxes	$ 1
Interest	2
Payroll taxes	4
Rent	5
Depreciation	6
Dividends	7
Undistributed profits	8
Corporate profits taxes	16
Materials	37
Wages and salaries	42
Sales of output	128

	Billions of dollars
Payroll taxes	$ 5
Interest	6
Rents	11
Dividends	11
Corporate profits after taxes	19
Corporate income taxes	24
Indirect business taxes	35
Depreciation	37
Sales to government	47
Proprietors' income	52
Sales to other businesses	58
Wages and salaries	186
Sales to consumers	270

ment provided at the bottom of this page. Compute any totals not provided above.

4. Arrange the data in the table at the top of the next column in a consolidated income statement for the business sector of the economy on the blank statement provided on page 50. Follow the form used in Table 7–8 in the text. Compute by addition or subtraction any figures not included in the data.

■ SELF-TEST

Circle the T if the statement is true, the F if it is false.

1. The personal distribution of income describes the manner in which society's total income is divided among wages, rent, interest, and profit.   **T   F**

2. Corporate profits over the years have tended to be an unstable percentage of national income.   **T   F**

3. A distribution of income which is based on the productivity of resources usually results in considerable *in*equality in the size of incomes.   **T   F**

4. In both relative and absolute terms, personal taxes have exceeded personal saving in recent years.   **T   F**

5. A "durable good" is defined as a good

Allocations		Receipts	
(1)	$_____	(8)	$_____
(2)	_____		
(3)	_____		
(4)	_____		
(5)	_____		
(6)	_____		
(a) $_____			
(b) _____			
(c) _____			
(7)	_____		
(a) _____			
(b) _____			
Total allocations	$_____	Total receipts	$_____

	Allocations			Receipts	
(1)		$_____	(8)		$_____
(2)		_____	(a)	$_____	
(3)		_____	(b)	_____	
(4)		_____	(c)	_____	
(5)		_____			
(a)	$_____				
(b)	_____				
(c)	_____				
(6)		_____			
(a)	_____				
(b)	_____				
(7)		_____			
	Total allocations $_____			Total receipts $_____	

which has an expected life of one year or more. **T F**

6. The upper 10 percent of families, ranked on the basis of size of income, account for most of the personal saving done in the United States. **T F**

7. *Dissaving* means that personal consumption expenditures exceed after-tax income. **T F**

8. A plant is defined as a group of firms under a single management. **T F**

9. An industry is a group of firms that produce the same or nearly the same products. **T F**

10. The corporate form of organization is the least used by firms in the United States. **T F**

11. Corporations account for over one-half the total output of the privately owned business firms in the United States. **T F**

12. The corporation in the United States today always has a tax advantage over other legal forms of business organization. **T F**

13. Whether a business firm should incorporate or not depends chiefly upon the amount of money capital it must have to finance the enterprise. **T F**

14. Most giant firms in the United States have grown and become big by internal growth rather than through combination with other firms. **T F**

15. Not all economists and observers agree that modern technology requires firms as large as some of those in the United States today. **T F**

16. On the receipts side of the business sector's consolidated income statement, the largest single item is sales to government. **T F**

Underscore the letter that corresponds to the best answer.

1. There are in the United States approximately how many households (families)? *(a)* 40 million; *(b)* 50 million; *(c)* 60 million; *(d)* 70 million.

2. When national income declines (as in a recession or depression): *(a)* wages remain constant and the other distributive shares of national income decrease; *(b)* wages decrease and the other distributive shares increase; *(c)* wages increase and other distributive shares decrease; *(d)* wages and the other distributive shares decrease.

3. Which of the following is *not* a factor affecting the amount of money income received by the individual household? *(a)* the quantity of resources the household has available to supply to business firms; (b) the amount of saving done by the household; (c) the prices paid for the various resources in the market; (d) the actual level of employment of the household's resources.

4. Expenditures for *nondurable* goods in recent years have amounted to approximately what percentage of personal consumption expenditures? (a) 30%; (b) 45%; (c) 60%; (d) 75%.

5. Which of the following is a true statement? (a) The durable goods and service parts of personal consumption expenditures vary more over time than do the expenditures for nondurables; (b) expenditures for nondurables vary more than do the expenditures for durable goods and services; (c) expenditures for nondurables vary more than the expenditures for services and less than the expenditures for durables; (d) expenditures for nondurables vary more than the expenditures for durables and less than the expenditures for services.

6. In recent years personal taxes have been approximately what percentage of total income? (a) 15%; (b) 18%; (c) 24%; (d) 30%.

7. If we include self-employed farmers and professional people, there are approximately how many million business firms in the United States? (a) 5; (b) 8; (c) 11½; (d) 15.

8. A group of three plants which is owned and operated by a single firm and which consists of a farm growing wheat, a flour milling plant, and a plant which bakes and sells bakery products is an example of: (a) a horizontal combination; (b) a vertical combination; (c) a conglomerate combination; (d) a corporation.

9. Limited liability is associated with: (a) only proprietorships; (b) only partnerships; (c) both proprietorships and partnerships; (d) only corporations.

10. Which of the following forms of business organization can most effectively raise money capital? (a) corporation; (b) partnership; (c) proprietorship; (d) vertical combination.

11. Which of the following industries has the largest number of firms? (a) agriculture, for-estry, and fishing; (b) manufacturing; (c) wholesale and retail trade; (d) mining.

12. Which of the following industries produces the largest percentage of the national income? (a) agriculture, forestry, and fishing; (b) manufacturing; (c) wholesale and retail trade; (d) government.

13. The 100 largest manufacturing firms in the United States today own approximately what percentage of the net capital assets of all manufacturing firms? (a) 30%; (b) 50%; (c) 60%; (d) more than 60%.

14. Approximately what percentage of the total sales of business firms consists of sales to consumers? (a) 40%; (b) 50%; (c) 60%; (d) 70%.

15. If a farmer produces $60 worth of wheat and sells it to a miller, who uses it to produce $80 worth of flour and in turn sells it to a baker, who produces bread which he sells for $150, the value of the production which has taken place is: (a) $60; (b) $80; (c) $150; (d) $290.

16. For the business sector of the economy as a whole, the largest allocation is for: (a) wages and salaries; (b) taxes; (c) depreciation; (d) profits.

■ DISCUSSION QUESTIONS

1. Explain the difference between a functional and a personal distribution of income.

2. The present personal distribution of income affects both the level of resource use and the allocation of resources in the economy. What is the connection between the distribution of income and the employment and allocation of resources?

3. What determines how large a money income an individual household will have? In what way is a household's income related to its productivity? Why does a personal distribution of income based on productivity lead to personal income inequality?

4. Which, in your opinion, would result in a greater total saving out of a national income of a given size: a more or less nearly equal distribution of income?

5. The purchase of what type of consumer goods is largely postponable? Why is this? How is it possible for a family's personal consumption expenditures to exceed its after-tax income?

6. What is meant by "consumer protection"? Why might consumer protection and increased consumer knowledge lead to a better allocation of resources? Are there any problems that might arise as a result of the imposition by government of quality standards for products?

7. What does it mean when it is said that the business population in the United States is both "diverse" and "fluid"?

8. What is the difference between a plant and a firm? Between a firm and an industry? Which of these three concepts is the most difficult to apply in practice? Why? Distinguish between a horizontal, a vertical, and a conglomerate combination.

9. What are the principal advantages and disadvantages of each of the three legal forms of business organization? Which of the disadvantages of the proprietorship and partnership account for the employment of the corporate form among the big businesses of the American economy?

10. Explain what "separation of ownership and control" of the modern corporation means.

What problems does this separation create for stockholders and the economy?

11. What figures can you cite to show that the typical firm engaged in agriculture is relatively small and that the average firm engaged in manufacturing is relatively large? Are firms engaged in wholesaling and retailing; mining; and finance, insurance, and real estate relatively large or relatively small?

12. Is manufacturing in the United States an industry dominated by big business? What evidence do you use to reach this conclusion?

13. What are the two opposing views often advanced in answer to the question, "Is big business bad for the economy"?

14. What are the seven main items which appear on the allocation side of an *individual* firm's income statement? One of these items has two subitems and another has three. What are these subitems?

15. There are seven main items on the allocation side of a *consolidated* income statement for the business sector of the economy, but they are not the same seven that appear in an individual firm's income statement. What item has been added and what item has been eliminated? Why is this done?

16. Explain carefully what is meant by depreciation.

THE FACTS
OF AMERICAN CAPITALISM:
THE PUBLIC SECTOR

The facts of public sector or government finance in the United States presented in Chapter 8 center on two questions: Where do governments get their incomes? On what do they spend these incomes?

The organization of the chapter is relatively simple. First, the trends which taxes collected and expenditures made by all levels of government—Federal, state, and local—have taken during the past thirty years are examined briefly. Second, a closer look is given to the major items upon which governments spend their incomes, the principal taxes they levy to obtain their incomes, and the relative importance of these taxes. Third, the chapter looks at revenue sharing as a means of reducing the mismatch between the fiscal needs and resources of the Federal government on the one hand, and the needs and resources of state and local government on the other hand. Fourth, the chapter examines the principles applied in levying taxes, the way tax rates vary as personal incomes change, who really pays the taxes levied against various groups in the economy, and how much of their incomes Americans pay to government in the form of taxes.

What should the student get out of this chapter? There are at least six important sets of facts: (1) the trend which taxes and government expenditures have taken in recent years and why; (2) the relative importance of the principal taxes and the relative importance of the various expenditure items in the budgets of the three levels of government; (3) the nature of the fiscal imbalance between the Federal government and state and local governments, how revenue sharing might remedy this imbalance; (4) the meaning and philosophy of the benefits-received and ability-to-pay principles; (5) the meaning of progressive, regressive, and proportional taxation, the shifting and incidence of taxes, and the incidence of the major types of taxes; and (6) the degree of progressiveness that exists in the taxing systems of Federal, state, and local government; and the percentages of income turned over to government by all households and by families with different incomes.

The student is cautioned again to avoid memorizing statistics. He should look instead for the trends and generalizations which these statistics illuminate. He should spend his time, also, on the terms used, the classifications employed, and the conclusions which are drawn and which embody these terms and classifications.

■ CHAPTER OUTLINE

1. Government's dual role in the economy consists of collecting revenue by taxation and expending this revenue for goods and services.

2. In both absolute and relative terms, government tax collections and spending have increased during the past forty-five years.

a. The increased tax collections and spending are the result of hot and cold wars, population increases, urbanization and the greater demand for social goods, pollution of the environment, and inflation.

b. Government spending consists of expenditures for goods and services and transfer payments.

3. At the Federal level of government:

a. Over 50% of the total expenditure is for military preparedness and about 25% is for income security.

b. The major sources of revenue are personal income, payroll, and corporate income taxes; and it has been suggested that a value-added tax be imposed to increase revenue.

c. Tax-exempt securities, capital gains, and depletion allowances are tax loopholes for some persons and firms.

4. At the other two levels of government:

a. State governments depend largely on sales and excise taxes and use a large part of their revenues for education and highways.

b. Local governments rely heavily upon property taxes and spend the greater part of their revenues for education.

5. Because of an imbalance between the ability of state and local governments to expand their tax collections and the growing need for these governments to deal with serious social and economic problems, the Federal government has increasingly resorted to revenue sharing to reduce this imbalance.

6. Although the overall level of taxes is important to the economy, the question of who pays the tax bill is equally important.

a. Two philosophies, the benefits-received principle and the ability-to-pay principle, are widely employed to determine how the tax bill should be apportioned among the economy's citizens.

b. Taxes can be classified as progressive, regressive, or proportional according to the way in which the *tax rate* changes as income increases.

c. A tax levied upon one person or group of persons may be shifted partially or completely to another person or group; to the extent that a tax can be shifted or passed on through lower prices paid or higher prices received, its incidence is passed on. The incidence of the four major types of taxes is only probable and is not known for certain.

d. Federal taxes tend to be progressive and state and local taxes regressive; and the tax system as a whole is roughly proportional. But when transfer payments received are deducted from the taxes paid the combined tax-transfer system is, on the whole, progressive.

■ IMPORTANT TERMS

Government transfer payment	Intergovernmental grant
Personal income tax	Categorical grant
Marginal tax rate	Unrestricted grant
Average tax rate	State and Local Fiscal Assistance Act
Payroll tax	
Corporation income tax	Benefits-received principle
Double taxation	Ability-to-pay principle
Sales tax	
Excise tax	Progressive tax
Value-added tax	Regressive tax
Tax-exempt security	Proportional tax
Capital gain	Tax incidence
Depletion allowance	Tax shifting
	Net taxes
Property tax	Combined tax-transfer system
Revenue sharing	

■ FILL-IN QUESTIONS

1. It is through the _____ and the _____ of government that the functions of government are most directly felt by the economy.

2. Transactions in the private sector of the economy are _____ while those in the public sector, by and large, are _____

3. Government transfer payments are _____

_____

4. The most important source of revenue for the Federal government is the _____ tax; next in importance are the _____ taxes. The major portion of Federal expenditures is for _____

5. Corporation income is said to be "taxed double" because _____

_____

6. A tax levied on the difference between the value of a firm's production and the value of the materials purchased by the firm from other firms is called a _____ tax.

7. State governments rely primarily upon _____ and _____ taxes for their incomes which they spend mostly on _____ and _____

8. At local levels of government the single most important source of revenue is the _____ tax and the single most important expenditure is for _____

9. List below three important Federal tax loopholes.

a. _____

b. _____

c. _____

10. To increase the incomes of state and local governments and enable them to expand their efforts to solve the serious social and economic problems facing them the Federal government has engaged in _____

11. The two philosophies of apportioning the tax burden which are most evident in the American economy are the _____ principle and the _____ principle.

12. As the income *decreases*, a proportional tax involves a _____ tax rate, a regressive tax, an _____

tax rate, and a progressive tax, a _____ _____ tax rate.

13. Indicate in the space to the right of each of the following taxes whether that tax (as applied in the United States) tends to be regressive (R) or progressive (P).

a. Personal income tax _____
b. Sales tax _____
c. Payroll tax _____
d. Property tax _____
e. Corporation income tax _____

14. What is the probable incidence of each of the following taxes?

a. Personal income tax: _____
b. Sales and excise tax: _____
c. Corporate income tax: _____
d. Property tax: _____

15. In the United States:
a. the tax systems of state and local governments tend to be _____
b. the tax system of the Federal government is _____
c. the tax system for all levels of government combined is roughly _____
d. the tax-transfer system for all levels of government combined is _____

■ PROBLEMS AND PROJECTS

1. Below are several levels of taxable income and hypothetical marginal tax rates applicable to each $1,000 increase in income. Compute for each income level the tax and the average tax rate.

Taxable income	Marginal tax rate, %	Tax	Average tax rate, %
$1,500	20	$300	20
2,500	22	_____	_____
3,500	25	_____	_____
4,500	29	_____	_____
5,500	34	_____	_____
6,500	40	_____	_____
7,500	47	_____	_____

Income	Tax A Tax paid	Av. tax rate %	Tax B Tax paid	Av. tax rate %	Tax C Tax paid	Av. tax rate %
$ 500	$ 15.00	_____%	$ 5.00	_____%	$ 50.00	_____%
1,500	45.00	_____	30.00	_____	135.00	_____
3,000	90.00	_____	90.00	_____	240.00	_____
5,000	150.00	_____	150.00	_____	350.00	_____
7,500	225.00	_____	187.50	_____	450.00	_____
10,000	300.00	_____	200.00	_____	500.00	_____
15,000	450.00	_____	300.00	_____	600.00	_____
Type of tax:	_____		_____		_____	

2. In the table above are seven levels of taxable income and the amount paid at each of the seven levels under three tax laws: A, B, and C. Compute for each of the three taxes the *average* rate of taxation of each of the seven income levels and indicate whether the tax is regressive, proportional, progressive, or some combination thereof.

3. Assume a government levies a 4 percent sales tax on all consumption expenditures. Consumption expenditures at six income levels are shown in the table below.

Income	Consumption expenditures	Sales tax paid	Average tax rate, %
$ 5,000	$5,000	$_____	_____
6,000	5,800	_____	_____
7,000	6,600	_____	_____
8,000	7,400	_____	_____
9,000	8,200	_____	_____
10,000	9,000	_____	_____

a. Compute the sales tax paid at each income.
b. Compute the average tax rate at each income.
c. Using income as the tax base, the sales tax is a _____ tax.

4. The table below shows the amount of taxes paid and the size of the government transfer payments received at five different levels of income. Taxes are proportional because the average tax rate is 30% at each income level.

Income	Taxes paid	Transfer payments received	Net taxes	Net tax rate
$ 2,000	$ 600	$1,000	$_____	_____%
4,000	1,200	800	_____	_____
10,000	3,000	600	_____	_____
15,000	4,500	300	_____	_____
25,000	7,500	0	_____	_____

a. Compute and enter in the table the net tax at each of the five income levels.
b. Now compute and enter in the table the average *net* tax rate at each income. (*Hint:* Divide the net tax at each income by the income to find the average net tax rate.)
c. The tax-transfer system is (progressive, regressive, proportional) _____ because the net tax rate _____ as the level of income increases.

■ SELF-TEST

Circle the T if the statement is true, the F if it is false.

1. Taxes collected by, and expenditures of, all levels of government in the United States exceed $375 billion per year.   T   F

2. For the public sector to play its dual role in the economy it must collect taxes and reduce the size of its debt.   T   F

3. The chief source of revenue for the Federal government is the corporation income tax.   T F

4. The level of Federal expenditures in 1974 was about $180 million.   T F

5. There is a major loophole in the Federal tax system because personal income tax rates are progressive.   T F

6. Total taxes collected by the Federal government are approximately equal to the amount of taxes collected by all state and local governments.   T F

7. The State and Local Fiscal Assistance Act of 1972 provides for categorical grants to state and local governments.   T F

8. The chief difficulty in applying the benefits-received principle of taxation is to determine who receives the benefits of many of the goods and services which government supplies.   T F

9. A sales tax generally turns out to be a proportional tax.   T F

10. The state and Federal taxes on gasoline are good examples of taxes levied on the benefits-received principle.   T F

Underscore the letter that corresponds to the best answer.

1. Today all government expenditures equal approximately what percentage of the American economy's total output? *(a)* 10%; *(b)* 18%; *(c)* 23%; *(d)* 33%.

2. Which of the following would *not* be a government transfer expenditure? *(a)* contributions of employers to support the social security program; *(b)* social security payments to the aged; *(c)* unemployment compensation benefits; *(d)* payments to the widows of war veterans.

3. Past, present, and future wars account for approximately what percentage of all Federal expenditures? *(a)* 47%; *(b)* 55%; *(c)* 60%; *(d)* 65%.

4. If a firm purchases $80,000 worth of materials to produce products which it sells for $100,000 and if the value-added tax rate is 5%, it must pay a value-added tax of *(a)* $1,000; *(b)* $4,000; *(c)* $5,000; *(d)* $9,000.

5. Which of the following pairs represents the chief source of income and the most important type of expenditure of *state* governments? *(a)* personal income tax and expenditures for education; *(b)* personal income tax and expenditures for highways; *(c)* sales and excise taxes and expenditures for public welfare; *(d)* sales and excise taxes and expenditures for education.

6. Which of the following pairs represents the chief source of income and the most important type of expenditure of *local* governments? *(a)* property tax and expenditures for highways; *(b)* property tax and expenditures for education; *(c)* sales and excise taxes and expenditures for public welfare; (d) sales and excise taxes and expenditures for police, fire, and general government.

7. Which of the following is *not* true of the ability-to-pay principle as applied in the United States? *(a)* it is more widely applied than the benefits-received principle; *(b)* income is generally taken as the measure of the ability to pay; *(c)* it is more widely applied by state and local than by Federal government; *(d)* as the tax base increases, taxes paid increase both absolutely and relatively.

8. Which of the following tends to be a progressive tax in the United States? *(a)* income tax; *(b)* property tax; *(c)* sales tax; *(d)* payroll tax.

9. Which of the following taxes can be least easily shifted? *(a)* personal income tax; *(b)* corporation income tax; *(c)* sales tax; *(d)* business property tax.

10. Which of the following is roughly proportional? *(a)* The state and local tax system; *(b)* the Federal tax system; *(c)* the American tax system as a whole; *(d)* the American tax-transfer system.

■ DISCUSSION QUESTIONS

1. What is meant by the "dual role" of government in the economy? How do transactions in the public sector differ from those in the private sector of the economy?

2. What have been the causes which have contributed to the absolute and relative in creases in government spending over the last forty-five years?

3. Government expenditures fall into two broad classes: expenditures for goods and services, and transfer payments. Explain the difference between these and give examples of expenditures which fall into each of the two classes.

4. Explain the difference between exhaustive and nonexhaustive government spending.

5. Explain precisely the difference between the marginal tax rate and the average tax rate.

6. Explain in detail the differences that exist between Federal, state, and local governments in the taxes upon which they primarily rely for their revenues and the major purposes for which they use these revenues.

7. What is a value-added tax? Why has the Federal government considered the use of and why have others argued against the imposition of this kind of tax?

8. What is a tax "loophole"? What are three principal loopholes in the Federal tax system?

How do these loopholes affect the distribution of income?

9. Why has the Federal government increasingly shared its tax revenues with state and local governments. Explain the difference between a categorical grant and an unrestricted grant; and the major provisions of the State and Local Fiscal Assistance Act of 1972.

10. What are the two basic philosophies for apportioning the tax burden in the United States? Explain each. What are the difficulties encountered in putting these philosophies into practice?

11. Explain the differences among progressive, regressive, and proportional taxes. Which taxes fall into each of these three categories? What can be said about the progressivity or regressivity of Federal taxes, state and local taxes, the overall tax system, and the combined tax-transfer system?

12. Which of the following taxes tends to be shifted? *(a)* personal income tax; *(b)* corporate income tax; *(c)* sales and excise taxes; *(d)* property tax. From whom is the tax shifted and upon whom is the tax incidence?

NATIONAL INCOME ACCOUNTING

National income (or social) accounting is the subject matter of Chapter 9. This type of accounting aims to measure or estimate five things: (1) the gross national product, the total output of all final goods and services in the economy during a year; (2) the net national product, the annual output of all final goods and services over and above (in excess of or "net of") the stock of capital goods with which the economy began the year; (3) the national income, the total income or output earned by owners of land and capital and suppliers of labor and entrepreneurial ability during a year; (4) personal income, the total income or output actually received—whether earned or unearned—by these suppliers of resources (or the total income earned and received plus unearned income) before the payment of personal taxes; and (5) disposable income, the total income or output available to resource suppliers after the payment of personal taxes.

This is national income (or social) accounting because it involves estimating output or income for the nation or society as a whole, rather than for an individual business firm or family. Note that the terms "output" and "income" are interchangeable because the nation's output and income are identical: The value of the nation's output equals the total expenditures for this output, and these expenditures become the receipts or the income of those in the nation who have produced this output. Consequently, there are two equally acceptable methods, both discussed in the chapter, for obtaining each of the five income-output measures listed above. These two methods are the output (or expenditures) method (or approach) and the income (or allocations) method (or approach).

Accounting is essentially a process of adding up. This chapter explains in detail and lists the items which must be added and/or subtracted to obtain by both methods each of the five income-output measures. It is up to the student to learn precisely *what* to add and subtract, i.e., how to compute GNP, NNP, NI, PI, and DI by both methods. This is a fairly difficult chapter, and the only way to learn the material is simply to sit down and learn it—memorize it if necessary! A careful reading of the chapter, however, will enable the student to avoid the necessity of memorizing. He should first try to understand what each of the five income-output measures attempts to measure and the two alternative approaches to these measurements. Then the item added and/or subtracted will be simpler.

In addition to explaining the two methods of computing the five income-output measures and each of the items used in the computation process, the chapter discusses the purpose of social accounting; the means by which income-output measures for different years may be adjusted to take account of changes in the price level so that comparisons between years are possible; and the shortcomings and dangers inherent in national income accounting. Chapter 9 is essential background for Parts Two and Three, which explain the history of and the factors determining the level of total output and income in the economy. The chapter is important in itself because it presents one of the several means of measuring or estimating the well-being of the economy and the individuals comprising the economy in a given year and over the years.

■ CHAPTER OUTLINE

1. National income (or social) accounting consists of concepts which enable those who use them to measure the economy's output, to compare it with past outputs, to explain its size and the reasons for changes in its size, and to formulate policies designed to increase it.

2. The gross national product (GNP) is the market value of all final goods and services produced in the economy during a year.

  a. GNP is measured in dollar terms rather than in terms of physical units of output.

  b. Because the value of the dollar (and the price level) changes over time, it is necessary to adjust dollar GNP figures when comparing GNPs in different years.

  c. To adjust dollar GNP figures for changes in the price level, divide the dollar GNP in any year by the price index for that year.

  d. To avoid double counting, GNP includes only *final* goods and services—goods and services that will not be processed further during the *current* year.

  e. Nonproductive transactions are not included in GNP; purely financial transactions and secondhand sales are, therefore, excluded.

  f. GNP is not a measure of social welfare for several reasons.

  g. Measurement of GNP can be accomplished by two methods—the expenditures and the income methods—but the same result is obtained by either method.

3. Computation of GNP by the expenditures method requires the accountant to add the four types of spending for final goods and services which occur in the economy: the personal consumption expenditures of households; government spending for goods and services; gross business spending for capital goods; and the *net* spending of foreign citizens, firms, and governments for American goods and services.

4. Computation of GNP by the income method requires the accountant to total the nine uses to which the income derived from the production and sale of final goods and services are put: depreciation, indirect business taxes, compensation of employees, rents, interest, proprietors' income, corporate income taxes, dividends, and undistributed corporate profits.

5. In addition to GNP, four other national income measures are useful and important in evaluating the output and health of the economy: the Net National Product, National Income, Personal Income, and Disposable Income. Each has a distinct and different meaning and can be computed by either the expenditures or the income method. All five are related to each other in a specific way, and each can be computed by making additions to or deductions from the other measures.

■ IMPORTANT ITEMS

National income (social) accounting

Gross national product

Real gross national product

Inflating

Deflating

Price index

Base year

Given year

Final goods

Intermediate goods

Double counting

Value added

Nonproductive transaction

Nonmarket transaction

Output (expenditures) approach

Income (allocations) approach

Personal consumption expenditures

Government purchases of goods and services

Gross private domestic investment

Noninvestment transaction

Net private domestic investment

Expanding (growing) economy

Stationary (static) economy

Declining (contracting) economy

Net exports

Nonincome charges

Capital consumption allowances

Indirect business taxes

Compensation to employees

Wage and salary supplements

Net national product

National income

Personal income

Disposable income

Personal saving

■ FILL-IN QUESTIONS

1. Social accounting is invaluable because it provides a means of keeping track of the ____

_____

and the information necessary to devise and put into effect _____

_____

2. Gross national product is a monetary measure of all final goods and services produced during a year; to measure the value of these goods and services, the goods and services are valued at their _____

3. In order to compare the gross national product in two different years, it is necessary to adjust money GNP because _____

_____

4. In measuring GNP only final goods and services are included; if intermediate goods and services were included, the accountant would be _____

5. A firm buys materials for $200 and produces from them a product which sells for $315. The $115 is the _____ by the firm.

6. The total value added to a product at all stages of production equals _____

_____

7. Public transfer payments, private transfer payments, and security transactions are all examples of the _____ type of nonproductive transactions.

8. Depreciation and indirect business taxes, by the income or allocations approach, are referred to as _____ charges or allocations.

9. Gross private domestic investment basically includes _____,

_____,

and _____
Net private domestic investment is less than gross private domestic investment by an amount equal to _____

10. If gross private domestic investment is greater than capital consumption, the economy is _____; and if it equals capital consumption, the economy is _____

11. The compensation of employees in the system of social accounting consists of actual wages and salaries and wage and salary ____ which are the payments employers make to

_____

and to _____

12. Corporate profits are disposed of in three ways: _____,

_____,

and _____

13. Gross national product overstates the economy's production in a given year because it fails to _____

14. Net national product equals gross national product minus _____

15. National income equals net national products minus _____; this deduction is made because national income is income _____ and the subtracted item is not considered to be a payment to a factor of production which contributes to the production of output.

16. *Transfer payments* include the following five items:

a. _____

b. _____

c. _____

d. _____

e. _____

17. Personal income equals national income

plus _____

and minus _____ ,

_____ ,

and _____ .

It also equals the sum of _____ ,

_____ ,

_____ ,

and _____

18. Disposable income equals personal in-

come minus _____ ;

disposable income also equals _____

plus _____

plus _____

19. Personal saving equals disposable in-

come minus _____

and _____

20. Net private domestic investment plus

_____

equals gross private domestic investment.

■ PROBLEMS AND PROJECTS

1. Price indices, deflating and inflating:
 a. Below are hypothetical figures for five
different years showing the prices of a typical
commodity for each of the five years.

Year	Price	Price index (1927 equals 100)	Price index (1935 equals 100)
1927	$ 9	_____	_____
1929	11	_____	_____
1931	6	_____	_____
1933	7	_____	_____
1935	8	_____	_____

(1) Using 1927 as the base year, compute
the index of prices in each of the five years.
 (2) Using 1935 as the base year, compute
the index of prices in each of the five years.
 b. Below are hypothetical figures for money
or unadjusted gross national product in each
of the five years.

Year	Money or unadjusted GNP, billions of dollars	Adjusted GNP in 1927 dollars	Adjusted GNP in 1935 dollars
1927	$ 90	$_____	$_____
1929	120	_____	_____
1931	60	_____	_____
1933	65	_____	_____
1935	70	_____	_____

(1) Compute the real (or adjusted) gross
national product measured in 1927 dollars.
 (2) Compute the real (or adjusted) gross
national product measured in 1935 dollars.

2. You are given the following national income accounting data.

	Billions of dollars
Personal taxes	$ 37
Social security contributions	10
Indirect business taxes	19
Corporate income taxes	38
Transfer payments	17
Gross national product	468
Undistributed corporate profits	34
Gross private domestic investment	74
Personal consumption expenditures	310
Net private domestic investment	51
Interest paid by consumers	8

Compute each of the following:
 a. Net national product: $_____
 b. National income: $_____
 c. Personal income: $_____
 d. Disposable income: $_____
 e. Personal saving: $_____

3. Following are hypothetical social accounting figures for the United States.

	Billions of dollars
Exports	$ 12
Interest paid by consumers	5
Dividends	13
Depreciation (capital consumption allowances)	22
Government expenditures for goods and services	71
Rents	9
Indirect business taxes	11
Compensation to employees	238
Gross private domestic investment	56
Personal saving	29
Corporate income taxes	15
Transfer payments	26
Interest	6
Proprietors' income	21
Personal consumption expenditures	217
Imports	7
Social security contributions	7
Undistributed corporate profits	14
Personal taxes	55

Complete the table below in which the five income-output measures are computed by both methods. Identify each of the several amounts which you add (and/or subtract) to compute each of the five measures.

4. Below is a list of items which may or may not be included in the five income-output measures. Indicate in the space to the right of each which of the income-output measures includes this item; it is possible for the item to be included in none, one, two, three, four, or all of the measures. If the item is included in none of the measures, indicate why it is not included.

a. Interest on the national debt _____

b. The sale of a used air conditioner _____

c. The production of shoes which are not sold by the manufacturer _____

d. The income of a bootlegger in a "dry" state _____

Income (allocations) method	Output (expenditures) method
Gross National Product	
(1) $	(1) $
(2)	(2)
(3)	(3)
(4)	(4)
(5)	Gross national product $_____
(6)	
(7)	
(8)	
(9)	
Gross national product $_____	
Net National Product	
(1) $	(1) $
(2)	(2)
(3)	(3)
(4)	(4)
(5)	Net national product $_____
(6)	
(7)	
(8)	
Net national product $_____	

Income (allocations) method		Output (expenditures) method	
National Income			
(1)	$	(1)	$
(2)		(2) Less:	
(3)		National income	$_____
(4)			
(5)			
(6)			
(7)			
National income	$_____		
Personal Income			
(1)	$	(1)	$
(2) Plus:		(2)	
(3) Less:		(2)	
(4) Less:		(4)	
(5) Less:		Personal income	$_____
Personal income	$_____		
Disposable Income			
(1)	$	(1)	$
(2) Less:		(2)	
Disposable income	$_____	(3)	
		Disposable income	$_____

e. The purchase of a share of common stock on the New York Stock Exchange _____

f. The interest paid on the bonds of the General Motors Corporation _____

g. The labor performed by a housewife _____ _____

h. The labor performed by a paid baby-sitter _____

i. The monthly check received by an idler from his rich aunt _____

j. The purchase of a new tractor by a farmer _____

k. The labor performed by an assembly-line worker in repapering his own kitchen _____ _____

l. The services of a lawyer _____

m. The purchase of shoes from their manufacturer by a shoe retailer _____

n. The monthly check received from the government by a student studying on the GI Bill of Rights _____

o. The rent a homeowner would receive if he did not live in his own home _____

■ SELF-TEST

Circle the T if the statement is true, the F if it is false.

1. Gross national product measures at their market value the total output of all goods and services produced in the economy during a year.   **T   F**

2. Comparison of gross national product with the gross national product of an earlier year when the price level has risen between the two years necessitates the "inflation" of the GNP figure in the later year.   **T   F**

3. To adjust money gross national product for a given year so that a comparison between GNP in that year and in the base year can be made, it is necessary to divide money GNP in the given year by the price index—expressed as a decimal—for that year.   **T   F**

4. The total value added to a product and the value of the final product are equal.   **T   F**

5. The two approaches to the measurement of the gross national product yield identical results because one approach measures the total amount spent on the products produced by business firms during a year while the second approach measures the total income of business firms during the year.   **T   F**

6. In computing gross national product, net national product, and national income by the expenditures (or output) approach, transfer payments are excluded because they do not represent payments for currently produced goods and services.   **T   F**

7. If gross private domestic investment is greater than depreciation during a given year, the economy has declined or contracted during that year.   **T   F**
The data in the table below should be used to answer true-false questions 8 through 10 and multiple-choice questions 8 through 10.

	Billions of dollars
Net private domestic investment	$ 32
Personal taxes	39
Transfer payments	19
Indirect business taxes	8
Corporation income taxes	11
Personal consumption expenditures	217
Depreciation	7
Interest paid by consumers	4
United States exports	15
Government purchase of goods and services	51
Undistributed corporate profits	10
Social security contributions	4
United States imports	17

8. Gross private domestic investment is equal to $25 billion.   **T   F**

9. National income equals the net national product minus $8 billion.   **T   F**

10. Disposable income is equal to $245 billion.   **T   F**

Underscore the letter that corresponds to the best answer.

1. Which of the following is *not* an important use to which social accounting is put? (*a*) provides a basis for the formulation and application of policies designed to improve the economy's performance; (*b*) permits measurement of the economic efficiency of the economy; (*c*) makes possible an estimate of the output of final goods and services in the economy; (*d*) enables the economist to chart the growth or decline of the economy over a period of time.

2. If both money gross national product and the level of prices are rising, it is evident that: (*a*) real GNP is constant; (*b*) real GNP is rising but not as rapidly as prices; (*c*) real GNP is declining; (*d*) no conclusion can be drawn concerning the real GNP of the economy on the basis of this information.

3. To include the value of the parts used in producing the automobiles turned out during a year in gross national product for that year would be an example of: (*a*) including a nonmarket transaction; (*b*) including a nonproductive transaction; (*c*) including a noninvestment transaction; (*d*) double counting.

4. The sale in 1969 of an automobile produced in 1968 would not be included in the gross national product for 1969; doing so would involve: (*a*) including a nonmarket transaction; (*b*) including a nonproductive transaction; (*c*) including a noninvestment transaction; (*d*) double counting.

5. The service a baby-sitter performs when she stays at home with her baby brother while her parents are out and for which she receives no payment is not included in the gross national product because: (*a*) this is a nonmarket transaction; (*b*) this is a nonproductive transaction; (*c*) this is a noninvestment transaction; (*d*) double counting would be involved.

6. Which of the following does *not* represent investment? (*a*) an increase in the quantity of shoes on the shelves of a shoe store; (*b*) the construction of a house which will be occupied by its owner; (*c*) the purchase of newly issued shares of stock in the General Motors Corporation; (*d*) the construction of a factory building using money borrowed from a bank.

7. A refrigerator is produced by its manufacturer in 1968, sold during 1968 to a retailer, and sold by the retailer to a final consumer in 1969. The refrigerator is: (*a*) counted as consumption in 1968; (*b*) counted as investment in 1969; (*c*) counted as investment in 1968 and consumption and disinvestment in 1969; (*d*) not included in the gross national product of 1968.

Questions 8 through 10 use the national income accounting data given in the table in the true-false section.

8. The net national product is equal to: (*a*) $298 billion; (*b*) $302 billion; (*c*) $317 billion; (*d*) $321 billion.

9. National income exceeds personal income by: (*a*) $6 billion; (*b*) $15 billion; (*c*) $21 billion; (*d*) $44 billion.

10. Personal saving is equal to: (*a*) −$24 billion; (*b*) −$7 billion; (*c*) $7 billion; (*d*) $24 billion.

■ DISCUSSION QUESTIONS

1. Of what use is national income accounting to the economist and to the policy makers in the economy?

2. Why are GNP, NNP, etc., monetary measures, and why is it necessary that they be monetary measures?

3. Why do economists find it necessary to inflate and deflate GNP when comparing GNP in different years? How do they do this?

4. Why is GNP not a measure of the social welfare of society? Are there any better measures? For what purposes are NNP, NI, PI, and DI used?

5. Why does GNP exclude nonproductive transactions? What are the two principal types of nonproductive transactions? List some examples of each.

6. Why are there two ways, both of which yield the same answers, of computing GNP, NNP, etc?

7. What is meant by a nonincome charge or allocation? What are the two principal nonincome charges included in GNP? Why are they excluded from NI?

8. Why are transfer payments excluded from GNP, NNP, and NI?

9. Is residential construction counted as investment or consumption? Why?

10. How do you define a static, an expanding, and a contracting economy? What is the relationship between gross private domestic investment and depreciation in these three economies?

11. Why are indirect business taxes "indirect"?

12. Under what conditions can personal saving be negative? How is this possible?

THE BUSINESS CYCLE:
UNEMPLOYMENT AND INFLATION

This chapter begins the explanation of what determines the level of gross national product, net national product, national income, etc., actually achieved in any year. In the preceding chapter the student learned how to compute these income-output measures and what each of them means. In the chapters that follow he should learn what causes income and output to be what they are, what causes them to fluctuate, and how they can be controlled for the welfare of the economy as a whole.

Chapter 10 is concerned with the ups and downs which occur in employment, output, income, and price level over the years. These ups and downs are usually referred to as the business cycle. The chapter is in part historical and descriptive. It examines recent American economic history to see how prices, employment, income, and output have changed; the relationships between changes in these variables; and the immediate causes of these changes. One purpose of the chapter is to give the student a few historical facts which will be used in the next three chapters as a basis for generalizations about the determinants of income and output. The chapter is not purely descriptive and historical, however. Sections of it deal with the reasons the economic variables behave the way they do and why certain relationships exist between them.

Particular attention should be paid to the following: (1) the basic cause of changes in employment, output, income, and the price level; (2) the relationship between the level of employment in the economy and the effect of increased spending upon prices and employment; (3) what full employment means; (4) the relationship between the level of employment in the economy and the effect of increased spending upon the output of durable and nondurable goods; (5) the effect of price inflation upon the real incomes of various groups in the economy; (6) who is hurt by and who benefits from inflation and deflation; (7) the specific causes of the periods of prosperity, depression, and inflation experienced by the American economy during the last fifty years or so; and (8) what seem to be the prospects for economic stability in the future.

The facts, relationships, and explanations in Chapter 10 are too important to be overlooked, and they must be mastered if the student is to understand the chapters that follow.

■ CHAPTER OUTLINE

1. The macroeconomic trilogy is evident in the history of the American economy: economic growth interrupted by price, employment, and output instability.

2. The levels of employment, output, and prices actually achieved by the economy depend upon the level of total spending or demand in the economy.

a. When the economy is suffering a severe recession an increase in total demand will increase both output and employment and have almost no effect on the price level.

b. As the economy approaches full employment increases in total demand will continue to increase output and employment and will result in premature inflation.

c. If the economy is fully employing all of its resources an increase in total demand will have no effect on output or employment and will bring about pure (or demand-pull) inflation.

d. At or near full employment decreases in total demand will decrease output and employment, but will not, however, reduce the price level.

3. Full employment does not mean that all workers in the labor force are employed and that there is no unemployment in the economy.

a. There is always some frictional unemployment; and this kind of unemployment is generally desirable.

b. And in addition there is the structural unemployment that is the result of changes in technology and in the types of goods and services consumers wish to buy.

c. Cyclical unemployment is the result of insufficient aggregate demand in the economy.

d. Because some structural and frictional unemployment is unavoidable, full employment means that 96% of the labor force is employed (and 4% is unemployed).

e. The economic cost of unemployment is unproduced output (a GNP gap); and this cost is unequally distributed among different groups in the economy.

f. Unemployment also leads to serious social problems.

4. Inflation and deflation mean increases and decreases, respectively, in the level of prices in the economy.

a. Even if the total output of the economy did not change, inflation and deflation would redistribute real income; and would benefit some groups and hurt other groups in the economy.

b. But inflation and deflation may also affect the total output of the economy.

c. Creeping inflation involves small annual increases in the level of prices and may or may not be desirable for the economy as a whole.

5. The business cycle means alternating periods of prosperity and depression. These recurrent ups and downs in employment, output, and prices are irregular in their occurrence and intensity.

a. Not all changes in employment and output which occur in the economy are cyclical; some are due to seasonal and secular influences.

b. The business cycle affects almost the entire economy, but it does not affect all parts in the same way and to the same degree. In particular, the production of durable and nondurable goods does not fluctuate to the same degree during the cycle.

6. Since 1920 the American economy has witnessed great changes in the levels of employment, output, and prices; these changes can best be understood by reviewing the ways in which total spending changed during this period and the reasons for these changes in total spending.

7. Most economists agree that the economy will be more stable in the future than in the past because of changes in its institutions and structure, the expansion of the public sector of the economy, and the growth of economic knowledge and better public policies.

■ IMPORTANT TERMS

Macroeconomic trilogy	Deflation
Demand-pull inflation	Money income
Premature inflation	Real income
Pure inflation	Creeping inflation
Frictional unemployment	Hyper-(galloping) inflation
Structural unemployment	Rule of 72
Cyclical unemployment	Inflationary psychosis
Full unemployment	Business cycle
GNP gap	Seasonal variation
Inflation	Secular trend
	Stagflation

■ FILL-IN QUESTIONS

1. The basic determinant of the levels of employment and output and of the price level

is the volume or level of _____ in the economy.

2. Complete the following chain (using such words as more, less, larger, smaller, increase, decrease, etc.): An increase in total spending in the economy will make it profitable for

business to produce a _____

output; to do this it must employ _____

resources and this _____ the incomes received in the economy and *may*

_____

the price level.

3. Increases in total spending when the economy is at *less* than full employment may result in a rise in the price level; this is

termed _____ inflation. Increases in spending when the economy is at full employment result only in a rise in the price

level; and this is called _____ inflation.

4. Full employment in the American economy

is achieved when approximately _____% of the labor force is employed and there is no

_____

unemployment; but even at full employment

there is always some _____ and _____ unemployment in the economy.

5. The GNP gap is equal to _____

GNP *minus* _____ GNP.

6. Inflation means a _____

and deflation a _____

_____

7. A person's's *real* income depends upon his

_____

and _____

_____

8. List under the appropriate headings in the table below as many of those groups as you can who are affected by inflation and deflation.

9. Creeping inflation means an increase in

the level of prices of from about _____

to _____%
per year.

10. If the business cycle is divided into four

phases, these phases are often called _____

_____,

_____,

_____,

and _____;
if it is divided into two phases, it is common

to call these phases _____

and _____

or _____

and _____

11. In addition to the changes brought about by the operation of the business cycle, changes in output and employment may be

due to _____

and _____

Inflation		Deflation	
Hurt	Benefit	Hurt	Benefit
_____	_____	_____	_____
_____	_____	_____	_____
_____	_____	_____	_____
_____	_____	_____	_____
_____	_____	_____	_____

12. Production and employment in the _____

_____ goods industries are affected to a greater degree by depression and expansion than they are in the _____ goods industries; prices vary to a greater extent in the (low-, high-) _____ concentration industries.

13. During the period from 1922 to 1929 in the United States, GNP tended to _____

_____ ,

unemployment was _____ ,

and prices were _____ .
The basic cause of these conditions was a

_____ level of

investment spending on _____

and _____

14. Three important factors contributing to the prosperity of the 1920s were:

a. _____

b. _____

c. _____

15. In the 1930s investment spending was low largely because of _____

_____

and _____

_____

16. By and large, the prosperity of the World War II years was due to increased government spending; during this period consumer

spending _____

and private investment spending _____

_____

17. Following World War II consumer spending in the United States greatly increased

because consumers had both _____

and _____

and because the level of prices was _____

_____

18. In addition to a high level of consumer spending, prosperity in the United States between 1946 and 1949 was due to:

a. _____

b. _____

c. _____

d. _____

19. The decade of the 1950s was, in general, a period of prosperity and rising *real* GNP.

But there were brief recessions in _____

and _____ ; and inflation was accompanied by a slowing down of the _____

_____ rate and a _____
level of unemployment.

20. The American economy in 1961 began a period of unprecedented economic expansion. The principal reasons for this expansion were:

a. _____

b. _____

c. _____

d. _____

e. _____

21. During the period of economic expansion that began in early 1961, the *rate* of growth

_____ and *un*employment

_____ .

Until 1965 the price level was _____ ;

but after 1965 the economy experienced _____

_____

22. In the early 1970s the real output of the United States did not grow and:

a. both the rate of _____ and the

_____ rate increased;

b. the macroeconomic conditon of the economy was referred to as _____

c. the Federal government introduced a _____

_____ Policy which included a(n)

(increase, decrease) _____

in taxes and the imposition of wage and price

d. many economists became convinced that it was impossible for the economy to achieve both _____ and _____

23. From an examination of the business cycle since 1920 it seems evident that _____ spending is the most variable component of total spending; that changes in the _____ supply affect the levels of output, employment, and prices; and that upswings and downswings in economic activity are _____

24. List three reasons why many feel the American economy is more stable today than it was 40 or 50 years ago.

a. _____

b. _____

c. _____

■ PROBLEMS AND PROJECTS

1. In the table below are statistics* dealing with population, the labor force, employment, etc., in the United States during the years 1971, 1972, and 1973. Make the computations necessary to complete the statistics. (Numbers of persons are in thousands.)
  a. How was it possible to have *both* employ-

* Board of Governors of the Federal Reserve System, Federal Reserve Bulletin, vol. 60, no. 3, March, 1974, p. A64.

ment and unemployment increase? _____

b. In relative terms, if unemployment increases employment will decrease. Why? ____

c. Would you say that these years were years of full employment? _____
  d. Why is the task of maintaining full employment over the years more than just a problem of finding jobs for those who happen to be involuntarily idle in any given year? ____

2. In the space below, indicate for each of the following situations the effects of an increase in total spending on *incomes, output, employment,* and the *price level,* respectively, using the following symbols: A, no effect or slight increase; B, increase; and C, sharp increase.
  a. Depression and widespread unemployment

_____ _____ _____ _____

b. Prosperity, but moderate unemployment

_____ _____ _____ _____

c. Prosperity and full employment

_____ _____ _____ _____

3. The table on page 72 gives the average prices charged and the outputs of two different industries during a boom year and a depression year. Indicate in the appropriate spaces the percentages by which prices and output de-

	1971	1972	1973
Total noninstitutional population over 15 years of age	142,596	145,775	148,263
Population not in the civilian labor force	55,666	56,785	57,222
Armed Forces	2,817	2,448	2,327
Civilian labor force	_____	_____	_____
Percent of noninstitutional population over 15 years of age in the civilian labor force	_____	_____	_____
Total employment	79,120	81,702	84,409
Total unemployment	_____	_____	_____
Percent of civilian labor force employed	_____	_____	_____
Percent of civilian labor force unemployed	_____	_____	_____

Industry	Prices			Output		
	Boom	Depression	% Decline	Boom	Depression	% Decline
A	$ .65	$ .43	_____	90,000	70,000	_____
B	7.50	7.00	_____	120,000	75,000	_____

clined between the boom year and the depression year in each of the two industries.

a. In which industry was the relative price decline the greatest? _____

b. In which industry was the relative output decline the greatest? _____

c. Of the two, which industry would you say produced "hard" goods (capital goods and consumer durable goods)? _____

d. Which industry of the two would you suspect was concentrated? _____

4. Indicate in the space to the right of each of the following the effect—beneficial (B), detrimental (D), or indeterminate (I)—of inflation and deflation on these persons:

a. A retired schoolteacher living on her savings _____ _____

b. A retired schoolteacher living on the dividends she receives on the shares of stock she owns _____ _____

c. A farmer who has mortgaged his farm at the local bank for $20,000, which must be paid off in ten years _____ _____

d. A pensioner _____ _____

e. A widow whose income consists entirely of interest received on the corporate bonds she owns _____ _____

f. A schoolteacher _____ _____

g. A union member who works in a steel plant _____ _____

h. A state government employee

_____ _____

5. Suppose that in 1984 the economy is at full employment and has a GNP of $1,200 billion. GNP is capable of growing at a rate of 5% per year.

a. Compute the economy's *potential* GNP in 1985 and 1986 and enter them in the table

below. (*Hint:* Potential GNP in any year is equal to 105% of the potential GNP in the previous year.)

Year	Potential GNP	Actual GNP	GNP gap
1984	$1,200	$1,200	$ 0
1985	_____	1,236	_____
1986	_____	1,286	_____

b. *Actual* GNP in 1985 and 1986 is shown in the table. Complete the table by computing the GNP gap in these two years.

6. Employing "the rule of 72," how many years would it take for the price level to double if the annual increases in the level of prices were:

a. 10%: _____ years

b. 7.2%: _____ years

c. 5%: _____ years

■ SELF-TEST

Circle the T if the statement is true, the F if it is false.

1. In practical terms, full employment means that 96% of the total work force is employed. **T F**

2. With a moderate amount of unemployment in the economy, an increase in total spending will generally increase both the price level and the output of the economy. **T F**

3. If the economy is operating at full employment a decrease in total spending can be expected to reduce both the price level and employment in the economy. **T F**

4. If the price level increases by 10% each year the price level will double every ten years. **T F**

5. Not all changes which occur in output and employment in the economy are due to the business cycle.   **T   F**

6. Industries which are highly concentrated show small relative decreases in output and large relative decreases in prices during a downswing of the business cycle.   **T   F**

7. Inflation tends to work to the advantage of those persons whose income is derived from corporate profits and to the disadvantage of those whose income is derived from interest on corporate bonds.   **T   F**

8. Economists agree that creeping inflation benefits the economy as a whole.   **T   F**

9. The 1920s, in general, were years of rising GNP and prices and little unemployment.

T   F

10. The World War II years were a period characterized by a high level of private investment spending.   **T   F**

11. During World War II the increased taxes paid by consumers and the increased saving done by consumers were significant factors contributing to inflation.   **T   F**

12. The economy's GNP gap is measured by deducting its actual GNP from its potential GNP.   **T   F**

13. Changes in the nation's money supply appear to have little or no effect upon the economy's output, employment, and price levels.   **T   F**

14. The New Economic Policy included both an increase in taxes and wage and price controls.   **T   F**

15. While mild recessions and inflation will be encountered by the American economy in the future there seems to be no reason why it should have to experience a major depression.   **T   F**

Underscore the letter that corresponds to the best answer.

1. Which of the following is *not* part of the macroeconomic trilogy? (*a*) price stability; (*b*) economic growth; (*c*) full employment; (*d*) full production.

2. If the resources of the economy are fully employed, an increase in total spending will cause: (*a*) output and employment to increase; (*b*) output and prices to increase; (*c*)

incomes and prices to increase; (*d*) employment and incomes to increase.

3. If the economy is experiencing a depression with substantial unemployment, an increase in total spending will cause: (*a*) a decrease in the *real* income of the economy; (*b*) little or no increase in the level of prices; (*c*) an increase in the *real* income and a decrease in the *money* income of the economy; (*d*) proportionate increases in the price level, output, and income in the economy.

4. In Range II there is (*a*) price stability; (*b*) premature inflation; (*c*) demand-pull inflation; (*d*) pure inflation.

5. Insufficient total demand results in (*a*) frictional unemployment; (*b*) structural unemployment; (*c*) seasonal unemployment; (*d*) cyclical unemployment.

6. Total employment in December of this year was greater than total employment in December of 1928. This is no doubt due to the effect of: (*a*) seasonal variations; (*b*) secular trend; (*c*) the business cycle; (*d*) the diverse impact of the business cycle.

7. If employment in the agricultural sector of the American economy during last August and September was 112% of what it normally is in those months, this is probably a consequence of: (*a*) seasonal variations; (*b*) secular trend; (*c*) the business cycle; (*d*) both seasonal variations and the business cycle.

8. Production and employment in which of the following industries would be least affected by a depression? (*a*) nondurable consumer goods; (*b*) durable consumer goods; (*c*) capital goods; (*d*) iron and steel.

9. Which of the following would *not* benefit from deflation? (*a*) those living on fixed incomes; (*b*) those who find prices falling faster than their incomes; (*c*) those who have money savings; (*d*) those who became debtors during a period when prices were higher.

10. In late 1929 and the early 1930s a severe depression occurred in the United States. Which of the following was *not* a factor which contributed to the depression? (*a*) a decline in residential construction; (*b*) an expansion in the nation's money supply; (*c*) excess industrial capacity; (*d*) a large volume of personal indebtedness.

11. Which of the following was characteristic of economic conditions in the United States during the 1920s? (a) a backlog of demand for capital; (b) excess industrial capacity; (c) diminishing consumer debt; (d) rising prices and wage rates.

12. Which of the following was characteristic of the American economy between 1946 and 1949? (a) decreased government spending and a rising price level; (b) decreased consumer spending and decreased private investment spending; (c) increased consumer spending and decreased net exports; (d) declining employment and a rising price level.

13. Which of the following was not characteristic of the decade of the 1950s? (a) inflation; (b) two recessions; (c) an increase in the rate of economic growth; (d) significant economic growth.

14. Which of the following was not characteristic of the American economy in the 1960s? (a) a decline in the level of consumer prices; (b) a decline in the percentage of the labor force that is unemployed; (c) an increased rate of economic growth; (d) increased spending by Federal, state, and local governments.

15. In the early 1970s (a) the unemployment rate increased; (b) the rate of inflation increased; (c) stagflation occurred; (d) all of the above took place.

■ DISCUSSION QUESTIONS

1. What is meant by the macroeconomic trilogy?

2. Explain why and how total spending determines output, employment, and income in the economy.

3. Explain what will tend to happen to employment, output, income, and the price level if total spending increases and the resources of the economy are: (a) widely unemployed, (b) moderately unemployed, (c) fully employed. If total spending decreased would the effects on employment, output, income, and the price level be just the opposite? Why?

4. Distinguish (a) between premature and pure inflation; and (b) between frictional, structural, and cyclical unemployment.

5. Why will the price level tend to increase as a consequence of an increase in total spending in the economy before all the resources of the economy are fully employed?

6. When is there full employment in the American economy? How are the concepts of frictional and structural unemployment related to this definition of full employment?

7. What are inflation and deflation? What groups benefit from and what groups are hurt by inflation and deflation? Why?

8. Why do some economists believe that creeping inflation is beneficial to the economy?

9. What are the two principal arguments against creeping inflation? How can creeping inflation turn into hyperinflation and eventually result in depression and unemployment?

10. What are the phases of the business cycle called? How often do business cycles occur?

11. The business cycle is only one of three general causes of changes in output, income, and employment in the economy. What are the other influences which affect these variables?

12. Compare the manner in which the business cycle affects output, prices, and incomes in the industries producing capital and durable goods with industries producing nondurable goods and services. What causes these differences?

13. The level of total spending in the economy is the basic determinant of the levels of income, output, employment, and prices. What were the fundamental factors affecting total spending during: (a) the 1920s; (b) the 1930s; (c) the 1940s; (d) the 1950s; (e) the 1960s?

14. What was the macroeconomic condition of the economy in the early 1970s? How did the New Economic Policy attempt to deal with this condition and how did it lead to the "disillusionment" of many economists?

15. After reviewing the upswings and downswings in the American economy during the past fifty years, what four observations can be made?

16. What reasons do economists offer to support their belief that the American economy will be more stable and less prone to depressions in the future than it has been in the past?

THE BACKGROUND AND ANALYTICAL TOOLS OF EMPLOYMENT THEORY

Chapters 11 and 12 are really one chapter which has been divided into two parts and are probably the most important and crucial chapters in the first half of the text. They both concern the critical question of what determines the actual levels of employment and output the economy achieves in a given year.

Most of the material contained in the two chapters deals with the Keynesian theory or modern explanation of how employment and output are determined. This modern explanation is not the only possible explanation, however. It is with an alternative explanation called the classical theory of employment that the first part of Chapter 11 deals. The classical theory is described there for several reasons: to impress upon the student the fact that an alternative theory does exist; to examine the assumptions upon which the theory rests; to point out the weaknesses—both in fact and in logic—of the explanation; to provide an understanding of the reasons lying behind the "cures" for depression often advanced both in the past and at the present time; and, finally and most important, to enable the student to understand and evaluate the modern theory.

The outstanding thing about the classical theory is its conclusion that the economy will *automatically* function to produce the maximum output the economy is capable of pro-

ducing and to provide employment for all those who are willing and able to work. Compare this with the conclusion drawn by the exponents of the modern theory that the economy functions in no such way, that both depression and inflation can prevail with no automatic tendency to be corrected, and that full employment and maximum output, when achieved, are accidental. Compare also the political philosophies of the proponents of the two theories. Those accepting the classical theory have advocated as little government interference with the economy as possible in the belief that such interference would only prevent the achievement of full employment and maximum output; adherents of the modern theory have proposed that government action is necessary to eliminate the periods of depression and periods of inflation that can occur.

In studying this part of Chapter 11 the student should focus his attention on the following: (1) the three specific assumptions listed on page 220 of the text which are used throughout Chapters 11 and 12 to simplify the explanation, (2) Say's Law, (3) how the classical economists were able to conclude that whatever part of their incomes people choose to save will nevertheless be spent, (4) the part played by flexible prices and flexible wages in ensuring that all workers will be employed and that the economy will produce its maximum output, and (5) why the classical theory is not a good explanation of how the economy actually operates.

The basic proposition contained in the modern theory is that the level of total spending (aggregate demand) in the economy determines the size of the economy's output (NNP) and the total amount of employment. The latter part of the chapter analyzes the economic factors which determine the two principal components of aggregate demand—consumption demand and investment demand. The student should pay particular attention to the relationships called the consumption schedule, the saving schedule, and their characteristics; and to the four propensity concepts as well as to the "nonincome" determinants of consumption and saving. Investment demand depends upon the rate of net profit which businessmen expect to earn from an investment and upon the rate of interest they have to pay for the use of money. Five factors which influence the profit expectations of businesses are analyzed; and the student should learn how changes in these factors will affect investment. The student should also know how and why changes in the rate of interest will affect the amounts firms spend for additional capital goods.

In the next chapter the tools and ideas developed and explained in Chapter 11 are put together to form a complete and coherent picture of how aggregate demand determines the level of NNP.

■ CHAPTER OUTLINE

1. The classical theory of employment reached the conclusion that the economy would automatically tend to employ its resources fully and produce a full-employment level of output; this conclusion was based on Say's Law and the assumption that prices and wages were flexible.

a. Say's Law stated that the production of goods produced an equal amount of income to buy these goods; changes in the rate of interest would ensure that all income not spent (that is, income saved) by consumers would be loaned to investors, who would spend these borrowed funds on capital goods.

b. If there were an excess supply of goods

or an excess supply of labor (unemployment), prices and/or wages would fall until the excesses were eliminated and full employment and maximum output again prevailed in the economy.

c. Believing that capitalism would automatically ensure a full-employment level of output, the classical economists saw no need for government interference with the operation of the economy.

2. J. M. Keynes, in his *General Theory of Employment, Interest, and Money,* denied that flexible interest rates, prices, and wages would automatically promote full employment; he set forth the modern theory that there was nothing automatic about full employment and that both depression and inflation might prevail without any tendency existing for them to be self-correcting.

3. Aggregate output and employment are directly related to the level of total spending in the economy; to understand what determines the level of total spending at any time it is necessary to explain the factors that determine the levels of consumption and investment spending, the two principal components of total spending.

4. Consumption is the largest component of total spending; saving is income not spent for consumer goods.

a. Disposable income is the most important determinant of both consumption and saving; the relationships between income and consumption and between income and saving are both direct (positive) ones.

b. The consumption schedule shows the amounts that households will spend for consumer goods at various levels of income, and the saving schedule shows the amounts they will save.

c. The average propensities to consume and to save and the marginal propensities to consume and to save can be computed from the consumption and saving schedules.

d. In addition to income, there are several other important determinants of consumption and saving; changes in these nonincome determinants will cause the consumption and saving schedules to change.

e. A change in the amount consumed (or saved) is not the same thing as a change in the consumption (or saving) schedule. If these schedules change they change in opposite directions (except when they change as a result of a change in taxation); but the schedules are very stable.

5. The two important determinants of the level of investment in the economy are the expected rate of net profit from the purchase of additional capital goods and the rate of interest.

a. At least five factors influence the net profit expectations of business firms.

b. When the expected rate of net profit from an investment is greater (less) than the rate of interest a business will (will not) invest because the investment will be profitable (unprofitable). For this reason, the lower (higher) the rate of interest, the greater (smaller) will be the level of investment spending in the economy.

c. Investment spending in the economy may also be either independent of or directly related to the economy's NNP.

d. Because the five factors that influence the expected rate of net profit from investment are subject to sudden and rapid change, investment spending is highly unstable.

■ IMPORTANT TERMS

Classical theory of employment	Marginal propensity to consume
Say's Law	Marginal propensity to save
Rate of interest	
Money market	Change in amount consumed
Saving	Change in amount saved
Investment	
Price-wage flexibility	Change in the consumption schedule
Consumption schedule	Change in the saving schedule
Saving schedule	Nonincome determinants of consumptions and saving
Average propensity to consume	
Average propensity to save	Expected rate of net profit

■ FILL-IN QUESTIONS

1. Three "simplifying assumptions" used throughout most of the chapter are that the economy is a _____,

that all saving is _____ saving, and that the government _____

_____

_____.

A consequence of these assumptions is that

_____ = _____ =

_____ = _____

2. According to Say's Law, the production of goods and services creates an equal _____

_____

3. Changes in _____, according to the classical economists, ensure that what is not spent on consumer goods is spent on capital goods.

4. In the classical theory, if saving is greater than investment the rate of interest will _____

_____

and if investment is greater than saving it will

_____;

the rate of interest will have a tendency to ___

_____

where saving and investment are equal.

5. Full employment, in the classical theory, was assured by _____

and _____

_____

6. According to the classical way of thinking, if the interest rate did not equate saving and investment, and if total output exceeded the level of spending, prices in the output markets would tend to _____ because of competition among business firms; this would make production unprofitable and temporarily cause _____ in resource markets; but competition among resource suppliers would tend to drive resource prices _____

and _____ employment. This process would continue until _____

7. Keynes, in attacking the classical theory of employment, contended that price-wage flexibility would not guarantee full employ-

ment, first, because _____

_____

and, second, because wage reductions would

simply lead to _____,

_____,

and _____

8. Reasoning that if a price and wage rate reduction would increase the output and employment of an individual firm, then a general reduction in prices and wages will increase output and employment in the economy as a

whole involves the fallacy called _____

_____

9. According to the modern theory of employment, saving and investment are done by

_____

and for _____

10. Keynes argued that _____
is the most important determinant of the level of saving in the economy and that saving will

_____

as this determinant increases in size.

11. The largest single component of total

spending is _____
spending.

12. As disposable income falls, the average

propensity to consume will _____

and the average propensity to save will _____

_____

13. The most important determinants of consumption spending, other than the level of disposable income, are:

a. _____

b. _____

c. _____

d. _____

e. _____

f. _____

14. A change in the consumption (or saving)

schedule means that _____

_____

while a change in the amount consumed (or

saved) means that _____

_____

15. Investment is defined as spending for

additional _____;
and the total amount of investment spending in the economy depends upon:

a. the _____ rate of net _____

b. the rate of _____

16. Five factors which affect the profit expectations of business firms are:

a. _____

b. _____

c. _____

d. _____

e. _____

17. A business firm will invest in more capital if the expected rate of net profit on this in-

vestment is (greater, less) _____
than the rate of interest it must pay for the use of money.

18. The relation between the rate of interest and the total amount of investment in the

economy is (direct, inverse) _____
This means that if the rate of interest:

a. rises investment will _____

b. falls investment will _____

19. The consumption schedule and the saving schedule tend to be (stable or unstable)

_____

while investment demand tends to be _____

_____

20. The demand for new capital goods tends

to be unstable because of the _____

of capital goods, the _____ of

innovation, and the _____ of actual
and expected profits.

NNP	C	S	APC, %	APS, %	MPC, %	MPS, %
$350	$351	_____	_____	_____		
360	360	_____	_____	_____	_____	_____
370	369	_____	_____	_____	_____	_____
380	377	_____	_____	_____	_____	_____
390	385	_____	_____	_____	_____	_____
400	392	_____	_____	_____	_____	_____
410	399	_____	_____	_____	_____	_____
420	405	_____	_____	_____	_____	_____

■ PROBLEMS AND PROJECTS

1. Above is a consumption schedule. Assume taxes and transfer payments are zero.

a. Compute saving, the average propensity to consume, and the average propensity to save for each of the eight levels of NNP.

b. Compute the marginal propensity to consume and the marginal propensity to save for each of the seven changes in NNP.

c. Graph the consumption schedule, the saving schedule, and the 45° line.

2. Indicate in the space to the right of each of the following events whether the event will tend to increase (+) or decrease (−) the saving schedule.

a. Development of consumer expectations that prices will be higher in the future _____

b. Gradual shrinkage in the stock of durable goods owned by consumers _____

c. Increase in the volume of consumer indebtedness _____

d. Growing belief that disposable income will be lower in the future _____

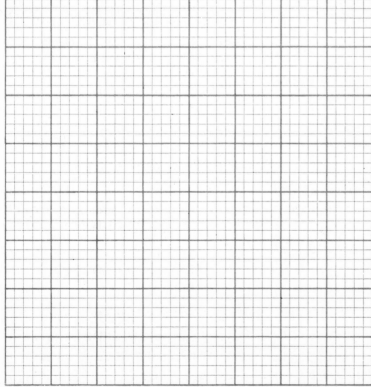

0   NNP

e. Rumors that a current shortage of consumer goods will soon disappear _____

f. Rise in the actual level of disposable income _____

g. A build-up in the dollar size of liquid assets owned by consumers _____

h. Development of a belief by consumers that the Federal government can and will prevent depressions in the future _____

3. The schedule below has nine different rates of net profit and the dollar amounts of investment expected to have each of these net-profit rates.

Rate of net profit	Amount of investment (millions)
9%	$1
8	2
7	3
6	4
5	5
4	6
3	7
2	8
1	9

In answering the questions that follow you may *assume* (1) there are no investments expected to have a rate of net profit greater than 9%; and (2) that businesses will not only make investments which they expect to be profitable but also any investments which they do not expect to be unprofitable.

a. If the rate of interest in the economy were 10%, business firms would plan to spend $_____ million for investment; but if the interest rate were 9% they would plan to spend $_____ million for investment.

b. Should the interest rate be 8% they would still wish to make the investments they were willing to make at interest rates of 10% and 9%; they would also plan to spend an additional $_____ million for investment; and their total investment would be $_____ million.

c. Were the rate of interest 7% they would make all the investments they had planned to make at higher interest rates plus an addi-

tional $_____ million; and their total investment spending would be $_____ million.

d. Complete the table below, employing the technique you learned above for determining how much investment would be planned at interest rates of 10, 9, and 8%, by computing the amount of planned investment at the six remaining interest rates.

Rate of interest	Amount of investment (millions)
10%	$ 0
9	1
8	3
7	6
6	_____
5	_____
4	_____
4	_____
2	_____
1	_____

e. Graph the schedule you completed above on the graph below. Plot the rate of interest on the vertical axis and the amount of investment planned at each rate of interest on the horizontal axis.

0

f. Both the graph and the table show that the relation between the rate of interest and the amount of investment spending in the economy is _____
This means that when the rate of interest:

(1) increases, investment will _____

(2) decreases, investment will _____

g. It also means that should we wish to:

(1) increase investment, we would need to

_____ the rate of interest

(2) decrease investment, we would have to

_____ the rate of interest

4. Indicate in the space to the right of each of the following events whether the event would tend to increase (+) or decrease (−) the net profit expectations of business firms.

a. Rising stock market prices   _____

b. Development of expectations by businessmen that business taxes will be higher in the future   _____

c. Step-up in the rates at which new products and new production processes are being introduced   _____

d. Business belief that wage rates may be lower in the future   _____

e. A mild recession   _____

f. A belief that business is "too good" and the economy is due for a period of "slow" consumer demand   _____

g. Rising costs in the construction industry   _____

h. A rapid increase in the size of the economy's population   _____

i. A period of a high level of investment spending which has resulted in productive capacity in excess of the current demand for goods and services   _____

■ SELF-TEST

Circle the T if the statement is true, the F if it is false.

1. Say's Law states that demand for goods and services creates an equal supply of goods and services.   **T   F**

2. In the classical theory, if saving exceeds investment the rate of interest will rise until saving and investment are equal.   **T   F**

3. According to the classical economists involuntary unemployment is impossible.   **T   F**

4. The level of saving in the economy depends primarily upon the level of disposable income.   **T   F**

5. The consumption schedule which is employed as an analytical tool is also a historical record of the relationship of consumption to disposable income.   **T   F**

6. Statistics show and economists agree that the marginal propensity to consume rises and the marginal propensity to save falls as disposable income rises.   **T   F**

7. An increase in the taxes paid by consumers will decrease both the amount they spend for consumption and the amount they save.   **T   F**

8. Both the consumption schedule and the saving schedule tend to be relatively stable over time.   **T   F**

9. A business firm will purchase additional capital goods if the rate of interest it must pay exceeds the expected rate of net profit from the investment.   **T   F**

10. An increase in an economy's income may induce an increase in investment spending.   **T   F**

Underscore the letter that corresponds to the best answer.

1. If government neither taxes nor spends, and all saving done in the economy is personal saving: (a) gross national product equals net national product; (b) gross national product equals national income; (c) net national product equals disposable income; (d) disposable income equals personal consumption expenditures.

2. Which of the following could *not* be called a classical economist? (a) John Maynard Keynes; (b) J. B. Say; (c) A. C. Pigou; (d) John Stuart Mill.

3. If the rate of interest did not equate saving and investment and total output was greater than total spending, the classical economists argued, competition would tend to force: (a) product and resource prices down; (b) product prices up and resource prices down; (c) product prices up and resource prices up; (d) product prices down and resource prices up.

4. Which of the following is *not* involved in Keynes's criticism of the classical theory of employment? (*a*) a reduction in wage rates will lead only to a reduction in total spending, not to an increase in employment; (*b*) investment spending is not influenced by the rate of interest; (*c*) prices and wages are simply not flexible downward in modern capitalistic economies; (*d*) saving in modern economies depends largely upon the level of disposable income and is little influenced by the rate of interest.

5. If consumption spending increases from $358 to $367 billion when disposable income increases from $412 to $427 billion, it can be concluded that the marginal propensity to consume is: (*a*) 0.4; (*b*) 0.6; (*c*) 0.8; (*d*) 0.9.

6. If when disposable income is $375 billion the average propensity to consume is 0.8, it can be concluded that: (*a*) the marginal propensity to consume is also 0.8; (*b*) consumption is $325 billion; (*c*) saving is $75 billion; (*d*) the marginal propensity to save is 0.2.

7. When the disposable income of consumers decreases (*a*) consumption increases and saving decreases; (*b*) consumption decreases and saving increases; (*c*) both consumption and saving increase; (*d*) both consumption and saving decrease.

8. Which of the following would *not* cause the consumption schedule to increase (that is, cause the consumption curve to rise)? (*a*) a decrease in consumers' stocks of durable goods; (*b*) an increase in consumers' ownership of liquid assets; (*c*) a decrease in the amount of consumers' indebtedness; (*d*) an increase in the income received by consumers.

9. A decrease in the level of investment spending would be a consequence of: (*a*) a decline in the rate of interest; (*b*) a decline in the level of wages paid; (*c*) a decline in business taxes; (*d*) a decline in stock market prices.

10. Which of the following relationships is an inverse one? (*a*) The relationship between consumption spending and disposable income; (*b*) the relationship between investment spending and the rate of interest; (*c*) the relationship between saving and the rate of interest; (*d*) the relationship between investment spending and net national product.

■ DISCUSSION QUESTIONS

1. According to the classical economists, what level of employment would tend to prevail in the economy? On what two basic assumptions did their analysis of the level of employment rest?

2. What is Say's Law? How were the classical economists able to reason that whatever is saved is spent?

3. In the classical analysis Say's Law made it certain that whatever was produced would be sold. How did flexible prices, flexible wages, and competition drive the economy to full employment and maximum output?

4. On what grounds did J. M. Keynes argue that flexible interest rates would not ensure the operation of Say's Law? What were his reasons for asserting that flexible prices and wages would not ensure full employment?

5. "Savers and investors are largely different groups and are motivated by different factors." Explain in detail who these groups are and what motivates them. Does the rate of interest play any role in determining saving and investment?

6. Explain briefly how the average propensity to consume and the average propensity to save vary as disposable income varies. Why do APC and APS behave this way? What happens to consumption and saving as disposable income varies?

7. Why do the sum of the APC and the APS and the sum of the MPC and the MPS always equal exactly one?

8. Explain briefly and explicitly *how* changes in the six nonincome determinants will affect the consumption schedule and the saving schedule and *why* such changes will affect consumption and saving in the way you have indicated.

9. Explain (*a*) when a business firm will or will not purchase additional capital goods; (*b*) how changes in the five determinants of the expected net profits of business firms will affect investment spending; and (*c*) why investment spending tends to rise when the rate of interest falls.

10. Why does the level of investment spending tend to be highly unstable?

THE EQUILIBRIUM
LEVELS OF OUTPUT,
EMPLOYMENT, AND INCOME

Chapter 12 explains in simple terms what determines the equilibrium level of NNP—the actual size of the NNP which will tend to be produced in the economy. The student *must* understand this chapter if he is to acquire an understanding of what causes NNP to rise and fall; of what causes unemployment, depression, inflation, and prosperity; and of what can be done to prevent recession and inflation and to foster price stability, full employment, and economic growth.

The equilibrium level of NNP is determined by the level of total spending or *aggregate demand* in the economy. In Chapter 11, the two principal components of aggregate demand, consumption demand and investment demand, were analyzed. In this chapter the equilibrium level of NNP is explained with both tables and graphs, first by using the aggregate demand–aggregate supply approach and then by employing the leakages-injections approach. These two approaches are complementary and are simply two different ways of analyzing the same process and of reaching the same conclusions. For each approach it is important for the student to know, given the consumption (or saving) schedule and the level of investment demand, *what* NNP will tend to be produced and *why* this will be the NNP which will be produced.

It is also important that the student under-

stand the significant distinctions between intended (planned) saving and actual (realized) saving; and between intended (planned) investment and actual (realized) investment. Actual saving is always equal to actual investment because both are defined in exactly the same way: the output of the economy minus its consumption. Intended saving and intended investment are not, however, equal by definition; they are equal only when NNP is at its equilibrium level. When NNP is *not* at its equilibrium level, intended saving and intended investment are *not* equal; but actual saving and investment will, as always, be equal because actual investment includes *unintended* (or *unplanned*) investment. Remember: Equilibrium NNP is achieved when *intended* saving and investment—*not actual* saving and investment—are equal.

The consumption (and the saving) schedule and investment demand—especially the latter —are subject to change, and when they change NNP will also change. The relationship between a change in investment (or a change in the consumption schedule) and a change in NNP is called the multiplier. Three things to note here are: *how* the multiplier is defined, *why* there is a multiplier effect, and upon *what* the size of the multiplier depends. Because of the multiplier, the paradoxical consequence of an attempt by the economy to save more is either no increase or a decrease in the level of saving in the economy. The explanation of this paradox will be evident to the student when he understands equilibrium NNP and the multiplier effect.

The final portion of the chapter emphasizes that equilibrium NNP is not necessarily the NNP at which full employment is achieved without the creation of inflationary pressures. Equilibrium NNP may be greater or less than full-employment NNP: if it is greater there is an inflationary gap, and if it is less there exists a recessionary gap. The next chapter deals with the fiscal policies that can be employed by government to eliminate these gaps. Chapter 12 has purposely ignored government and assumed an economy in which government neither taxes nor spends. But Chapter 13 does not ignore the role of government in the economy and discusses fiscal policies and their effects upon equilibrium NNP.

■ CHAPTER OUTLINE

1. Two alternative approaches are used to explain what level of NNP will tend to prevail in the economy (that is, will be the equilibrium NNP). Both approaches yield the same answer. Using the aggregate demand–aggregate supply approach, equilibrium NNP will be that NNP at which aggregate quantity demanded (planned consumption + planned net investment) equals aggregate quantity supplied or NNP (planned consumption + planned saving).

2. Using the leakages-injections approach, equilibrium NNP will be that NNP at which planned saving and planned net investment are equal.

3. The saving and investment schedules indicate what consumers and investors *plan* to do; if planned saving and planned net investment are not equal, NNP will change until they become equal. *Realized* saving and net investment are always equal.

4. Changes in the net investment schedule or in the consumption and saving schedules will cause the equilibrium level of NNP to change.
a. If net investment changes, NNP will change in the same direction by an amount greater than the change in net investment; this is called the multiplier effect; the size of

the simple multiplier depends upon the size of the marginal propensity to save.
b. The paradox of thrift is that an increase in the saving schedule results in no increase, and may result in a decrease, in saving; the increase in the saving schedule causes a multiple contraction in NNP and at the lower NNP the same amount or even less saving takes place.

5. The equilibrium level of NNP may turn out to be an equilibrium at less than full employment, at full employment, or at full employment with inflation.
a. If the equilibrium NNP is *less* than the NNP consistent with full employment, there exists a recessionary gap; the size of the recessionary gap equals the amount by which aggregate demand must increase to increase *real* equilibrium NNP to full-employment NNP.
b. If equilibrium NNP is *greater* than the NNP consistent with stable prices there is an inflationary gap. The size of the inflationary gap equals the amount by which aggregate demand must decrease to decrease *money* NNP without reducing *real* NNP or creating unemployment.
c. As aggregate demand increases and moves the economy closer to full employment both the economy's real NNP and its price level tend to rise; and this premature inflation makes it impossible to achieve both full employment and price stability.

■ IMPORTANT TERMS

Aggregate demand	Actual (realized) saving
Aggregate supply	
Aggregate quantity demanded	Actual (realized) investment
Aggregate quantity supplied	Equilibrium level of NNP
Aggregate demand–aggregate supply approach	Multiplier effect
	Multiplier
	Complex multiplier
Leakages-injections approach	Simple multiplier
Leakage	Paradox of thrift
	Supermultiplier
Injection	Recessionary gap
Planned (intended) saving	Inflationary gap
	Demand-pull inflation
Planned (intended) investment	Premature inflation

■ FILL-IN QUESTIONS

1. Two complementary approaches which are employed to explain the equilibrium level of output, employment, and income are the ____

_____

approach and the _____
approach.

2. In the modern theory of employment, income, employment, and output depend directly upon the level of _____
in the economy.

3. Assuming a governmentless economy, the equilibrium level of NNP is that NNP at which

NNP equals _____

plus _____

4. When the leakages-injections approach is used:
  a. in this chapter the only leakage considered is _____ and the only injection considered is _____
  b. in later chapters two additional:

  (1) leakages considered are _____

and _____

  (2) injections considered are _____

and _____

5. If:
  a. Aggregate quantity demanded is greater than aggregate quantity supplied, planned

saving is _____

planned investment, and NNP will tend to __

_____

  b. Aggregate quantity demanded is less than aggregate quantity supplied, planned saving is

_____

planned investment, and NNP will tend to __

_____

  c. Aggregate quantity demanded is equal to aggregate quantity supplied, planned saving is

_____

planned investment, and NNP will tend to __

_____

6. At every level of NNP _____

saving and _____ investment
are equal. But if planned investment is greater
than planned saving by $10, NNP will tend to

_____

by an amount _____
$10; and if planned saving is greater than
planned investment by $5, NNP will tend to

_____

by _____

7. When full employment has been achieved, if aggregate quantity demanded is greater than aggregate quantity supplied, planned in-

vestment will be _____

planned saving, prices will tend to _____,

output to _____,

income to _____,

employment to _____,

and _____
will be the result.

8. The value of the simple multiplier equals

_____

or _____.
The fact that NNP will increase by more than
an increase in investment demand is due to

two facts: _____

and _____

9. If the economy decides to save more (consume less) at every level of NNP, the equilib-

rium NNP will _____
and the equilibrium level of saving in the

economy will either _____

or _____;
this consequence of an increased desire to

save is called the _____

10. A recessionary gap exists when equilib-

rium NNP is (greater, less) _____

than the full-employment NNP; to bring NNP to the full-employment level, aggregate demand must _____ by an amount equal to the difference between equilibrium and full-employment NNP divided by _____

_____

11. When equilibrium money NNP is greater than the full-employment NNP at which prices are stable, there is a(n) _____

_____ gap; to eliminate this gap _____ must decrease by

_____

divided by the multiplier.

12. When the economy is at:
a. full employment and the price level has risen because of an increase in aggregate demand it is called _____ inflation.
b. less than full employment and the price level has risen because of an increase in aggregate demand it is called _____ inflation.

■ PROBLEMS AND PROJECTS

1. The table below shows consumption demand at various levels of NNP. Assume taxes and government spending are zero and that investment demand is $22.
a. Complete the saving, investment, and consumption-plus-investment columns.

NNP	C	S	I	C + I
$300	$290	$____	$____	$____
310	298	____	____	____
320	306	____	____	____
330	314	____	____	____
340	322	____	____	____
350	330	____	____	____
360	338	____	____	____
370	346	____	____	____
380	354	____	____	____
390	362	____	____	____
400	370	____	____	____

b. The equilibrium level of NNP will be
$_____
c. The marginal propensity to consume is

_____ ,

and the marginal propensity to save is _____
d. The value of the simple multiplier is _____
e. If investment demand should increase by $3, NNP would increase by $_____
f. If investment demand should decrease by $4, NNP would decrease by $_____
g.
(1) On the graph at the top of page 87, plot, C, C + I, and aggregate supply, and indicate the equilibrium NNP.
(2) On the graph below, plot S and I and indicate the equilibrium NNP.

0   NNP

2. Assume the marginal propensity to consume is 0.8 and the change in investment demand is $10. Complete the table on next page, modeled after Table 12–2 in the textbook.

3. On the next page are a saving schedule and two investment schedules—one (I_a) indicating that investment spending is constant and the other (I_i) indicating that the investment demand schedule is upsloping.

0   NNP

	Change in income	Change in consumption	Change in saving
Increase in investment of $10	+ 10	_____	_____
Second round	_____	_____	_____
Third round	_____	_____	_____
Fourth round	_____	_____	_____
Fifth round	_____	_____	_____
All other rounds	_____	_____	_____
Totals	_____	_____	_____

NNP	S	I_a	I_i
$300	$ 5	$15	$10
310	7	15	11
320	9	15	12
330	11	15	13
340	13	15	14
350	15	15	15
360	17	15	16
370	19	15	17
380	21	15	18
390	23	15	19
400	25	15	20

a. Using either investment schedule, the equilibrium NNP is $_____ and saving is $_____

b. The marginal propensity to save is _____ and the simple multiplier is _____
c. A $2 rise in the I_a schedule will cause NNP to rise by $_____, while a $2 rise in the level of the I_i schedule will cause NNP to rise by $_____

d. The value of the supermultiplier in the second case is, therefore, ______

e. Use the two investment schedules given in the table and assume a $2 increase in the saving schedule in the table—that is, planned saving at every NNP increases by $2.

(1) If the investment schedule is I_a, equilibrium NNP will ______ to $______ and at this NNP saving will be $______

(2) If the investment schedule is I_i, equilibrium NNP will ______ to $______ and at this NNP saving will be $______

(3) The effect of the increase in the saving schedule is to ______ equilibrium NNP and either to ______ or to ______ saving; this is called the ______

(4) The amount by which NNP changes depends upon the size of the change in the saving schedule and the size of ______

4. In the table below are consumption and saving schedules. Assume that the level of NNP at which full employment without inflation is achieved is $590.

NNP	C	S
$550	$520	$30
560	526	34
570	532	38
580	538	42
590	544	46
600	550	50
610	556	54
620	562	58
630	568	62

a. The value of the multiplier is ______

b. If investment demand is $58, equilibrium NNP is $______ and exceeds the full-employment noninflationary NNP by $______. There is a(n) ______ gap of $______

c. If investment demand is $38, equilibrium NNP is $______ and is less than full-employment NNP by $______. There is a(n) ______ gap of $______

■ SELF-TEST

Circle the T if the statement is true, the F if it is false.

1. Both the saving schedule and the investment schedule are schedules of plans rather than schedules of saving and investment actually realized. **T F**

2. The larger the marginal propensity to consume, the larger the size of the multiplier. **T F**

3. Actual saving at any level of NNP equals planned investment plus unintended investment (or minus unintended disinvestment). **T F**

4. The existence of a recessionary gap in the economy is characterized by the full employment of labor. **T F**

The following two questions are based on the data supplied for multiple-choice questions 1 and 2.

5. If saving at each level of NNP decreased by $5 and if investment demand remained constant at $24, equilibrium NNP would decrease by $16⅔ and saving in the economy would decrease by $5. **T F**

6. If consumption spending at each level of NNP increased by $10, the equilibrium level of NNP would tend to rise by $30. **T F**

7. If NNP were to decline by $40, consumers would probably reduce their consumption expenditures by an amount less than $40. **T F**

8. Realized saving and realized investment are always equal. **T F**

Underscore the letter that corresponds to the best answer.

Questions 1 and 2 below, as well as true-false questions 5 and 6, are based on the following consumption schedule.

NNP	C
$200	$200
240	228
280	256
320	284
360	312
400	340
440	368
480	396

1. If investment demand is $60, the equilibrium level of NNP will be: (a) $320; (b) $360; (c) $400; (d) $440.

2. If investment demand were to increase by $5, NNP would increase by: (a) $5; (b) $7½; (c) $15; (d) $16⅔.

3. If the value of the marginal propensity to consume is 0.6 and NNP falls by $25, this was caused by a decrease in aggregate demand of: (a) $10; (b) $15; (c) $16⅔; (d) $20.

4. The paradox of thrift means that: (a) an increase in saving lowers the level of NNP; (b) an increase in the average propensity to save lowers or leaves unchanged the level of savings; (c) an increase in the marginal propensity to save lowers the value of the multiplier; (d) an increase in NNP increases investment demand.

5. If the marginal propensity to consume is 0.6⅔ and if both investment demand and the saving schedule increase by $25, NNP will: (a) increase by $75; (b) not change; (c) decrease by $75; (d) increase by $25.

6. If NNP is $275 billion, consumption $250 billion, and investment $20 billion, NNP: (a) will tend to remain constant; (b) will tend to increase; (c) will tend to decrease; (d) equals aggregate demand.

7. If planned saving is greater than planned investment: (a) businesses will be motivated to increase their investments; (b) aggregate quantity demanded will be greater than aggregate quantity supplied; (c) NNP will be greater than planned investment plus planned consumption; (d) realized saving will tend to increase.

8. To eliminate an inflationary gap of $50 in an economy in which the marginal propensity to save is 0.1 it will be necessary to: (a) decrease aggregate demand by $50; (b) decrease aggregate demand by $5; (c) increase aggregate demand by $50; (d) increase aggregate demand by $5.

■ DISCUSSION QUESTIONS

1. Explain why the equilibrium level of NNP is that level of NNP at which NNP equals aggregate demand and at which saving equals investment. What will cause NNP to rise if it is below this level and what will cause it to fall if it is above this level?

2. Explain what is meant by a leakage and by an injection. What are the three major leakages and the three major injections in the flow of income in the American economy? Which leakage and which injection are considered in this chapter? Why is the equilibrium NNP the NNP at which the leakages equal the injections?

3. What is meant by "the distinction between saving and investment plans or intentions and the actual amounts which households manage to save and businesses to invest"? Are the saving schedule and the investment schedule planned or realized saving and investment? What adjustment causes planned and realized saving and investment to become equal?

4. What is the multiplier effect? Why does there tend to be a multiplier effect (that is, on what basic economic facts does the multiplier effect depend)? What determines how large the simple multiplier effect will be?

5. What is meant by the paradox of thrift? When would an increase in the saving schedule cause saving (at equilibrium) to decrease?

6. What relationship is there between the equilibrium level of NNP and the level of NNP at which full employment without inflation is achieved?

7. Explain what is meant by a recessionary gap and an inflationary gap. What economic conditions are present in the economy when each of these gaps exists? How is the size of each of these gaps measured?

8. How does premature inflation differ from demand-pull inflation? What are the consequences of premature inflation if two of the economic goals of the United States are full employment and price stability?

FISCAL POLICY
AND THE PUBLIC DEBT

Chapter 13 is really a continuation of the two preceding chapters and is concerned with the chief practical application of the principles discussed in those chapters.

It is worth recalling that principles of economics are generalizations about the way the economy works; and that these principles are studied in order that policies may be devised to solve real problems. Over the past one-hundred or so years the most serious problems encountered by the American economy have been those problems that resulted from the business cycle. Knowing what determines the output, employment, and price levels of an economy and what causes them to fluctuate makes it possible to discover ways to "control" the economy and to bring about full employment, maximum output, and stable prices. Economic principles, in short, suggest the policies that will eliminate both recessionary and inflationary gaps.

Government spending and taxing have a strong influence on the economy's output and employment and its price level. Federal expenditure and taxation policies designed to affect total production and employment and the level of prices are called fiscal policies. (The Federal Reserve Banks are also able to affect these variables by applying monetary

policy; but the study of monetary policy must wait until the effect of banks on the operation of the economy is examined in Chapters 14, 15, and 16.)

Talking about fiscal policies and the amounts the Federal government spends and taxes is really a discussion of the Federal budget. Chapter 13 opens with an examination of three budget philosophies. The student should learn from this section what each of the philosophies is and how they differ. He should also discover the effects of applying each philosophy upon national output, employment, and the price level; and upon the size of the public debt. The second and brief section makes it clear that Congress in the Employment Act of 1946 committed the Federal government to using fiscal (and monetary) policy to achieve a trio of economic goals—economic growth, stable prices, and full employment. This act also established the Council of Economic Advisors to advise the President and the Joint Economic Committee to advise Congress on matters pertaining to national economic policy.

The section entitled "Discretionary Fiscal Policy" is the crucial part of Chapter 13. It introduces government taxing and spending into the analysis of equilibrium NNP. It is important to note that government spending for goods and services adds to aggregate demand; and that taxation reduces the disposable income of consumers, and thereby reduces both the amount of consumption and the amount of saving that will take place at any level of NNP. Both "approaches" are again employed, and the student is again warned that he must know *what* NNP will tend to be produced and *why*. Special attention should be directed to the exact effect taxes have upon the consumption and saving schedules and the multiplier effects of changes in government spending and taxes.

An important point needs to be made here. Fiscal policy affects aggregate demand either directly or indirectly. Changes in government spending for goods and services alter aggregate demand directly by the same amount and in the same direction as the changes in government spending and have a multiplier effect on NNP. Changes in taxes alter aggregate demand indirectly, change the consumption schedule by an amount equal to the change in taxes times the marginal propensity to consume (which is less than 1.0), and change it in the opposite direction. This change in the consumption schedule then has a multiplier effect on NNP.

Once the student learns how government spending and taxing affect the equilibrium NNP it is fairly simple to understand what fiscal policies will be expansionary and reduce a recessionary gap and what fiscal policies will be contractionary and lessen an inflationary gap. It is at this point that the distinction between discretionary and nondiscretionary fiscal policy becomes significant. Discretionary fiscal policy requires that Congress take action to change tax rates, transfer payment programs, or expenditures for goods and services. Nondiscretionary fiscal policy does not require Congress to take any action; and is a built-in stabilizer of the economy. Because *net* tax receipts (tax collections less the transfer payments made) automatically increase (decrease) when the NNP rises (falls), fluctuations in national output and employment are not as large as they otherwise would be.

Unfortunately, nondiscretionary fiscal policy by itself is not able to eliminate any recessionary or inflationary gap that might develop; and discretionary fiscal policy will be neces-

sary if the economy is to produce its full-employment and noninflationary NNP. But the same built-in stabilizers of the economy make it more difficult to use discretionary fiscal policy to achieve this goal. The built-in stabilizers produce what is called fiscal drag. The student should understand why they result in fiscal drag. The student will then see that the built-in stabilizers may create the illusion that the Federal government's discretionary fiscal policy is expansionary or contractionary when in fact its policy is just the opposite of what it appears to be. Because of the illusions produced by the built-in stabilizers economists developed the full-employment budget. The full-employment budget enables us to discover whether Federal fiscal policy was actually expansionary or contractionary and to discover what policy it should have followed in order to create full employment without inflation in the economy.

In addition to this, what else should the student learn about fiscal policy from Chapter 13? He should be aware (1) that if the government has a budget deficit or surplus there are several ways of financing the deficit or disposing of the surplus, and that the way the deficit or surplus is handled can affect the economy's operation as much as the size of the deficit or surplus; (2) that which taxes and which expenditures government changes when it employs discretionary fiscal determines how effective its fiscal policy will be; and (3) that there are quite a few specific problems connected with the actual application of fiscal policy and what some of the most important of these problems are.

Whenever the Federal government applies fiscal policy and incurs either a budget deficit or a budget surplus, the size of the public (i.e., the national) debt is affected. Budget deficits lead to an increase in the public debt, while surpluses cause the debt to decrease. In the final section of the chapter the public debt is considered. Here the student should become aware of how large the debt and interest on the debt are, both absolutely and relatively; why an internally held public debt is a debt to ourselves and a public credit; and how and why the debt has grown. He should understand that the existence of the public debt both causes several economic problems and has its economic advantages— but that the problems are *not* those of bankrupting the government or of shifting the cost of a war (or of other government programs) to future generations.

It is clear that an increasing public debt is the result of government borrowing private saving. Private saving by business firms and by households is constantly increasing as the NNP grows. To maintain full employment and growth, all this saving must be borrowed and spent. To the extent that businesses and households fail to borrow all that is saved at full employment, government must take up the slack by borrowing and increasing the public debt if we are to continue to have full employment and economic growth.

Overall, it should become apparent that the size of the national debt is not of great importance. Changes in its size are important because they are the result of either deficits or surpluses; and a deficit or a surplus reflects the application of fiscal policy to affect the performance of the economy.

▪ CHAPTER OUTLINE

1. Fiscal policy is the manipulation by the Federal government of its expenditures and tax receipts in order to affect total spending in the economy (and thereby to affect output, employment, and prices).

2. Three budgetary philosophies may be followed by a government; the adoption of any of these philosophies will affect the employment, the output, and the price level of the economy.

a. Proponents of an annually balanced budget would have government expenditures and tax revenues equal in every year; but such a budget is pro- rather than countercyclical.

b. Those who advocate a cyclically balanced budget propose matching surpluses (in years of prosperity) with deficits (in depression years) to stabilize the economy; but there is no assurance that the surpluses will equal the deficits over the years.

c. Advocates of functional finance contend that deficits, surpluses, and the size of the debt are of minor importance; that the goal of full employment without inflation should be achieved regardless of the effects of the nec-

essary fiscal policies upon the budget and the size of the national debt.

3. The Employment Act of 1946 set the goals of American fiscal policy and provided for a Council of Economic Advisors to the President.

4. Discretionary fiscal policy involves congressional changes in tax rates and expenditure programs in order to eliminate recessionary and inflationary gaps.

a. Government expenditures for goods and services add to aggregate demand and increase equilibrium NNP; an increase in these expenditures has a multiplier effect upon equilibrium NNP.

b. Taxes decrease planned consumption and aggregate demand by the amount of the tax times the MPC; an increase in taxes thus decreases equilibrium NNP by a multiplier which is equal to MPC/MPS.

c. If the government both taxes and spends, equilibrium NNP will be the NNP at which

(1) Aggregate quantity demanded (planned consumption + planned investment + government spending for goods and services) equals aggregate quantity supplied (NNP or planned consumption + planned saving + net taxes).

(2) Planned investment + government spending for goods and services equals planned saving + net taxes.

d. Equal increases (decreases) in taxes and in government expenditures increase (decrease) equilibrium NNP by the amount of the change in taxes (or in expenditures).

e. The elimination of the inflationary recessionary) gap is accomplished by contractionary (expansionary) fiscal policy and by increasing (decreasing) taxes, decreasing (increasing) expenditures, and incurring budget surpluses (deficits).

5. In the American economy net tax revenues (tax receipts minus government transfer payments) are not a fixed amount or lump sum; they increase as the NNP rises and decrease as the NNP falls.

a. This net tax system serves as a built-in stabilizer of the economy because it reduces purchasing power during periods of inflation and expands purchasing power during periods of recession.

b. But built-in stability:

(1) can only reduce and cannot eliminate economic fluctuations;

(2) creates fiscal drag and makes it difficult to reduce unemployment during a recession and to maintain full employment in a growing economy;

(3) and requires that the full-employment budget be used to determine whether the Federal budget is actually expansionary or contractionary.

6. For a better understanding of fiscal policy it is necessary to include two important refinements.

  a. In addition to the size of the deficit or surplus, the manner in which the government finances its deficit or disposes of its surplus affects the level of total spending in the economy.

  b. And the types of taxes and the types of expenditures upon which the government relies to operate its fiscal policy help to determine the effectiveness of that fiscal policy in promoting economic stability.

7. Certain other specific complications arise in enacting and applying fiscal policy, and the degree of success achieved in solving these problems determines whether fiscal policy will actually be employed and whether it will be appropriate and effective.

8. Any government surplus or deficit automatically affects the size of the public debt.

  a. The public debt has grown substantially since 1929.

  (1) This debt is primarily the result of Federal borrowing during wartime; and is only secondarily the consequence of expansionary fiscal policies.

  (2) It is almost entirely internally held.

  (3) The relative size of the public debt and the interest payments on it have not grown so rapidly as the absolute size of the debt and the interest payments; and it has grown less rapidly than private debt.

  b. The contentions that a large debt will eventually bankrupt the government and that borrowing to finance expenditures passes the cost onto future generations are myths.

  c. There are, however, a number of real economic problems which a large public debt creates.

  d. But, on the other hand, there are several desirable aspects to this debt.

■ IMPORTANT TERMS

Fiscal policy
Annually balanced budget
Cyclically balanced budget
Functional finance
Employment Act of 1946
Council of Economic Advisors
Joint Economic Committee
Discretionary fiscal policy
Balanced-budget multiplier
Expansionary fiscal policy

Contractionary fiscal policy
Nondiscretionary fiscal policy
Net taxes
Built-in stability
Fiscal drag
Full-employment budget
Internally held public debt
Externally held public debt
Retiring the public debt
Refinancing the public debt

■ FILL-IN QUESTIONS

1. An annually balanced budget is procyclical rather than countercyclical because _____

_____

2. A cyclically balanced budget suggests that to ensure full employment without inflation, the government incur deficits during periods of _____ and surpluses during periods of _____

with the deficits and surpluses equaling each other over the business cycle. The budget over the cycle may not balance, however, because

_____

3. Functional finance has as its main goal the achievement of _____; and would regard budget _____ and increases in the _____ as of secondary importance.

4. The use of monetary and fiscal policy to reduce inflationary and recessionary gaps became national economic policy in the _____

_____ Act of _____.

This act also established the _____

to the President and the _____
in Congress.

5. Taxes tend to reduce consumption demand at each level of NNP by an amount

equal to the taxes multiplied by the _____

_____ ;

saving will decrease by an amount equal to

the taxes multiplied by the _____

_____

6. In an economy in which government both
taxes and spends, the equilibrium level of
NNP is the NNP at which:

a. NNP is equal to _____

plus _____

plus _____ ;

b. _____ plus _____

equals _____ plus _____

7. Equal reductions in taxes and government

spending will _____

NNP by an amount equal to _____

8. In order to increase NNP during a period

of recession, taxes should be _____

and government expenditures _____ ;
to decrease NNP during a period of inflation,

taxes should be _____

and government expenditures _____

9. If fiscal policy is to have a countercyclical

effect, a budget _____
should be incurred during a recession and a

budget _____ during inflation.

10. Net taxes:

a. equal _____ minus _____

b. in the United States will (increase, de-

crease) _____ as the NNP rises and will

_____ as the NNP falls.

11. When net tax receipts are directly related

to the NNP the economy has some _____
stability because:

a. when the NNP rises, leakages (increase,

decrease) _____ and the budget surplus

will _____ (or the budget deficit

will _____)

b. when the NNP falls, leakages _____

and the budget deficit will _____

(or the budget surplus will _____)

12. The built-in stability of the American net
tax system:

a. is not by itself capable of _____

_____ ;

b. results in _____ ;
c. makes it difficult to determine from an
examination of the Federal budget whether
discretionary fiscal policy has or has not been

_____

13. Fiscal drag means that when net tax receipts vary directly with the NNP and are not
a lump sum it is more difficult for discretion-

ary fiscal policy to raise the level of _____

_____ in the short run and to maintain

_____ in the long run.

14. The full-employment budget:

a. indicates what the Federal _____

_____ would have been if the economy

had operated at _____ during
the year;

b. tells us whether the Federal budget was

in fact _____ or _____

15. The two principal means available to
the Federal government for financing budget

deficits are _____

and _____ ;

the (former, latter) _____

is least contractionary because _____

_____

16. If the MPS were 0.2, a $1 billion increase in government expenditures for goods and services would increase NNP by $________ billion; but a $1 billion increase in transfer payments would increase by only $________ billion.

17. Most, though not all, economists would agree that a $10 billion increase in a (progressive, regressive) ______________ tax would be the more contractionary.

18. There is a problem of timing in the use of discretionary fiscal policy because of the ______________, ______________, and ____________________ lags.

19. The public debt of the United States is almost entirely ________________ held.

20. Today the public debt is about ________ percent, and interest charges on the debt are approximately ________ percent of GNP in the United States.

21. The cost of World War II was not passed on to future generations because the generation that fought the war had to go without ____________________________

22. As the full-employment NNP of the economy increases, the amount of saving done at full employment ____________________.
To maintain full employment, all this saving must be ____________________ and ____________________________

23. If the saving done at full employment is not all borrowed and spent by business and consumers, ____________________ must borrow and spend the saving. If it:

a. does *not* borrow and spend it, NNP and the rate of economic growth will ____________

b. does borrow and spend it, the public debt will ________________________

24. The existence of a large public debt may dampen ________________________ incentives in the economy, increase ____________________________, and make it difficult to use ________________ to control inflation.

25. The existence of a large public debt is desirable to the extent that it provides ____________________________, cushions the impact of ____________________, and provides a means of applying ____________________________ policies.

■ PROBLEMS AND PROJECTS

1. On page 96 is a consumption function.

a. Assume the government levies $10 in taxes at all levels of NNP and the marginal propensity to consume remains constant. Compute the new consumption column (C'), the saving column (S'), and the saving plus taxes column ($S + T$) at each of the 13 levels of NNP.

b. Suppose that investment demand is $15 and government spending for goods and services is $20. Complete the investment-plus-government-spending column ($I + G$) and the consumption-plus-investment-plus-government-spending column ($C' + I + G$).

c. On the graphs on the next two pages plot:

(1) C', $I + G$ and $C' + I + G$, and aggregate supply. Show the equilibrium NNP.

(2) $S' + T$ and $I + G$. Show the equilibrium NNP.

d. The equilibrium level of NNP will be $____________________
(To answer the question below it is not necessary to recompute C, S, $S + T$, and $C + I + G$. Use the multipliers.)

e. If taxes remained at $10 and government expenditures rose by $10, NNP would rise by $____________________

f. If government expenditures remained at $20 and taxes increased by $10, NNP would fall by $____________________

g. The effect of a $10 increase in taxes *and* a $10 increase in government spending

NNP	C	C′	S′	S′ + T	I + G	C′ + I + G
$350	$325	_____	_____	_____	_____	_____
360	334	_____	_____	_____	_____	_____
370	343	_____	_____	_____	_____	_____
380	352	_____	_____	_____	_____	_____
390	361	_____	_____	_____	_____	_____
400	370	_____	_____	_____	_____	_____
410	379	_____	_____	_____	_____	_____
420	388	_____	_____	_____	_____	_____
430	397	_____	_____	_____	_____	_____
440	406	_____	_____	_____	_____	_____
450	415	_____	_____	_____	_____	_____
460	424	_____	_____	_____	_____	_____
470	433	_____	_____	_____	_____	_____

0   NNP

0   NNP

is to _____ NNP by an amount

equal to $_____

2. In the table below are nine NNPs and the net tax receipts of government at each NNP.

NNP	Net tax receipts	Government expenditures	Government surplus
$ 800	$160	$____	$____
850	170	____	____
900	180	____	____
950	190	____	____
1,000	200	____	____
1,050	210	____	____
1,100	220	____	____
1,150	230	____	____
1,200	240	____	____

  a. Looking at the two columns on the left of the table, it can be seen that:

(1) when NNP increases by $50, net tax receipts (increase, decrease) _____

by $_____

(2) when NNP decreases by $100, net tax receipts _____ by $_____

(3) the relation between NNP and net tax receipts is (direct, inverse) _____

  b. Assume the investment multiplier has a value of 10 and that investment spending in the economy decreases by $10.

(1) *If* net tax receipts remained constant, the equilibrium NNP would decrease by

$_____

(2) But when NNP decreases, net tax receipts also decrease; and this decrease in net tax receipts will tend to (increase, decrease)

_____ the equilibrium NNP.

(3) And, therefore, the decrease in NNP brought about by the $10 decrease in investment spending will be (more, less) _____ than $100.

(4) The direct relationship between net tax receipts and NNP has (lessened, expanded)

_____ the impact of the $10 decrease in investment spending on NNP.

c. Suppose the government expenditures multiplier is also 10 and government wishes to increase the equilibrium NNP by $50.

(1) If net tax receipts remained constant, government would have to increase its expen-

ditures for goods and services by $_____

(2) But when NNP rises, net tax receipts also rise; and this rise in net tax receipts will

tend to (increase, decrease) _____
the equilibrium NNP.

(3) The effect, therefore, of the $5 increase in government expenditures will be to increase

the equilibrium NNP by (more, less) _____
than $50.

(4) The direct relation between net tax receipts and NNP has (lessened, expanded)

_____ the effect of the $5 increase in government expenditures; and to raise the equilibrium NNP by $50 government will have to increase its expenditures by (more, less)

_____ than $5.

d. Imagine that the full-employment NNP of the economy is $1,150 and that government expenditures for goods and services are $200.

(1) Complete the table on page 97 by entering the government expenditures and by computing the budget surplus at each of the NNPs. (Show a government deficit by placing a minus sign in front of the amount by which expenditures exceed net tax receipts.)

(2) The full-employment surplus equals

$_____

(3) Were the economy in a recession and producing an NNP of $900, the budget would

show a (surplus, deficit) _____ of

$_____

(4) This budget deficit or surplus makes it appear that government is pursuing a(n) (ex-

pansionary, contractionary) _____
fiscal policy; but this deficit or surplus is not the result of countercyclical fiscal policy but

the result of the _____

(5) If government did not change its net tax rates it could increase the equilibrium NNP

from $900 to the full-employment NNP of $1,050 by increasing its expenditures by (approximately) $70. At the full-employment NNP the budget would show a (surplus,

deficit) _____ of $_____

(6) If government did not change its expenditures it could increase the equilibrium NNP from $900 to the full-employment NNP of $1,050 by decreasing net tax receipts at all NNPs by a lump sum of (approximately) $80. The full-employment budget would have a

(surplus, deficit) _____ of $_____

3. Indicate in the space to the right of each of the following the effect—increase (+), decrease (−), or no effect (0)—on money NNP, output, and employment.

a. The economy is at less than full employment and:

(1) Government reduces its expenditures

for goods and services   ___ ___ ___

(2) Government reduces net taxes

___ ___ ___

(3) Investment increases

___ ___ ___

(4) Households plan to save more

___ ___ ___

(5) Households plan to consume more

___ ___ ___

b. The economy is operating at full employment and:

(1) Government increases its expenditures

for goods and services   ___ ___ ___

(2) Government increases transfer payments

___ ___ ___

(3) Investment increases

___ ___ ___

(4) Households plan to save more

___ ___ ___

(5) Households plan to consume less

___ ___ ___

■ SELF-TEST

Circle the T if the statement is true, the F if it is false.

1. Proponents of functional finance argue that a balanced budget, whether it is balanced annually or over the business cycle, is of

minor importance when compared with the objective of full employment without inflation. **T F**

2. There is no assurance that a nation can both use fiscal policy to promote full employment and balance its budget cyclically. **T F**

3. The Employment Act of 1946 commits the Federal government to using monetary and fiscal policy to achieve economic stability. **T F**

4. If the MPS were 0.3 and taxes were levied by the government so that consumers paid $20 in taxes at each level of NNP, consumption expenditures at each level of NNP would be $14 less. **T F**

5. If taxes only are reduced by $10 at all levels of NNP and the marginal propensity to save is 0.4, equilibrium NNP will rise by $25. **T F**

6. Even a balanced budget can be a weapon in fighting depression and inflation. **T F**

7. A governmental deficit is contractionary. **T F**

8. Built-in stabilizers are not sufficiently strong to prevent recession or inflation, but they can reduce the severity of recession or inflation. **T F**

9. A regressive tax system is more conducive to built-in stability than a progressive one. **T F**

10. The full-employment budget indicates how much government must spend and tax if there is to be full-employment in the economy. **T F**

11. It is generally believed that public works expenditures have a greater expansionary effect than transfer payments and that regressive taxes are more contractionary than progressive taxes. **T F**

12. The fiscal policies of state and local governments have tended to assist and reinforce the efforts of the Federal government to mitigate depression and inflation. **T F**

13. The public debt is about $470 billion. **T F**

14. The primary reason for the large increase in the public debt since 1930 is the deficit

spending during the years of the Great Depression. **T F**

15. A nation can experience prosperity and growth in its real output even though its national debt is increasing rapidly. **T F**

16. The chief disadvantage of the public debt of the United States is that as the debt becomes payable, the government may be unable to tax or to borrow sufficient money to redeem its securities. **T F**

17. The amount of saving done at full employment increases in a growing economy. **T F**

18. To maintain full employment in a growing economy it is necessary for the total of public and private debt to increase. **T F**

Underscore the letter that corresponds to the best answer.

1. Which of the following would involve reducing government expenditures and increasing tax rates during a depression? (*a*) an annually balanced budget policy; (*b*) functional finance; (*c*) cyclically balanced budget policy; (*d*) a policy employing built-in stability .

The next four questions are based on the consumption schedule below.

2. If taxes were zero, government expenditures for goods and services $10, and investment $6, equilibrium NNP would be: (*a*) $310; (*b*) $320; (*c*) $330; (*d*) $340.

NNP	C
$300	$290
310	298
320	306
330	314
340	322
350	330
360	338

3. If taxes were $5, government expenditures for goods and services $10, and investment $6, equilibrium NNP would be: (*a*) $300; (*b*) $310; (*c*) $320; (*d*) $330.

4. Assume investment is $42, taxes $40, and government spending for goods and services zero. If the full-employment level of NNP is $340, the gap can be eliminated by reducing taxes by: (*a*) $8; (*b*) $10; (*c*) $13; (*d*) $40.

5. Assume that investment is zero, that taxes

are zero, and that government spending for goods and services is $20. If the full-employ-ment-without-inflation level of NNP is $330, the gap can be eliminated by decreasing gov-ernment expenditures by: (a) $4; (b) $5; (c) $10; (d) $20.

6. Which of the following policies would do the *most* to reduce inflation? (a) increase taxes by $5 billion; (b) reduce government ex-penditures for goods and services by $5 bil-lion; (c) increase taxes and government ex-penditures by $5 billion; (d) reduce both taxes and government expenditures by $5 billion.

7. If the government wishes to increase the level of NNP, it might: (a) reduce taxes; (b) reduce its expenditures for goods and serv-ices; (c) reduce transfer payments; (d) reduce the size of the budget deficit.

8. If the marginal propensity to consume is 0.6⅔ and both taxes and government expendi-tures for goods and services increase by $25, NNP will: (a) fall by $25; (b) rise by $25; (c) fall by $75; (d) rise by $75.

9. If the economy is to have built-in stability, when NNP falls: (a) tax receipts and govern-ment transfer payments should fall; (b) tax receipts and government transfer payments should rise; (c) tax receipts should fall and government transfer payments should rise; (d) tax receipts should rise and government transfer payments should fall.

10. A direct relation between net tax receipts and NNP (a) automatically produces budget surpluses during a recession; (b) makes it easier for discretionary fiscal policy to move the economy out of a recession and toward full employment; (c) makes it easier to main-tain full employment in a growing economy; (d) reduces the effect of a change in invest-ment spending upon the national output and employment.

11. Which of the following by itself is the most expansionary (least contractionary)? (a) redemption of government bonds held by the public; (b) borrowing from the public to fi-nance a budget deficit; (c) a build-up in the size of the government's checking account in the central banks; (d) creating new money to finance a budget deficit.

12. Which of the following would be the most

contractionary? (a) increased personal income taxes, the receipts being used to retire part of the national debt; (b) increased sales and excise taxes, the receipts being used to retire part of the national debt; (c) increased per-sonal income taxes, the receipts being used to increase the cash balance of the govern-ment; (d) increased sales and excise taxes, the receipts being used to increase the cash balance of the government.

13. As a percentage of the gross national product, the public debt and interest on the debt are, respectively, about : (a) 50% and 1%; (b) 40% and 2%; (c) 105% and 3%; (d) 125% and 6%.

14. Incurring internal debts to finance a war does not pass the cost of the war on to future generations because: (a) the opportunity cost of the war is borne by the generation that fought it; (b) the government need not pay interest on internally held debts; (c) there is never a need for government to refinance the debt; (d) wartime inflation reduces the rela-tive size of the debt.

15. Which of the following is a consequence of the public debt of the United States? (a) it increases incentives to work and invest; (b) it provides some built-in stability during a recession; (c) it reduces income inequality; (d) it leads to greater saving at the various levels of disposable income.

16. Which of the following would be a conse-quence of the total retirement of the public debt? (a) a reduction in the nation's produc-tive capacity; (b) a reduction in the nation's standard of living; (c) a redistribution of the nation's wealth among its citizens; (d) an in-crease in aggregate demand in the economy.

17. Suppose the average propensity to save is constant and equal to 0.2 of NNP. If the full-employment NNP increases from $1,200 billion to $1,260 billion, saving at full em-ployment will increase by: (a) $3 billion; (b) $6 billion; (c) $9 billion; (d) $12 billion.

18. Suppose the multiplier is 3. Were the amount of saving done at full employment to increase by $20 and were private borrowing to increase by $5, to maintain full employ-ment, public borrowing and the public debt would have to increase by: (a) $5; (b) $15; (c) $45; (d) $60.

■ DISCUSSION QUESTIONS

1. What is meant by fiscal policy? What methods can government use to increase NNP? What policies can it follow to reduce NNP?

2. Explain why an annually balanced budget is not "neutral" and how it can intensify, rather than reduce the tendencies for NNP to rise and fall.

3. How does a cyclically balanced budget philosophy differ from the philosophy of functional finance?

4. Why do advocates of functional finance argue that budget deficits and a mounting public debt are of secondary importance?

5. In the Employment Act of 1946, (a) what responsibility was given to the Federal government; (b) what tasks were assigned to the Council of Economic Advisors and the Joint Economic Committee; and (c) what specific kinds of policy were to be used to achieve the goals established by the act?

6. Explain why, with government taxing and spending, the equilibrium NNP is that NNP at which NNP equals aggregate demand (consumption plus investment plus government spending for goods and services); and saving plus taxes equals investment plus government spending. What will cause NNP to move to its equilibrium level?

7. What is the exact effect which taxes will have on the consumption schedule? On the saving schedule?

8. If both taxes and government spending increase by equal amounts, NNP will increase by that amount. Why?

9. What is the difference between discretionary and nondiscretionary fiscal policy? How do the built-in stabilizers work to reduce rises and falls in the level of NNP?

10. What kind of tax system works best to promote built-in stability? Why? Which tax system does the least to promote built-in stability? Why?

11. Explain why a tax system in which net tax receipts vary directly with the level of NNP makes it difficult to achieve and to sustain full employment.

12. What is the full-employment budget? What was the problem which the use of the full-employment budget was designed to solve?

13. What are the alternative means of financing deficits and disposing of surpluses available to the Federal government? What is the difference between these methods insofar as their expansionary and contractionary effect is concerned?

14. In what sense has state and local fiscal policy been procyclical rather than countercyclical? What accounts for this fiscal perversity?

15. How big is the national debt of the United States absolutely and relatively? How large are the interest charges on the debt absolutely and relatively? What has happened to the size of the debt and interest charges since 1930? Why?

16. Explain the difference between an internally held and an externally held public debt. If the debt is internally held government borrowing to finance a war does not pass the cost of the war on to future generations. Why?

17. What are the principal advantages and disadvantages of a public debt internally held? Which of its disadvantages seems most important to you at this point in your study of economics?

18. In what ways does the existence of a large public debt contribute to inflation? Why does an increase in the size of the debt abet inflation? Which tends to be more inflationary, the existence of the debt or increases in its size?

19. What tends to happen to the absolute and the relative amounts of saving done at full employment as the full-employment NNP grows?

20. Why, in a growing economy, must borrowing and debt increase in order to maintain full employment and economic growth? What will happen to NNP if private borrowing and private debt do not increase? What must government do to maintain full employment if private borrowers do not increase their borrowings and debt enough to maintain full employment? What will this do to the public debt?

MONEY AND BANKING
IN AMERICAN CAPITALISM

By and large, Chapter 14 is descriptive and factual. It contains no explanation of how the banking system affects the operation of the economy. The purpose of this chapter is, however, to prepare the student for such an explanation. Of special importance are many terms and definitions which will probably be new to the student. These must be learned if the following two chapters and their analysis of how the banking system affects the performance of the economy are to be clearly understood. Chapter 14 also contains a factual description of the institutions which comprise the American banking system—the Board of Governors of the Federal Reserve System, the Federal Reserve Banks, and the commercial banks—and the functions of these institutions.

The student will do well to pay particular attention to the following points: (1) what money is and the functions it performs, what types of money exist in the American economy and their relative importance, and what constitutes the money supply; (2) what gives value to or "backs" American money; and (3) the three principal institutions of the American banking system, their functions, and their relationships.

Several points are worth repeating here because so much depends upon their being fully understood. First, money is whatever performs the three functions of money, and in the United States money consists of the debts (promises to pay) of the Federal government or of banks. In the United States, this money is "backed" by no more than the goods and services for which its owners can exchange it—not by gold, because Americans cannot exchange their money for gold.

Second, the central bank in the United States is the twelve Federal Reserve Banks and the Board of Governors of the Federal Reserve System, which oversees their operation. These banks, while privately owned by the commercial banks, are operated more or less as an agency of the Federal government —not for profit, but primarily to regulate the nation's money supply in the best interests of the economy as a whole and secondarily to perform other services for the banks, the government, and the economy. They are able to perform their primary function because they are bankers' banks where commercial banks can deposit and borrow money. They do not deal directly with the public.

Third, commercial banks, like many other financial institutions, accept deposits and make loans, but they also—and this distinguishes them from other financial institutions —are literally able to create money by lending demand deposits. Because they are able to do this, they have a strong influence on the size of the money supply and the value of money. The Federal Reserve Banks exist primarily to regulate the money supply and its value by influencing and controlling the amount of money commercial banks create.

Finally, banks—both Federal Reserve and commercial—are dealers in debt. Their assets consist almost entirely of the debts of others —the Federal government, other banks, or private borrowers—in the form of currency, bonds, and other types of promises to pay; their liabilities are debts to others in the form of currency and deposits (which "the others" consider assets).

■ CHAPTER OUTLINE

1. Money is whatever performs the three basic functions of money: a medium of exchange, a standard of value, and a store of value.

2. In the American economy the supply of money consists (in order of relative importance) of demand deposits, paper money, and coins—not owned by banks or the government.

  a. Currency (paper money plus coins) is money created by the government, and demand deposits are money which has been created by private commercial banks.

  b. Such paper assets as government bonds and savings accounts are near-monies because they can easily and quickly be converted into money; the amount of near-money is important because it affects consumer saving and spending and because changes in the money supply would occur if near-money were converted.

3. In the United States:

  a. Money is the promise of either some bank or the Federal government to pay (it is a bank or government debt), but these debts cannot be redeemed for anything tangible.

  b. Money has value only because people can exchange it for desirable goods and services.

  c. The value of money is inversely related to the price level.

  d. Money is "backed" by the confidence which the public has that the value of money will remain stable; and the Federal government can use monetary and fiscal policy to keep the value of money relatively stable.

4. The centralized American banking system consists of thousands of privately owned and operated commercial banks and the twelve Federal Reserve Banks, which are owned by the commercial banks and whose operation is directed by the Board of Governors of the Federal Reserve System.

  a. The banking system is centralized because the absence of centralization in the past led to an inflexible supply of money, a multitude of different kinds of money, and a mismanagement of the money supply which caused recurrent financial panics and speculation.

  b. The Federal Reserve System is composed of:

  (1) The Board of Governors, which exercises control over the supply of money and the banking system.

  (2) The Federal Reserve Banks, which are central, quasi-public, bankers' banks

  (3) Over 13,000 commercial banks—either state or national banks—which perform the two essential functions of holding deposits and making loans

  c. The Board of Governors and the Federal Reserve Banks perform six functions aimed at providing certain essential services, supervision of the private commercial banks, and the regulation of the supply of money.

■ IMPORTANT TERMS

Medium of exchange	Federal Open Market Committee
Standard of value	
Store of value	Federal Advisory Committee
Token money	Federal Reserve Bank
Intrinsic value	Central bank
Face value	Quasi-public bank
Paper money	Bankers' bank
Federal Reserve Note	Commercial bank
Treasury currency	State bank
Currency	National bank
Bank money	Member bank
Demand deposit	Member bank deposits (or reserves)
Near-money	
Time deposit	Collection of checks
Money supply	Quantitative credit controls
Fiat money	
Legal tender	Qualitative (selective) credit controls
Board of Governors	

■ FILL-IN QUESTIONS

1. Three functions of money are:

a. _____

b. _____

c. _____

2. The supply of money in the United States

consists of _____,

_____,

and _____

not owned by _____

or _____

3. Money in the United States consists of

the debts of _____

or the debts of _____

4. Insofar as their dollar size is concerned, the two most important near-monies in the

United States are _____

and _____

5. Money in the United States has value be-

cause _____

_____;

the value of money varies _____

with changes in the _____

6. Money = _____ + _____

7. Two groups which help the Board of Governors of the Federal Reserve System to

formulate its policies are the _____

_____ and the _____

_____.

8. What are the three basic quantitative controls employed by the Federal Reserve Banks?

a. _____

b. _____

c. _____

9. The three principal characteristics of the Federal Reserve Banks are:

a. _____

b. _____

c. _____

10. If a bank is a bankers' bank it means

that _____

and _____

11. The six major functions of the Federal Reserve Banks are:

a. _____

b. _____

c. _____

d. _____

e. _____

f. _____

12. Commercial banks are banks which ____

_____

and _____

and in doing so _____

13. Commercial banks differ from other financial institutions (savings banks, savings

and loan associations, etc.) because they ____

_____

and _____

and the other institutions do not.

14. When it is said that the Federal Reserve Banks act as a fiscal agent for the Federal government, it is meant that the Federal Re-

serve Banks _____,

_____,

and _____

15. The most important of the functions which the Federal Reserve Banks perform is

that of _____

■ PROBLEMS AND PROJECTS

1. From the data in the table on the next page, it can be concluded that on the date to which the figures pertain:

	Billions of dollars
Total Federal Reserve Notes outstanding	$ 64.3
Total savings accounts of the public	345.8
Total treasury coin outstanding	7.2
Commercial bank reserves at the Federal Reserve Banks	27.2
Demand deposits of the Federal government at the Federal Reserve Banks	3.4
Currency owned by commercial banks	7.1
Currency owned by the Federal Reserve Banks	4.4
Total treasury paper money outstanding	0.8
Demand deposits of the public in commercial banks	203.2
Government bonds owned by the public	173.5
Currency owned by the Federal government	0.8

a. The money supply is $_____ billion.

b. The amount of near-money is $_____ billion.

2. If you were to deposit $500 in currency in your checking account in a commercial bank, the *size* of the supply of money, as a consequence of your deposit, would have _____

_____;

and the *composition* of the money supply would have _____

3. If the price level:
a. Fell by 20%, the value of money would

_____ by _____ percent.
b. Rose by 10%, the value of money would

_____ by _____ percent.

■ SELF-TEST

Circle the T if the statement is true, the F if it is false.

1. If a coin is "token money," its face value is less than its intrinsic value.　　T　F

2. The larger the volume of near-monies owned by consumers, the larger will be their average propensity to save.　　T　F

3. If money is to have a fairly stable value, its supply must be limited relative to the demand for it.　　T　F

4. The Board of Governors of the Federal Reserve System is appointed by the President of the United States and confirmed by the Senate.　　T　F

5. The Federal Reserve Banks are owned and operated by the United States government.
　　T　F

6. All national banks are members of the Federal Reserve System.　　T　F

7. The most important function of the Federal Reserve Banks is the control of the size of the economy's money supply.　　T　F

8. Federal Reserve Banks are bankers' banks because they make loans to and accept deposits from commercial banks.　　T　F

Underscore the letter that corresponds to the best answer.

1. Which of the following constitutes the largest element in the nation's money supply? (a) treasury currency; (b) Federal Reserve Notes; (c) time deposits; (d) demand deposits.

2. Demand deposits are money because they are (a) legal tender; (b) fiat money; (c) a medium of exchange; (d) token money.

3. Which of the following *best* describes the "backing" of money in the United States? (a) the gold bullion stored at Fort Knox, Kentucky; (b) the belief of holders of money that it can be exchanged for desirable goods and services; (c) the willingness of banks and the government to surrender something of value in exchange for money; (d) the faith and confidence of the public in the ability of government to pay its debts.

4. If a person deposits $75 in currency in his checking account at a commercial bank, the supply of money has (a) decreased by $75; (b) increased by $75; (c) not changed in any way; (d) not changed in amount, but its composition has changed.

5. Which of the following is *not* a quantitative credit control? (*a*) regulation of consumer credit for purchasing homes; (*b*) open-market operations; (*c*) setting of the reserve requirement; (*d*) setting of the discount rate.

6. Which of the following functions distinguishes a commercial bank from other financial institutions? (*a*) accepts deposits; (*b*) creates and destroys money; (*c*) makes loans; (*d*) deals in debts.

7. Less than one-half of all commercial banks are members of the Federal Reserve System; these member banks have about what percentage of all deposits in commercial banks? (*a*) 20%; (*b*) 40%; (*c*) 60%; (*d*) 80%.

8. If the price level increases 20 percent, the value of money decreases: (*a*) 14½%; (*b*) 16⅔%; (*c*) 20%; (*d*) 25%.

■ DISCUSSION QUESTIONS

1. How would you define money? What constitutes the supply of money in the United States? Which of these is the largest element in the money supply?

2. Why are savings accounts (time deposits) and United States government bonds near-monies? Of what importance is the existence of near-monies?

3. For what reasons are demand deposits included in the money supply?

4. What "backs" the money used in the United States? What determines the value of money? Explain the relationship between the value of money and the price level.

5. Why is it necessary to have central banks in the United States?

6. Outline the structure of the Federal Reserve System and the chief functions of each of the segments of the system.

7. As briefly as possible outline the characteristics of the Federal Reserve Banks and explain the meaning of these chartcteristics.

8. How are commercial banks *like* other financial institutions? How do commercial banks *differ* from other financial institutions?

9. What are the chief functions which the Federal Reserve Banks perform? Explain briefly the meaning of each of these functions. Which function is the most important?

10. What is a commercial bank? What functions does it perform in the United States?

HOW BANKS CREATE MONEY

Chapter 14 outlined the institutional structure of banking in the United States today, the functions which banks and money perform, and the composition of the money supply in the United States. Chapter 15 explains how banks literally create money—checking account money—and the factors which determine and limit the money-creating ability of commercial banks.

The device (and a most convenient and simple device it is) employed to explain commercial banking operations and money creation is the balance sheet. All banking transactions affect this balance sheet, and the first step to understanding how money is created is to understand how various simple and typical transactions affect the commercial bank balance sheet.

In reading this chapter the student must analyze for himself the effect upon the balance sheet of each and every banking transaction discussed. The important items in the balance sheet are demand deposits and reserves, because demand deposits *are* money, and the ability of a bank to create new demand deposits is conditioned by the amount of reserves the bank owns. Expansion of the money supply depends upon the possession by commercial banks of excess reserves. Excess reserves do not appear explicitly in the balance sheet but do appear there implicitly because excess reserves are the difference between the actual reserves and the required reserves of commercial banks.

Three cases—the single commercial bank, the monopoly bank, and the banking system —are presented in order to help the student build an understanding of banking and money creation slowly and methodically. It is important here to understand that the money-creating potential of a single commercial bank differs in an important way from the money-creating potential of a monopoly bank and the entire banking system; it is equally important to understand how the money-creating ability of many single commercial banks is *multiplied* and results in the money-creating ability of the banking system as a whole.

Certain assumptions are used throughout most of the chapter to analyze money-creating ability; in certain instances these assumptions may not be completely realistic and may need to be modified. The chapter concludes with a discussion of how the earlier analysis must be modified—but not changed in its essentials— to take account of these slightly unrealistic assumptions.

■ CHAPTER OUTLINE

1. The balance sheet of the commercial bank is a statement of the assets, liabilities, and net worth of the bank at a specific point in time.

2. By examining the ways in which the balance sheet of the commercial bank is affected by various transactions, it is possible to understand how a single commercial bank in a multibank system can create money.

a. Certain reserve concepts are vital to this understanding.

(1) The *legal reserve deposit* (required reserve) which a commercial (member) bank must maintain at its Federal Reserve Bank (or as vault cash—which can be ignored) equals the reserve ratio multiplied by the deposit liabilities of the commercial bank.

(2) *Excess reserves* equal the *actual* deposit (reserve) of a commercial bank at the Federal Reserve Bank (plus the vault cash—which can be ignored) less its required reserve.

b. The deposit of cash in a commercial bank does not affect the total money supply; it only changes its composition, substituting demand deposits (bank money) for currency in circulation.

c. The writing of a check upon one bank and its deposit in a second bank results in a loss of reserves and deposits for the first and gain in reserves and deposits for the second bank.

d. A single commercial bank loans (or buys securities) in an amount equal to its excess reserves because it fears the loss of reserves and deposits to other banks. When lending (or buying securities), a bank increases its own deposit liabilities and, therefore, the supply of money by the amount of the loan.

3. A monopoly bank can make loans (or buy securities) and thus increase its deposit liabilities and the supply of money by an amount equal to its excess reserves multiplied by the reciprocal of the reserve ratio. The monopoly bank can lend more than can a single commercial bank because it does not lose reserves to other banks.

4. The lending ability of a banking system composed of many individual banks is the same as the lending ability of a monopoly bank.

a. The system can lend (or buy securities), thereby creating money and deposits, in an amount equal to the excess reserves of the system multiplied by the deposit multiplier (the reciprocal of the reserve ratio).

b. The banking system as a whole can do this even though no single commercial bank lends an amount greater than its excess reserves because the banking system, like the monopoly bank, does not lose reserves.

c. The potential lending ability of the banking system may not be fully achieved because of "leakages."

■ IMPORTANT TERMS

Balance sheet	The lending potential of a monopoly bank
Vault cash (till money)	
Legal (required) reserve	Commercial banking system
Reserve ratio	The lending potential of the banking system
Fractional reserve	
Actual reserve	Profit vs. liquidity
Excess reserve	Deposit multiplier
The lending potential of an individual commercial bank	Leakage
	Willingness vs. ability to lend
Monopoly bank	

■ FILL-IN QUESTIONS

1. The balance sheet of a commercial bank is a statement of the bank's _____ and _____ at some specific point in time.

2. The coins and paper money which a bank has in its possession are called _____ _____ or _____

3. Another name for a checking account is a _____ ___; a savings account is also called a _____ _____

4. The legal reserve deposit of a commercial bank (ignoring vault cash) must be kept in the _____ and must equal (at least) its _____

multiplied by the _____

5. The excess reserves of a commercial bank

equal its _____

less its _____

6. If commercial banks are allowed to accept (or create) deposits in excess of their reserves, the banking system is operating under

a system of _____
reserves.

7. When a person deposits cash in a commercial bank and receives a demand deposit in return, the size of the money supply has

(increased, decreased, not changed) _____

_____

8. When a check is drawn upon bank X, deposited in bank Y, and cleared, the reserves of bank X are (increased, decreased, not

changed) _____

and the reserves of bank Y are _____ ;

deposits in bank X are _____

and deposits in bank Y are _____

9. A single commercial bank in a multibank system can make loans equal in amount to

the _____
of that commercial bank.

10. When a commercial bank makes a new

loan of $10,000, it (increases, decreases) ___

_____

the supply of money by $_____

11. When a commercial bank sells a $2,000 government bond to a private business firm the supply of money (increases, decreases)

_____ .

by $_____

12. A bank ordinarily pursues two conflicting

goals; they are _____

and _____

13. A monopoly bank can make loans and create money in an amount equal to its excess

reserves multiplied by the _____

_____

14. The greater the reserve ratio is, the

(larger, smaller) _____
is the deposit multiplier.

15. If the required reserve ratio is 16⅔ percent, the banking system is $6 million short of reserves and the banking system is unable to increase its reserves, the banking system

must _____

the money supply by $_____

■ PROBLEMS AND PROJECTS

1. Below is a simplified balance sheet for a commercial bank. Assume that the figures given show the balance sheet of the bank *prior* to each of the following transactions. Draw up the balance sheet as it would appear after each of the transactions is completed, and place the balance sheet figures in the appropriate column.

	(1)	(2)	(3)	(4)
Assets:				
Cash	$100 $__	$__	$__	$__
Reserves	200 __	__	__	__
Loans	500 __	__	__	__
Securities	200 __	__	__	__
Liabilities:				
Demand deposits	900 __	__	__	__
Capital stock	100 __	__	__	__

   a. A check for $50 is drawn by one of the depositors of the bank, given to a person who deposits it in another bank, and cleared (column 1).
   b. A depositor withdraws $50 in cash from the bank, and the bank restores its vault cash by obtaining $50 in additional cash from its Federal Reserve Bank (column 2).
   c. A check for $60 drawn on another bank is deposited in this bank and cleared (column 3).
   d. The bank sells $100 in government bonds to the Federal Reserve Bank in its district (column 4).

2. In column 1 below are several reserve ratios. Compute the deposit multiplier for each of the reserve ratios and enter the figures in column 2. In column 3 show the maximum amount by which a single commercial bank in a multibank system can increase its loans for each dollar's worth of excess reserves it possesses. In column 4 indicate the maximum amount by which the banking system can increase its loans for each dollar's worth of excess reserves in the system.

3. Below are five balance sheets for a commercial bank (columns 1a–5a). The required reserve ratio is 20%.

a. Compute the required reserves (A) and—ignoring vault cash—the excess reserves* (B) of the bank.

b. If this bank is one bank in a multibank system, compute the amount of new loans it can extend (C).

c. If this bank is a monopoly bank, compute the amount of new loans it can extend (D).

d. Draw up for the individual bank in a multibank system the five balance sheets as they appear after the bank has made the new loans that it is capable of making (columns 1b–5b).

e. Draw up for the monopoly bank the balance sheet as it would appear after the bank has made the new loans that it is capable of making (columns 1c–5c).

* If the bank is short of reserves and must reduce its loans or obtain additional reserves, show this by placing a minus sign in front of the amounts by which it is short of reserves.

(1)	(2)	(3)	(4)
12½%	——	$——	$——
16⅔%	——	——	——
20%	——	——	——
25%	——	——	——
30%	——	——	——
33⅓%	——	——	——

	(1a)	(2a)	(3a)	(4a)	(5a)
Assets:					
Cash	$ 10	$ 20	$ 20	$ 20	$ 15
Reserves	40	40	25	40	45
Loans	100	100	100	100	150
Securities	50	60	30	70	60
Liabilities:					
Demand deposits	175	200	150	180	220
Capital stock	25	20	25	50	50
A. Required reserve	$ ——	$ ——	$ ——	$ ——	$ ——
B. Excess reserve	——	——	——	——	——
C. New loans—single bank	——	——	——	——	——
D. New loans—monopoly bank	——	——	——	——	——

	(1b)	(1c)	(2b)	(2c)	(3b)	(3c)	(4b)	(4c)	(5b)	(5c)
Assets:										
Cash	$——	$——	$——	$——	$——	$——	$——	$——	$——	$——
Reserves	——	——	——	——	——	——	——	——	——	——
Securities	——	——	——	——	——	——	——	——	——	——
Liabilities:										
Demand deposits	——	——	——	——	——	——	——	——	——	——
Capital stock	——	——	——	——	——	——	——	——	——	——

4. Below is a simplified consolidated balance sheet for all commercial banks in the economy. The reserve ratio is 20%. Assume that this is the balance sheet as it appears *prior* to the following transactions.

a. The public deposits $5 in cash in the banks and the banks send the $5 to the Federal Reserve, where it is added to their reserves. Fill in column 1. If the banking system extends the new loans it is capable of extending, show in column 2 the balance sheet as it would then appear.

posit in return; an hour later the Lincoln Coal and Iron Company borrows $300 from the same bank. The money supply has increased $300 as a result of the two transactions. **T F**

3. A single commercial bank in a multibank system of banking can loan an amount equal to its excess reserves multiplied by the required reserve ratio. **T F**

4. A commercial bank which is a member of the Federal Reserve System may maintain its

		(1)	(2)	(3)	(4)	(5)	(6)
Assets:							
Cash	$ 50	$___	$___	$___	$___	$___	$___
Reserves	100	___	___	___	___	___	___
Loans	200	___	___	___	___	___	___
Securities	200	___	___	___	___	___	___
Liabilities:							
Demand deposits	500	___	___	___	___	___	___
Capital stock	50	___	___	___	___	___	___
Loans from Federal Reserve	0	___	___	___	___	___	___
Excess reserves		___	___	___	___	___	___
Maximum possible expansion of the money supply		___	___	___	___	___	___

b. The banking system sells $8 worth of securities to the Federal Reserve. Complete column 3. Assuming the system extends the maximum amount of credit of which it is capable, fill in column 4.

c. The Federal Reserve lends $10 to the commercial banks; complete column 5. Complete column 6 showing the condition of the banks after the maximum amount of new loans which the banks are capable of making is granted.

■ SELF-TEST

Circle the T if the statement is true, the F if it is false.

1. The balance sheet of a commercial bank shows the transactions in which the bank has engaged during a given period of time. **T F**

2. Tom Roberts deposits $300 in cash in a commercial bank and receives a demand de-

legal reserve either as a deposit in its Federal Reserve Bank or as government bonds in its own vault. **T F**

5. The legal reserve which a commercial bank maintains must equal at least its own deposit liabilities multiplied by the required reserve ratio. **T F**

6. The actual reserves of a commercial bank equal excess reserves plus required reserves. **T F**

7. A commercial bank's assets plus its net worth equal the bank's liabilities. **T F**

8. The reserve of a commercial bank in the Federal Reserve Bank is an asset of the Federal Reserve Bank. **T F**

9. A check for $1,000 drawn on bank X by a depositor and deposited in bank Y will increase the excess reserves of bank Y by $1,000. **T F**

10. To say that a commercial bank seeks *profits* and *liquidity* is an example of dual terminology—using two different words to mean the same thing.　　　**T　F**

11. When a borrower repays a loan of $500, either in cash or by check, the supply of money is reduced by $500.　　　**T　F**

12. The granting of a $5,000 loan and the purchase of a $5,000 government bond from a private citizen by a commercial bank have the same immediate effect on the money supply.　　　**T　F**

13. If a monopoly bank has $10 million in excess reserves and if the reserve ratio is 25%, it can increase its loans by $40 million.　　　**T　F**

14. While a single commercial bank in a multibank system can only increase its loans by an amount equal to its excess reserves, the entire banking system can increase its loans by an amount equal to its excess reserves multiplied by the reciprocal of the reserve ratio.　　　**T　F**

15. When borrowers from a commercial bank wish to have cash rather than demand deposits, the money-creating potential of the banking system is increased.　　　**T　F**

Underscore the letter that corresponds to the best answer.

1. A bank has excess reserves of $3,000 and deposit liabilities of $30,000; the required reserve ratio is 20%. The actual reserves of the bank are: (a) $3,000; (b) $6,000; (c) $9,000; (d) $10,000.

2. A bank has excess reserves of $5,000 and deposit liabilities of $50,000 when the required reserve ratio is 20%. If the reserve ratio is raised to 25%, the bank's excess reserves will be: (a) $1,000; (b) $1,500; (c) $2,000; (d) $2,500.

3. A depositor places $750 in cash in a bank, and the reserve ratio is 33⅓%; the bank sends the $750 to the Federal Reserve Bank. As a result, the *reserves* and the *excess reserves* of the bank have been increased, respectively, by: (a) $750 and $250; (b) $750 and $500; (c) $750 and $750; (d) $500 and $500.

4. A bank has deposit liabilities of $100,000, reserves of $37,000, and a required reserve ratio of 25%. The amount by which a *single commercial bank* and the amount by which a *monopoly bank* can increase their loans are, respectively: (a) $12,000 and $48,000; (b) $17,000 and $68,000; (c) $12,000 and $60,000; (d) $17,000 and $85,000.

5. A bank has no excess reserves to start with, but then a depositor places $600 in cash in the bank, and the bank adds the $600 to its reserves by sending it to the Federal Reserve Bank. The bank then loans $300 to a borrower. As a consequence of these transactions the size of the money supply has: (a) not been affected; (b) increased by $300; (c) increased by $600; (d) increased by $900.

6. A bank has excess reserves of $500 and a required reserve ratio of 20%; it grants a loan of $1,000 to a borrower. If the borrower writes a check for $1,000 which is deposited in another bank, the first bank will be short of reserves, after the check has been cleared, in the amount of: (a) $200; (b) $500; (c) $700; (d) $1,000.

7. A monopoly bank has excess reserves of $700 and decides it can make new loans of $2,100 and be just meeting its reserve requirements. The required reserve ratio is: (a) 20%; (b) 25%; (c) 30%; (d) 33⅓%.

8. A bank sells a $1,000 government security to a private business firm. The business firm pays for the bond in cash, which the bank adds to its vault cash. The money supply has: (a) not been affected; (b) decreased by $1,000; (c) increased by $1,000; (d) increased by $1,000 multiplied by the reciprocal of the required reserve ratio.

9. The commercial banking system, because of a recent change in the reserve ratio required, finds that it is $50 million short of reserves. Before the change in the reserve ratio, it was loaned up but not short of reserves. It has deposit liabilities of $500 million and reserves of $100 million. The change in the reserve ratio which took place was from 20% to (a) 25%; (b) 30%; (c) 33⅓%; (d) 40%.

10. Only one bank in the commercial banking system has excess reserves, and its excess reserve is $100,000. This bank makes a new loan equal to the maximum amount it can loan. The borrower receives half the loan in the form of a demand deposit and half in cash, which the bank obtains from its Federal Reserve Bank. The required reserve ratio for all banks is 20%, and the cash is *not* redeposited in a bank. The maximum amount that the money supply can be expanded by the banking system as a result of the entire transaction is: (*a*) $250,000; (*b*) $300,000; (*c*) $500,000; (*d*) $600,000.

■ DISCUSSION QUESTIONS

1. Commercial banks seek both profits and safety. Explain how the balance sheet of the commercial banks reflects the desires of bankers for income and for liquidity.

2. Do the reserves held by commercial banks satisfactorily protect the deposits of the bank's depositors? Are the reserves of commercial banks needed, and are they sufficient to ensure the safety of deposits? Explain your answers.

3. Explain why the granting of a loan by a commercial bank increases the supply of money. Why does the repayment of a loan decrease the supply of money?

4. A store owner writes a check on his account in a New York City bank and gives it to one of his suppliers, who deposits it in his bank in Albany, New York. How does the Albany bank obtain payment from the New York City bank? If the two banks were in New York City and San Francisco, how would one bank pay the other? How are the excess reserves of the two banks affected?

5. Why is a single commercial bank in a multibank system only able to loan an amount equal to its excess reserves, while a monopoly bank can loan an amount equal to its excess reserve multiplied by the reciprocal of the reserve ratio required?

6. In a multibank system of banking, no one commercial bank ever lends an amount greater than its excess reserve, but the banking system as a whole is able to extend loans and expand the money supply by an amount equal to the system's excess reserves multiplied by the reciprocal of the reserve ratio. Explain why this is possible and how the multiple expansion of credit and money takes place.

7. On the basis of a given amount of excess reserves and a given reserve ratio, a certain expansion of the money supply may be possible. What are two reasons why the potential expansion of the money supply may not be fully achieved?

THE FEDERAL RESERVE
BANKS AND MONETARY POLICY

Chapter 16 is the third chapter dealing with money and banking. It explains how the Board of Governors of the Federal Reserve System and the Federal Reserve Banks affect output, income, employment, and the price level in the economy. Central-bank policies designed to affect these variables are called monetary policies, the goal of which in the present economy is full employment without inflation.

The student should have little difficulty with this chapter if he has understood the material in Chapter 15. In Chapter 16 attention should be concentrated on the following: (1) the cause-effect chain between monetary policy; commercial bank reserves and excess reserves; the supply of money; the cost and availability of credit; and investment spending, aggregate demand, output, employment, and the price level; (2) the principal items on the balance sheet of the Federal Reserve Banks; (3) the three major quantitative controls available to the Federal Reserve Banks, and how employment of these controls can affect the reserves, excess reserves, the actual money supply, and the money-creating potential of the banking system; (4) the minor qualitative controls which the Federal Reserve banks use or have used to influence the

economy; (5) the actions the Federal Reserve would take if it were pursuing a tight money policy to curb inflation, and the actions it would take if it were pursuing an easy money policy to prevent or eliminate depression; and (6) the relative effectiveness of the various types of monetary controls and of monetary policy in general in curbing inflation and depression.

In order to acquire a thorough knowledge of the manner in which each of the Federal Reserve transactions affects reserves, excess reserves, the actual money supply, and the potential money supply, the student must study very carefully each of the sets of balance sheets which are used to explain these transactions. On these balance sheets the items to watch are again reserves and demand deposits! Be sure that you know why each of the balance-sheet changes is made and are able, *on your own*, to make the appropriate balance-sheet entries to trace through the effects of any transaction.

To increase the student's understanding of how changes in the money supply affect the output of an economy and its price level, Chapter 16 offers the student an alternative way of looking at the economic forces that determine output and prices. This is the monetary approach. It employs the equation of exchange to reach conclusions that do not differ from those obtained from the leakages-injections (or aggregate demand–aggregate supply) approach. But it emphasizes the effects of a change in the money supply rather than the effects of changed saving and investment plans upon NNP and prices. Changes in saving and investment plans affect either V (the income velocity of money), M (the money supply) or both V and M in the equation of exchange and thereby affect either output (Q), the price level (P), or both. V and M are the connecting link between the two approaches. The student should learn how and why changes in saving and investment plans affect V and M. In addition, the student must understand the equation of exchange and each of its four terms and how a change in any one of the four terms affects the other terms in the equation.

■ CHAPTER OUTLINE

1. The objective of monetary policy is full employment in the economy without inflation; the Federal Reserve Banks attempt to accomplish this objective by exercising control over the size of commercial bank reserves, thereby influencing the size of the money supply, the rate of interest, investment, and the level of total spending.

2. By examining the consolidated balance sheet and the principal assets and liabilities of the Federal Reserve Banks, an understanding of the ways in which the Federal Reserve can control and influence the reserves of commercial banks and the money supply can be obtained.

3. The Federal Reserve Banks employ three quantitative controls to affect the total amount of bank credit and the size of the money supply.

   a. The Federal Reserve can change the reserve ratio.

   b. It can buy and sell government bonds in the open market.

   c. And it can also change the discount rate.

   d. Changes in the discount rate and the purchase and sale of government bonds affect the amount of Reserve Bank credit and the amount of commercial bank reserves.

   e. A tight (easy) money policy involves increasing (decreasing) the reserve ratio, selling (buying) bonds in the open market, and increasing (decreasing) the discount rate.

4. The Federal Reserve also employs qualitative controls to affect the volume of credit available for and the amount of spending on certain types of goods and securities.

   a. These controls consist of setting the margin requirements for the purchase of stocks, the terms of credit available to purchasers of homes and durable consumer goods, and the maximum interest rate commercial banks may pay on time deposits.

   b. In addition, moral suasion is used to influence commercial bank lending.

5. Open-market operations are the most effective device for controlling credit and the money supply.

6. An alternative approach to the relationships between the money supply, national output, and the price level employs the equation of exchange ($MV = PQ$).

   a. The equation of exchange looks at the $C + I_n + G = $ NNP equation from the money point of view; and tells us that total spending for the national output (MV) equals the money value of the output (PQ). If V is constant, an increase (decrease) in M will increase (decrease) P, Q, or both P and Q.

   b. While the Federal Reserve can control M, they cannot control V because V depends upon the resting time of money in the private sector of the economy.

   c. The value of V in the American economy has tended to rise historically; but it has not been determined whether V is relatively stable or unstable during short periods of time.

   d. The value of the multiplier in any time period depends directly on the magnitude of V.

   e. The leakages-injections and equation-of-exchange approaches yield the same conclusions and reinforce each other; but each approach emphasizes the economic forces underemphasized by the other.

7. Whether monetary policy is effective in promoting full employment without inflation is a debatable question, but monetary policy has both shortcomings and strengths in fighting recession and inflation.

■ IMPORTANT TERMS

Monetary policy

Easy money policy

Tight money policy

Gold certificates

Quantitative control

Qualitative control

Reserve Bank credit

Open-market opera-
tions

Discount rate

Moral suasion

Margin requirement

Regulation Q

Equation of exchange

Income (circuit)
velocity of money

Resting time of money

Monetary approach

Financial interme-
diaries

Cost-push inflation

■ FILL-IN QUESTIONS

1. The general objective of monetary policy

in the United States is _____ ;

the _____

is generally responsible for the monetary poli-

cies which are put into effect by _____

_____

2. To eliminate inflation the monetary au-

thority should seek to _____
the reserves of commercial banks, which

would _____
the supply of money, causing the rate of in-

terest to _____

and investment spending to _____

3. The two largest assets of the Federal Re-

serve Banks are _____

and _____. Their two largest

liabilities are _____ and

_____

4. Government securities are bought and sold
in the open market by the Federal Reserve

Banks in order to _____

and to _____

5. Reserve Bank credit is the sum of _____

_____

and _____

6. The three quantitative (or major) controls employed by the monetary authority are

changing _____,

charging _____,

and _____

7. Changes in the reserve ratio affect the
ability of commercial banks to create money

in two ways: they affect the _____

_____

and the _____

8. To increase the supply of money, the Fed-

eral Reserve Banks should _____

the reserve ratio, _____

the discount rate, and/or _____
government securities in the open market; to

decrease the supply of money, it should _____

_____

the reserve ratio, _____

the discount rate, and/or _____
securities in the open market.

9. If the Federal Reserve Banks were to sell
$10 million in government bonds to the public
and the reserve ratio were 25%, the supply
of money would immediately be reduced

$_____,
the reserves of commercial banks would be

reduced $_____,
and the excess reserves of the banks would be

reduced $_____;
if these bonds were sold to the commercial
banks, the supply of money would immediately

be reduced $_____,
the reserves of the banks would be reduced

$_____,
and the excess reserves of the banks would be

reduced $_____

10. Indicate in the space to the right of each
of the following transactions whether it will
increase (+) or decrease (−) commercial
bank excess reserves.

  a. Federal Reserve sells bonds in the open

market _____

b. Commercial banks borrow from the Federal Reserve _____

c. Federal Reserve reduces the reserve ratio

_____

11. The qualitative or minor controls are changes in:

a. _____

b. _____

c. _____

12. In the equation of exchange, $MV = PQ$, indicate below what each of the four letters in the equation represents.

M: _____

V: _____

P: _____

Q: _____

13. Indicate in the spaces provided the effects—increase (+), decrease (−), or no change (0)—upon P and Q of the following:

a. The economy is at full employment, M increases, and V remains constant.

_____ _____

b. The economy is in a severe recession, V increases, and M remains constant.

_____ _____

c. The economy is close to but not at full employment, and both M and V increase.

_____ _____

d. The economy is in a severe recession, M increases, and V remains constant.

_____ _____

e. The economy is at full employment, and both M and V increase.   _____ _____

14. If each firm and household wishes to hold an amount equal to $\frac{1}{12}$ of its annual income:

a. The "resting time" of a dollar in each firm and household would be _____

b. V would be _____

15. The value of V:

a. depends upon _____

b. has tended to (rise, fall, remain constant) _____ in the United States since 1947.

c. (is, is not, may be) _____ relatively constant during short time periods.

16. Suppose the marginal propensity to consume is 0.9. If V is 4, a \$10 billion increase in investment will increase the NNP by \$_____ during the *first* year following the investment.

17. Monetary policy will *not* be effective in pulling a nation out of a depression if commercial banks _____ or if the public _____

18. One of the advantages of monetary policy is that it tends to have more _____ than fiscal policy.

■ PROBLEMS AND PROJECTS

1. Below are various items which belong in the balance statement of the Federal Reserve Banks. Place them in their proper place in the blank balance sheet, listing them either on the asset or on the liabiilty side and in the order of their dollar importance.

Member bank reserves	Treasury deposits
Securities	Cash
Loans to member banks	Gold certificates
Federal Reserve Notes	

Assets	Liabilities
_____	_____
_____	_____
_____	_____
_____	_____

2. Assume that the consolidate balance sheet below is for all commercial banks. Assume also that the required reserve ratio is 25%, that cash is *not* a part of the commercial banks' legal reserve, and that the demand schedule below shows the amounts of commercial bank loans from the Federal Reserve that will be outstanding at various rates of interest.

Assets		Liabilities	
Cash	\$ 50	Demand deposits	\$400
Reserves	100	Loans from Federal	
Loans	150	Reserve	25
Securities	200	Net worth	75
	\$500		\$500

Discount rate, %	Amounts commercial banks will owe to the Federal Reserve
3.0	$ 0.0
2.5	12.5
2.0	25.0
1.5	37.5
1.0	50.0
0.5	62.5

a. To increase the supply of money by $100, the Federal Reserve Banks could *either:*

(1) _____

the reserve ratio to _____ %

(2) _____

securities worth $_____ in the open market

(3) _____

the discount rate to _____ %

b. To reduce the supply of money by $50, the Federal Reserve Banks could *either:*

(1) _____

the reserve ratio to _____ %

(2) _____

securities worth $_____ in the open market

(3) _____

the discount rate to _____ %

3. Below are the initial consolidated balance sheets of the Federal Reserve and of commercial banks. Assume that the reserve ratio for commercial banks is 25%, that cash is *not* a part of a bank's legal reserve, and that the

	(1)	(2)	(3)	(4)	(5)	(6)
Federal Reserve Banks						
Assets:						
Gold certificates	$ 25	$___	$___	$___	$___	$___
Securities	30	___	___	___	___	___
Loans to commercial banks	10	___	___	___	___	___
Liabilities:						
Reserves of commercial banks	50	___	___	___	___	___
Treasury deposits	5	___	___	___	___	___
Federal Reserve Notes	10	___	___	___	___	___
Commercial Banks						
Assets:						
Reserves	$ 50	$___	$___	$___	$___	$___
Securities	70	___	___	___	___	___
Loans	90	___	___	___	___	___
Liabilities:						
Demand deposits	200	___	___	___	___	___
Loans from Federal Reserve	10	___	___	___	___	___
A. Required reserves		___	___	___	___	___
B. Excess reserves		___	___	___	___	___
C. Initial change in the money supply		___	___	___	___	___
D. Total potential change in the money supply		___	___	___	___	___

balance-sheet figures in column 1 prevail at the start of each of the following problems. Place the new balance-sheet figures in the appropriate columns and complete A, B, C, and D. *Do not cumulate your answers!*

a. The Federal Reserve Banks sell $3 in securities to the public, which pays by check (column 2).

b. The Federal Reserve Banks buy $4 in securities from the commercial banks (column 3).

c. The Federal Reserve Banks lower the required reserve ratio for commercial banks to 20% (column 4).

d. The U.S. Treasury buys $5 worth of goods from American manufacturers and pays the manufacturers by checks drawn on its accounts at the Federal Reserve Banks (column 5).

e. Because the Federal Reserve Banks have raised the discount rate, commercial banks repay $6 which they owe to the Federal Reserve (column 6).

4. In the table below are the values of three of the four terms in the equation of exchange during six different years.

Year	M	V	P	Q
1	$300	3	$2	——
2	400	3	——	600
3	400	——	2²⁄₇	700
4	——	5	3	750
5	600	5	——	750
6	600	6	4⁸⁄₁₀	——

a. Complete the table by computing the value of the term not given in each year.

b. Between years:

(1) 1 and 2, a 33⅓% increase in M caused _____ to increase by _____%.

(2) 2 and 3, a 33⅓% increase in V caused _____ to increase by _____% and _____ to increase by _____%.

(3) 3 and 4, a 12½% increase in M and a 25% increase in V caused P to increase by _____% and Q to increase by _____%.

(4) 4 and 5, a 33⅓% increase in M caused _____ to increase by _____%.

(5) 5 and 6, a 20% increase in V caused _____ to increase by _____%.

■ SELF-TEST

Circle the T if the statement is true, the F if it is false.

1. Consumer spending is more sensitive to changes in the rate of interest than is investment demand. **T F**

2. If the monetary authority wished to follow a tight money policy, it would seek to reduce the reserves of commercial banks. **T F**

3. The securities owned by the Federal Reserve Banks are almost entirely U.S. government bonds. **T F**

4. A change in the reserve ratio will affect the multiple by which the banking system can create money, but it will not affect the actual or excess reserves of member banks. **T F**

5. If the Federal Reserve Banks buy $15 in government securities from the public in the open market, the effect will be to increase the excess reserves of commercial banks by $15. **T F**

6. If the reserve ratio is lowered, some required reserves are turned into excess reserves. **T F**

7. Statistical evidence reveals that the income velocity of money has remained almost constant from one year to the next. **T F**

8. An increase in the private sector's demand for money or cash balances tends to increase the velocity of money. **T F**

9. The policies of the Federal Reserve Banks during a period of inflation are reinforced by the desire of the United States Treasury to keep interest rates low. **T F**

10. It is generally agreed that fiscal policy is more effective than monetary policy in controlling the business cycle because fiscal policy is more flexible. **T F**

Underscore the letter that corresponds to the best answer.

1. The agency directly responsible for monetary policy in the United States is: (a) the twelve Federal Reserve Banks; (b) the Board of Governors of the Federal Reserve System; (c) the Congress of the United States; (d) the U.S. Treasury.

2. The largest single asset in the Federal Reserve Banks' consolidated balance sheet is: (a) securities; (b) gold certificates; (c) cash; (d) the reserves of member banks.

3. The largest single liability of the Federal Reserve Banks is: (a) the reserves of member banks; (b) the deposits of the U.S. Treasury; (c) Federal Reserve Notes; (d) loans to member banks.

4. If the banking system had actual reserves of $140 and excess reserves of $20, to eliminate the excess reserves the Federal Reserve Banks would have to: (a) raise the reserve ratio from 18 to 20%; (b) raise the reserve ratio from 20 to 23⅓%; (c) raise the reserve ratio from 23⅓ to 25%; (d) raise the reserve ratio from 25 to 27½%.

5. Assuming that the Federal Reserve Banks sell $20 million in government securities to member banks and the reserve ratio is 20%, then the effect will be: (a) to reduce the actual supply of money by $20 million; (b) to reduce the actual supply of money by $4 million; (c) to reduce the potential money supply by $20 million; (d) to reduce the potential money supply by $100 million.

6. Which of the following acts would *not* have the same general effect upon the economy as the other three? (a) the Federal Reserve Banks sell bonds in the open market; (b) the Federal Reserve increases the discount rate; (c) the Federal Reserve lowers the down payments required for the purchase of consumer durables; (d) the Federal Reserve raises the reserve ratio.

7. If V in the equation of exchange is constant, an increase in M will necessarily increase; (a) P; (b) Q; (c) both P and Q; (d) P times Q.

8. If the monetary authorities believe that the income velocity of money is 3, to increase NNP by $15 billion they should (a) decrease M by $45 billion; (b) decrease M by $5 billion; (c) increase M by $45 billion; (d) increase M by $5 billion.

9. If the "resting time" of a dollar in each firm and household in the economy is 3 months, (a) firms and households wish to hold an amount of money equal to ⅓ of their annual incomes; (b) firms and households

wish to hold an account of money equal to ½ of their annual incomes; (c) the velocity of money is 3; (d) the velocity of money is 2.

10. If the income velocity of money is 4 and the marginal propensity to consume is 0.8, a $10 increase in planned investment will *during the first year* increase NNP by: (a) $18; (b) $24.40; (c) $29.52; (d) $50.

■ DISCUSSION QUESTIONS

1. Explain how the Board of Governors and the Federal Reserve Banks can influence investment, output, employment, and the price level. In your explanation, employ the following concepts: reserves, excess reserves, the supply of money, the availability of bank credit, and the rate of interest.

2. Why are changes in the rate of interest more likely to affect investment spending than consumption and saving?

3. What are the principal assets and liabilities of the Federal Reserve Banks? Which of these items seems most crucial in its effect on the levels of income, output, employment, and prices in the economy?

4. What is Reserve Bank credit? Why is it so called? How is it related to commercial bank reserves and the supply of money?

5. Explain how the quantitative controls of the Federal Reserve Banks would be used to contract the supply of money. How would they be used to expand the supply of money?

6. What is the difference between the effects of the Federal Reserve's buying (selling) government securities in the open market from (to) commercial banks and from (to) the public?

7. How do the selective or qualitative controls differ from general or quantitative controls? What are the principal selective controls? Explain how the Federal Reserve would use these controls in following a tight and an easy money policy.

8. Explain how the Federal Reserve employs Regulation Q to prevent the impact of a tight money policy from falling heavily upon the residential construction industry.

9. Which of the control devices available to the Federal Reserve is most effective? Why is it more effective than other quantitative controls?

10. Explain the terms in the equation of exchange and why the equation is a restatement, from the money point of view, of the $C + I_n + G =$ NNP equation.

11. Explain how a change in M or in V in the equation of exchange will affect P and Q during a recession, during a period of prosperity without full employment, and during a period of full employment. What causes V to change?

12. Why is monetary policy more effective in controlling inflation than in reducing unemployment?

13. Why did the Federal Reserve and the Treasury disagree in the post–World War II period of inflation over the policy the Federal Reserve should follow with respect to its open-market operations?

14. If the Federal Reserve is following a tight money policy and trying to reduce the reserves of commercial banks, but the commercial banks are acquiring new reserves by selling government securities to the Federal Reserve Banks, is there anything the Federal Reserve can do to prevent this?

15. Looking back at your answer to question 1, explain why monetary policy may be ineffectual in controlling inflation and preventing depression.

ECONOMIC STABILITY:
THEORY AND POLICY

Chapter 17 is in part a summary of the previous eight chapters. The first two major sections of the chapter recall for the student the main outline of the theory of employment and the principal public policies that may be used to promote full employment without creating inflation. They help the student to see that the various principles discussed in the previous chapters are *not* separate theories but are, in fact, connected parts of the one theory of employment; and that the public policies discussed in earlier chapters are *not* really separate policies but are alternative means of achieving the goal of economic stabilization.

This one theory of employment and the alternative means of achieving this one goal are summarized for the student in Figure 17–1. This is probably the single most important figure in the textbook. But the student should be aware that it *is* a summary and that a summary necessarily sacrifices detail and completeness in exchange for generality and briefness. A few of the "Complications and Problems" which are hidden by Figure 17–1 and which are an essential part of a full understanding of the theory of employment and of stabilization policy are reviewed for the student in the third section of the chapter.

In order to increase the student's comprehension of this single theory in its entirety

and the alternative fiscal and monetary policies which are available to promote economic stability, the "Problems and Projects" section of the *Study Guide* contains a series of three numerical problems. The problems begin with familiar concepts and principles and from these familiar ideas develop several entirely new concepts and tools. These new concepts enable the student to understand better the theory of employment and public policy as a whole—rather than in parts—and to see the connections between the parts. In working these new and more difficult problems the student cannot rely on the textbook for help. Instead he must depend on what he has already learned and on carefully following the instructions given him in the problems. The only words of caution that need be given are: (1) start at the beginning of the series of problems; and (2) check your answer with those in the Answers section (at the back of the *Study Guide*) at every step of the way.

The fourth section of Chapter 17 examines two sharply opposing views. Keynesians stress the impact of the Federal budget on national output and the price level; and they believe that the way to achieve full employment without inflation is fiscal policy. Monetarists stress the impact of the money supply on output and price levels; and they contend that monetary policy is the best way to achieve these goals. The theories employed by the Keynesians and the Monetarists are really one theory. The student should try to see that what divides them is not the theory but the question of what method, fiscal or monetary policy, is the best means of promoting economic stability.

In the final section of the chapter the student will find a brief discussion of the ways in which the monetary and fiscal policies employed to bring about full employment and a stable price level affect the composition of the national output and the distribution of that output among the citizens of the economy. The point to be stressed is this. There are a number of different ways we can combine monetary and fiscal policies to eliminate unemployment and prevent serious inflation; but each of these different combinations or mixes results in a different answer for the *what is to be produced* question and a different answer for the *how is output to be distributed* question. The actual mix of policies selected, therefore, helps to determine our answers for these two questions. This final section ends with what may be an obvious conclusion: the monetary and fiscal policies we choose to employ should not work against (or oppose) each other but should be coordinated to reinforce and support each other.

■ CHAPTER OUTLINE

1. The income, employment, output, and prices of an economy are positively related to the level of aggregate demand, which has three principal components.

   a. Consumption spending depends upon the income of the economy and the several factors which affect the location of the consumption schedule.

   b. Investment spending is the more unstable component because it depends upon profit expectations which are themselves highly variable.

   c. Government spending depends partly on what level of spending is necessary to achieve full employment and price stability.

2. To achieve economic stability, government employs both fiscal and monetary policy.

   a. Fiscal policy utilizes both automatic and discretionary changes in government spending and in net taxes.

   b. Monetary policy utilizes both quantitative and selective controls to affect the money supply and interest rates.

3. The use of the theory of employment to achieve economic stability is complicated by several considerations.

   a. The connections between cause and effect are more complex and interdependent than the theory may suggest.

   b. The quantitative relationships between the components of the theory can only be estimated; and stabilization policies will, therefore, never be completely successful.

   c. Economic stabilization is but one goal of the American economy, and at times it may be made subordinate to other more pressing goals.

4. Economists disagree over whether fiscal or monetary policy is the more effective means of stabilizing the economy.

   a. Keynesians believe fiscal policy is more effective.

   b. The Monetarists believe monetary policy is more effective and argue that:

   (1) because the demand for money is a stable percentage of national income

   (2) the velocity of money is, therefore, stable; and the level of national income can be controlled by controlling the money supply

   (3) the economic history of the United States show that the changes in the money supply caused the observed changes in national income

   (4) fiscal policy is ineffective unless accompanied by changes in the money supply and it is, therefore, money-supply change that changes the level of economic activity

   (5) discretionary changes in the money supply bring about instability and a fixed rate of growth in the money supply is necessary for stability

   c. The Keynesians reply that velocity is not constant and that it tends to decrease during recessions and to increase during booms; and that if the money supply were to grow at a fixed rate national income would fluctuate as a result of the unstable velocity of money.

5. The mix of monetary and fiscal policies selected to stabilize the economy also affects the composition of the NNP (and, therefore, the allocation of resources) and the distribution of the national income. In selecting the mix to achieve stabilization it is essential that the monetary and fiscal policies be coordinated and congenial.

■ IMPORTANT TERMS

Keynesian position   Allocative effect
Monetarist position   Distributive effect
Monetary rule

■ FILL-IN QUESTIONS

1. The levels of output, employment, income, and prices depend upon the level of _____ _____ which in turn depends (in a closed economy) upon the amounts of

_____ ,

_____ , and _____

2. The theory of employment explains each of the three primary components of aggregate demand as follows:
   a. Consumption depends upon the level of

   _____ and the position of the

   _____

   b. Net investment depends upon the _____ rate of _____ of business firms and the rate of _____

   c. Government expenditures for goods and services depend upon _____

   _____

3. Government seeks to stabilize the economy by employing _____ and _____ policies.

4. Fiscal policy entails changing:
   a. _____ spending to affect

   _____ directly.

   b. _____ revenues in order to affect the _____ and _____ components of aggregate demand.

5. Monetary policy entails changing the supply of _____ to bring about a change in

the _____ and thereby affect

_____ spending in the economy.

6. Applying fiscal and monetary policies to achieve stability is difficult because economic

relations are more _____ than the theory suggests, the economic relations are hard to _____

and the economy also pursues _____ goals.

7. The Keynesian position is that while both fiscal and monetary policies affect the level

of economic activity, _____ policy is a more effective means of stabilizing the economy.

8. Monetarists:
   a. argue that because the _____ for

   money is stable, the _____ of money is

   also stable; and that the _____ of money determines the level of activity in the economy;

   b. would have the supply of money increase at the same annual rate as the potential rate

   of growth of _____ ,

   a rate of from _____ to _____% a year.

9. The use of monetary and fiscal policy to bring about full employment and price-level

stability affects the _____ of

_____ and the _____ of

   _____

10. If both monetary and fiscal policies are to be employed to stabilize the economy it is necessary that these two kinds of policy be

_____

■ PROBLEMS AND PROJECTS

1. Assume that the economy engages in no international trade—that its exports and imports are both zero; that government expenditures for goods and services are $50; that net taxes are also $50; and that the consumption

schedule of the economy *before* taxes is that shown in the table below.

NNP	C	C'	S'	i	I
$200	$190	___	___	5.0%	$ 0
250	230	___	___	4.5	10
300	270	___	___	4.0	20
350	310	___	___	3.5	30
400	350	___	___	3.0	40
450	390	___	___	2.5	50
500	430	___	___	2.0	60
550	470	___	___	1.5	70
600	510	___	___	1.0	80

a. Assume that all taxes are personal taxes. Given the marginal propensities to consume and to save evident in the consumption schedule, compute saving and consumpton *after* taxes at each level of NNP and enter them in the table.

b. Assume that the level of investment in the economy depends only upon the rate of interest according to the table above. Recalling that the government spends $50 for goods and services, what is the equilibrium level of NNP if the rate of interest happens to be 5%?

c. Now compute the equilibrium NNP at each of the other eight rates of interest given in the table; and enter the equilibrium NNPs opposite the appropriate rate of interest in the table below. (*Hint:* After computing NNP at

i	Equilibrium NNP
5.0%	___
4.5	___
4.0	___
3.5	___
3.0	___
2.5	___
2.0	___
1.5	___
1.0	___

5%, the other NNPs can be determined by using the multiplier.)

d. Plot the schedule obtained in (c) on the graph below. Place *i* on the vertical axis and NNP on the horizontal axis; and label the curve *IS* (because planned Investment and Saving are equal at the rates of interest and NNPs indicated by the curve).

e. Using your knowledge of the multiplier, what would be the effect—increase (+) or decrease (−)—on the equilibrium NNP at any given rate of interest of each of the following:

(1) A tax increase? ___ A tax decrease? ___

(2) An increase in government expenditures? ___ A decrease in government expenditures? ___

(3) An increase in the amount of investment at each rate of interest? ___ A decrease in investment demand at each rate of interest? ___

(4) An increase in the consumption schedule (that is, an increase in consumption at each level of NNP)? ___ A decrease in the consumption schedule? ___

f. Utilizing your answers in (e) immediately above, how would each of the following affect—increase (+) or decrease (−)—the entire *i*-equilibrium NNP schedule you calculated in (c)? (An increase in the schedule means that NNP at each *i* increases; a decrease means that NNP at each *i* decreases.)

(1) A tax increase? _____ A tax decrease?

_____

(2) An increase in government expenditures? _____ A decrease? _____

(3) An increase in investment demand?

_____ A decrease? _____

(4) An increase in the consumption schedule? _____ A decrease? _____

g. How would each of the eight changes listed in (f) above affect the *IS* curve? Assuming that the initial *IS* curve in the diagram below is IS_2, which four of the eight changes would move it to IS_1? _____

_____

Which four would move it to IS_3? _____

_____

2. Assume that the total supply of money (*M*) in the economy is equal to $100. Suppose also that the total demand for money (*L*) depends upon both the level of NNP and the prevailing rate of interest (*i*) in the economy.

The quantity of money demanded for *transaction* purposes (L_t) depends upon the level of NNP and is shown in the schedule above. The quantity of money demanded for *speculative* purposes (L_s) depends upon the rate of interest and is also shown in the same table. The total demand for money (*L*) equals the transactions demand plus the speculative demand ($L_t + L_s$).

NNP	L_t	*i*	L_s
$200	$20	5.0%	$40
250	25	4.5	45
300	30	4.0	50
350	35	3.5	55
400	40	3.0	60
450	45	2.5	65
500	50	2.0	70
550	55	1.5	75
600	60	1.0	80

a. The greater the NNP of the economy, the

_____ (greater, smaller) is the quantity of money demanded for transaction purposes; and vice versa.

b. The higher the rate of interest in the

economy, the _____ (greater, smaller) is the quantity of money demanded for speculative purposes; and vice versa.

c. If NNP were $200,

(1) L_t would be equal to _____
(2) In order that the supply of money ($100) equal the *total* demand for money ($L_t + L_s$), the speculative demand (L_s) would

have to be equal to _____

and the rate of interest equal to _____
(*Hint:* Subtract L_t from $100 to determine L_s; and then examine the schedule to discover what *i* must be to cause this L_s). Enter this rate of interest opposite the NNP of $200 in the table on page 127.

d. Now repeat the process followed in (c) above for NNPs from $250 through $600. Determine for each of these NNPs:

(1) The transactions demand (L_t) for money at this NNP.

(2) The amount of money from the total money supply (of $100) remaining to satisfy the speculative demand for money (L_s).

(3) What the rate of interest (*i*) would have to be in order that the L_s be the amount indicated in (2); and enter this *i* opposite the appropriate NNP in the table.

i	Equilibrium NNP
_____	$200
_____	250
_____	300
_____	350
_____	400
_____	450
_____	500
_____	550
_____	600

e. Plot the schedule obtained in (d) above on the graph below. Place i on the vertical axis and NNP on the horizontal axis; and label the curve LM because the quantity of money demanded and the supply of money are equal at the rates of interest and NNPs indicated by the curve.

f. If the supply of money (M) should:

(1) Increase from $100 to $105; the i op-

posite every NNP would _____

(increase, decrease) by _____ percentage points.

(2) Decrease from $100 to $95, the i op-

posite every NNP would _____

by _____ percentage points.

g. Using the knowledge gained in (f) above concerning the effects of a change in the sup-

ply of money upon the LM schedule; and using the LM_2 curve given in the diagram below, draw:

(1) An LM curve that would result from an increase in the money supply and label it LM_3

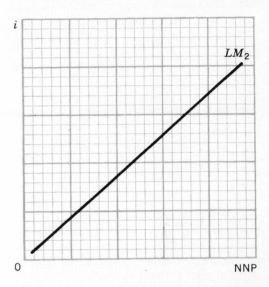

(2) An LM curve that would result from a decrease in the money supply and label it M_1

3. Assume the following: the existence of the consumption and investment schedules given in question 1 above; the existence of the transactions and speculative demand for money schedules given in question 2 above; that government expenditures for goods and services are $50; that net taxes are $50; and that the supply of money is $100.

a. Using the tables which you completed in questions (1 c) and (2 d) above, what NNP and what rate of interest will ensure both that the aggregate quantity of goods and services demanded equals the aggregate quantity supplied; and that the total quantity of money demanded equals the supply of money? (Hint: At what i is the NNP the same in both schedules? Or at what NNP is the i the same in both schedules?)

(1) NNP: $_____

(2) i: _____%

b. Plot both the IS and the LM curves on the following graph. These curves cross at an

(1) NNP of $_____

(2) i of _____%

c. Look back to your answers to questions (1 f) and (2 g) above. What would be the effect—increase (+), decrease (−), no change (0), or indeterminate (?)—upon NNP, i, C, and I of each of the following?

	Effect upon			
	NNP	i	C	I
(1) An increase in government expenditures for goods and services	___	___	___	___
(2) An increase in net taxes	___	___	___	___
(3) An increase in the money supply	___	___	___	___
(4) A decrease in the investment schedule	___	___	___	___
(5) An increase in the consumption schedule	___	___	___	___

d. If the NNP of the economy consistent with both full employment and the absence of inflation were $450, what monetary and fiscal measures might be taken to bring the economy's NNP to this level? _____

e. If the NNP of the economy consistent with both full employment and the absence of inflation were $350, what monetary and fiscal measures might be taken to bring the economy's NNP to this level? _____

_____

■ SELF-TEST

Circle the T if the statement is true, the F if it is false.

1. Inappropriate levels of aggregate demand are not the only causes of inflation and unemployment. **T F**

2. Keynesians believe that monetary policy cannot be used to lessen inflationary pressures. **T F**

3. A budget deficit, according to Keynesians, will bring about a rise in interest rates unless the money supply increases. **T F**

4. The chief proponent of the Monetarist position is Milton Friedman. **T F**

5. According to the Monetarists, the money supply is the single most important factor affecting output, employment, and prices. **T F**

6. From the Monetarist viewpoint, the economy is in equilibrium when the amount of money people want to hold is equal to the supply of money. **T F**

7. From the Monetarist way of looking at the economy, increasing M will increase Q in the equation of exchange. **T F**

8. Keynesians contend that the velocity of money is unstable. **T F**

9. In moving the economy to full employment it makes very little difference whether government increases its expenditures or decreases net taxes to achieve this result. **T F**

10. If the money supply is reduced to combat inflation the rate of growth of the economy is likely to decrease. **T F**

Underscore the letter that corresponds to the best answer.

1. Which of the following is *not* one of the difficulties encountered in achieving full employment without inflation? (a) the pursuit of noneconomic goals; (b) the inability to quantify economic relationships; (c) the nonoperational character of the policy implications of the theory of employment; (d) the looseness of the cause-effect relations in macroeconomic theory.

2. Expansion of the money supply, according to Keynesians, would dampen the impact of

(or would not be congenial with) (a) a decrease in personal income tax rates; (b) a reduction in government expenditures; (c) increased government transfer payments; (d) a budget deficit.

3. If the demand for money is stable and equal to 25% of national income, a $10 billion increase in the money supply will increase the national income by (a) $20 billion; (b) $30 billion; (c) $40 billion; (d) $50 billion.

4. Were the demand for money a stable 12.5% of national income and the level of national income at which full employment without inflation is achieved $480 billion, the appropriate money supply, according to the Monetarists would be (a) $40 billion; (b) $50 billion; (c) $60 billion; (d) $80 billion.

5. Suppose the stable demand for money is 20% of national income, the actual national income is $600 billion, and the money supply is $100 billion. From the viewpoint of the Monetarists, national income would tend to (a) increase; (b) decrease; (c) remain unchanged; (d) be unstable.

6. Were the Federal government to incur a budget surplus to fight inflation and use the surplus to retire (or buy back) government securities owned by the public, the price level, in the opinion of Monetarists, would (a) not be affected; (b) rise more slowly; (c) rise more rapidly; (d) decrease.

7. The monetary rule suggested by the Monetarists is that the money supply should increase at the same rate as (a) the price level; (b) the real output of the economy; (c) the velocity of money; (d) none of the above.

8. Keynesians believe that adherence to the monetary rule of the Monetarists would result in (a) inflation; (b) unemployment; (c) economic instability; (d) an unstable velocity of money.

9. To fight recession government decreases personal income tax rates for the lower income classes. This policy will *not* (a) increase the allocation of resources to the public sector; (b) increase the allocation of resources to industries producing nonluxury goods; (c) increase the extent of income inequality; (d) stimulate investment in the private sector of the economy.

10. Which of the following are coordinated policies? (a) an increase in government expenditures and in the money supply; (b) a decrease in personal tax rates and in the money supply; (c) an increase in transfer payments and a decrease in the money supply; (d) an increase in corporate tax rates and in the money supply.

■ DISCUSSION QUESTIONS

1. Explain as briefly as possible what determines the level of national output in the American economy.

2. Distinguish between fiscal and monetary policy and explain how we may use each of them to achieve reasonably full employment and relatively stable prices.

3. What complications and problems are encountered in using monetary and fiscal policy to eliminate inflationary and recessionary gaps.

4. What is the Keynesian position in their controversy with the Monetarists?

5. Why has interest in the role of money as a determinant of the level of economic activity revived in recent years?

6. Explain the Monetarist position. Include in your explanation (a) their analysis of the demand for money and the equilibrium level of national income, (b) the evidence they use to support their position, (c) their analysis of fiscal policy, and (d) their monetary rule.

7. What criticisms do the Keynesians make of the Monetarist position?

8. Explain how the several different fiscal policies that might be employed to bring the economy out of a recession would affect (a) the composition of output and the allocation of resources in the economy and (b) the distribution of the national income.

9. How would a reduction in the money supply that would eliminate inflationary pressures in the economy affect investment and the rate of economic growth?

10. What does it mean when it is said that monetary and fiscal policy should be coordinated? Can a full-employment NNP or price stability be achieved without such coordination?

FULL EMPLOYMENT
VERSUS INFLATION:
THE ECONOMICS
OF WAGE-PRICE POLICIES

Chapter 18 does not really require a long introduction. It is almost enough to say that until a few years ago most economists believed that it was possible for the American economy to have both full employment and stable prices. This belief was based on the assumption that the price level would not rise until the labor force was fully employed. All that was necessary if there was to be full employment without inflation was just the right level of aggregate demand. Fiscal and monetary policy, thought economists, could be used to assure that aggregate demand was adequate but not excessive.

But the assumption which was the basis of the economists belief that monetary and fiscal policy could guarantee a stable price level and the full employment of the labor force was not at all realistic. The price level rises before full employment is achieved; and the closer the economy moves to full employment the more rapid appears to be the rate at which prices rise. This premature inflation (that is, inflation *before* full employment is reached) seems to be the result of the ability of big unions to raise wage rates, of the power of big business firms to raise prices, and of the fact that

some types of labor become fully employed while other kinds of workers have not yet all found jobs. But no matter what the causes of this premature inflation, the economy finds itself on the spot. It can have full employment with inflation or it can have stable prices with unemployment; *but* it can't have both full employment and stable prices.

Is there any way for the economy to avoid this problem? It may be possible for the economy to avoid both horns of this dilemma; but whether the suggested policies for escaping from both inflation and unemployment will work is still quite uncertain. These policy suggestions (or options) make up the major portion of this chapter. The economy has, in general, two major policy options. It can try to eliminate the causes of premature inflation; and the student should be sure he understands these causes. Or instead of attacking the causes, the economy can attack the symptoms by imposing voluntary or mandatory ceilings on the rates at which wage rates and prices are allowed to rise each year; and here the student should study the arguments on both sides of the wage-price policy debate.

It may turn out that we have no real alternative to putting up with premature inflation at times and with unemployment at other times. (If this is the only realistic possibility, then we can still use fiscal and monetary policies to cool the economy down when inflation becomes too severe and to heat it up when the unemployment rate becomes too high.) But we should not give up and concede that there is no way to solve the premature inflation problem. One of the several policy options discussed in this chapter may prove to be a solution for the problem; and it is for this reason that these options are explored. Even if none of these policies is capable of solving the problem we can be quite certain that fiscal and monetary policies are equally incapable of "fine tuning" the economy to the full employment without inflation channel.

■ CHAPTER OUTLINE

1. Modern economics often assumes that the price level is stable until the economy achieves full employment; and that excess aggregate demand is the sole cause of inflation.

2. But the experiences of the American and other economies indicate that inflation occurs before aggregate demand becomes excessive and before full employment has been achieved. The Phillips Curve shows that the unemployment rate and the rate of inflation are inversely related; and suggests that to reduce unemployment (inflation) the economy must indure greater inflation (unemployment).

   a. There are at least two reasons why inflation occurs before the economy reaches full employment.

   (1) Scarcities of some kinds of labor develop before the economy's entire labor force is fully employed; and these scarcities increase wage rates, production costs, and prices.

   (2) Labor unions and business firms have market power and they raise wage rates and prices as the economy approaches full employment.

   b. Only if increases in wage rates exceed the increases in the productivity of labor do labor costs rise and contribute to cost-push inflation.

   c. While fiscal and monetary policy can be employed to change aggregate demand and to affect unemployment and the rate of inflation,

the nation faces a serious policy dilemma: full employment without inflation and price stability without unemployment are both impossible and a choice must be made between inflation and unemployment.

3. To make possible the achievement of both full employment and price level stability it will be necessary to introduce new policies to supplement fiscal and monetary policy.

   a. Market policies would try to eliminate the causes of premature inflation and would include:

   (1) manpower policies to reduce the scarcities of particular kinds of labor that occur before the labor force is fully employed;

   (2) pro-competition policies to reduce the power of labor unions and business firms to raise wage rates and prices.

   b. Wage-price (or income) policies would try to restrict increases in wages and prices by utilizing either guideposts or controls.

   (1) Wage-price guideposts are voluntary restraints; would restrict wage increases in all industries to the rate at which the productivity of labor in the economy has increased; and would allow an industry to increase the price of its product by an amount equal to the increase in its unit labor cost.

   (2) Wage-price controls are mandatory (or legal) restraints; and were employed after August of 1971 as a part of the New Economic Policy designed to eliminate the inflationary recession in the American economy.

   c. Whether to employ wage-price policies to limit inflation has been a vigorously debated issue; and the proponents and opponents have based their arguments on the questions of workability and compliance, allocative efficiency, economic freedom of choice, and equity.

   d. In addition to market and wage-price policies, the economy has at least two other options.

   (1) It might impose an excess wage settlement tax on firms which increase wage rates by more than the increase in the productivity of labor.

   (2) It might decide to live with either full employment with inflation or price stability with unemployment and employ a stop-and-go stabilization policy to prevent either inflation or unemployment from becoming excessively great.

■ IMPORTANT TERMS

Demand-pull inflation	Wage-price guideposts
Premature inflation	Wage-price controls
Phillips Curve	Wage guidepost
Stagflation	Price guidepost
Cost- (wage-, profit-) push inflation	New Economic Policy
Stabilization policy dilemma	Excess wage settlement tax
Wage-price (income) policy	Stop-and-go stabilization policy

■ FILL-IN QUESTIONS

1. In the traditional view of inflation,
a. prices would not rise until the economy reached _____.

b. inflation was the result of excess _____
_____ and was, therefore, called
_____ inflation.

2. Premature inflation:

a. means that prices rise _____
_____

b. is the result of the market power of _____
_____ and _____ and of
imbalances or bottlenecks in _____
markets.

3. The Phillips Curve:
a. is the relation between the annual rate of
increase in the _____
and the _____ rate;

b. has a (positive, negative) _____
slope;
c. shows that the economy is subject to
(demand-pull, premature) _____
inflation.

4. Labor market adjustments do not eliminate the bottlenecks which develop in some labor markets before the full employment of the labor force is achieved because unemployed workers cannot enter these markets with sufficient _____, because training for

a new occupation is _____, because
they are not _____ of the shortage
in other labor markets, and because there
may be artificial _____ to their
entry into these other labor markets.

5. The cost-push theory explains inflation as follows: labor unions possessing considerable
_____ are able to obtain
wage increases from employers who also possess considerable _____
during periods in which there is _____
_____ in the economy; these
wage increases plus _____
are passed on to buyers in the form of _____
_____

6. In the equation $L = W/P_L$:

a. L is _____
b. W is _____
c. P_L is _____
d. If W increases at a rate:
(1) greater than the rate at which P_L increases, L will (increase, decrease, remain constant) _____
(2) less than the rate at which P_L increases,
L will _____
(3) equal to the rate at which P_L increases,
L will _____

7. The policy dilemma faced by the American economy is that to have full employment it
must also have _____,
and to have stable prices it must tolerate
_____

8. The two categories of policies designed to
reduce premature inflation are _____
and _____ policies; and would, if successful, move the Phillips Curve to the _____
_____

9. Market policies to limit inflation include:

a. _____ policies to reduce

_____ in labor markets;

b. and _____ policies to decrease

the _____ of business firms and labor unions.

10. List three kinds of programs that would provide a better matching of workers and jobs.

a. _____

b. _____

c. _____

11. Two things that might be done to reduce the market power of:

a. big business firms are to apply the _____

_____ laws more vigorously and to

eliminate _____

b. labor unions are to apply the _____ laws to unions and to prohibit labor unions

from _____

12. Wage-price policies:

a. are sometimes called _____

policies because _____

b. involve either:

(1) wage-price _____ which rely

upon the _____ cooperation of labor unions and business firms:

(2) or wage-price _____ which have

the force of _____ to make them effective.

13. The wage-price guideposts for curbing inflation limit wage increases in an industry to

the overall rate of increase in the _____ of labor and limit price increases in an industry to an amount equal to the increase in

_____ in that industry.

14. The New Economic Policy of 1971:

a. aimed to increase _____ and

_____ in the economy and to prevent an increase (or to decrease) the rate

of _____

b. made it illegal to increase _____

and _____, _____, and _____

15. Critics of wage-price (or incomes) policies contend that such policies are _____

and difficult to _____, prevent the

efficient _____ of resources, limit

economic _____, and result in _____

16. When the maximum legal price that may be charged for a product is set below the price that would be charged in a free and competitive market:

a. there will be a persistent _____

of the product, the liklihood that a _____ market for the product will develop, and the

possibility that government will _____ the product; and

b. an increase in demand (will, will not) _____

_____ result in the increased production of the product and there will be an (over-,

under-) _____ allocation of resources to the industry producing the product.

17. Suppose the national income is $1,000, that labor's share of this national income is 75% or $750, and that the nonlabor share is 25% or $250.

a. If national income increases by 10% to $1,100 and labor income also increases by 10%:

(1) labor income will be $_____ or _____% of national income; and nonlabor income will

be $_____ or _____% of national income; and

(2) there (will, will not) _____ have been any change in the distribution of the national income.

b. But if when national income increases by 10% to $1,100, labor income remains at $750:

(1) labor income will be _____% and nonlabor income will be _____% of the national income;

(2) and labor's share will have _____

18. Instead of employing either market or wage-price policies to limit inflation, government might:

a. impose an_____ tax, or

b. employ a _____-and-_____ stabilization policy which would utilize _____

and _____ policies to cool the economy during periods of excessive _____ and to heat it during periods in which there is excessive _____

■ PROBLEMS AND PROJECTS

1. Below is a Phillips Curve.

a. At full employment (a 4% unemployment rate) the price level would rise by _____% each year.

b. If the price level were stable (increasing by 0% a year) the unemployment rate would be _____%.

c. Which of the combinations along the Phillips Curve would you choose for the economy? _____ Why would you select this combination? _____

_____

2. Assume that the overall rate of increase

in the productivity of labor in the economy is 4% per year.

a. The general level of wages in the economy can increase by _____% a year without increasing unit labor costs and inducing cost-push inflation.

b. If the wage rate were increased by this percentage,

(1) In an industry in which the productivity of labor had increased 3%, labor costs per unit would _____; and the price of the product produced by this industry would _____

(2) In an industry in which the productivity of labor had increased 5%, labor costs per unit would _____; and the price of the product would _____

(3) In an industry in which the productivity of labor had increased 4%, labor costs per unit would _____; and the product price would _____

c. Granting all workers in the economy this same percentage increase in wages regardless of the rate of productivity increase in their industry means that

(1) The general level of prices in the economy will _____

(2) Prices in the various industries will ____

_____ , _____ ,

or _____ depending upon whether productivity increases in these industries were less than, greater than, or the same as the economy's rate of productivity increase.

3. Below are the demand and supply schedules for a product that is bought and sold in a competitive market.

Quantity demanded (pounds)	Price (per pound)	Quantity supplied (pounds)
3,000	$14.00	6,000
3,500	13.00	5,500
4,000	12.00	5,000
4,500	11.00	4,500
5,000	10.00	4,000
5,500	9.00	3,500
6,000	8.00	3,000

a. In a free market the equilibrium price of this product would be $_____ per pound and _____ pounds of the product would be bought and sold.

b. Suppose that government decrees that the maximum price that may be legally charged for this product is $9.00 a pound.

(1) At this price the quantity demanded is _____ pounds and the quantity supplied is _____ pounds;

(2) The legal price of $9.00 has resulted in a (shortage, surplus) _____ of _____ pounds.

c. Put another way, buyers are paying only $9.00 per pound for each of the 3,500 pounds supplied them but are willing to pay a price of $_____ a pound for this quantity.

d. If the shortage is to be eliminated without government rationing or the development of a black market, the legal maximum price for this product must be lifted to at least $_____ per pound. Were this done the quantity supplied would increase by _____ pounds and the quantity demanded would decrease by _____ pounds.

e. The increase in the quantity supplied would require that (more, fewer, the same amount of) _____ resources be allocated to the industry producing this product.

■ SELF-TEST

Circle the T if the statement is true, the F if it is false.

1. In the demand-pull theory of inflation, at less than full employment an increase in MV (in the equation of exchange) results in an increase in both *P* and *Q*.   **T F**

2. As the economy approaches full employment, some types of labor become fully employed before all of the labor force is fully employed.   **T F**

3. According to the Phillips Curve the rate of inflation increases as the level of unemployment decreases.   **T F**

4. Stagflation refers to a situation in which the price level is rising and the output of the economy is either falling or constant (and below the full-employment output).   **T F**

5. When the money wage rate increases at a rate greater than the rate at which the productivity of labor increases, the unit labor cost will rise.   **T F**

6. Because of the negative slope of the Phillips Curve fiscal and monetary policies cannot be used to increase employment or to reduce the rate of inflation in the economy.   **T F**

7. Of the new policies that might be employed to deal with inflation, both market and wage-price policies are designed to move the Phillips Curve to the left.   **T F**

8. Application of the antitrust laws has proved effective in the past in curbing the market power of big business; and so it is a promising technique for fighting premature inflation.

9. Voluntary restraint by business and labor leaders is not apt to be effective in preventing price and wage increases because such restraint requires them to abandon their major goals.   **T F**

10. The wage-price guideposts for preventing cost-push inflation are to limit wage increases to the overall rate of increase in labor productivity in the economy.   **T F**

11. Application of the wage-price guideposts would increase "capital's" share and decrease labor's share of the national income.   **T F**

12. The excess wage settlement tax would impose a 3% surtax on the personal incomes of union members who receive inflationary wage increases.

Underscore the letter that corresponds to the best answer.

1. If inflation is explained solely by the demand-pull theory, then: (*a*) price changes occur only if there is full employment; (*b*) inflation is the result of chronic unemployment; (*c*) inflation is the result of wage increases obtained by labor unions; (*d*) an increase in the level of prices results from the monopoly power of large business firms.

2. Premature inflation is the result of (*a*) excess aggregate demand; (*b*) full employment; (*c*) chronic unemployment; (*d*) market power.

3. The Phillips Curve (a) shows the inverse relation between the rate of increase in the price level and the unemployment rate; (b) makes it possible for the economy to achieve full employment and stable prices; (c) indicates that prices do not rise until full employment has been achieved; (d) slopes upward from left to right.

4. If inflation during periods of less than full employment is to be explained by the cost-push theory, it must be assumed that: (a) only unions possess considerable market power; (b) only employers possess considerable market power; (c) both unions and employers possess considerable market power; (d) neither unions nor employers possess considerable market power.

5. Labor-market adjustments do not eliminate bottleneck problems when there is less than full employment in the economy. Which of the following is *not* one of the reasons for these labor-market imbalances? (a) Unemployed workers often lack the skills or training needed for a new occupation; (b) the demand for workers in the markets in which there are labor shortages is inadequate; (c) there are artificial restrictions which prevent unemployed workers from filling the job openings; (d) unemployed workers do not know of the shortages of workers in other labor markets in the economy.

6. The public policy dilemma illustrated by a Phillips Curve is the mutual inconsistency of: (a) more employment and price stability; (b) a higher unemployment rate and price stability; (c) inflation and more employment; (d) inflation and a lower unemployment rate.

7. Which of the following is *not* one of the manpower policies that might reduce premature inflation? (a) Application of antimonopoly laws to labor unions; (b) removal of racial discrimination as an obstacle to employment; (c) improvement of the flow of job information between workers without jobs and employers with unfilled positions; (d) expansion of job training programs.

8. Which one of the following proposals for fighting inflation is aimed more at demand-pull inflation than at premature inflation? (a) restriction of total spending; (b) restriction of the market power of labor unions; (c) restric-tion of the market power of business firms; (d) restriction by government of price and wage increases.

9. If the wage rate in an industry increases from $6.00 to $6.30 an hour while the hourly productivity of labor increases from 40 to 42, the unit labor cost (a) has decreased; (b) has not changed; (c) has increased; (d) cannot be determined from this information;

10. Suppose the overall rate of increase in the productivity of labor in the economy is 4%. If the productivity of labor in a particular industry has increased at a rate of only 3%, the wage-price guideposts would allow this industry (a) to increase both the wage rate and the price of its product by 3%; (b) to increase the wage rate by 3% and would allow no increase in price; (c) to increase the wage rate by 4% and would allow no increase in price; (d) to increase the wage rate by 4% and to increase price by about 1%.

11. If the maximum price that may be legally charged for a product is below the price that would prevail in a competitive market (a) there will be a surplus of the product; (b) there will be an overallocation of resources to the industry producing the product; (c) the supply of the product will tend to increase; (d) some kind of rationing of the product will be necessary.

12. If the Phillips Curve cannot be moved to the left by the employment of market or wage-price policies it will be necessary for the economy (a) to suffer from continuing inflation; (b) to have less than full employment and to produce less than the maximum output; (c) to employ a stop-and-go stabilization policy; (d) to experience either a or b.

■ DISCUSSION QUESTIONS

1. What does the traditional demand-pull theory of inflation regard as the cause of inflation? What monetary and fiscal policies will prevent this kind of inflation?

2. Explain what is meant by premature inflation and the two major causes of this variety of inflation. Include in your explanation a definition and explanation of cost-push inflation.

3. What is a Phillips Curve? What is the public policy dilemma illustrated by this curve?

4. When are increases in money wage rates inflationary?

5. What are the two kinds of market policies that might be employed to shift the Phillips Curve to the left? Within each of these two categories, what specific things might be done to reduce the causes of premature inflation?

6. Explain (a) what is meant by wage-price policy; (b) why wage-price policy is often called income policy; and (c) the difference between wage-price guideposts and wage-price controls.

7. What (a) was the wage guidepost; (b) the price guidepost; and (c) were the methods employed by the Federal government to encourage business firms and labor unions to conform to the guideposts?

8. What wages and prices were controlled during the period of the New Economic Policy? Why did it seem necessary to control them?

9. State the cases *for* and *against* the use of wage-price (or incomes) policy to limit inflation. Build each case upon the four points around which the wage-price policy debate has centered.

10. Instead of wage-price or market policies, what other policy options are there? Include in your answer the views of the "inflationists" and the "accelerationists" and an explanation of "stop-and-go" stabilization policy.

THE SIMPLE ANALYTICS
OF ECONOMIC GROWTH

This is the first of three chapters dealing with the important and controversial topic of economic growth. Chapter 19 presents the theory of growth; Chapter 20 examines the American economic growth record and the controversy surrounding further growth in the United States; and Chapter 21 explains the special problems which underdeveloped nations encounter in their attempts to grow.

The purpose of Chapter 19 is to explain what makes economic growth possible. After briefly defining and pointing out the significance of growth, the text analyzes the six factors that make growth possible. The four *supply* factors increase the output potential of the economy. Whether the economy actually produces its full potential—that is, whether the economy has both full employment and full production —depends upon two other factors: the level of aggregate demand (the *demand* factor) and the efficiency with which the economy reallocates resources (the *allocative* factor).

The crucial thing to note about the supply factors is that when labor increases more rapidly than natural resources, or capital, or both of these, the economy will be subject to diminishing returns and eventually to decreasing output per person and to a declining standard of living. This will breed the misery and poverty forecast by Malthus over 175

years ago. Diminishing returns can, however, be offset—and more than offset—by increasing the amount of capital the economy possesses, by technological progress, and by improving the quality of the labor force at a more rapid rate. This is the way to achieve growth, and diminishing returns have been *more* than offset by those nations which have experienced economic growth. The nations which have not experienced growth have found the force of diminishing returns too great for them: their improvements in technology, capital, and labor just barely offset the effect of diminishing returns. And in some nations, these improvements were so weak that diminishing returns were dominant and the standard of living actually fell.

Probably the most important principle or generalization developed in the chapter employs the theory of output and employment already presented in Chapter 12. Here we discover that the maintenance of full employment in an economy whose productive capacity is increasing annually requires that investment increase annually to ensure a sufficient aggregate demand for the expanding full-employment output. And because investment increases an economy's productive capacity, not only must investment increase from year to year, but it must also increase by increasing amounts to assure the production of the full-employment output. The student must be sure he understands the "why" of this principle, because it is fundamental to an understanding of full employment without inflation in the growing economy.

Actually, Chapter 19 contains very little that is really new. It uses a few of the ideas, terms, and theories found in earlier chapters to explain what makes an economy capable of growing (that is, what increases the size of its full-employment or capacity output) and what is necessary if it is actually to grow (that is, if it is to produce all which its expanding capacity allows). With careful reading the student should have little or no trouble with Chapter 19, providing he has done a good job on the earlier chapters and providing he keeps in mind the fundamental distinction between the supply factors and the demand and allocative factors.

■ CHAPTER OUTLINE

1. While modern employment theory is concerned with the short run and an economy with a given productive capacity, growth economics deals with the long run and changes in productive capacity over time.

a. Economic growth means an increase in either the total or the per capita real output of an economy.

b. Economic growth is important because it lessens the burden of scarcity: it provides the means of satisfying existing wants more fully and of fulfilling new needs.

c. One or two percentage point differences in the rate of growth result in substantial differences in annual increases in the economy's output.

2. Whether economic growth *can* occur depends upon four supply factors; and whether it *will* occur depends upon the demand factor and the allocative factor.

3. The amount by which total output can increase depends upon the amount and the proportion in which resources are increased.

a. In an economy where the quantities of land and capital are relatively fixed, the law of diminishing returns operates so that increases in the quantity of labor employed

eventually result in declining increases in total output per additional unit of labor.

b. A proportionate increase in all resources moves the production possibilities curve to the right in the same proportion. But a disproportionate increase in resources moves it to the right by a percentage less than the percentage by which the most expanded resource has increased.

c. When diminishing returns set in and the marginal product of labor declines, the average product of labor will eventually decline.

d. The optimum population is the population at which the average product of labor (or real output per capita) is at a maximum.

e. Because of diminishing returns and the tendency for population to increase, Malthus predicted widespread poverty as time passed.

f. But growth can occur and poverty can be avoided if diminishing returns are offset by the increases in the productivity of workers that are brought about by more capital, better methods, and an improved labor force.

4. The amount the actual output of the economy increases depends not only upon the supply factors but also upon the demand factor.

a. To maintain full employment without inflation aggregate demand must grow at the same rate as the economy's productive capacity.

b. In the simple macroeconomic growth model the full-employment rate of growth equals the average propensity to save divided by the capital-output ratio; and achievement of the full-employment rate of growth requires that net investment grow at the same rate.

5. For economic growth to be possible, the economy must also be capable of reallocating its resources with reasonable speed and completeness.

■ IMPORTANT TERMS

Economic growth	**Increasing returns**
Supply factor	**Optimum population**
Demand factor	**Income-creating aspect of investment**
Allocative factor	
Law of diminishing returns	**Capacity-creating aspect of investment**
Marginal product	**Capital-output ratio**
Average product	**Full-employment rate of growth**

■ FILL-IN QUESTIONS

1. Keynesian (or modern) employment theory assumes the productive capacity of the economy is _____; while growth economics is concerned with an economy whose productive capacity _____ _____ over time.

2. Economic growth can mean an increase in either the _____ or the _____ of an economy.

3. An increase in output per capita _____ _____ the standard of living and _____ the burden of scarcity in the economy.

4. Assume an economy has a GNP of $600 billion. If the growth rate is 5%, GNP will increase by $_____ billion a year; but if the rate of growth is only 3%, the annual increase in GNP will be $_____ billion. A two percentage point difference in the growth rate results in a $_____ billion difference in the annual increase in GNP.

5. The four supply factors in economic growth are _____, _____, _____, and _____.

The other two growth factors are the _____ _____ factor and the _____ factor.

6. If there are no diseconomies or economies of scale and if *all* resources expand by 8%, the productive capacity of the economy will increase by _____%.

7. The law of diminishing returns says that when additional equal quantities of one resource are used along with fixed quantities of other resources, total output (beyond some

point) will _____ by _____ amounts.

8. Assume an economy employs only two resources. One of these increases by 10% and the other increases by 3%. Technology and the quality of the resources are fixed. If this economy is subject to diminishing returns, its productive capacity will increase by less than _____%.

9. When an economy is subject to diminishing returns and the marginal product of labor decreases, the _____ product of labor will sooner or later _____.

10. The population size which results in the maximum output per capita (or the maximum average product of labor) is the _____ _____.

11. Malthus predicted that because of diminishing returns and the tendency for the _____ of an economy to increase, the standard of living would _____ _____.

12. The tendency for the standard of living to fall as the population increases can be lessened or even overcome by increasing the ____ _____ of workers.

13. In an economy increasing its productive capacity each year it is necessary that ____ _____ increase by the right amount each year if full employment is to be maintained.

14. Expenditures for new capital goods both increase _____ and add to the _____ of the economy; the amount by which investment expenditures expand the latter depend upon the volume of investment expenditures and the _____ _____.

15. To have the economic growth which the

supply and demand factors make possible, an economy must also be able to _____ its resources from one use to another with

_____

and _____

■ PROBLEMS AND PROJECTS

1. The table below shows the total production of an economy as the quantity of labor employed increases. The quantities of all other resources employed are constant.

Units of labor	Total production	Marginal product of labor	Average product of labor
0	0		0
1	80	_____	_____
2	200	_____	_____
3	330	_____	_____
4	400	_____	_____
5	450	_____	_____
6	480	_____	_____
7	490	_____	_____
8	480	_____	_____

a. Compute the marginal products of the first through the eighth unit of labor and enter them in the table.

b. There are increasing returns to labor from the first through the _____ unit of labor and decreasing returns from the _____ through the eighth unit.

c. When total production is increasing, marginal product is (positive, negative) _____ and when total production is decreasing, marginal product is _____

_____

d. Now compute the average products of the various quantities of labor and enter them in the table.

e. When the marginal product of labor is greater than the average product, average

product is (increasing, decreasing) _____

_____; and when the marginal product is less than the average product, average product is _____

f. The optimum population in this economy would be _____ units of labor, because with this many units of labor the _____

_____

of labor is _____

2. Column 1 of the table below lists the various quantities of labor an economy might employ. Columns 2 and 3 show total production and the average product of labor for each quantity of labor.

(1) Quantity of labor	(2) Total production	(3) Average product of labor	(4) New total production	(5) New average product of labor
0	0	0	0	0
1	80	80	100	_____
2	200	100	220	_____
3	330	110	360	_____
4	400	100	500	_____
5	450	90	600	_____
6	480	80	660	_____
7	490	70	700	_____
8	480	60	720	_____

a. Assume the economy has and employs 4 units of labor. The average product of labor is

_____

b. Now suppose the total productivity of workers increases from the figures shown in column 2 to those given in column 4. Compute the new average products of labor and enter them in column 5.

c. If the economy continued to employ 4 units of labor, the average productivity of labor would have increased by _____%.

d. This increase in the productivity of workers could be due to more _____

_____, improved _____, better _____, or any two or three of these.

e. As a result of this increase in productivity the optimum population for this economy has

_____ from 3 to _____ units of labor.

f. If, while the productivity of workers increased, the number of units of labor this economy had, and employed, increased from 4 to:

(1) 5, the average product of labor would have (increased, decreased) _____

from 100 to _____

(2) 7, the average product of labor would have _____

(3) 8, the average product of labor would have _____

3. Assume that in an economy in which aggregate demand contains only consumption and net investment components the average propensity to consume is 0.80, that in year 1 the economy's equilibrium output (NNP) is its full-employment of $1,000, and that the supply factors make it possible for the full employment output to increase at a rate of 10% per year.

a. Complete the table below by computing:

(1) the full-employment output in year 2 and in year 3.

(2) the amounts that would be spent for consumption and saved if the economy produced its full-employment output in year 2 and in year 3.

(3) the amounts that would have to be invested and aggregate demand in years 2 and 3 if the equilibrium output of the economy is to equal its full-employment output. (Investment will have to be equal to the saving done when the economy produces a full-employment out-

put; and $C + I$ must equal the full-employment output.)

b. Examination of the table completed above reveals that to maintain full employment in an economy in which the average propensity to save is a constant and in which the full-employment output is growing at the rate of 10% annually:

(1) aggregate demand must grow at a rate of _____% per year; and

(2) net investment must grow at an annual rate of _____%.

c. Further examination of the completed table above shows that when the:

(1) average propensity to consume is constant and equal to 0.8, the marginal propensity to consume is equal to _____

and is _____

(2) average propensity to save is constant and equal to 0.2, the marginal propensity to save is equal to _____ and is

_____

(3) the value of the investment multiplier is equal to _____

d. Employing your knowledge of the multiplier, had net investment increased by 5% from $200 to $210 between year 1 and year 2, the equilibrium output of the economy would have increased from $1,000 to $_____

(1) This is a _____% increase in NNP.

(2) The equilibrium NNP is (greater than, less than, equal to) _____ the full-employment output of the economy.

(3) There is in year 2 _____ in the economy.

e. Still employing the multiplier, if net investment increased by 15% from $200 to $230 between year 1 and year 2, the equi-

Year	Full-employment Output (NNP)	Consumption	Saving	Investment	Aggregate demand $(C + I)$
1	$1,000	$800	$200	$200	$1,000
2	_____	_____	_____	_____	_____
3	_____	_____	_____	_____	_____

librium output of the economy would have

tried to increase from $1,000 to $_____
(1) This equilibrium output is (greater than,

less than, equal to) _____
the full-employment output and (can, cannot)

_____ actually be produced.

(2) There will in year 2 be _____
in the economy.

f. Still further examination of the table completed above reveals that for the economy to grow at any given rate—such as 10%—the *amount* that net investment must increase

(increases, decreases, remains constant) ____

---

4. This problem is much like problem 3 above; but it is a little more difficult because it does not ignore the capacity-creating aspect of investment as problem 3 did.

Assume in an economy in which the only two components of aggregate demand are consumption and saving that the average propensity to consume is 0.7, the capital-output ratio is 3, and in year 1 the economy is producing a full-employment output of $900.

a. In the table below compute the amount of saving that would be done in year 1 if the economy produced its full-employment output and the amount of investment that would be needed if the economy were to produce an equilibrium output equal to its full-employment output; and enter these two figures in the table.

b. Now compute the increase in full-employment output between year 1 and year 2 that results from the investment undertaken in year 1. (*Hint:* Divide the investment in year 1 by the capital-output ratio.)

c. Add the increase in full-employment output that results from the investment in year 1

to the full-employment output of year 1 to find the full-employment output of year 2; and calculate the amount of saving that would be done at full employment in year 2, the amount of investment needed to bring about full employment, and the increase in the full-employment output between year 2 and year 3.

d. Find the full-employment output and saving in year 3, the necessary amount of investment in year 3, and the increase in full-employment output between year 3 and year 4.

e. This economy's full-employment rate of growth is 10% and:

(1) will be achieved if _____
grows at a rate of 10%
(2) can be calculated by dividing the econ-

omy's _____

by the _____
f. Were the economy's average propensity to save 0.1 and its capital-output ratio 4 its full-employment rate of growth would be equal

to _____%.

■ SELF-TEST

Circle the T if the statement is true, the F if it is false.

1. Growth economics is concerned with an economy in which productive capacity is not fixed. **T F**

2. The best of the two definitions of economic growth is an increase in the per capita real output of the economy. **T F**

3. Suppose two economies both have GNPs of $500 billion. If the GNPs grow at annual rates of 3% in the first and 5% in the second economy, the difference in their amounts of growth in one year is $10 billion. **T F**

4. The demand factor in economic growth re-

| | Full-employment | | | Increase in |
Year	Output (NNP)	Saving	Investment	full-employment output
1	$900	$____	$____	$____
2	____	____	____	____
3	____	____	____	____

fers to the ability of the economy to expand its production as the demand for products grows.   **T   F**

5. The allocative factor in economic growth refers to the ability of the economy to move resources from one use to another as the productive capacity of the economy grows. **T   F**

6. Diminishing returns for a resource are the eventual result of increasing the employment of that resource by larger percentages than the employment of other resources is increased.   **T   F**

7. The effect of diminishing returns to labor upon the standard of living is overcome whenever the average productivity of labor is increased.   **T   F**

8. When average product is falling, marginal product is greater than average product. **T   F**

9. When marginal product is negative, total production (or output) is decreasing.   **T   F**

10. If the volume of investment expands more rapidly than is necessary to keep the full-employment output of the economy expanding at the rate which the supply factors allow, the result will be unemployment.   **T   F**

11. Other things being constant, the productive capacity of an economy will increase by an amount equal to net investment multiplied by the capital-output ratio.   **T   F**

12. One of the requirements for allocative efficiency is the reasonably rapid and complete employment of the new workers in the labor force.   **T   F**

Underscore the letter that corresponds to the best answer.

1. Which of the following is *not* one of the benefits of economic growth to a society? (a) everyone enjoys a greater real income; (b) the standard of living in that society increases; (c) the burden of scarcity decreases; (d) the society is better able to meet new needs.

2. Suppose an economy has a GNP of $700 billion and an annual growth rate of 5%. Over a two-year period GNP will increase by: (a) $14 billion; (b) $35 billion; (c) $70 billion; (d) $71¾ billion.

3. If the production possibilities curve of an economy moves from *AB* to *CD* on the graph below, and the economy changes the combination of goods it produces from *X* to *Y*, there has been: (a) improvement in both the supply and the other growth factors; (b) an improvement in only the supply factor; (c) an improvement in only the demand and allocative growth factors; (d) an improvement in the level of total employment in the economy.

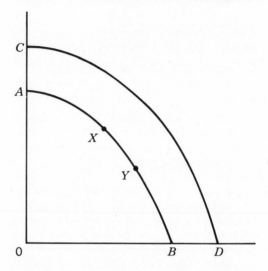

4. Which of the following is *not* a supply factor in economic growth? (a) an expansion in purchasing power; (b) an increase in the economy's stock of capital goods; (c) more natural resources; (d) technological improvements.

For questions 5 and 6 use the data given in the table below.

Units of labor	Total production
0	0
1	50
2	110
3	160
4	200
5	230
6	250
7	260
8	265

5. The marginal product of the fifth unit of labor is: (a) 40; (b) 30; (c) 20; (d) 10.

6. The average product of 4 units of labor is: (a) 70; (b) 60; (c) 50; (d) 40.

7. The law of diminishing returns says that as increased quantities of one resource are added to fixed quantities of other resources, there will eventually be a decrease in: (a) total production; (b) marginal product; (c) average product; (d) the optimum population.

8. The "optimum population" of an economy is: (a) the largest population the resources of that economy are capable of supporting; (b) the level of population which enables the economy to produce the largest possible output; (c) the level of population which enables the economy to produce the largest possible per capita output; (d) the level of population which results in the greatest amount of natural resources and capital equipment per capita in the economy.

9. Which of the following will *not* usually increase the average product of labor? (a) technological improvements; (b) an expanded labor force; (c) an increase in the amount of capital per worker; (d) better-educated workers.

10. If an economy is to maintain a constant *rate* of economic growth, assuming that the average propensity to consume is constant: (a) the volume of investment spending must increase at a more rapid rate; (b) the volume of investment spending must increase at the same rate; (c) the volume of investment spending need only remain constant; (d) the volume of investment spending must increase by the same amount that the output of the economy increases.

■ DISCUSSION QUESTIONS

1. What is meant by economic growth? Why should the citizens of the United States be concerned with economic growth?

2. How does growth economics differ from the theory of employment (or the theory of national income determination)?

3. What are the six basic ingredients of economic growth? What is the essential difference

between the supply factors and the other two factors? Is there any relationship between the strength of the supply factor and the strength of the demand factor?

4. State the law of diminishing returns. What is the cause of diminishing returns?

5. What does an expansion in the quantity of resources employed do to the production possibilities curve if: (a) all resources expand proportionally and (b) all resources do not expand proportionally?

6. Define the marginal and the average product of labor. If marginal product at first increases and then decreases as more labor is employed, what will happen to the average product? Why will average product behave this way?

7. What is an optimum population? Why is this concept important?

8. What predictions did Malthus make for the economic future of mankind? On what bases did he make this prediction?

9. What can be done to offset or overcome the tendency for the average product of labor and the standard of living to decline as the employment of labor and the population increase?

10. Explain why an increasing level of aggregate demand is necessary in an economy whose productive capacity is increasing if full employment is to be maintained. Why does the maintenance of full employment in a growing economy in which the average propensity to save is constant require that investment increase at the same rate as the full-employment output?

11. What determines (a) how much the investment of one year will increase the full-employment output of the economy; (b) the full-employment rate of growth in an economy? What two events would bring about an increase in the full-employment rate of growth?

12. What is meant by allocative efficiency? Why is this kind of efficiency important if there is to be economic growth?

20

ECONOMIC GROWTH:
FACT AND CONTROVERSY

Chapter 20 is the second of the three chapters concerned with economic growth. It is concerned primarily with economic growth in the United States.

Using the two definitions of growth found in Chapter 19, Chapter 20 begins by describing how much and how fast the American economy has grown. That it has grown is fairly obvious. Real GNP has increased by over 500% in the past six decades; and per capita real GNP has expanded by about 150% in the same sixty-year period. Since 1870 real GNP has increased, on the average, by 3.6% per year; and real GNP per capita, again on the average, has grown by 1.9% annually. The net result of this rapid growth in the United States is that Americans now enjoy the highest standard of living in the world.

Why has the United States grown economically? Because the six growth factors explained in Chapter 19 have made growth possible. The four supply factors in economic growth have increased the productive capacity of the economy more rapidly than the population has expanded. More capital, a larger and better labor force, additional natural resources, and technological advance all have contributed to increased productive capabilities. In addition, aggregate demand has expanded sufficiently to bring about most of the

actual growth that the supply factors made possible. And the economy has been able to reallocate its resources with enough speed and completeness to realize the better part of the growth which the supply and demand factors gave the economy power to achieve.

The latter part of Chapter 20 asks three important questions. Whether further economic growth is *desirable* in the already affluent American economy is the first of these questions. The controversy over whether growth should be a social goal with a high priority in the United States has, of course, two sides to it. The case for and the case against growth are both considered. The student will have to decide for himself which case is the stronger and whether the social benefits from growth are worth the costs.

The second question is whether further economic growth in the world is *possible*. Here the author looks at the dismal predictions of the MIT-Club of Rome. The Club of Rome is an informal group of all kinds of people from all over the world who first met in that city in 1968 and later commissioned a team of professors from the Massachusetts Institute of Technology to prepare a report on the "Predicament of Mankind." Their report, a book entitled *The Limits To Growth*, has aroused a storm of controversy throughout the world.

Their prediction is that given the way things are going throughout the world today, not only will world growth end within the next 100 years but population and the standard of living will also suddenly decline or collapse. In addition to noting the trends or assumptions upon which such a pessimistic forecast is made, the student should also take note of the policies which the MIT-Club of Rome believes are necessary if Doomsday is to be avoided. More optimistically, the critics of the Doomsday model point out that there are good reasons to be suspicious of these dismal predictions. The end of the world may not be at hand.

The final question is what caused the energy crisis of 1973. The Doomsday explanation of the crisis is simple and pessimistic: the world is running out of the petroleum from which the greater part of its energy is created; and the predictions of the MIT-Club of Rome are about to be realized. This explanation is probably *too* simple. It ignores the events of 1972 and 1973 which brought about the energy crisis. And it is *too* pessimistic. It ignores the ability of a price system and modern technology to adapt to natural resource scarcities. But it does not ignore the one aspect of reality most relevant to the future of the American economy: abundant and inexpensive energy are gone with the wind.

■ CHAPTER OUTLINE

1. Over the last sixty or so years the growth record of the American economy has been impressive and per capita real income in the United States is now higher than in any other nation; but American growth in recent years has been slower than in many of the developed nations.

2. The six growth factors are the source of the impressive growth of the American economy.
    a. Natural resources have been generally abundant.
    b. The human resources of the economy have increased in quantity and improved in quality.
    c. Technological progress has increased the

efficiency with which natural, human, and capital resources are employed.
    d. Investment has expanded the American economy's stock of capital goods and thereby provided the American worker with more tools, equipment, and machinery with which to work.
    e. Variations in the rate of economic growth and a growth rate less than what the supply factors made possible were largely the result of insufficient increases in aggregate demand.
    f. The social, political, and cultural environment surrounding the economy has been conducive to economic change. It has encouraged new products, new production processes, and new capital equipment; and the economy has been sufficiently flexible to provide for the reallocation of resources required by these changes.
    g. Between 1948 and 1968, increases in the quantities of labor and capital accounted for about 45%, improvements in technology and in the quality of the labor force for about 40%, and resource reallocations and economies of scale for the remainder of the increases in the total output of the American economy.

3. Americans today debate whether economic growth is or is not desirable.
    a. Those opposed to rapid economic growth contend that it imposes great spillover costs on society; it is not needed to resolve domestic problems; it makes people more anxious and insecure; and, while providing more goods and services, it does not result in a better life.
    b. Those in favor of growth argue that the benefits from growth—a higher standard of living—outweigh the costs of growth; that growth is not the cause of pollution and a decline in the quality of life; and that growth is the easiest way to bring about a more equitable distribution of income.

4. The Doomsday models (based upon current trends in population, output, and pollution and upon the availability of natural resources and the ability of the environment to absorb pollution) not only forecast the end of economic growth but also predict sudden collapses in the world's population and its capacity to produce goods and services within the next 100 years.
    a. To avoid this future collapse the Doomsday forecasters advocate policies to reduce

the current rates of economic and population growth to zero.

b. Critics of the Doomsday models argue that the forecasters have made unrealistic assumptions, underestimated future technological progress, and made inadequate allowances for existing feedback mechanisms.

5. Energy shortages brought about an energy crisis in 1973 and drove energy prices upward.

a. In the Doomsday interpretation of the crisis, the demand for energy has outrun the fixed supplies of energy resources.

b. The economy, taking a more optimistic view, will adapt to the shortages by applying technology to increase useable supplies and by employing the price system to expand production and reduce consumption.

c. Some believe that the firms of the petroleum industry created the crisis by conspiring to restrict supply in order to increase prices and profits.

■ IMPORTANT TERMS

R and D   ZEG
Doomsday model   ZPG

■ FILL-IN QUESTIONS

1. Over the last sixty years in the United States:

a. Real GNP has increased _____ fold.

b. Real GNP per capita has increased _____ _____ fold.

2. Since 1870 the rates of growth in real GNP and per capita real GNP have, on the average, been _____% and _____%, respectively.

3. Figures showing the real GNP and the per capita real GNP of the United States over the last sixty years fail to take account of improvements in the _____ of the products produced, increases in the amount of _____ Americans have, deterioration in the _____

of the United States, or a possible decline in the quality of _____

4. One of the supply factors explaining past American economic growth is the relatively fixed but generous quantity and quality of the _____ with which the economy was endowed.

5. The size of the nation's labor force depends basically upon the _____ while the quality of the labor force seems to depend upon such factors as its _____ _____, _____, and _____

6. Technological progress means that we learn how to employ given quantities of resources to obtain greater _____; and, more often than not, this progress requires _____ in new machinery and equipment.

7. The average American worker today has about $_____ worth of capital equipment with which to work; and about _____ times as much capital per man-hour of labor is employed today as was employed at the end of the nineteenth century.

8. When aggregate demand does not increase as much as the productive capacity of the economy increases, the result is a _____ gap and a _____ rate of growth.

9. The social environment of a society must meet two requirements if there is to be economic growth in that society; these requirements are that _____ and _____; reallocation in the United States has been accomplished by the _____

10. Since 1948 about _____% of American economic growth has been due to increases in the quantities of capital and labor;

the remainder has been due to _____

_____,

_____,

_____,

and _____

11. Influential economists arguing against the need for growth in the United States believe that growth has adverse _____, does not lead to the solution of _____ _____, breeds _____ and _____, and does not result in the _____

12. Those who favor growth for the American economy argue that the _____ from growth exceed the _____ of this growth, that economic growth does not necessarily reduce the _____, and that growth is the only practical way of obtaining a more _____ distribution of _____

13. The Doomsday models:
   a. are based on current and projected trends in world _____,

_____, _____,

_____, and _____

   b. predict that within the next _____ years there will be a sudden collapse in the world's _____ and _____

14. To avoid the collapse predicted by the Doomsday models it is necessary, the forecasters say, to have _____ and _____

15. The criticisms of the Doomsday models are that the models employ _____ assumptions, underestimate future _____, and make inadequate allowance for _____ mechanisms.

16. The energy crisis was the _____

and sharply rising _____ of energy that occurred during 1973.
   a. The Doomsday interpretation of the crisis is that the demand for energy has _____ while the world's endowment of exhaustable energy resources has remained _____
   b. A more optimistic view is that _____ _____ progress and the operation of the _____ system will enable the American economy to adjust to resource scarcities.
   c. The crisis may be the result of a _____ _____ in the petroleum industry to restrict supply in order to increase the _____ _____ of the firms in the industry.

■ PROBLEMS AND PROJECTS

1. Suppose the real GNP and the population of an economy in seven different years were those shown in the table below.

Year	Population, millions	Real GNP, billions of dollars	Per capita real GNP
1	30	$ 9	$____
2	60	24	____
3	90	45	____
4	120	66	____
5	150	90	____
6	180	99	____
7	210	105	____

   a. How large would the real per capita GNP of the economy be in each of the seven years? Put your figures in the above table.
   b. What would have been the size of the optimum population of this economy? _____
   c. What was the *amount* of growth in:
   (1) Real GNP between year 1 and year 2? $_____
   (2) Real GNP per capita between year 2 and year 3? $_____

d. What was the *rate* of growth in:

(1) Real GNP between year 3 and year 4?
_____%

(2) Real GNP per capita between year 4 and year 5? _____%

2. Column 2 of the table below gives the productive capacities of an economy *in constant dollars* during the four different years shown in column 1. Productive capacity is growing at a constant rate of 10%.

(1) Year	(2) Productive capacity*	(3) Aggregate demand*	(4) Output of economy*
1	$200.0	$200.0	$_____
2	220.0	210.0	_____
3	242.0	265.0	_____
4	266.2	266.2	_____

* In billions of constant dollars.

a. Aggregate demand, also *in constant dollars,* during these four years is shown in column 3. Given that an economy will produce an output equal to the level of aggregate demand up to the limits of the productive capacity of the economy, what were the *actual* outputs of this economy *in constant dollars* in each of the four years? Place these outputs in column 4.

b. Between year 1 and year 2 the rate of growth in output was _____%. This rate of growth was (more, less) _____ than the rate of growth of productive capacity, because _____

_____

c. In year 2:

(1) The economy had an unused productive capacity of _____ billion constant dollars.

(2) About _____% of its productive capacity was idle.

d. Between years 2 and 3:

(1) The economy had an increase in productive capacity equal to _____ billion constant dollars.

(2) Aggregate demand increased by _____ billion constant dollars.

(3) The increase in aggregate demand was (more, less) _____ than the combined increase in productive capacity and the idle productive capacity in year 2.

(4) The actual rate of growth in output was about _____%.

(5) The price level would tend to _____
_____ because _____

_____

(6) How could output increase by more than the increase in productive capacity? _____

_____

_____

e. In year 4:

(1) Aggregate demand was _____ than in year 3 and was _____ the productive capacity of the economy.

(2) The price level would tend to _____

_____

(3) There (would, would not) _____ be full employment and the absence of unused productive capacity.

3. To understand the predictions of Doomsday made by the MIT-Club of Rome models, look at Figure 20–3 on page 415 of the text.

a. From 1900 until the present the world's:

(1) population, pollution, food output per capita, and industrial output per capita have all (increased, decreased) _____
by (increasing, decreasing, constant) _____
_____ amounts.

(2) natural resources have _____
by _____ amounts.

b. If these trends continue, the models predict that within the next 100 years (somewhere between the year 2000 and the year 2100):

(1) population and food and industrial output per capita will begin to _____

(2) as a result _____ will begin to _____

(3) while _____ continue to decrease.

c. To limit increases in pollution and decreases in natural resources between now and the future and to prevent the eventual collapse of per capita food and industrial production and of population predicted by the models requires, as can be seen in Figure 20–4 on page 417 of the text, that steps be taken now to end all further increases in the

world's _____ and in per capita _____

■ SELF-TEST

Circle the T if the statement is true, the F if it is false.

1. Real GNP has tended to increase more rapidly than per capita GNP in the United States.　　　　　　　　**T　F**

2. Growth and rates of growth estimates generally attempt to take account of changes in the quality of goods produced and in the amount of leisure members of the economy enjoy.　　　　　　　　**T　F**

3. The quantity and quality of the natural resources with which the United States was endowed can accurately be described as generous.　　　　　　　　**T　F**

4. The population of the United States has increased by 300% since 1900.　　**T　F**

5. More often than not technological progress requires the economy to invest in new machinery and equipment.　　　**T　F**

6. The American economy has a stock of capital with a value which exceeds $20 trillion.　　　　　　　　**T　F**

7. Changes in the supply factors do not cause changes in the demand factor, and vice versa.　　　　　　　　**T　F**

8. The American social, cultural, and political environment has, in general, worked to slow the economic growth of the United States.　　　　　　　　**T　F**

9. The most important single source of the growth of the total output of the American economy since 1948 has been the improved training and education of its labor force.　　　　　　　　**T　F**

10. Since 1948 improved technology has ac-counted for a little over 40% of the growth of total real output in the United States.　　　　　　　　**T　F**

11. The MIT-Club of Rome model predicts that if present trends continue the world's population and its per capita outputs of industrial products and food will decline before the year 2100.　　　　　　　　**T　F**

12. To prevent the collapse predicted by the Doomsday models from coming about the MIT-Club of Rome recommends that the current rate of growth of the economy be increased and that there be no increase in the world's population.　　　　　　　　**T　F**

Underscore the letter that corresponds to the best answer.

1. Since 1915 real GNP in the United States has increased about (a) threefold; (b) fourfold; (c) fivefold; (d) sixfold.

2. Since about 1870 the total output of the American economy has increased at an average *annual* rate of about: (a) ½ of 1%; (b) 2%; (c) 3½%; (d) 5%.

3. Total output per capita in the United States since 1870 has increased at an average annual rate of about: (a) 1%; (b) 2%; (c) 3%; (d) 4%.

4. The supply of which of the following is the most nearly fixed? (a) natural resources; (b) labor; (c) capital; (d) money.

5. There are in the American labor force approximately how many million workers? (a) 75; (b) 85; (c) 93; (d) 205.

6. Approximately what percentages of the labor force have completed high school and four years of college; (a) 45% and 8%; (b) 44% and 13%; (c) 60% and 8%; (d) 68% and 13%.

7. The United States currently spends about what percentage of its gross national product on research and development? (a) 2%; (b) 2.4%; (c) 2.8%; (d) 5%.

8. Which of the following is *not* one of the consequences when aggregate demand increases by less than the productive capacity of the economy? (a) inflation; (b) a GNP gap; (c) a slower rate of economic growth; (d) unemployed labor.

9. Which of the following is *not* an artificial impediment to economic growth? (*a*) labor union restrictions on the size of their membership; (*b*) government-supported prices for agricultural products; (*c*) the reluctance of workers to move to new communities and to take new jobs; (*d*) unfair competition by firms in an industry to prevent the entry of new firms into the industry.

10. About what percentage of the increase in the total output of the American economy since 1948 was due to increases in the quantities of capital and labor employed? (*a*) 20%; (*b*) 23%; (*c*) 30%; (*d*) 43%.

11. Which of the following is *not* a part of the case against economic growth? (*a*) Growth produces pollution and other adverse spillovers; (*b*) growth impedes the increased production of consumer goods; (*c*) growth prevents the attainment of a better life; (*d*) growth is not needed to provide us with the means of solving domestic social problems.

12. Which of the following is *not* a part of the case in defense of economic growth? (*a*) Growth lessens the unlimited wants-scarce resources problem; (*b*) growth lessens the extent of anxiety and insecurity; (*c*) growth need not be accompanied by the pollution of the environment; (*d*) growth is the only practical way to reduce poverty.

■ DISCUSSION QUESTIONS

1. What has been the growth record of the American economy over the past five or six decades and since 1870? Compare recent American growth rates with those in other nations.

2. Some economists contend that the natural resources of the United States explain much of its past economic growth *and* they will limit its economic growth in the future. Explain how natural resources made past growth possible and may slow future growth.

3. What long-run changes have occurred in the size of the American population and labor force? What qualitative changes have occurred?

4. Why are technological advance and capital formation closely related processes?

5. What are the economic consequences if aggregate demand increases more than the productive capacity of the economy increases? If aggregate demand increases less than productive capacity increases?

6. In what ways has the American social environment been conducive to economic growth?

7. What role does the price-market system play in promoting the reallocation of scarce resources? What impediments are there in the United States to the reallocation of resources which must occur if there is to be economic growth?

8. What have been the sources of the economic growth which the United States has experienced since 1948?

9. What arguments can be presented on both sides of the question of whether growth in the United States is desirable?

10. What are the assumptions and conclusions of the MIT-Club of Rome models? What policies do they suggest to avoid the Doomsday which the models predict? What have the critics had to say about the models and their predictions?

11. What was the energy crisis of 1973? According to the Doomsday interpretation, what was the cause and what would be the consequences of the crisis?

12. Explain the two ways the American economy can adapt to the scarcity of energy resources. What aggravated this scarcity?

13. Why and how did the American petroleum industry allegedly create the energy crisis? What is the response of the major oil firms to these allegations.

GROWTH AND THE
UNDERDEVELOPED NATIONS

Chapter 21 is the third of the three chapters concerned with economic growth. Chapter 19 dealt with the theory of growth; and Chapter 20 examined the record and problems of economic growth in the United States.

This chapter looks at the problem of raising the standard of living faced by the underdeveloped nations of the world. Economic growth both in these underdeveloped nations and in the developed or the advanced nations requires that the nation's resources and technological knowledge be expanded. Application of this very simple principle in the underdeveloped nations, however, faces a set of obstacles quite different from those that limit economic growth in the United States. The emphasis in this chapter is on the obstacles to economic growth in the poor and underdeveloped nations of the world. The student should concentrate his attention on these obstacles. He will then understand why increasing the quantity and quality of resources and improving technology is especially difficult in the world's underdeveloped nations.

The existence of these special obstacles does not mean that increases in the living standards of the underdeveloped nations are impossible. What it does mean is that the underdeveloped nations are going to have to do things that did not need to be done in

the United States (or in the other developed nations) in order to grow. Governments of the poor countries will have to take an active role in promoting growth. Population increases are going to have to be limited. And dramatic changes in social practices and institutions will be required. If these things are not done it will not be possible to eliminate or reduce the obstacles to growth.

No matter how successful the underdeveloped nations are in eliminating these obstacles they probably will still not be able to grow very rapidly without the help of the developed nations. There seem to be at least two reasons why the developed nations will offer the less developed ones some amount of assistance. The citizens of the more advanced nations feel some moral obligation to aid the less fortunate peoples of the world; and they may feel it is in their own self-interest to aid the poor of the world. (It is just this motive for extending aid—the self-interest of those extending the aid—that leads the radical economist to fear foreign aid, and to argue that foreign aid is nothing more than a new form of imperialism designed to return the underdeveloped nations to an inferior status.)

The question that always remains to be answered is the one posed in the final section of this chapter. Will the poor nations increase their standards of living by substantial amounts in the future? What appears to be the best available answer—no one can really see into the future—is well expressed by the term "cautious optimism." Many of the underdeveloped nations will raise their living standards substantially *if* they do the many things that have to be done. The terrible *if!* Will these things be done?

On this note of uncertainty we conclude the topic of economic growth and end our study of macroeconomics. An examination of microeconomic principles, problems, and policies begins in the next chapter.

■ CHAPTER OUTLINE

1. The underdeveloped nations of the world comprise two-thirds of the world's population.

a. Most of the countries of Asia, Africa, South America, and Southeastern Europe are underdeveloped, and all of them have one common characteristic—poverty (that is, a low per capita income or standard of living).

b. Because of an increasing disparity between the standards of living in the developed and the underdeveloped nations, and because many of the underdeveloped nations have recently become politically independent, these nations are discontented and determined to raise their standards of living.

c. The economic and social environment of the underdeveloped nations is vastly different from that in which the United States found itself when it began its development; consequently, the underdeveloped nations cannot develop merely by following the examples of the United States and other advanced nations.

2. Economic development requires that the quantity and quality of economic resources be increased and that technological knowledge be expanded; but there are many special obstacles to such a program in the underdeveloped nations.

a. Many (but not all) underdeveloped nations possess inadequate natural resources and this limits their ability to develop.

b. The typical underdeveloped nation is overpopulated, is plagued with disguised unemployment, and has a poor quality labor force.

c. Usually very short of capital goods, underdeveloped nations find it difficult to accumulate capital because of their low saving potentials and the absence of investors and incentives to invest.

d. Technological knowledge is primitive in underdeveloped nations; and they might adopt the technologies employed in the advanced nations if obstacles to technological advance did not exist.

e. In addition, a nation must have a strong desire to develop and be willing to alter its own social and institutional environment to grow economically.

3. In summary, underdeveloped nations save little and, therefore, invest little in real and human capital because they are poor; and because they do not invest, their output per capita remains low and they remain poor. Even if this vicious circle were to be broken, a rapid increase in population would leave the standard of living unchanged.

4. It is probable that the governments of these nations will have to play a major role by sponsoring and directing many of the early development plans if the obstacles to growth are to be overcome.

5. The advanced nations of the world can in a number of ways help the poor nations to develop.

a. They can lower the barriers which prevent the underdeveloped nations from selling their products in the developed nations.

b. The flow of private capital from the advanced nations helps the underdeveloped nations increase their productive capacities and per capita outputs.

c. Loans and grants from governments and international organizations also enable the underdeveloped nations to accumulate capital.

d. Radical economists believe that the help extended by the advanced nations of the Western world is designed to exploit the underdeveloped nations.

6. In the 1960s real GNP increased at about the same rate in developed and underdeveloped nations; but the rate of growth in per capita output was much less in underdeveloped nations. The outlook for future growth in the latter nations is cautiously optimistic.

■ IMPORTANT TERMS

Underdeveloped nation	Basic social capital
Disguised unemployment	Capital-saving technological advance
Investment in human capital	Capital-using technological advance
Domestic capital formation	World Bank
	1% rule
Nonfinancial investment	Green revolution

■ FILL-IN QUESTIONS

1. The common characteristic of underdeveloped nations is _____

2. The underdeveloped nations are found chiefly in the following areas of the world:

_____,

_____,

_____,

and _____;

and they account for approximately _____

_____

of the world's population.

3. To grow, every economy must increase its _____,

_____,

and _____

and improve its _____

4. Which resource is *least* easily increased in the typical underdeveloped nation? _____

_____

5. Three characteristics of the human resources in underdeveloped nations are:

a. _____

b. _____

c. _____

6. The per capita standard of living = _____

_____

and social unrest = _____

minus _____

7. Disguised unemployment means that the marginal product of workers is _____

_____

8. If the process of capital accumulation is "cumulative," this means that _____

_____

9. Domestic capital accumulation requires that a nation _____

and _____.
The former is difficult in underdeveloped nations because of a _____
and the latter is difficult because of a lack of

_____

and _____

10. Nonfinancial investment involves the transfer of surplus labor from _____

to _____

or _____

11. Technological advance in an underdeveloped nation does not ordinarily require an expensive program of research and development because _____

_____

12. If technological advances make it possible to replace a worn-out plow, costing $10 when new, with a new $5 plow, the technological advance is _____

13. The "will to develop" in underdeveloped nations involves a willingness to change the

_____

of the nation.

14. In the typical underdeveloped nation saving is small because the _____ per capita is small. Because saving is small,

_____ in real and human capital is also small. And for this reason the _____

_____ of labor and the _____ per capita remain small.

15. List six reasons why the role of government in fostering economic development will need to be large in the underdeveloped nations, especially during the early stages of development:

a. _____

b. _____

c. _____

d. _____

e. _____

f. _____

16. The three major ways in which the United States can assist economic development in the underdeveloped nations are _____

_____,

_____,

and _____

17. The "1% rule" of the UN recommends that public and private flows of capital from the developed to the underdeveloped nations equal 1% of the _____ of the developed nations.

18. During the 1960s real GNP in the underdeveloped nations grew at an average annual rate of _____% and per capita real GNP increased annually about _____%.

■ PROBLEMS AND PROJECTS

1. While economic conditions are not identical in all underdeveloped nations, there are certain conditions common to or typical of all. In the spaces after each of the following characteristics, indicate briefly the nature of this characteristic in the typical underdeveloped nation.

a. Standard of living (per capita income).

_____

b. Average life expectancy. _____

_____

c. Extent of unemployment. _____

d. Endowment of natural resources. _____

_____

e. Agricultural techniques employed. _____

_____

f. Percentage of the population engaged in agriculture. _____

g. Size of the population relative to the land and capital available. _____

h. The birth and death rates. _____

i. Quality of the labor force. _____

j. Amount of capital equipment relative to the labor force. _____

k. Level of saving. _____

l. Incentive to invest. _____

m. Amount of basic social capital. _____

_____

n. Extent of industrialization. _____

_____

o. Size and quality of the entrepreneurial class and the supervisory class. _____

_____

2. Suppose that it takes a minimum of 5 units of food to keep a person alive for a year, that the population can double itself every 10 years, and that the food supply can increase every 10 years by an amount equal to what it was in the beginning.

Year	Food supply	Population
0	200	20
10	_____	_____
20	_____	_____
30	_____	_____
40	_____	_____
50	_____	_____
60	_____	_____

a. Assume that both the population and the food supply grow at these rates. Complete the table by computing the size of the population and the food supply in years 10 through 60.

b. What happens to the relationship between the food supply and the population in the 30th year? _____

c. What would actually prevent the population from growing at this rate following the 30th year? _____

d. Assuming that the actual population growth in the years following the 30th does not outrun the food supply, what would be the size of the population in:

(1) Year 40: _____

(2) Year 50: _____

(3) Year 60: _____

e. Explain why the standard of living failed to increase in the years following the 30th even though the food supply increased by 75% between years 30 and 60. _____

_____

■ SELF-TEST

Circle the T if the statement is true, the F if it is false.

1. Among the larger nations of the world the United States has the highest per capita income. **T F**

2. The difference between the per capita incomes in the underdeveloped nations and the per capita incomes in the developed nations has been decreasing over the past years. **T F**

3. It is impossible to achieve a high standard of living with a small supply of natural resources. **T F**

4. Nations with large populations are overpopulated. **T F**

5. The chief factor preventing the elimination of disguised unemployment in the agricultural sector of underdeveloped nations is the small number of job openings available in industry. **T F**

6. The marginal propensity to consume of the mass of the people in underdeveloped nations is less than 1.0. **T F**

7. Before private investment can be increased in underdeveloped nations it is necessary to reduce the amount of investment in basic social capital. **T F**

8. The policies of the governments of underdeveloped nations have often tended to reduce the incentives of foreigners to invest in the underdeveloped nations. **T F**

9. Underdeveloped nations will not need foreign aid if the developed nations will reduce tariffs and import quotas on the goods which the underdeveloped nations export. **T F**

10. An increase in the output and employment of the United States works to the advantage of the underdeveloped nations because it provides the underdeveloped nations with larger markets for their exports. **T F**

11. Private and public capital flows from the United States to the underdeveloped nations have consistently exceeded the amounts suggested by the "1% rule." **T F**

12. Radical economists believe that the foreign aid extended by the developed to the underdeveloped nations is designed to increase profits in the former and to exploit the latter nations. **T F**

Underscore the letter that corresponds to the best answer.

1. Which of the following is the most underdeveloped nation? (*a*) U.S.S.R.; (*b*) Israel; (*c*) Canada; (*d*) India.

2. Which of the following is the most serious obstacle to economic growth in underdeveloped nations? (*a*) the supply of natural resources; (*b*) the size and quality of the labor force; (*c*) the supply of capital equipment; (*d*) technological knowledge.

3. An increase in the total output of consumer goods in an underdeveloped nation may not increase the average standard of living because; (*a*) of diminishing returns; (*b*) it may provoke an increase in the population; (*c*) of disguised unemployment; (*d*) the quality of the labor force is so poor.

4. Which of the following *best* describes disguised unemployment? (*a*) an agricultural worker in an underdeveloped nation; (*b*) a worker whose marginal product is zero or less than zero; (c) an agricultural worker who cannot find employment in industry; (d) a worker whose productivity is subject to diminishing returns.

5. Which of the following is *not* a reason for placing special emphasis on capital accumulation in underdeveloped nations? (a) the inflexible supply of arable land; (b) the low productivity of workers; (c) the low marginal productivity of capital equipment; (d) the possibility that capital accumulation will be "cumulative."

6. Which of the following is *not* a factor limiting saving in underdeveloped nations? (a) the incomes of the mass of people are too low to allow saving; (b) those who are able to save are unwilling to save; (c) the highly unequal distribution of income; (d) the low marginal productivity of capital equipment.

7. Which of the following is an example of basic social capital? (a) a steel plant; (b) an electric power plant; (c) a farm; (d) a demand deposit in a commercial bank.

8. Which of the following seem to be the *most* needed and widespread institutional change required of underdeveloped nations? (a) adoption of birth control; (b) development of strong labor unions; (c) increase in the nation's basic social capital; (d) land reform.

9. Suppose the average propensity to save in an underdeveloped nation is .09 and that the capital-output ratio is 3. At what rate can total real output increase? (a) 2.7%; (b) 3.0%; (c) 3.3%; (d) 3.9%.

10. Assume the total real output of an underdeveloped economy increases from $100 billion to $115.5 billion while its population expands from 200 million to 210 million people. Real income per capita has, as a result, increased by (a) $50; (b) $100; (c) $150; (d) $200.

11. The role of government in the early stages of economic development will probably be a major one for several reasons. Which one of the following is *not* one of these reasons? (a) only government can provide a large amount of the needed basic social capital; (b) the absence of private entrepreneurs to accumulate capital and take risks; (c) the necessity of creating *new* money to finance capital ac-

cumulation; (d) the slowness and uncertainty of the price system in fostering development.

12. Which of the following was *not* true during the 1960s? (a) Real GNP increased at about the same average rate in developed and underdeveloped nations; (b) real GNP increased more rapidly than population in the underdeveloped nations; (c) the rate of growth of real GNP per capita was more rapid in the developed than in the underdeveloped nations; (d) real GNP per capita was approximately constant in the underdeveloped nations.

■ DISCUSSION QUESTIONS

1. What nations of the world can be called "developed"? Which can be classified as "semideveloped"? Where are the "underdeveloped" nations of the world found?

2. What recent events have increased the desire of the underdeveloped nations to improve their standard of living? Why should social unrest increase in the underdeveloped nations even though their standards of living have been increasing?

3. Why is advice to the underdeveloped nations to follow the example of the United States inappropriate and unrealistic?

4. What must any nation, developed or underdeveloped, do if it is to increase its standard of living? Answer in terms of the production possibilities curve concept.

5. What obstacles do the human resources of underdeveloped natons place in the path of economic development? Why is it difficult to eliminate disguised unemployment in underdeveloped nations?

6. What reasons exist for placing special emphasis on capital accumulation as a means of promoting economic growth in underdeveloped nations?

7. Why is domestic capital accumulation difficult in underdeveloped nations? Answer in terms of both the saving side and the investment side of capital accumulation. How does a lack of basic social capital inhibit investment in underdeveloped nations?

8. In addition to the obstacles which limit domestic investment, what other obstacles tend to limit the flow of foreign capital into underdeveloped nations?

9. Why is it possible for underdeveloped nations to improve their technology without engaging in slow and expensive research?

10. What is meant by the "will to develop"? How is it related to social and institutional change in underdeveloped nations?

11. Explain the "vicious circle" of poverty found in the underdeveloped nations. How does population growth make an escape from this vicious circle difficult.

12. Why is the role of government expected to be a major one in the early phases of development in underdeveloped nations?

13. How can the United States help underdeveloped nations? What types of aid can be offered?

14. Discuss the World Bank in terms of its purposes, characteristics, sources of funds,

promotion of private capital flows, and success. What are its affiliates and their purposes?

15. How is it possible for the United States to assist underdeveloped nations without spending a penny on "foreign aid"? Is this type of aid sufficient to ensure rapid and substantial development in the underdeveloped nations?

16. How much does the United States contribute in relative and absolute amounts to underdeveloped nations? How much do you think it should contribute?

17. How do the radical economists interpret the foreign aid extended by the advanced capitalistic nations to the world's underdeveloped nations?

18. What was the growth record of the underdeveloped nations during the 1960s and what are their prospects for growth during the 1970s?

THE MARKET STRUCTURES
OF AMERICAN CAPITALISM

In this chapter the text shifts from the study of macroeconomics to the study of microeconomics; from an analysis of national output and the price level to an analysis of the output and prices of firms and industries; and from an examination of the economy as a whole to an examination of the parts of the economy. In addition, the central question to be answered is no longer what will be the level of resource employment, but how are resources allocated among different products, by whom and by what methods will these products be produced, and how will the income generated in their production be distributed among the owners of various resources.

It has been pointed out more than once that price and the price system are the particular devices which American capitalism employs to answer these questions, and that price depends upon the supply of and the demand for the different products. If the operation of the economy and the method by which it answers the basic economic questions are to be understood, it is necessary to discover what determines supply and demand. The supply of products depends basically upon two factors: the cost of producing the product, and the characteristics of the market in which the

product is sold. Chapter 22 focuses attention upon the different market structures under which products are sold. Because demand is also influenced by the characteristics of the market in which goods and services are purchased, some attention is paid to the relationship between demand and the character of the market.

Chapter 22's first major section describes four market situations from the point of view of sellers. Although these four situations are no more than generalized categories into which almost all real market situations can be placed, the student should concentrate his attention upon the five major characteristics of each of the four market situations. Most of the analysis in later chapters is based on an understanding of these categories and their characteristics. To facilitate the learning process, a table—Table 22–1—is provided in the summary at the end of the chapter.

The second section of the chapter describes four generalized market situations from the buyers' side of the market. Each of these situations is defined solely in terms of the number of buyers—one, few, fairly many, or very many—and they are, therefore, quite easy to learn and remember.

The third section of the chapter points out

that the degree of competitiveness or non-competitiveness of a market depends not only upon the five characteristics of each market category but also upon the geographic size of the market, how much competition there is between firms and products in *different* industries, the extent of nonprice competition, and how much competition there is *over time* from new products, processes, and firms. In evaluating the competitiveness of any market the reader will do well to keep these four factors in mind.

The final topic with which the chapter is concerned is the reasons why any industry or market becomes the type of market or industry it is. Four general factors are suggested as causes for the actual development of a market into one of the four categories.

■ CHAPTER OUTLINE

1. On the sellers' side of the market, markets fall into one of four categories: pure competition, pure monopoly, monopolistic competition, and oligopoly. The distinction between market categories depends upon the number of sellers, the type of product, the degree of control which one seller has over price, the ease of entry into the market, and the extent of nonprice competition.

2. On the buyers' side of the market, markets also fall into one of four categories: pure competition, pure monopsony, monopsonistic competition, and oligopsony; the distinction between market categories depends solely upon the number of buyers.

3. How competitive these markets are depends upon four additional elements: the geographic extent of the market and the amount of interindustry, nonprice, and technological competition.

4. The type of market which develops for the exchange of any good or service depends upon such things as the government's laws, regulations, and policies; the practices and behavior of the firms in the market; the technology employed in producing the product; and the institutions of the capitalistic economy.

■ IMPORTANT TERMS

Pure competition
Pure monopoly
Monopolistic competition
Oligopoly
Standardized product
Nonprice competition
Product differentiation
Price-taker
Price-setter
Monopsony
Monopsonistic competition
Oligopsony
Bilateral monopoly
Quality competition
Interindustry competition

■ FILL-IN QUESTIONS

1. List the five characteristics of pure competition:

a. _____
b. _____
c. _____
d. _____
e. _____

2. Oligopoly is a market model viewed from the _____ side of the market and monopsonistic competition is a model viewed from the _____ side.

3. The efficient management of economic resources requires that the resources be both _____ and _____; the present chapter begins the study of the (latter, former) _____ aspect of the efficient use of resources.

4. The products produced by purely competitive firms are _____ while those produced by monopolistically competitive firms are _____; the product produced by the pure monopolist has no _____

5. A pure monopolist has no close rivals or

competitors because _____

_____

6. The advertising done by a pure monopolist tends to be of a _____

or _____

nature.

7. Monopolistic competition is like pure competition because _____

and _____,

but like pure monopoly because _____

_____

8. List the five characteristics of pure monopoly:

a. _____

b. _____

c. _____

d. _____

e. _____

9. In order for the number of firms in a monopolistically competitive industry to be

considered "large," it is necessary that _____

_____

10. List the five characteristics of monopolistic competition:

a. _____

b. _____

c. _____

d. _____

e. _____

11. Pure competition and monopolistic competition differ chiefly because _____

_____

12. The product produced by the firms in an oligopoly may be either _____

or _____

13. Oligopolistic firms which produce a standardized product are typically found in those

industries which produce either _____

_____

or _____

14. The number of firms in an oligopoly is

_____

and each firm supplies _____
of the total market supply.

15. The degree of control which an oligopolistic firm possesses over the price of its

product depends upon two factors: _____

_____

and _____

16. In column (1) of the table below, list the four market models viewed from the buyers' side of the market. In column (2) opposite each of the four market models, list their distinguishing characteristic.

(1)\n Market model	(2)\n Distinguishing\n characteristic
_____	_____
_____	_____
_____	_____
_____	_____

17. In addition to the type of product, the number of sellers, the ease of entry, and the degree of control over price, the competitiveness or noncompetitiveness of a market depends upon _____,

_____,

_____,

and _____

18. The four factors that have been important determinants of market structures in the United States are:

a. _____

b. _____

c. _____

d. _____

■ PROBLEMS AND PROJECTS

1. Employing the following set of terms, complete the table below by inserting the appropriate letter or letters in the blanks.

a. one
b. few
c. many
d. a very large number
e. standardized
f. differentiated
g. some

h. considerable
i. very easy
j. blocked
k. fairly easy
l. fairly difficult
m. none

2. Listed below are several firms or types of firms. In the blanks, indicate (1) into what market type—from the sellers' side of the market—this firm falls and (2) the chief reason(s) for placing it in this classification.

a. A local dry-cleaning firm _____

_____

b. A manufacturer of toothpaste _____

_____

c. A farmer raising pigs _____

_____

d. The Ford Motor Company _____

_____

e. A used-car dealer _____

_____

f. A steel producer _____

_____

3. Indicate for each of the following industries whether its firms compete in any significant way with firms in other industries and what the competing industries are.

a. Airlines _____

b. Silk _____

c. Plastics _____

d. Television sets _____

e. Copper _____

■ SELF-TEST

Circle the T if the statement is true, the F if it is false.

1. Every industry in the American economy falls clearly into one of four market models.
T F

2. The definition of competition is one of the very few economic concepts upon which the layman and the economist find it easy to agree.
T F

3. Although no individual purely competitive firm is able to influence the market price of the product which it produces, all the firms in a purely competitive industry can influence the market price.
T F

4. A large number of sellers does not necessarily mean that the industry is purely competitive.
T F

5. Only in a purely competitive industry do individual firms have no control over the price of their product.
T F

6. Because he is the sole supplier of a product, the pure monopolist cannot affect the market price of his product.
T F

7. Insofar as pure monopoly is concerned, the industry and the firm are one and the same.
T F

Market characteristics	Market situation			
	Pure competition	Pure monopoly	Monopolistic competition	Oligopoly
Number of firms	_____	_____	_____	_____
Type of product	_____	_____	_____	_____
Control over price	_____	_____	_____	_____
Entry	_____	_____	_____	_____
Nonprice competition	_____	_____	_____	_____

8. There are no substitutes for the product produced by the pure monopolist.   **T   F**

9. The monopolistic competitor has only a limited amount of control over the price of his product.   **T   F**

10. Entry into the monopolistically competitive industry is usually quite difficult.   **T   F**

11. The greater the degree of product differentiation in an oligopoly, the larger will be the amount of control a firm has over the price of its product.   **T   F**

12. If an oligopolistic firm is producing a differentiated product, it is more likely to engage in advertising and sales promotion than a firm producing a standardized product.
   T   F

13. The existence of just two sellers in a market is called "bilateral monopoly."   **T   F**

14. The policies of the Federal government have been consistently directed at preventing or eliminating monopoly and at encouraging competition.   **T   F**

15. The economics of mass production and the role of research in the development of new products and techniques of production generally lead to an increase in the number of firms in an industry and a decrease in the size of these firms.   **T   F**

Underscore the letter that corresponds to the best answer.

1. Which of the following is *not* one of the four market models as viewed from the sellers' side of the market? (*a*) pure competition; (*b*) monopoly; (*c*) monopolistic competition; (*d*) oligopsony.

2. Which of the following is characteristic of monopolistic competition? (*a*) standardized product; (*b*) very few firms; (*c*) entry is fairly easy; (*d*) very little nonprice competition.

3. Which of the following is *not* characteristic of pure competition? (*a*) large number of sellers; (*b*) differentiated product; (*c*) easy entry; (*d*) no advertising.

4. If the product produced by an industry is standardized, the market structure can be: (*a*) pure competition or monopolistic competition; (*b*) pure competition or oligopoly; (*c*) monopolistic competition or oligopoly; (*d*) pure competition, monopolistic competition, or oligopoly.

5. Into which of the following industries is entry least difficult? (*a*) pure competition; (*b*) pure monopoly; (*c*) monopolistic competition; (*d*) oligopoly.

6. Which of the following industries comes *closest* to being purely competitive? (*a*) wheat; (*b*) shoes; (*c*) retailing; (*d*) farm implements.

7. Which of the following is the *best* example of a pure monopoly? (*a*) the local telegraph company; (*b*) the local water company; (*c*) the Aluminum Company of America; (*d*) the United States Steel Corporation.

8. With respect to which of the following characteristics are purely competitive industries and monopolistically competitive industries most similar? (*a*) type of product; (*b*) number of firms; (*c*) difficulty of entry; (*d*) extent of nonprice competition.

9. Which of the following industry classifications encompasses the greatest number of actual market situations in the American economy? (*a*) pure competition; (*b*) pure monopoly; (*c*) monopolistic competition; (*d*) oligopoly.

10. Which of the following is an example of an oligopoly producing a differentiated product? (*a*) automobiles; (*b*) steel; (*c*) shoes; (*d*) women's dresses.

11. From the buyers' side of the market, the market for automobile workers in Detroit would be: (*a*) purely competitive; (*b*) monopsonistic; (*c*) monopsonistically competitive; (*d*) oligopsonistic.

12. Under which of the following pairs of conditions would the oligopolistic firm have the greatest degree of control over the price of its product? (*a*) no collusion between firms in the industry and a standardized product; (*b*) no collusion between firms in the industry and a differentiated product; (*c*) collusion between firms in the industry and a standardized product; (*d*) collusion between firms in the industry and a differentiated product.

■ DISCUSSION QUESTIONS

1. What does it mean when it is said that "the purely competitive firm is at the mercy of the market"? In your answer explain the difference between a price-taker and a price-setter; and why firms outside of purely competitive industries are not at the complete mercy of the market.

2. Why do purely competitive firms do little advertising? Why do monopolistically competitive firms do so much?

3. Explain in what sense the monopolistically competitive firm is competitive and in what sense it is monopolistic.

4. What seems to be the most important factor in preventing rivals from developing to compete with pure monopolists?

5. What are the barriers to entry typically found in oligopolistic markets?

6. How has the Federal government contributed to the formation of monopolies? In what ways has it attempted to limit their formation or to regulate them?

7. Why might an industry which at first glance seems to be purely competitive or monopolistically competitive because of its large number of firms at second glance turn out to be monopolistic or oligopolistic?

8. What determines whether an oligopolist will engage in extensive advertising and other forms of sales promotion?

9. What are the four market models as seen from the buyers' side of the market and their distinguishing characteristics?

10. In assessing the competitiveness or non-competitiveness of a market, what factors should be considered?

11. How does competition over *time* differ from competition *at a point in time?*

12. What factors are important in determining the type of market or industry a particular group of firms will become?

13. Why is it dangerous to employ just four market models—from the sellers' side of the market—in classifying and analyzing American industries?

14. What limits the ability of a monopolistically competitive firm to control the price of its product?

15. Why is entry into a monopolistically competitive industry more difficult than into a purely competitive industry?

16. "Clear-cut mutual interdependence" is one of the characteristics peculiar to oligopoly. What does this mean?

DEMAND, SUPPLY,
AND ELASTICITY:
SOME APPLICATIONS

Before the student begins to read Chapter 23, he is urged (he would be commanded if this were possible) to read and study Chapter 4 again. It is absolutely necessary that the student have mastered Chapter 4 if the new material of this chapter is to be understood and digested.

As might be guessed, Chapter 23 is, in a sense, a continuation of Chapter 4. In the earlier part of the book it was necessary for the student to have only an elementary knowledge of supply and demand. Now the economic principles, problems, and policies to be studied require a more detailed examination and analysis of supply and demand principles. Of particular importance and value in studying much of the material found in the remainder of the text is the concept of elasticity, to which the major portion of Chapter 23 is devoted.

With respect to the concept of elasticity of demand, it is essential for the student to understand (1) what elasticity measures; (2) how the price-elasticity formula is applied to measure the elasticity of demand precisely; (3) the difference between elastic, inelastic, and unitary elasticity of demand; (4) how total revenue varies in each of these three cases;

and (5) the meaning of perfect elasticity and perfect inelasticity. In addition to the analysis of the concept of elasticity of demand, the student will find a discussion of the principal factors which influence the elasticity of demand and several examples of the importance of this concept in practical economic questions.

When the student has become thoroughly acquainted with the elasticity of demand concept, he will find he has very little trouble understanding the elasticity of *supply* and that the transition requires no more than the substitution of the words "quantity supplied" for the words "quantity demanded." Here attention should be concentrated upon the meaning of elasticity of supply, its measurement, and its principal determinant.

In the final section of the chapter three topics are discussed. The first of these topics is legal price ceilings and minimums. The student should note that these ceilings and minimums prevent supply and demand from determining the equilibrium price of a commodity and from determining the quantity of the commodity which will be bought and sold in the market. The consequences will be shortages or surpluses of the commodity.

The incidence of a sales or excise tax is the

second topic. Incidence means "who ends up paying the tax." The most important thing the student will learn is that the elasticities of demand and of supply determine how much of the tax will be paid by buyers and how much of it will be paid by sellers. The student should be especially careful to learn and to understand how the two elasticities affect the incidence of a tax.

The third topic introduces the student to several important new revenue concepts. These concepts are a necessary part of the analysis of the behavior of the business firm under the four sets of market conditions discussed in Chapters 26 through 29, and the student should master them now if he is to understand what follows. Here it is important to distinguish between the way in which the individual pure competitor sees the demand for his product and the way in which the imperfect competitor sees the demand for the product of his firm. After this distinction is understood, the further distinction between the nature of the demand, total-revenue, average-revenue, and marginal-revenue schedules confronting the pure competitor and those confronting the imperfect competitor needs to be made. First learn the revenue concepts, and then learn the difference between the ways in which the pure and the imperfect competitor see them.

■ CHAPTER OUTLINE

1. It is necessary to review the analysis of supply and demand and the concepts found in Chapter 4 before studying this chapter.

2. Price elasticity of demand is a measure of the sensitivity of quantity demanded to changes in the price of the product.

a. The exact degree of elasticity can be measured by using a formula to compute the elasticity coefficient. Demand is either elastic, inelastic, or of unitary elasticity.

b. The way in which total revenue changes (increases, decreases, or remains constant) when price changes is a test of the elasticity of demand for a product.

c. The elasticity of demand for a product depends upon the number of good substitutes the product has, its relative importance in the consumer's budget, whether it is a necessity or a luxury, its durability, and the period of time under consideration.

d. Elasticity of demand is of great practical importance in matters of public policy and in the setting of prices by the individual business firm.

e. Price elasticity of supply is a measure of the sensitivity of quantity supplied to changes in the price of the product; while there is no total-revenue test, the formula used to measure elasticity of demand can also be used to measure elasticity of supply.

3. Supply and demand analysis and the elasticity concepts have many important applications.

a. Legal price ceilings and price minimums prevent price from performing its rationing function.

(1) A price ceiling results in a shortage of the commodity; may bring about formal rationing by government and a black market; and causes a misallocation of resources.

(2) A price minimum creates a surplus of the commodity; and may induce government to undertake measures either to increase the demand for or to decrease the supply of the commodity.

b. The imposition of a sales or excise tax on a commodity decreases the supply of the commodity and increases its price. The amount of the price increase is the portion of the tax paid by the buyer; the seller pays the rest.

(1) The more elastic (inelastic) the demand for the commodity, the greater (smaller) is the portion paid by the seller.

(2) The more elastic (inelastic) the supply of the commodity, the greater (smaller) is the portion paid by the buyer.

c. The way in which the individual firm sees the demand for its product depends upon whether the firm is a pure competitor or an imperfect competitor.

(1) Under conditions of pure competition, it sees demand as perfectly elastic, average revenue and marginal revenue as equal and constant at the fixed market price, and total revenue as constantly increasing as the firm's output increases.

(2) Under conditions of imperfect competition, it sees demand as less than perfectly elastic, marginal revenue as less than average revenue, both decreasing as the firm's output increases, and total revenue as increasing at first but then decreasing as its output increases.

■ IMPORTANT TERMS

Review

Demand	Rationing function of prices
Supply	
Law of demand	Change in demand
Law of supply	Change in supply
Equilibrium price	Change in quantity demanded
Equilibrium quantity	
Competition (competitive market)	Change in quantity supplied

New

Price elasticity of demand	Elastic supply
	Inelastic supply
Elastic demand	Market period
Inelastic demand	Short run
Total-revenue test	Long run
Elasticity coefficient	Price ceiling
Elasticity formula	Price support
Unitary elasticity	Tax incidence
Perfect inelasticity of demand	Total revenue
	Average revenue
Perfect elasticity of demand	Marginal revenue
Price elasticity of supply	Imperfect competition

Note: Before answering the Fill-in, Self-test, and Discussion questions and working out the Problems and Projects, the student should return to Chapter 4 in this study guide and review the terms and concepts, answer the questions, and rework the problems.

■ FILL-IN QUESTIONS

1. If a relatively large change in price results in a relatively small change in quantity demanded, demand is _____;
if a relatively small change in price results in a relatively large change in quantity demanded, demand is _____

2. When demand is elastic, buyers are relatively (sensitive, insensitive) _____ to change in the price of the product; when demand is inelastic, they are relatively _____

_____ to changes in price.

3. If demand is elastic, price and total revenue are _____ related; if demand is inelastic, they are _____ _____ related.

4. Complete the summary table.

If demand is	The elasticity coefficient is	If price rises, total revenue will	If price falls, total revenue will
Elastic	___	___	___
Inelastic			
Of unitary elasticity	___	___	___

5. If a change in price causes no change in quantity demanded, demand is _____;
if an extremely small change in price results in an extremely large change in quantity demanded, demand is _____.
When the former is graphed, the demand curve is _____;
a graph of the latter demand curve is _____

6. If the price of a commodity declines,
a. When demand is inelastic the loss of revenue due to the lower price is _____ _____ the gain in revenue due to the greater quantity demanded.
b. When demand is elastic the loss of revenue due to the lower price is _____ _____ the gain in revenue due to the greater quantity demanded.
c. When demand is of unitary elasticity the loss of revenue due to the lower price is _____ _____ the gain in revenue due to the greater quantity demanded.

7. List five determinants of the elasticity of demand:
a. _____
b. _____

c. _____

d. _____

e. _____

8. The most important factor affecting the elasticity of supply is _____

9. If the demand and supply schedules for a certain product are as given in the table, answer the following questions.

Quantity demanded	Price	Quantity supplied
12,000	$10	18,000
13,000	9	17,000
14,000	8	16,000
15,000	7	15,000
16,000	6	14,000
17,000	5	13,000
18,000	4	12,000

a. The equilibrium price of the product is

$_____ and the equilibrium

quantity is _____

b. If the government imposes a price ceiling of $5 on this product, there would be a

_____

of _____
units.

c. If the government imposes a minimum

price of $8, there would be a _____

_____

of _____
units.

10. Price ceilings imposed by the United States government have usually occurred dur-

ing _____

periods, result in _____
of the commodities, and require that the gov-

ernment institute _____
to prevent this.

11. Price ceilings and price minimums pre-

vent prices from performing their _____
function.

12. The two most common examples of gov-

ernment-imposed minimum prices are _____

_____

and _____

13. A minimum price imposed by the govern-

ment on a commodity causes a _____
of the commodity and requires that the gov-

ernment either _____

or _____
to eliminate this.

14. When a sales or excise tax is levied on a commodity, the amount of the tax borne by

buyers of the commodity is equal to _____

_____.

The incidence of such a tax depends on the elasticity of demand and of supply.

a. The buyer's portion of the tax is larger

the (more, less) _____ elastic

the demand and the _____
elastic the supply.

b. The seller's portion of the tax is larger

the _____ elastic the demand

and the _____ elastic the supply.

15. An individual firm which is purely com-petitive finds that as it increases its output,

the price it must charge to sell this output ___

_____,
while the imperfectly competitive firm finds that the price it must charge to sell a larger

output _____;
for this reason the purely competitive firm

finds that marginal revenue is _____
average revenue, and the imperfectly competi-

tive firm finds that marginal revenue is ___

_____
average revenue.

16. On the demand schedule which is less than perfectly elastic, the elasticity of demand typically varies with price. Demand tends to

be _____

in the upper range of prices, _____
in the lower range, and of unitary elasticity at a price between the two ranges.

■ PROBLEMS AND PROJECTS

1. If the supply and demand schedules for a certain product are as given in the table, answer the following questions.

Quantity demanded	Price	Quantity supplied
300	$1.00	800
400	.90	700
500	.80	600
600	.70	500
700	.60	400
800	.50	300
900	.40	200

a. The equilibrium price of the product will

be between $_____ and $ _____

or approximately $ _____

b. The equilibrium quantity of the product

will be between _____

and _____

or approximately _____

c. In the following table, using the demand data given, complete the table by computing total revenue at each of the seven prices and the six elasticity coefficients between each of the seven prices, and indicate whether demand is elastic, inelastic, or of unitary elasticity between each of the seven prices.

Price	Quantity de-manded	Total revenue	Elasticity coeffi-cient	Character of demand
$1.00	300	$____		
.90	400	____	____	____
.80	500	____	____	____
.70	600	____	____	____
.60	700	____	____	____
.50	800	____	____	____
.40	900	____		

d. Using the supply data derived from the schedules above, complete the following table by computing the six elasticity-of-supply coefficients between each of the seven prices, and indicate whether supply is elastic, inelastic, or of unitary elasticity.

Price	Quantity supplied	Elasticity coefficient	Character of supply
$1.00	800		
.90	700	____	____
.80	600	____	____
.70	500	____	____
.60	400	____	____
.50	300	____	____
.40	200	____	____

e. If the government imposed a:

(1) Price ceiling of $.60, there would be a

_____

of _____

units of the product in the market.

(2) Price minimum of $1, there would be a

_____

of _____

units of the product in the market.

2. On the graph below are three different supply curves (S_1, S_2, and S_3) for a product bought and sold in a competitive market.

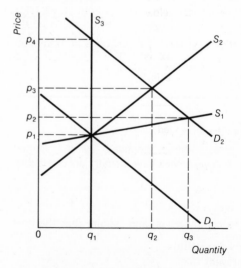

a. The supply curve for the:

(1) market period is the one labeled _____

(2) short run in the one labeled _____

(3) long run is the one labeled _____

b. No matter what the period of time under consideration, if the demand for the product were D_1, the equilibrium price of the product would be _____ and the equilibrium quantity would be _____.

c. Were demand to increase from D_1 to D_2:
(1) in the market period the equilibrium price would increase to _____ and the equilibrium quantity would _____
(2) in the short run the price of the product would increase to _____ and the quantity would increase to _____
(3) in the long run the price of the product would be _____ and the quantity would be _____

d. The longer the period of time allowed to sellers to adjust their outputs the (more, less) _____ elastic is the supply of the product.

e. The more elastic the supply of a product, the (greater, less) _____ is the effect on equilibrium price and the _____ is the effect on equilibrium quantity of an increase in demand.

3. In the table below are the demand and supply schedules for copra in the New Hebrides Islands.

a. Before a tax is imposed on copra, its equilibrium price is $_____

b. The government of the New Hebrides now imposes an excise tax of $.60 per pound on copra. Complete the after-tax supply schedule in the right-hand column of the table below.

c. After the imposition of the tax, the equilibrium price of copra is $_____

d. Of the $.60 tax, the amount borne by
(1) the buyer is $_____ or _____%
(2) the seller is $_____ or _____%

4. Below are two graphs.
a. On the first graph draw a perfectly elastic demand curve and a normal upsloping supply curve for a commodity.
(1) Now impose an excise tax on the com-

0

Quantity demanded (pounds)	Price (per pound)	Before-tax quantity supplied (pounds)	After-tax quantity supplied (pounds)
150	$4.60	900	_____
200	4.40	800	_____
250	4.20	700	_____
300	4.00	600	_____
350	3.80	500	_____
400	3.60	400	_____
450	3.40	300	0
500	3.20	200	0
550	3.00	100	0

modity, and draw the new supply curve that would result.

(2) As a consequence of the tax, the price of the commodity has _____

(3) It can be concluded that when demand is perfectly elastic, the buyer bears _____ of the tax and the seller bears _____ of the tax.

(4) Thus the *more* elastic the demand, the

_____ is the portion of the tax

borne by the buyer and the _____ is the portion borne by the seller.

(5) But the *less* elastic the demand, the

_____ is the portion borne by

the buyer and the _____ is the portion borne by the seller.

b. On the second graph draw a perfectly elastic supply curve and a normal downsloping demand curve.

(1) Again impose an excise tax on the commodity and draw the new supply curve.

(2) As a result of the tax, the price of the

commodity has _____

(3) From this it can be concluded that when supply is perfectly elastic, the buyer

bears _____ of the tax and

the seller bears _____ of the tax.

(4) Thus the *more* elastic the supply, the

_____ is the portion of the

tax borne by the buyer and the _____ is the portion borne by the seller.

(5) But the *less* elastic the supply, the ____

_____ is the portion borne by

the buyer and the _____ is the portion borne by the seller.

5. If the demand schedule confronting an individual firm is as shown in the table below, complete the following questions.

a. Complete the table by computing average revenue, total revenue, marginal revenue, and the coefficient of the price elasticity of demand.

b. Is this firm operating in a market which

Price	Quantity demanded	Average revenue	Total revenue	Marginal revenue	Elasticity coefficient
$11	0	$_____	$_____		
10	1	_____	_____	$_____	_____
9	2	_____	_____	_____	_____
8	3	_____	_____	_____	_____
7	4	_____	_____	_____	_____
6	5	_____	_____	_____	_____
5	6	_____	_____	_____	_____
4	7	_____	_____	_____	_____
3	8	_____	_____	_____	_____
2	9	_____	_____		

is purely or imperfectly competitive? _____

How can you tell? _____

c. On the graph below plot the demand schedule, average revenue, total revenue, and marginal revenue; label each of these curves. (*Note:* Plot marginal revenue at ½, 1½, 2½, etc., units of output rather than at 1, 2, 3, etc.)

d. By examination of the total-revenue, marginal-revenue, and price elasticity of demand coefficients, it can be seen that:

(1) Where total revenue is increasing as price falls, demand is _____

and marginal revenue is _____

(2) Where total revenue is decreasing as price falls, demand is _____

and marginal revenue is _____

(3) Where total revenue is constant as price falls, demand is _____

and marginal revenue is _____

e. Using the tables above, explain why marginal revenue is less than average revenue.

6. Below is another demand schedule for an individual firm.

Price	Quantity demanded	Average revenue	Total revenue	Marginal revenue
$10	0	$_____	$_____	
10	1	_____	_____	$_____
10	2	_____	_____	_____
10	3	_____	_____	_____
10	4	_____	_____	_____
10	5	_____	_____	_____
10	6	_____	_____	_____

a. Complete the table by computing average revenue, total revenue, and marginal revenue.

b. Is this firm operating in a market which is purely or imperfectly competitive? _____

How can you tell? _____

Dollars

0   Quantity

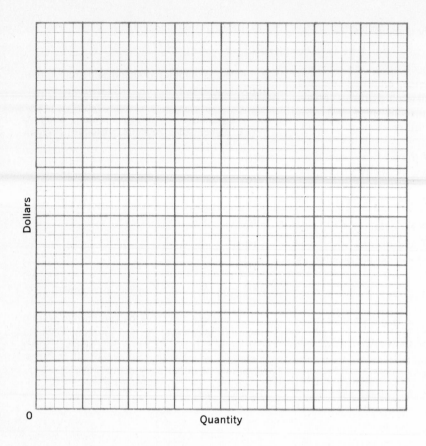

Dollars

0

Quantity

c. On the graph above plot the demand schedule, average revenue, total revenue, and marginal revenue; label each of these curves. (*Note:* Plot marginal revenue at ½, 1½, 2½, etc., units of output rather than 1, 2, 3, etc.)

d. The coefficient of the price elasticity of demand is the same between every pair of quantities demanded. How much is it? _____

e. What relationship exists between average revenue and marginal revenue? _____

■ SELF-TEST

Circle the T if the statement is true, the F if it is false.

1. Demand tends to be inelastic at high prices and elastic at low prices. **T F**

2. Total revenue will not change if the elasticity of demand is unitary. **T F**

3. If the relative change in price is greater than the relative change in quantity demanded, the elasticity coefficient is greater than one. **T F**

4. Elasticity of demand and the slope of the demand curve are two different things. **T F**

5. The demand for most agricultural products is inelastic. Consequently, an increase in supply will reduce the total income of producers of agricultural products. **T F**

6. If an increase in product price results in no change in the quantity supplied, supply is perfectly elastic. **T F**

7. If the government imposes a price ceiling above what would be the free-market price of a commodity, a shortage of the commodity will develop. **T F**

8. The purely competitive firm views an average-revenue schedule which is identical to its marginal-revenue schedule. **T F**

9. As an imperfectly competitive firm increases its output, it finds that its total revenue at first decreases, and that after some output level is reached, its total revenue begins to increase.   **T F**

10. In the range of prices in which demand is inelastic, marginal revenue is a negative amount.   **T F**

11. When an excise tax is placed on a product bought and sold in a competitive market, the portion of the tax borne by the seller equals the amount of the tax less the rise in the price of the product due to the tax. **T F**

12. The more elastic the demand for a good, the greater will be the portion of an excise tax on the good borne by the seller.   **T F**

Underscore the letter that corresponds to the best answer.

1. If when the price of a product rises from $1.50 to $2, the quantity demanded of the product decreases from 900 to 1,000, the elasticity of demand coefficient is: (*a*) 3.00; (*b*) 2.71; (*c*) 0.37; (*d*) 0.33.

2. If a 1 percent fall in the price of a commodity causes the quantity demanded of the commodity to increase 2%, demand is: (*a*) inelastic; (*b*) elastic; (*c*) of unitary elasticity; (*d*) perfectly elastic.

3. Which of the following is *not* characteristic of a commodity the demand for which is elastic? (*a*) the elasticity coefficient is less than unity; (*b*) total revenue decreases if price rises; (*c*) buyers are relatively sensitive to price changes; (*d*) the relative change in quantity is greater than the relative change in price.

4. Which of the following is *not* characteristic of a good the demand for which is inelastic? (*a*) there are a large number of good substitutes for the good; (*b*) the buyers spends a small percentage of his total income on the good; (*c*) the good is regarded by consumers as a necessity; (*d*) the period of time for which demand is given is very short.

5. If a 5% fall in the price of a commodity causes quantity supplied to decrease by 8%, supply is: (*a*) inelastic; (*b*) of unitary elasticity; (*c*) elastic; (*d*) perfectly inelastic.

6. If supply is inelastic and demand decreases, the total revenue of sellers will: (*a*) increase; (*b*) decrease; (*c*) decrease only if demand is elastic; (*d*) increase only if demand is inelastic.

7. If the government sets a minimum price for a commodity and this minimum price is less than the equilibrium price of the commodity, the result will be: (*a*) a shortage of the commodity; (*b*) a surplus of the commodity; (*c*) neither a shortage nor a surplus of the commodity; (*d*) an increase in total receipts from the sale of the commodity if demand is inelastic.

8. The demand schedule or curve confronted by the individual purely competitive firm is: (*a*) perfectly inelastic; (*b*) inelastic but not perfectly inelastic; (*c*) perfectly elastic; (*d*) elastic but not perfectly elastic.

9. The imperfectly competitive firm finds that marginal revenue is: (*a*) less than average revenue; (*b*) greater than average revenue; (*c*) equal to average revenue; (*d*) sometimes greater and sometimes less than average revenue.

10. The chief determinant of the elasticity of supply of a product is: (*a*) the number of good substitutes the product has; (*b*) the length of time producers have to adjust to a change in price; (*c*) whether the product is a luxury or a necessity; (*d*) whether the product is a durable or a nondurable good.

11. In a competitive market the portion of an excise tax borne by a buyer is equal to: (*a*) the amount the price of the product rises as a result of the tax; (*b*) the amount of the tax; (*c*) the amount of the tax less the amount the price of the product rises as a result of the tax; (*d*) the amount of the tax plus the amount the price of the product rises as a result of the tax.

12. Which of the following statements is correct? (*a*) the more elastic the supply, the greater the portion of an excise tax borne by the seller; (*b*) the more elastic the demand, the greater the portion of an excise tax borne by the seller; (*c*) the more inelastic the supply, the greater the portion of an excise tax borne by the buyer; (*d*) the more inelastic the demand, the greater the portion of an excise tax borne by the seller.

■ DISCUSSION QUESTIONS

1. Define and explain the elasticity of demand concept in terms of each of the following: (a) the relative sensitiveness of quantity demanded to changes in price; (b) the behavior of total revenue when price changes; (c) the elasticity coefficient; (d) the relationship between the relative (percentage) change in quantity demanded and the relative (percentage) change in price.

2. In computing the elasticity coefficient, it usually makes a considerable difference whether the higher price and lower quantity or the lower price and higher quantity are used as a point of reference. What have economists done to eliminate the confusion which would arise if the elasticity of demand coefficient varied and depended upon whether a price rise or price fall were being considered?

3. Why does the government from time to time impose price ceilings and minimum prices on certain goods and services? What are the consequences of these ceilings and minimums if they are not set at the price which would prevail in the free market?

4. Explain what determines the elasticity of supply of an economic good or service.

5. What are the important factors which affect the elasticity of demand for a product?

6. Of what practical importance is the concept of elasticity of demand?

7. Explain the basic difference between the way in which purely competitive and imperfectly competitive individual firms see the demand for their products in terms of (a) price elasticity of demand; (b) the relation of average to marginal revenue; and (c) the behavior of total, average, and marginal revenue as the output of the firm increases.

8. Explain why marginal revenue is always less than average revenue when demand is less than perfectly elastic and how marginal revenue can be computed.

9. What is meant by perfectly elastic demand? By perfectly inelastic demand? What does the demand curve look like when demand is perfectly elastic and when it is perfectly inelastic?

10. When the price of a commodity declines, the quantity demanded of it increases. When demand is elastic, total revenue is greater at the lower price; but when demand is inelastic, total revenue is smaller. Explain why total revenue will sometimes increase and why it will sometimes decrease.

11. Explain the effect which the imposition of an excise tax has upon the supply of a commodity bought and sold in a competitive market. How do you find what part of the tax is passed on to the buyer and what part is borne by the seller? What determines the division of the tax between buyer and seller?

12. What is the relationship between the elasticity of demand for a commodity and the portion of an excise tax on a commodity borne by the buyer and by the seller? What is the relationship between the elasticity of supply and the incidence of the tax?

FURTHER TOPICS IN THE THEORY
OF CONSUMER DEMAND

In several earlier chapters it was pointed out that consumers typically buy more of a product as its price decreases and less of it as its price increases. Chapter 24 looks behind this law of demand and explains why consumers behave this way. Two explanations are presented. One, developed in terms of the income effect and the substitution effect, is a general and simple explanation. The other, developed in terms of the concept of marginal utility, is a more detailed explanation and is more difficult to understand.

The marginal-utility explanation requires that the student first understand the concepts and assumptions upon which this theory of consumer behavior rests, and second, do some rigorous reasoning using these concepts and assumptions. It is an exercise in logic, but be sure that you follow the reasoning. To aid you, several problems are provided so that you can work things out for yourself.

Of course no one believes that consumers actually perform these mental gymnastics before they spend their incomes or make a purchase. But the marginal-utility approach to consumer behavior is studied because consumers behave "as if" they made their purchases on the basis of very fine calculations. Thus, this approach explains what we do in fact observe, and makes it possible for us to

forecast with a good deal of precision how consumers will react to changes in their incomes and in the prices of products. Several criticisms of the marginal-utility theory are set down in the text. However, before you discard the theory as unrealistic or overly cumbersome, ask yourself whether it "works," that is, whether it enables us to envision the way consumers will behave and their reasons for behaving this way.

■ CHAPTER OUTLINE

1. The law of consumer demand can be explained by employing either the income-effect and substitution-effect concepts, or the concept of marginal utility.

a. Consumers buy more of a commodity when its price falls because their money income will go further (the income effect) and because the commodity is now less expensive relative to other commodities (the substitution effect).

b. The essential assumption made in the alternative explanation is that the more the consumer buys of any commodity, the smaller becomes the marginal (extra) utility he receives from it.

2. The assumption (or law) of diminishing marginal utility is the basis of the theory that explains how a consumer will spend his income.

a. The typical consumer, it is assumed, is rational, knows his marginal-utility schedules for the various goods available, has a limited money income to spend, and must pay a price to acquire each of the goods which give him utility.

b. Given these assumptions, the consumer maximizes the total utility he receives when the marginal utility of the last dollar spent on a commodity is the same for all commodities.

c. Algebraically, his total utility is a maximum when the marginal utility of the last unit of a commodity purchased divided by its price is the same for all commodities.

3. To find a consumer's demand for a product the utility-maximizing rule is applied to determine the amount of the product he will purchase at different prices, his income and tastes and the prices of other products remaining constant.

■ IMPORTANT TERMS

Income effect

Substitution effect

Utility

Marginal utility

Law of diminishing marginal utility

Rational

Budget restraint

Utility-maximizing rule

■ FILL-IN QUESTIONS

1. A fall in the price of a product tends to

_____ the *real* income of a consumer, and a rise in

its price tends to _____

his real income. This is called the _____

effect.

2. When the price of a product increases, the

product becomes relatively (more, less) _____

expensive than it was and the prices of other

products become relatively (higher, lower) ___

than they were; the consumer will, therefore,

buy (less, more) _____

of the product in question and _____

of the other products. This is called the _____

_____

effect.

3. The marginal-utility theory of consumer

behavior assumes that the consumer is _____

_____

and that he has certain _____

for various goods.

4. A consumer cannot buy all he wishes of every good and service because his income is

_____

and goods and services have _____ ;

these facts are called the _____

_____

5. When the consumer is maximizing the utility which his income will obtain for him,

the _____

is the same for all the products he buys.

6. The two factors (other than the price of the product and the tastes of the consumer) which determine how much of a particular product a consumer will buy are:

a. _____

b. _____

7. If the marginal utility of the last dollar spent on one product is greater than the marginal utility of the last dollar spent on another

product, the consumer should _____

his purchases of the first and_____
his purchases of the second.

8. The law of diminishing marginal utility

is that _____ will _____
as the consumer increases his consumption of a particular commodity.

■ PROBLEMS AND PROJECTS

1. Suppose that when the price of bread is 50 cents per loaf, the Robertson family buys six loaves of bread in a week.

a. When the price of bread falls to 40 cents, the Robertson family will increase their bread consumption to seven loaves.

(1) Measured in terms of bread, the fall in

Good A			Good B			Good C		
Quantity	Utility	Marginal utility	Quantity	Utility	Marginal utility	Quantity	Utility	Marginal utility
1	21	_____	1	7	_____	1	23	_____
2	41	_____	2	13	_____	2	40	_____
3	59	_____	3	18	_____	3	52	_____
4	74	_____	4	22	_____	4	60	_____
5	85	_____	5	25	_____	5	65	_____
6	91	_____	6	27	_____	6	68	_____
7	91	_____	7	28.2	_____	7	70	_____

the price of bread will _____

their real income by _____
loaves. (*Hint:* How many loaves of bread *could* they now buy without changing the amount they spend on bread?)

(2) Is the Robertsons' demand for bread

elastic or inelastic? _____

b. When the price of bread rises from 50 to 60 cents per loaf, the Robertson family will decrease their bread consumption to four loaves.

(1) Measured in terms of bread, this rise in

the price of bread will _____

their real income by _____
loaves.

(2) Is the Robertsons' demand for bread

elastic or inelastic? _____

2. Assume that Palmer is confronted with three goods, A, B, and C, and that the amounts of utility which their consumption will yield him are as shown in the table above. Compute the marginal utilities for successive units of A, B, and C and enter them in the appropriate columns.

3. Using the marginal-utility data for goods A, B, and C which you obtained in problem 2, assume that the prices of A, B, and C are $5, $1, and $4, respectively, and that Palmer has an income of $37 to spend.

a. Complete the table below by computing the *marginal utility per dollar* for successive units of A, B, and C.

b. Palmer would not buy 4 units of A, 1

unit of B, and 4 units of C because _____

_____

c. Palmer would not buy 6 units of A, 7

units of B, and 4 units of C because _____

_____

d. When Palmer is maximizing his utility he

Good A		Good B		Good C	
Quantity	Marginal utility per dollar	Quantity	Marginal utility per dollar	Quantity	Marginal utility per dollar
1	_____	1	_____	1	_____
2	_____	2	_____	2	_____
3	_____	3	_____	3	_____
4	_____	4	_____	4	_____
5	_____	5	_____	5	_____
6	_____	6	_____	6	_____
7	_____	7	_____	7	_____

will buy: (1) _____ units of A, (2) _____ units of B, (3) _____ units of C; his total utility will be _____ _____ and the marginal utility of the last dollar spent on each good will be ___

_____

e. If Palmer's income increased by $1, he would spend it on good _____, assuming he can buy fractions of a unit of a good, because

_____

4. In the table below are Thompson's marginal-utility schedules for goods A, B, C, and D and for saving.

a. Assume that the prices of A, B, C, and D are $3, $2, $4, and $5, respectively. Compute the marginal utility per dollar (MU/$) for the four goods and saving. (*Hint:* The price of saving $1 is $1.)

b. If Thompson's income is $69, to maximize his utility he will purchase: (1) _____ units of A, (2) _____ units of B, (3) _____ units of C, (4) _____ units of D, and save $_____. His total utility will be _____

c. Suppose that instead of good A being priced at $3, its price is one of those listed below. How much of good A will Thompson purchase at each of these prices, his income and the prices of other goods remaining constant? (*Hint:* It will be necessary for you to compute marginal utility per dollar spent on A at each of these four prices.) The different

prices are: (1) $6: _____ units of A, (2) $4: _____ units of A, (3) $2: _____ units of A, (4) $1.50: _____ units of A.

d. Combine the information you have obtained concerning the amounts of A that Thompson would purchase at various prices in the graph and table below. What is this relationship between price and quantity called?

Price of A	Quantity of A demanded
$_____	_____
_____	_____
_____	_____
_____	_____
_____	_____

Unit of good or saving	Good A MU	Good A MU/$	Good B MU	Good B MU/$	Good C MU	Good C MU/$	Good D MU	Good D MU/$	Saving MU	Saving MU/$
1	45	___	12	___	40	___	40	___	6	___
2	30	___	11	___	36	___	34	___	5	___
3	20	___	10	___	32	___	30	___	4	___
4	15	___	9	___	28	___	27	___	3	___
5	12	___	8	___	24	___	25	___	2	___
6	10	___	7	___	20	___	23	___	1	___
7	9	___	6	___	16	___	20	___	½	___
8	7½	___	5	___	12	___	15	___	¼	___

■ SELF-TEST

Circle the T if the statement is true, the F if it is false.

1. An increase in the real income of a consumer will result from an increase in the price of a product which the consumer is buying.
 T F

2. Utility and usefulness are not synonymous.
 T F

3. All consumers are subject to the budget restraint. **T F**

4. When the consumer is maximizing his total utility, the marginal utilities of the last unit of every product he buys are identical. **T F**

5. Because utility cannot actually be measured, the marginal-utility theory cannot really explain how consumers will behave. **T F**

6. To find a consumer's demand for a product, the price of the product is varied while his tastes and income and the prices of other products remain unchanged. **T F**

Underscore the letter that corresponds to the best answer.

1. The reason the substitutions effect works to encourage a consumer to buy more of a product when its price decreases is: (a) the real income of the consumer has been increased; (b) the real income of the consumer has been decreased; (c) the product is now relatively less expensive than it was; (d) other products are now relatively less expensive than they were.

2. Which of the following best expresses the law of diminishing marginal utility? (a) the more a person consumes of a product, the smaller becomes the utility which he receives from its consumption; (b) the more a person consumes of a product, the smaller becomes the utility which he receives as a result of consuming an additional unit of the product; (c) the less a person consumes of a product, the smaller becomes the utility which he receives from its consumption; (d) the less a person consumes of a product, the smaller becomes the utility which he receives as a result of consuming an additional unit of the product.

3. Which of the following is *not* an essential assumption of the marginal-utility theory of consumer behavior? (a) the consumer has a small income; (b) the consumer is rational; (c) goods and services are not free; (d) goods and services yield decreasing amounts of marginal utility as the consumer buys more of them.

4. Assume a consumer has the marginal utility schedules for goods X and Y given below, that the prices of X and Y are $1 and $2, respectively, and that the income of the consumer is $9. When the consumer is maximizing the total utility he receives, he will buy (a) 7X and 1Y; (b) 5X and 2Y; (c) 3X and 3Y; (d) 1X and 4Y.

Good X		Good Y	
Quantity	MU	Quantity	MU
1	8	1	10
2	7	2	8
3	6	3	6
4	5	4	4
5	4	5	3
6	3	6	2
7	2	7	1

5. When the consumer in multiple-choice question 4 above purchases the combination of X and Y that maximizes his total utility, his utility is (a) 36; (b) 45; (c) 48; (d) 52.

6. Suppose that the prices of A and B are $3 and $2, respectively, that the consumer is spending his entire income and buying 4 units of A and 6 units of B, and that the marginal utility of both the 4th unit of A and the 6th unit of B is 6. It can be concluded that: (a) the consumer is in equilibrium; (b) the consumer should buy more of A and less of B; (c) the consumer should buy less of A and more of B; (d) the consumer should buy less of both A and B.

■ DISCUSSION QUESTIONS

1. Explain, employing the income-effect and substitution-effect concepts, the reasons consumers buy more of a product at a lower price than at a higher price, and vice versa.

2. Why is utility a "subjective concept"? How does the subjective nature of rationality limit

the practical usefulness of the marginal-utility theory of consumer behavior?

3. What essential assumptions are made about consumers and the nature of goods and services in developing the marginal-utility theory of consumer behavior? What is meant by "budget restraint"?

4. When is the consumer in equilibrium and maximizing his total utility? Explain why any deviation from this equilibrium will decrease the consumer's total utility.

5. Using the marginal-utility theory of consumer behavior, explain how an individual's demand schedule for a particular consumer good can be obtained. Why does a demand schedule obtained in this fashion almost invariably result in an inverse or negative relationship between price and quantity demanded?

THE COSTS OF PRODUCTION

In previous chapters the factors which influence the demand for any product purchased by consumers have been examined in some detail. Chapter 25 turns to the other side of the market and begins the investigation of the forces which determine the amounts of any particular product a business firm will offer to sell at various prices. In short, this chapter looks behind supply. The examination of supply is not completed in this chapter, however. One of the factors affecting the supply of any product is the type of market in which the product is sold, and in the next four chapters supply is examined in four different types of product market.

The most important determinant of the supply of any product is the cost of producing the product. Chapter 25 is simply an examination of the way in which the costs of the firm change as the output of the firm changes. This chapter is extremely important if the chapters which follow it are to be understood. For this reason it is necessary for the student to master the material dealing with the costs of the firm.

The student will probably find that he has some difficulty with the new terms and concepts. Particular attention, therefore, should be given to them. These new terms and concepts, which are listed below, are used in the explanation of the costs of the firm and will be used over and over again in later chapters. If the student will try to learn them in the order in which he encounters them he will have little difficulty because the later terms build on the earlier ones.

After the new terms and concepts are well fixed in the student's mind, understanding the generalizations made about the relationships between cost and output will be much simpler. Here the important things to note are: (1) that the statements made about the behavior of costs are *generalizations* (they do not apply to any particular firm or enterprise, but are more or less applicable to every business firm); and (2) that the generalizations made about the relationships between particular types of cost and the output of the firm are fairly precise generalizations. When attempting to learn these generalizations, the student will find it worthwhile to draw rough graphs (with cost on the vertical and output on the horizontal axis) which describe the cost relationships. Try it especially with the following types of costs: short-run fixed cost, short-run variable cost, short-run total cost, short-run average fixed cost, short-run average variable cost, short-run average total cost, short-run marginal cost, and long-run average cost.

One last cue: In addition to learning *how* the

costs of the firm vary as its output varies, be sure to understand *why* the costs vary the way they do. In this connection note that the behavior of short-run costs is the result of the law of diminishing returns and that the behavior of long-run costs is the consequence of economies and diseconomies of scale.

■ CHAPTER OUTLINE

1. Because resources are scarce and may be employed to produce many different products, the cost of using resources to produce any one of these products is the amount of other products that cannot be produced.

a. In money terms, the costs of employing resources to produce a product are the payments a firm must make to the owners of resources to attract these resources away from their best alternative opportunities for earning incomes; and these costs may be either explicit or implicit.

b. Normal profit is an implicit cost for a firm.

c. Economic or pure profit is any income which a firm receives in excess of all its economic (explicit plus implicit) costs.

d. The firm's economic costs vary as the firm's output varies; and the way in which costs vary with output depends upon the type of changes (that is, short-run or long-run) the firm is able to make in the amounts of resources it employs.

2. In the short run the firm cannot change the size of its plant and can vary its output only by changing the quantities of the variable resources it employs.

a. The law of diminishing returns is the most important factor influencing the manner in which the costs of the firm change as it changes its output in the short run.

b. The total short-run costs of a firm are partly fixed and partly variable costs; the former are costs which do not change and the latter are costs which do change as the firm's output changes.

c. Average fixed, variable, and total cost are equal, respectively, to the firm's fixed, variable, and total costs divided by the output of the firm.

d. Marginal cost is the extra cost involved in producing one additional unit of output.

3. In the long run all the resources employed

by the firm are variable resources, and all its costs, therefore, are variable costs.

a. As the firm expands its output by increasing the size of its plant, average cost tends to fall at first because of the economies of large-scale production; but as this expansion continues, sooner or later, average cost begins to rise because of the diseconomies of large-scale production.

b. The economies and diseconomies encountered in the production of different goods are important factors influencing the size of firms and the number of firms actually found in various industries.

■ IMPORTANT TERMS

Economic cost	Variable resource
Alternative (opportunity) cost doctrine	Fixed cost
	Variable cost
Explicit cost	Total cost
Implicit cost	Average fixed cost
Normal profit	Average variable cost
Economic (pure) profit	Average (total) cost
Short run	Marginal cost
Long run	Economies of large scale
Law of diminishing returns	Diseconomies of large scale
Fixed resource	

■ FILL-IN QUESTIONS

1. The cost of producing a particular product is the quantity of _____ that cannot be produced. This way of looking at costs is called the _____ or the _____ cost doctrine.

2. The money cost of producing a product is the amount of money the firm must pay to resource owners to _____ from alternative employments. These costs may be either _____ or _____ costs.

3. Normal profit is an _____ cost because it is the payment the firm must make to obtain _____; but economic profit is the amount by which a firm's total receipts exceed its _____ costs, the sum of its _____ and

_____ costs.

4. In the short run the firm can change its

output by changing the _____

it employs, but it cannot change _____

5. In the long run firms can _____

or _____

an industry, but in the short run the number

of firms in an industry is _____

6. The law of diminishing returns states that

as successive units of a _____

are added to a _____ ,

beyond some point the _____

attributable to each additional unit of the __

_____

will _____

7. The short-run costs of a firm are either

_____

costs or _____

costs, but in the long run all costs are _____

_____

costs.

8. In the short run, total variable costs at first

_____

by _____

amounts, but after some level of output is

reached, they _____

by _____

amounts.

9. On the graph at the top of the next column sketch the manner in which fixed cost,
variable cost, and total cost vary with the output the firm produces in the short run.

10. The law of diminishing returns causes a

firm's _____

cost, _____

cost, and _____

cost to decrease at first and then to increase
as the output of the firm increases. On the
next graph sketch these three cost curves in

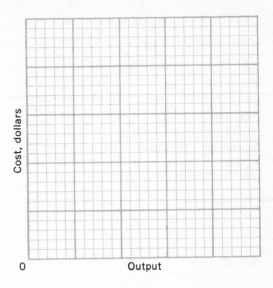

such a way that their proper relationship to
each other is shown.

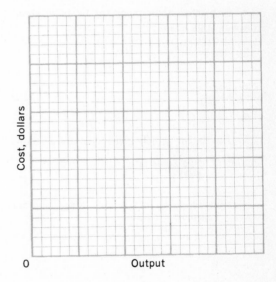

11. Marginal cost is the increase in either

_____

cost or _____

which occurs when the firm increases its output by one unit.

12. If marginal cost is less than average

variable cost, average variable cost will be __

_____ ,

but if average variable cost is less than marginal cost, average variable cost will be _____

_____

13. The long-run average cost of producing a product is equal to the lowest of the short-run costs of producing that product after the

firm has _____.
Below are the short-run average-cost curves of producing a product with three different sizes of plants, plant 1, plant 2, and plant 3. Draw the firm's long-run average-cost curve.

14. List below four important types of economy of large scale:

a. _____

b. _____

c. _____

d. _____

15. The factor which gives rise to diseconomies of large scale is _____

■ PROBLEMS AND PROJECTS

1. Below is a production-possibilities table for an economy. Employing the doctrine of alternative or opportunity cost:

Good X	0	1	2	3	4	5	6	7	8	9	10
Good Y	55	54	52	49	45	40	34	27	19	10	0

a. What is the *total* cost of producing 5 units of X? _____

b. If 2 units of good X are produced, what is the *average* cost of a unit of X? _____

c. Were the economy to increase its output of good X from 6 to 7 units, the *marginal* cost of the additional unit of X would be

_____

2. Assume that a firm has a plant of fixed size and that it can vary its output only by varying the amount of labor it employs. The table below shows the relationship between the amount of labor employed and the output of the firm.

a. Compute the ten marginal products of labor and enter these figures in the table.

b. Assume each unit of labor costs the firm $10. Compute the total cost of labor for each quantity of labor the firm might employ, and enter these figures in the table.

c. Now determine the marginal cost of the firm's product as the firm increases its output.

Quantity of labor employed	Total output	Marginal product of labor	Total cost of labor	Marginal cost of product
0	0		$_____	
1	5	_____	_____	$_____
2	11	_____	_____	_____
3	18	_____	_____	_____
4	24	_____	_____	_____
5	29	_____	_____	_____
6	33	_____	_____	_____
7	36	_____	_____	_____
8	38	_____	_____	_____
9	39	_____	_____	_____
10	39½	_____	_____	_____

Output	Fixed cost	Variable cost	Total cost	Average fixed cost	Average variable cost	Average total cost	Marginal cost
$ 0	$200	$ 0	$_____				
1	200	50	_____	$_____	$_____	$_____	$_____
2	200	90	_____	_____	_____	_____	_____
3	200	120	_____	_____	_____	_____	_____
4	200	160	_____	_____	_____	_____	_____
5	200	220	_____	_____	_____	_____	_____
6	200	300	_____	_____	_____	_____	_____
7	200	400	_____	_____	_____	_____	_____
8	200	520	_____	_____	_____	_____	_____
9	200	670	_____	_____	_____	_____	_____
10	200	900	_____	_____	_____	_____	_____

Divide the *increase* in total labor cost by the *increase in total output* to find the marginal cost. Enter these figures in the table.

d. When the marginal product of labor:

(1) Increases, the marginal cost of the firm's product _____

(2) Decreases, the marginal cost of the firm's product _____

3. In the table above you will find a schedule of a firm's fixed cost and variable cost.

a. Complete the table by computing total cost, average fixed cost, average variable cost, average total cost, and marginal cost.

b. On the small graph below, plot and label fixed cost, variable cost, and total cost.

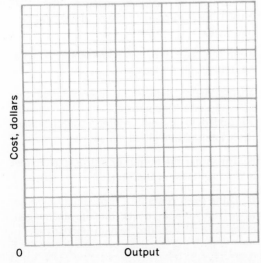

c. On the large graph (at the top of page 188), plot average fixed cost, average variable cost, average total cost, and marginal cost; label the four curves.

4. Below are the short-run average-total-cost schedules for three plants of different size which a firm might build to produce its product. Assume that these are the only possible sizes of plants which the firm might build.

Plant size A		Plant size B		Plant size C	
Output	ATC	Output	ATC	Output	ATC
10	$ 7	10	$17	10	$53
20	6	20	13	20	44
30	5	30	9	30	35
40	4	40	6	40	27
50	5	50	4	50	20
60	7	60	3	60	14
70	10	70	4	70	11
80	14	80	5	80	8
90	19	90	7	90	6
100	25	100	10	100	5
110	32	110	16	110	7
120	40	120	25	120	10

a. Complete the *long-run* average-cost schedule for the firm on page 188.

b. For outputs between:

(1) _____ and _____, the firm should build plant A.

Cost, dollars

0   Output

(2) _____ and _____, the firm should build plant B.

(3) _____ and _____, the firm should build plant C.

Output	Average cost
10	$_____
20	_____
30	_____
40	_____
50	_____
60	_____
70	_____
80	_____
90	_____
100	_____
110	_____
120	_____

■ SELF-TEST

Circle the T if the statement is true, the F if it is false.

1. Economic or pure profit is an explicit cost, while normal profit is an implicit cost.   **T   F**

2. The economic costs of a firm are the payments it must make to resource owners to attract their resources from alternative employments.   **T   F**

3. In the short run, firms are unable to enter an industry or to leave it.   **T   F**

4. The law of diminishing returns states that as successive amounts of a variable resource are added to a fixed resource, beyond some point total output will diminish.   **T   F**

5. The larger the output of a firm, the smaller is the fixed cost of the firm.   **T   F**

6. If the fixed costs of a firm should increase while its variable costs remain unchanged, marginal cost will also remain unchanged.

T   F

7. Marginal cost is equal to average variable cost at the output at which average variable cost is a minimum. **T F**

8. When the marginal product of a variable resource increases, the marginal cost of producing the product will decrease; and when marginal product decreases, marginal cost will increase.

9. One of the explanations of why the long-run average-cost curve of a firm rises after some level of output has been reached is the law of diminishing returns.

10. A firm can avoid the diseconomies of large scale by becoming a multiplant firm. **T F**

Underscore the letter that corresponds to the best answer.

1. In the following production-possibilities table the *average* cost of 5 units of good B is: (*a*) 4 units of A; (*b*) 5 units of A; (*c*) 7 units of A; (*d*) 9 units of A.

Good A	0	11	21	30	38	45	51	56	60	63	65
Good B	10	9	8	7	6	5	4	3	2	1	0

2. Using the same production-possibilities data given in question 1, the *marginal* cost of the second unit of B is: (*a*) 2 units of A; (*b*) 3 units of A; (*c*) 4 units of A; (*d*) 5 units of A.

3. Which of the following is most likely to be a long-run adjustment for a firm which manufactures jet fighter planes on an assembly-line basis? (*a*) an increase in the amount of steel the firm buys; (*b*) a reduction in the number of "shifts" of workers from three to two; (*c*) a changeover from the production of one type of jet fighter to the production of a later-model jet fighter; (*d*) a changeover from the production of jet fighters to the production of sports cars.

4. Assume that the only variable resource is labor and that as the amount of labor employed by a firm increases, the output of the firm increases in the way shown in the table. The marginal product of the fourth unit of labor is: (*a*) 3 units of output; (*b*) 3¾ units of output; (*c*) 4 units of output; (*d*) 15 units of output.

Amount of labor	Amount of output
1	3
2	8
3	12
4	15
5	17
6	18

5. Because the marginal product of a resource at first increases and then decreases as the output of the firm increases: (*a*) average fixed cost declines as the output of the firm increases; (*b*) average variable cost at first increases and then decreases; (*c*) variable cost at first increases by increasing amounts and then increases by decreasing amounts; (*d*) total cost at first increases by decreasing amounts and then increases by increasing amounts.

For questions 6 and 7 use the data given in the table below. The fixed cost of the firm is $500 and the firm's variable cost is indicated in the table.

Output	Variable cost
1	$ 200
2	360
3	500
4	700
5	1,000
6	1,800

6. The average total cost of the firm when 4 units of output are being produced is: (*a*) $175; (*b*) $200; (*c*) $300; (*d*) $700.

7. The marginal cost of the sixth unit of output is: (*a*) $200; (*b*) $300; (*c*) $700; (*d*) $800.

8. In the table on page 190 three short-run cost schedules are given for three plants of different sizes which a firm might build in the long run. What is the *long-run* average cost of producing 40 units of output? (*a*) $7; (*b*) $8; (*c*) $9; (*d*) $10.

9. Using the data given for question 8, at what output is long-run average cost a minimum? (*a*) 20; (*b*) 30; (*c*) 40; (*d*) 50.

Plant 1		Plant 2		Plant 3	
Output	ATC	Output	ATC	Output	ATC
10	$10	10	$15	10	$20
20	9	20	10	20	15
30	8	30	7	30	10
40	9	40	10	40	8
50	10	50	14	50	9

10. Which of the following is *not* a factor which results in economies of scale? (a) more efficient utilization of the firm's plant; (b) more efficient utilization of the firm's by-products; (c) greater specialization and division of labor in the management of the firm; (d) utilization of more efficient equipment.

■ DISCUSSION QUESTIONS

1. Explain the difference between the opportunity and the money cost of producing a product and the difference between an explicit and an implicit cost. How would you determine the implicit money cost of a resource?

2. What is the difference between normal and economic profit? Why is the former an economic cost?

3. What type of adjustments can a firm make in the long run that it cannot make in the short run? What adjustments can it make in the short run? How long is the short run?

4. Why is the distinction between the short run and the long run important?

5. State precisely the law of diminishing returns. Exactly what is it that diminishes, and why does it diminish?

6. Distinguish between a fixed cost and a variable cost. Why are short-run total costs partly fixed and partly variable costs, and why are long-run costs entirely variable?

7. Why do short-run variable costs increase at first by decreasing amounts and later increase by increasing amounts? How does the behavior of short-run variable costs influence the behavior of short-run total costs?

8. Describe the way in which short-run average fixed cost, average variable cost, average total cost, and marginal cost vary as the output of the firm increases.

9. Why is marginal cost "a very strategic concept"? What is the connection between marginal product and marginal cost? How will marginal cost behave as marginal product decreases and increases?

10. What is the precise relationship between marginal cost and minimum average variable cost and between marginal cost and minimum average total cost? Why are these relationships necessarily true?

11. What does the long-run average-cost curve of a firm show? What relationship is there between long-run average cost and the short-run average total-cost schedules of the different-sized plants which a firm might build?

12. Why is the long-run average-cost curve of a firm U-shaped?

13. What is meant by an economy of large scale? What are some of the more important types of such an economy?

14. What is meant by and what causes diseconomies of large scale?

15. Why are the economies and diseconomies of scale of great significance, and how do they influence the size of firms in an industry and the number of firms in an industry?

26

PRICE AND OUTPUT
DETERMINATION:
PURE COMPETITION

Chapter 26 is the first of four chapters which bring together a specific market model and the study of production costs found in Chapter 25. Each of these four chapters analyzes and draws conclusions for a different market situation. The questions which are analyzed and for which *both short-run and long-run* answers are sought are the following: given the costs of the firm, what output will it produce; what will be the market price of the good; what will be the output of the entire industry; what will be the profit received by the firm; and what relationships will exist between market price, average total cost, and marginal cost.

In addition to finding the answers to these questions the student should attempt to discover *why* the questions are answered the way they are in each of the market models and in what way the answers obtained in one model *differ* from those obtained in the other models.

Actually, the answers are obtained by applying relatively simple logic to different sets of assumptions. It is important, therefore, to note specifically how the assumptions made in one model differ from those of other models. Each model assumes that every firm is guided in making its decisions solely by the desire to maximize its profits, and that the costs of the firm are not materially affected by the type of market in which it *sells* its out-

put. The important differences in the models which account for the differing answers involve (1) the characteristics of the market, such as the number of sellers, the ease of entry into and exodus from the industry, and the kind of product (standardized or differentiated) being produced; and (2) the way in which the *individual firm* sees the demand for *its* output.

A few special words need to be said about Chapter 26. It begins by noting that there are several good reasons for studying pure competition, not the least of which is that in the long run, pure competition—subject to certain exceptions—results in an ideal or perfect allocation of resources. After obtaining the answers to the questions mentioned in the first paragraph above, the author returns at the end of the chapter to explain in what sense competitive resource allocation is ideal and in what cases it may be less than ideal. In Chapters 27 and 28, which concern monopoly and monopolistic competition, respectively, it will be found that in these market situations resource allocation is less than ideal. The student, therefore, should pay special attention in Chapter 26 to what is meant by an ideal allocation of resources and why perfect competition results in this perfect allocation.

Several other hints might be given to help the student with the material in Chapter 26.

1. The output the firm will produce in order to maximize its profits is analyzed in both the short run and the long run. Be sure that you understand exactly what is meant by these two terms.

2. Be aware that the output the firm will produce, its costs and profits, and the market price of the product may be different in the long run from what they are in the short run.

3. Remember that the sole principle which it is assumed governs the behavior of the firm in both the short run and the long run is its desire to maximize its total profits.

4. The two approaches which are employed to examine the behavior and decisions of the firm result in exactly the same conclusions.

5. The individual firm's short-run supply curve is obtained from the firm's short-run marginal-cost curve, and the market supply curve is the sum of all the individual firms' supply curves.

6. Short-run market supply and market demand determine the price and the output of the purely competitive industry in the short run.

7. Three *specific* cases are employed in each approach in order to obtain a general principle about the firm's most profitable output.

8. It is the entry and exit of firms which forces a competitive industry to produce an ideal output in the long run.

9. Whether an increased demand for the product of a competitive industry results in a constant or higher market price depends upon whether the entry of new firms increases or does not affect the cost curves of the firms in the industry.

■ CHAPTER OUTLINE

1. Pure competition is a situation in which a large number of independent firms, no one of which is able by itself to influence market price, sell a standardized product in a market which firms are free to enter and which firms are free to leave in the long run. Although pure competition is rare in practice, there are at least three good reasons for studying this "laboratory case."

2. There are two complementary approaches to the analysis of the output that the purely competitive firm will produce in the short run.

a. Employing the total-revenue—total-cost approach, the firm will produce that output at which total profit is the greatest or total loss is the least, provided that the loss is less than the firm's fixed costs (that is, provided that total revenue is greater than total variable cost). If the firm's loss is greater than its fixed cost, it will lessen its loss by producing no output.

b. Employing the marginal-revenue—marginal-cost approach, the firm will produce that output at which marginal revenue (or price) and marginal cost are equal, provided price is greater than average variable cost. If price is less than average variable cost, the firm will shut down to minimize its loss. The short-run supply curve of the individual firm is that part of its short-run marginal-cost curve which is above average variable cost.

c. Table 26-6 in the text summarizes the principles which the competitive firm follows when it decides what output to produce in the short run.

d. The short-run supply curve of the industry (which is the sum of the supply curves of the individual firms) and the total demand for the product determine the short-run equilibrium price and equilibrium output of the industry; and the firms in the industry may be either prosperous or unprosperous in the short run.

3. In the long run the price of a product produced under conditions of pure competition will equal the minimum average total cost, and firms in the industry will neither receive profits nor suffer losses.

a. If profits are being received in the industry during the short run, firms will enter the industry in the long run (attracted by the profits), increase total supply, and thereby force price down to the minimum average total cost.

b. If losses are being suffered in the industry during the short run, firms will leave the industry in the long run (seeking to avoid losses), reduce total supply, and thereby force price up to the minimum average total cost.

c. If an industry is a constant-cost industry, the entry of new firms will not affect the average-total-cost schedule or curve of firms in the industry. Hence an increase in demand will result in no increase in the long-run equilibrium price, and the industry will be able to supply any quantity of output at a constant price.

d. If an industry is an increasing-cost industry, the entry of new firms will raise the average-total-cost schedule or curve of firms in the industry. Hence an increase in demand will result in an increase in the long-run equilibrium price, and the industry will supply larger quantities only at higher prices.

4. In the long run, each purely competitive firm is compelled by competition to produce that output at which price (or marginal revenue), average total cost, and marginal cost are equal and average total cost is a minimum.

a. An economy in which all industries were purely competitive would tend to result in an ideal or perfect allocation of resources.

(1) Goods are most efficiently produced when the average total cost of producing them is a minimum; and buyers benefit most from this efficiency when they are charged a price just equal to minimum average total cost.

(2) Goods are produced in such quantities that the total satisfaction obtained from the economy's resources is a maximum when the price of every good is equal to its marginal cost.

b. Even in a purely competitive economy, resource allocation may, for at least four reasons, be somewhat less than ideal.

■ IMPORTANT TERMS

Total-receipts—total-cost approach

Marginal-revenue—marginal-cost approach

The profit-maximizing case

Break-even point

The loss-minimizing case

The close-down case

MR = MC rule

P = MC rule

The firm's short-run supply curve (schedule)

The competitive industry's short-run supply curve (schedule)

Short-run competitive equilibrium

Long-run competitive equilibrium

Constant-cost industry

Increasing-cost industry

Long-run supply

Ideal allocation of resources

■ FILL-IN QUESTIONS

1. What are the four specific conditions which characterize pure competition?

a. _____

b. _____

c. _____

d. _____

2. Economic profit is equal to _____

_____

3. The two approaches which may be used to determine the most profitable output for any firm are the _____ approach and the _____ approach.

4. A firm should produce in the short run if _____;

it should produce that output at which _____

_____,

or, said another way, that output at which ___

_____

5. A firm is willing to produce at a loss in the short run if the price which sellers receive is greater than _____

6. In the short run the individual firm's supply curve is _____;

the short-run market supply curve is _____

_____

7. The short-run equilibrium price for a product produced by a purely competitive industry is the price at which _____

_____

and _____

are equal; the equilibrium quantity is _____

_____

8. In the short run in a purely competitive industry, the number of firms in the industry and the sizes of their plants are _____,

while in the long run they are _____

9. When the purely competitive industry is in long-run equilibrium _____

and _____

and _____

of the individual firm are equal to the long-run average total cost of the firm, and long-run average total cost is _____

10. Firms tend to enter an industry in the long run if _____

and leave it if _____

11. If the entry of new firms into an industry tends to raise the costs of all firms in the industry, the industry is said to be a(n) _____

_____

industry.

12. An industry is apt to be a constant-cost industry if _____

or if _____

13. If resources are "ideally" allocated in an economy, _____ is a maximum; this occurs in a purely competitive economy, it is contended, because the goods which the economy produces are those which _____ ,

and these goods are produced in _____ way.

14. The most efficient method of production, it is argued, means that:

a. _____ technology is used.

b. _____ and _____ are equal.

c. the only costs involved are those which

_____

d. each firm produces that output at which its average total cost is a _____

15. The "right" goods (the goods consumers want most) are produced in an economy if the

_____

and the _____
of each good are equal.

16. List four reasons why resource allocation in a purely competitive economy may be less than ideal.

a. _____

b. _____

c. _____

d. _____

■ PROBLEMS AND PROJECTS

1. Assume that a purely competitive firm has the schedule of costs given in the table below.
  a. Complete the first table on page 195 showing the total revenue and total profit of the firm at each level of output the firm might produce, assuming market prices of $55, $120, and $200.
  b. Indicate what output the firm would produce and what its profits would be at a:

(1) Price of $55: output of _____

and profit of _____

(2) Price of $120: output of _____

and profit of _____

(3) Price of $200: output of _____

and profit of _____

Output	TFC	TVC	TC	AFC	AVC	ATC	MC
0	$300	$ 0	$ 300				
1	300	100	400	$300	$100	$400	$100
2	300	150	450	150	75	225	50
3	300	210	510	100	70	170	60
4	300	290	590	75	73	148	80
5	300	400	700	60	80	140	110
6	300	540	840	50	90	140	140
7	300	720	1,020	43	103	146	180
8	300	950	1,250	38	119	156	230
9	300	1,240	1,540	33	138	171	290
10	300	1,600	1,900	30	160	190	360

Output	Market price = $55		Market price = $120		Market price = $200	
	Revenue	Profit	Revenue	Profit	Revenue	Profit
0	$_____	$_____	$_____	$_____	$_____	$_____
1	_____	_____	_____	_____	_____	_____
2	_____	_____	_____	_____	_____	_____
3	_____	_____	_____	_____	_____	_____
4	_____	_____	_____	_____	_____	_____
5	_____	_____	_____	_____	_____	_____
6	_____	_____	_____	_____	_____	_____
7	_____	_____	_____	_____	_____	_____
8	_____	_____	_____	_____	_____	_____
9	_____	_____	_____	_____	_____	_____
10	_____	_____	_____	_____	_____	_____

c. Complete the supply schedule of a firm in the table below and indicate what the profit of the firm will be at each price.

Price	Quantity supplied	Profit
$360	_____	$_____
290	_____	_____
230	_____	_____
180	_____	_____
140	_____	_____
110	_____	_____
80	_____	_____
60	_____	_____

d. If there are 100 firms in the industry and all have the same cost schedule:

(1) Complete the market supply schedule in the table in the next column.

(2) Using the demand schedule given in (1): (a) what will the market price of the product be? $_____; (b) what quantity will the individual firm produce? _____;

(c) how large will the firm's profit be? $_____;
(d) will firms tend to enter or leave the indus-

Quantity demanded	Price	Quantity supplied
400	$360	_____
500	290	_____
600	230	_____
700	180	_____
800	140	_____
900	110	_____
1,000	80	_____

try in the long run? _____ Why?

_____

2. If the total costs assumed for the individual firm in problem 1 were long-run total costs and if the industry were a constant-cost industry:

a. What would be the market price of the product in the long run? $_____

b. What output would each firm produce when the industry is in long-run equilibrium?

_____

c. Approximately how many firms will there be in the industry in the long run, given the present demand for the product? _____

d. If the following were the market demand

schedule for the product, how many firms would there be in the long run in the industry?

Price	Quantity demanded
$360	500
290	600
230	700
180	800
140	900
110	1,000
80	1,100

e. On one graph draw the long-run supply curve of this industry. On the second graph draw a long-run supply curve for an increasing-cost industry.

0

0

■ SELF-TEST

Circle the T if the statement is true, the F if it is false.

1. One of the reasons for studying the pure competition model is that many industries are almost purely competitive. **T F**

2. A firm will produce in the short run the output at which marginal cost and marginal revenue are equal provided that the price of the product is greater than its average variable cost of production. **T F**

3. If a firm is producing an output less than its profit-maximizing output, marginal revenue is greater than marginal cost at that output. **T F**

4. The short-run supply curve tends to slope upward from left to right because of the law of diminishing returns. **T F**

5. A firm wishing to maximize its profits will always produce that output at which marginal cost and marginal revenue are equal. **T F**

6. Because the individual purely competitive firm is unable to influence the market price of the product it produces, the market price will change only if the demand for the product changes. **T F**

7. When firms in an industry are earning profits which are less than normal, the supply of the product will tend to decrease in the long run. **T F**

8. Given the short-run costs of firms in a purely competitive industry, the profits of these firms depend solely upon the level of the total demand for the product. **T F**

9. Pure competition, if it could be achieved in all industries in the economy, would result in the most efficient allocation of resources. **T F**

10. Under conditions of pure competition firms are forced to employ the most efficient production methods available to them if they are to earn no more than normal profits. **T F**

11. The marginal costs of a firm in producing a product are society's measure of the marginal worth of alternative products. **T F**

12. There is no scientific basis for determining which distribution of total money income results in the greatest satisfaction of wants in the economy. **T   F**

Underscore the letter that corresponds to the best answer.

1. In a purely competitive industry: *(a)* each of the firms will engage in various forms of nonprice competition; *(b)* new firms find no obstacles to entering the industry in the short run; *(c)* the individual firms do not have a "price policy"; *(d)* each of the firms produces a differentiated (nonstandardized) product.

2. A firm will be willing to produce at a loss in the short run if: *(a)* the loss is no greater than its total fixed costs; *(b)* the loss is no greater than its average fixed costs; *(c)* the loss is no greater than its total variable costs; *(d)* the loss is no greater than its average variable cost.

3. The MC $=$ P rule *cannot* be used to determine the most profitable output of a firm: *(a)* when price and marginal revenue are equal; *(b)* in purely competitive industries; *(c)* when demand is perfectly elastic; *(d)* when average revenue is greater than marginal revenue.

4. The individual firm's short-run supply curve is that part of its marginal-cost curve lying above its: *(a)* average-total-cost curve; *(b)* average-variable-cost curve; *(c)* average-fixed-cost curve; *(d)* average-revenue curve.

5. If a single purely competitive firm's most profitable output in the short run were an output at which it was neither receiving a profit nor suffering a loss, one of the following would *not* be true. Which one? *(a)* marginal cost and average total cost are equal; *(b)* marginal cost and average variable cost are equal; *(c)* marginal cost and marginal revenue are equal; *(d)* marginal cost and average revenue are equal.

6. Which one of the following statements is true of a purely competitive industry in short-run equilibrium? *(a)* price is equal to average total cost; *(b)* total quantity demanded is equal to total quantity supplied; *(c)* profits in the industry are equal to zero; *(d)* output is equal to the output at which average total cost is a minimum.

7. When a purely competitive industry is in long-run equilibrium, one of the following statements is *not* true. Which one? *(a)* firms in the industry are earning normal profits; *(b)* price and long-run average total cost are equal to each other; *(c)* long-run marginal cost is at its minimum level; *(d)* long-run marginal cost is equal to marginal revenue.

8. Increasing-cost industries find that their costs rise as a consequence of an increased demand for the product because of: *(a)* the diseconomies of scale; *(b)* diminishing returns; *(c)* higher resource prices; *(d)* a decreased supply of the product.

9. Which one of the following is *most likely* to be a constant-cost industry? *(a)* agricultural and extractive industries; *(b)* an industry in the early stages of its development; *(c)* an industry which employs a significant portion of the total supply of some resource; *(d)* the steel and oil industries.

10. It is contended that which of the following triple identities results in an ideal allocation of resources? *(a)* P $=$ AC $=$ MC; *(b)* P $=$ AR $=$ MR; *(c)* P $=$ MR $=$ MC; *(d)* AC $=$ MC $=$ MR.

11. An economy is producing the goods most wanted by society when, for each and every good, their: *(a)* price and average cost are equal; *(b)* price and marginal cost are equal; *(c)* marginal revenue and marginal cost are equal; *(d)* price and marginal revenue are equal.

12. The operation of a competitive price system accurately measures *(a)* both spillover costs and spillover benefits; *(b)* spillover costs but not spillover benefits; *(c)* spillover benefits but not spillover costs; *(d)* neither spillover costs nor spillover benefits.

■ DISCUSSION QUESTIONS

1. Explain exactly what the economist means by pure competition.

2. If pure competition is so rare in practice, why are students of economics asked to study it?

3. Why is a firm willing to produce at a loss in the short run if the loss is no greater than the fixed costs of the firm?

4. Explain how the short-run supply of an individual firm and of the purely competitive industry are determined.

5. What determines the equilibrium price and quantity of a purely competitive industry in the short run? Will economic profits in the industry be positive or negative?

6. Why do the MC = MR rule and the MC = P rule mean the same thing under conditions of pure competition?

7. What are the important distinctions between the short run and the long run and between equilibrium in the short run and in the long run in a competitive industry?

8. When is the purely competitive industry in long-run equilibrium? What forces the purely competitive firm into this position?

9. What is a constant-cost industry? What is an increasing-cost industry? Under what eco-

nomic conditions is each likely to be found? What will be the nature of the long-run supply curve in each of these industries?

10. What is meant by an ideal or the most efficient allocation of resources? Why is it said that a purely competitive economy results in this type of allocation.

11. What did Adam Smith mean when he said that self-interest and competition bring about results which are in the best interest of the economy as a whole without government regulation or interference?

12. Even if an economy is purely competitive, the allocation of resources may not be ideal. Why?

13. Does pure competition *always* promote both the use of the most efficient technological methods of production and the development of better methods?

PRICE AND OUTPUT
DETERMINATION:
PURE MONOPOLY

Chapter 27 is the second of the four chapters which deal with specific market models and is concerned with what economists call pure monopoly. Like pure competition, pure monopoly is rarely found in the American economy. But there are industries which are very close to being pure monopolies, and an understanding of pure monopoly is helpful in understanding the more realistic situations of monopolistic competition and oligopoly.

It is only possible for pure monopoly, approximations of pure monopoly, and oligopoly to exist if firms are prevented in some way from entering an industry in the long run. Anything which tends to prevent entry is referred to as a "barrier to entry." The first part of Chapter 27 is devoted to a description of the more important types of barriers to entry. Remember that barriers to entry not only make it possible for monopoly to exist in the economy but also explain why so many markets are oligopolies. These barriers to entry should be recalled by the student when he begins his study of Chapter 29.

Like the preceding chapter, this chapter tries to answer certain questions about the firm. These are: what output will the firm produce; what price will it charge; what will be the profit received by the firm; and what will be the relationships between price, average total cost, and marginal cost. In answering these questions for the monopoly firm and in comparing pure competition and pure monopoly note the following:

1. Both the competitive and monopoly firm try to maximize profits by producing that output at which marginal cost and marginal revenue are equal.

2. The monopolist *is* the industry, and the competitor is but one of many firms in the industry.

3. The individual competitor sees a perfectly elastic demand for his product at the going market price, which it cannot influence by itself; the monopolist sees a demand schedule which is less than perfectly elastic. The former, therefore, has *only* an output policy, while the latter is able to determine the price at which it will sell its output (that is, the output it decides to sell will determine the price at which it can sell, or the price at which it decides to sell will determine the size of the output it will be able to sell).

4. When demand is perfectly elastic, price is equal to marginal revenue and is constant; but when demand is less than perfectly elastic, marginal revenue is less than price and both decrease as the output of the firm increases.

5. Because entry is blocked in the long run,

firms cannot enter a monopolistic industry to compete away profits as they can under conditions of pure competition.

Chapter 27 also assesses resource allocation under monopoly conditions by comparing it with resource allocation under purely competitive conditions. Here it is important to see that (with one exception) under monopoly conditions the price of the product will be greater than both the minimum long-run average cost and marginal cost. For these reasons the output of the monopolist will be neither efficiently produced nor produced in an amount which efficiently allocates resources.

Because monopoly does cause a misallocation of resources, many of the natural monopolies are public utilities. Public utilities have the maximum prices they may charge set by agencies of government. The aim of regulation is a better allocation of the economy's resources. The final section of Chapter 27 introduces the student to the problem of determining the maximum price a monopolist may charge. The dilemma of regulation is that setting the ceiling price equal to *marginal* cost improves resource allocation but may force the monopolist to suffer economic losses (and government to subsidize him); and that setting price equal to *average* cost eliminates the losses of the monopolist, but results in a less efficient allocation of resources.

■ CHAPTER OUTLINE

1. Pure monopoly is a market situation in which a single firm sells a product for which there are no close substitutes. While it is rare in practice, the study of monopoly provides an understanding of firms which are "almost" monopolies and is useful in understanding monopolistic competition and oligopoly.

2. Pure monopoly (and oligopoly) can exist in the long run only if potential competitors find there are barriers which prevent their entry into the industry. There are at least six types of entry barriers, but they are seldom perfect in preventing the entry of new firms. Efficient production may, in some cases, require that firms be prevented from entering an industry.

3. The pure monopolist employs his cost and demand data to determine his most profitable output and the price he will charge.

a. Unlike the pure competitor, the monopolist has a price policy. Because he is the sole supplier, the price he charges will determine the amount of the product he can sell (or the amount he decides to produce and sell will determine the price at which he can sell it). Consequently, marginal revenue is less than price (or average revenue), and both decrease as the output of the monopolist increases.

b. Monopoly power in the sale of a product does not by itself affect the prices the monopolist pays or his costs of production.

c. The monopolist produces that output at which marginal cost and marginal revenue are equal; he charges that price at which this profit-maximizing output can be sold.

d. It is not true that a monopolist charges as high a price as is possible, and it is not true that his profit per unit is as large as it might be; a monopoly, in fact, may not be profitable at all.

e. To avoid public criticism and pressure or to deter the entry of competitors a monopolist may set a price below the one that would maximize his profits.

4. Pure monopoly is likely to have the following economic effects:

a. Because it produces smaller outputs and charges higher prices than would result from conditions of pure competition and because price will be greater than both average total and marginal cost, resources are misallocated.

b. Monopoly contributes to income inequality in the economy.

c. Monopolists may or may not use more efficient (less costly) methods of production, and they may or may not inhibit technological progress.

5. The prices charged by monopolists are often regulated by governments to reduce the misallocation of resources.

a. A ceiling price determined by the intersection of the marginal-cost and demand schedules improves the allocation of resources.

b. This ceiling price may force the firm to produce at a loss; and so government may set the ceiling at a level determined by the intersection of the average-cost and demand schedules to allow the monopolist a fair return.

c. The dilemma of regulation is that the ceiling price which results in the more efficient allocation of resources may cause losses for the monopolist, and that a fair-return price results in a less efficient allocation.

■ IMPORTANT TERMS

Pure monopoly

Barrier to entry

Natural monopoly

Tying agreement

Unfair competition

The economies of being established

Socially optimum price

Fair-return price

Dilemma of regulation

■ FILL-IN QUESTIONS

1. The study of pure monopoly is important because some industries are _____ of pure monopoly and because it enables the student better to understand _____

_____

and _____

2. How would you characterize (weak, non-existent, strong, or strongest) the long-run barriers to entry into each of the following?

a. Pure competition: _____

b. Pure monopoly: _____

c. Monopolistic competition: _____

d. Oligopoly: _____

3. What are the six most important types of barrier to entry?

a. _____

b. _____

c. _____

d. _____

e. _____

f. _____

4. If there are substantial economies of scale in the production of a product, a small-scale firm will find it difficult to enter into and survive in such an industry because _____

_____

and a firm will find it difficult to start out on

a large scale in the industry because _____

_____

5. Public utility companies tend to be _____ monopolies, and they receive their franchises from and are _____ by governments.

6. If a company with a patent on a certain product agrees to sell the product only to those who buy from it other products on which it does not have a patent, there is a _____

_____ between the company with the patent and those who buy from it.

7. Unfair methods of competition (or cutthroat tactics) such as _____,

_____, _____,

and _____ may force a firm's rivals from an industry or prevent the establishment of new firms in the industry.

8. If there are economies of being established, this means that established firms have

_____

which may be due to _____,

_____, _____,

or _____

9. The demand schedule confronting the pure monopolist is _____ perfectly elastic; this means that marginal revenue will be _____ than average revenue and that both marginal revenue and average revenue _____ as output increases.

10. When the profits of a monopolist are being maximized _____

and _____ are equal and price (or average revenue) is

_____ than marginal cost.

11. Three common fallacies about the pure monopolist are that:

a. He charges the _____ price.

b. His average (or per unit) profit is _____

_____

c. He always receives a _____

12. A monopolist may refuse to set his price and output at the level that would maximize his profits in order to prevent _____

_____

and _____

13. In the long run the price charged by a monopolist is not forced down to the level of average cost because there is no _____

_____

to force price downward.

14. The output produced by a monopolist is inefficiently produced because the average total cost of producing the product is not _____

_____,

and resources are not efficiently allocated because _____

is not equal to _____

15. Resources can be said to be more efficiently allocated by pure competition than by pure monopoly only if the _____

_____

of the purely competitive firm and the monopolist are the same; they will not be the same if the monopolist, by virtue of being a large firm, enjoys _____
not available to the pure competitor.

16. Monopoly seems to result in a greater inequality of income than there would be

otherwise because _____

17. Monopoly is, on the one hand, conducive to technological advance because monopolists have the _____
to finance research and development and their

monopoly position will protect _____

_____ that results
from the introduction of new products and

techniques. On the other hand, the absence of competitors means that there is no _____

_____ to technological advance.

18. In an economy in which technological progress is important, the economic efficiency of pure competition can be said to be _____

_____

19. The misallocation of resources that results from monopoly can be *eliminated* if a ceiling price for the monopolist's product is

set equal to _____ ;
such a price is, however, usually less than

_____

20. If a regulated monopolist is allowed to earn a fair return, the ceiling price for his

product is set equal to _____ ;
such a price reduces but does not eliminate

_____

■ PROBLEMS AND PROJECTS

1. The demand schedule for the product produced by a monopolist is given in the table below.

Price	Quantity demanded	Total revenue	Marginal revenue
$700	0	$_____	
650	1	_____	$_____
600	2	_____	_____
550	3	_____	_____
500	4	_____	_____
450	5	_____	_____
400	6	_____	_____
350	7	_____	_____
300	8	_____	_____
250	9	_____	_____
200	10	_____	_____

a. Complete the table by computing total revenue at each of the eleven prices and the ten marginal revenue figures.

b. Using the table of costs given in problem 1 of Chapter 26:

(1) What output will the monopolist produce? _____

(2) What price will the monopolist charge? $_____

(3) What total profit will the monopolist receive? $_____

(4) What average profit will the monopolist receive? $_____

c. Using the same table of costs and demand schedule, how large a total profit would the monopolist receive if he produced the outputs listed in the table below?

Output	Profit	Output	Profit
1	_____	6	_____
2	_____	7	_____
3	_____	8	_____
4	_____	9	_____
5	_____	10	_____

2. Again employing the cost schedule given in problem 1, Chapter 26, and the demand schedules given in the following table, complete the second table below for each set of demand data.

Demand schedule 2		Demand schedule 3	
Price	Quantity demanded	Price	Quantity demanded
$210	0	$80	0
190	1	75	1
170	2	70	2
150	3	65	3
130	4	60	4
110	5	55	5
90	6	50	6
70	7	45	7
50	8	40	8
30	9	35	9
10	10	30	10

	Demand 2	Demand 3
Output of the firm	_____	_____
Price it will charge	_____	_____
Total profit	_____	_____
Average profit	_____	_____

3. In the table below are cost and demand data for a pure monopolist.

Quantity demanded	Price	Marginal revenue	Average cost	Marginal cost
0	$17.50			
1	16.00	$16.00	$24.00	$24.00
2	14.50	13.00	15.00	6.00
3	13.00	10.00	11.67	5.00
4	11.50	7.00	10.50	7.00
5	10.00	4.00	10.00	8.00
6	8.50	1.00	9.75	8.50
7	7.00	−2.00	9.64	9.00
8	5.50	−5.00	9.34	9.25
9	4.00	−8.00	9.36	9.50

a. An unregulated monopolist would produce _____ units of his product, sell it at a price of _____, and receive a total profit of _____

b. If this monopolist were regulated and the maximum price he would charge were set equal to marginal cost, he would produce _____ units of his product, sell it at a price of _____, and receive a total profit of _____. Such regulation would either _____ the firm or require that the regulating government _____ the firm.

c. If the monopolist were regulated and allowed to charge a fair-return price, he would produce _____ units of product, charge a price of _____, and receive a profit of _____

d. From which situation—a, b, or c—does the most efficient allocation of resources result? _____ From which situation does the least efficient allocation result? _____ In practice, government would probably select situation _____

■ SELF-TEST

Circle the T if the statement is true, the F if it is false.

1. The pure monopolist produces a product for which there are no substitutes.　　T　F

2. The weaker the barriers to entry into an industry, the more competition there will be in the industry, other things being equal.

T F

3. The dilemma of monopoly regulation is that the production by a monopolist of an output that causes no misallocation of resources may force the monopolist to suffer an economic loss. **T F**

4. Monopoly is always undesirable unless it is regulated by government. **T F**

5. The monopolist can increase the sale of his product if he charges a lower price. **T F**

6. The monopolist determines his profit-maximizing output by producing that output at which marginal cost and marginal revenue are equal and sets his product price equal to marginal cost and marginal revenue at that output. **T F**

7. When a monopolist is maximizing his total profit he is also producing that output at which his per unit (or average) profit is a maximum. **T F**

8. A monopolist may refrain from maximizing his total profits in order to discourage the entry of new firms into the industry. **T F**

9. Resources are misallocated by a monopoly because price is not equal to marginal cost.

T F

10. In a society in which technology is not changing and the economies of scale can be employed by both pure competitors and monopolists, the purely competitive firm will use the more efficient methods of production.

T F

Underscore the letter that corresponds to the best answer.

1. Which of the following is the *best* example of a pure monopoly? (a) your neighborhood grocer; (b) the telephone company in your community; (c) the manufacturer of a particular brand of toothpaste; (d) the only airline furnishing passenger service between two major cities.

2. Which of the following is *not* an important characteristic of a natural monopoly? (a) substantial economies of scale are available; (b) very heavy fixed costs; (c) it is a public utility; (d) competition is impractical and/or would be very expensive for the consumer.

3. A monopolist who is limited by the imposition of a ceiling price to a fair return sells his product at a price equal to: (a) average total cost; (b) average variable cost; (c) marginal cost; (d) average fixed cost.

4. Monopoly can probably exist over a long period of time only if: (a) it is based on the control of raw materials; (b) it controls the patents on the product; (c) cut-throat competition is employed to eliminate rivals; (d) government assists the monopoly and prevents the establishment of rival firms.

5. Which of the following is *not* true with respect to the demand data confronting a monopolist? (a) marginal revenue is greater than average revenue; (b) marginal revenue decreases as average revenue decreases; (c) demand is less than perfectly elastic; (d) average revenue (or price) decreases as the output of the firm increases.

6. Assume the cost and demand data for a pure monopolist as given in the table below. How many units of output will the firm produce? (a) 1; (b) 2; (c) 3; (d) 4.

Output	Total cost	Price
0	$ 500	$1,000
1	520	600
2	580	500
3	700	400
4	1,000	300
5	1,500	200

7. If the monopolist for whom cost and demand data are given in question 6 above were forced to produce the socially optimum output by the imposition of a ceiling price, the ceiling price would have to be: (a) $200; (b) $300; (c) $400; (d) $500.

8. When the monopolist is maximizing his total profits *or* minimizing his losses: (a) total revenue is greater than total cost; (b) average revenue is greater than average total cost; (c) average revenue is greater than marginal cost; (d) average total cost is less than marginal cost.

9. A monopolist does not *produce* his product as efficiently as is possible because: (a) the average total cost of producing it is not a minimum; (b) the marginal cost of producing the last unit is less than its price; (c) he is earning a profit; *(d)* average revenue is greater than the cost of producing an extra unit of output.

10. Over time monopoly *may* result in greater technological improvement than would be forthcoming under conditions of pure competition for several reasons. Which of the following is *not* one of these reasons? *(a)* technological advance will lower the costs and enhance the profits of the monopolist, and these increased profits will not have to be shared with rivals; *(b)* technological advance will act as a barrier to entry and thus allow the monopolist to continue to be a monopolist; *(c)* technological advance requires research and experimentation, and the monopolist is in a position to finance them out of his profits; *(d)* technological advance is apt to make existing capital equipment obsolete, and the monopolist can reduce his costs by speeding up the rate at which his capital becomes obsolete.

■ DISCUSSION QUESTIONS

1. What is pure monopoly? Why is it studied if it is so rare in practice?

2. What is meant by a barrier to entry? What kinds of such barriers are there? How important are they in pure competition, pure monopoly, monopolistic competition, and oligopoly?

3. Why are the economies of scale a barrier to entry?

4. Why are most natural monopolies also public utilities? What does government hope to achieve by granting exclusive franchises to and regulating such natural monopolies?

5. What is meant by unfair competition? What kinds of unfair competition are there? How is unfair competition used to create monopolies and to bar the entry of new firms into industries?

6. Why is it said that the "monopoly power achieved through patents may well be cumulative"?

7. What advantage does the going, established firm have over the new, immature firm in an industry?

8. Compare the pure monopolist and the individual pure competitor with respect to: *(a)* their demand schedule; *(b)* their marginal-revenue schedule; *(c)* the relationship between marginal revenue and average revenue; *(d)* their price policy; *(e)* their ability to administer price.

9. What output will the monopolist produce? What price will he charge?

10. Why does the monopolist not charge the highest possible price for his product? Why does the monopolist not set the price for his product in such a way that his average profit is a maximum? Why are some monopolies unprofitable?

11. Why would any monopolist refrain from setting his price and producing an output that would maximize his total profits?

12. In what sense is resource allocation and production more efficient under conditions of pure competition than under monopoly conditions? Does pure competition *always* result in greater efficiency?

13. How does monopoly affect the distribution of income in an economy?

14. Does monopoly, when compared with pure competition, result in more rapid or less rapid technological progress? What are the arguments on *both* sides of this question? What evidence is there to support the two views?

15. Explain under what conditions you would prefer monopoly to pure competition.

16. How do public utility regulatory agencies attempt to eliminate the misallocation of resources that results from monopoly? Explain the dilemma that almost invariably confronts the agency in this endeavour; explain also why a fair-return price only reduces but does not eliminate the misallocation.

PRICE AND OUTPUT
DETERMINATION:
MONOPOLISTIC COMPETITION

Chapter 28 is the third of the four chapters which deal with specific market situations. As its name implies, monopolistic competition is a blend of pure competition and pure monopoly; and one of the reasons for studying those relatively unrealistic market situations was to prepare the student for the more realistic study of monopolistic competition. It must be pointed out that monopolistic competition is not a realistic description of all markets; but the study of it does help the student to understand the many markets which are nearly monopolistically competitive. It also helps him to understand why oligopoly is prevalent in the American economy and how oligopoly differs from monopolistic competition.

The first task is to learn exactly what is meant by monopolistic competition. Next the student should examine the demand curve which the monopolistically competitive firm sees for its product and note how and why it differs from the demand curves faced by the purely competitive firm and by the monopolist. In this connection it is important to understand that as the individual firm changes the character of the product it produces or changes the extent to which it promotes the sale of its product, both the costs of the firm and the demand for the product may change.

A firm confronts a different demand curve every time it alters its product or its promotion of that product.

With the product and promotional campaign of the firm *given*, the price-output analysis of the monopolistic competitor is relatively simple. In the short run this analysis is identical with the analysis of the price-output decision of the pure monopolist in the short run. It is only in the long run that the competitive element makes itself apparent: The entry (or exit) of firms forces the price the firm charges down (up) *toward* the level of average cost. This price is not equal either to *minimum* average cost or to marginal cost; and consequently monopolistic competition, on these two scores, can be said to be less efficient than pure competition.

A relatively large part of Chapter 28 is devoted to a discussion of nonprice competition. This is done for very good reasons. In monopolistically competitive industries much of the competitive effort of individual firms is given over to product differentiation, product development, and product advertising. Each firm has three things to manipulate—price, product, and advertising—in trying to maximize its profits. While monopolistic competition may not be so economically efficient as pure competition in terms of a *given* product and the promotion of it, when all the economic effects—good and bad—of differentiation, development, and advertising are considered this shortcoming may or may not be offset. Whether it is actually offset is an unanswerable question. If Chapter 28 has one central idea it is this: Monopolistic competition cannot be compared with pure competition solely on the basis of prices charged at any given moment of time; it must also be judged in terms of whether it results in better products, in a wider variety of products, in better-informed consumers, in lower-priced radio and television programs, magazines, and newspapers, and other redeeming features.

In short, the study of monopolistic competition is a realistic study and for that reason it is a difficult study. Many factors have to be considered in explaining how such a group of firms behaves and in appraising the efficiency with which such an industry allocates scarce resources.

■ CHAPTER OUTLINE

1. A monopolistically competitive industry is one in which a fairly large number of independent firms produce differentiated products, in which both price and various forms of nonprice competition occur, and into which entry is relatively easy in the long run. While there are many industries which approximate monopolistic competition, many more industries are blends of monopolistic competition and oligopoly.

2. Assume—for this part of the analysis only —that the products the firms in the industry are producing and the amounts of promotional activity in which they are engaged are given.

a. The demand curve confronting each firm will be highly but not perfectly elastic because each firm has many competitors who produce close but not perfect substitutes for the product it produces.

b. In the short run the individual firm will produce that output at which marginal cost and marginal revenue are equal and charge the price at which that output can be sold; either profits or losses may result in the short run.

c. In the long run the entry and exodus of firms will *tend* to change the demand for the product of the individual firm in such a way that profits are eliminated (price and average cost are made equal to each other).

3. Monopolistic competition among firms producing a *given* product and engaged in a *given* amount of promotional activity results in less economic efficiency and more waste than does pure competition. Although average cost and price are equal, the individual firm produces an output smaller than the output at which marginal cost and price are equal and smaller than the output at which average cost is a minimum.

4. In addition to setting its price and output so that its profit is maximized, each individual firm also attempts to differentiate its product and to promote (advertise) it in order to increase the firm's profit; these additional activities give rise to nonprice competition among firms.

a. Product differentiation and product development, as devices which firms employ in the hope of increasing their profit, may offset the wastes of monopolistic competition to the extent that they result in a wider variety and better quality of products for consumers.

b. Whether the advertising of differentiated products results in economic waste or in greater economic efficiency is debatable; there are good arguments on both sides of this question and there is no clear answer to it.

c. The monopolistically competitive firm tries to adjust its price, its product, and the promotion of its product so that the amount by which the firm's total revenue exceeds the total cost of producing and promoting a product is a maximum.

■ IMPORTANT TERMS

Monopolistic competition	**Informative advertising**
Product differentiation	**Competitive advertising**
Nonprice competition	

■ FILL-IN QUESTIONS

1. In a monopolistically competitive market

a _____

number of producers sell _____

products; these producers do not _____

and they engage in both _____
and _____
competition. In the long run, entry into the
industry is _____

2. The fact that monopolistically competitive
firms sell differentiated products results in
each firm having _____
control over the price of its product and ____
_____
between the firms.

3. Given the product being produced and
the extent to which that product is being promoted, in the *short run:*
a. The demand curve confronting the monopolistically competitive firm will be _____
_____
elastic than that facing a monopolist and ____
_____
elastic than that facing a pure competitor.
b. The elasticity of this demand curve will
depend upon _____ and
_____
c. The firm will produce that output at
which _____
and _____
are equal.

4. In the long run, the *entry* of new firms
into a monopolistically competitive industry
will _____
the demand for the product being produced
by each firm in the industry and _____
_____
the elasticity of that demand.

5. In the long run, *given* the product and
the amount of product promotion, the price
being charged by the individual firm will tend
to _____,
its economic profits will tend to _____
_____
and its average cost will be _____
than the minimum average cost of producing
and promoting the product.

6. Given the product and the extent of product promotion, monopolistic competition is
wasteful because _____
and because _____

7. In the long run, the monopolistic competitor cannot protect and increase his profits by
varying his product's price or output, but he
can try to protect and increase his profits
through _____
and _____

8. Product differentiation and product development tend to result in the consumer's being
offered _____
at any given moment of time and _____
_____
over a period of time.

9. Advertising that accurately describes the
price and qualities of products is called ____
_____
advertising, while that which makes unsub-
stantiated claims for products is _____
_____
advertising.

10. Those who argue that advertising expenditures are socially desirable contend that
advertising (a) increases the _____
_____ of consumers;
(b) supports _____;
(c) promotes the development of _____
_____; (d) results
in lower _____; and
(e) induces a high level of _____
which leads to greater total employment.

11. The critics of advertising argue (a) that
most advertising is persuasive but not ____
_____; (b) that advertising
_____ resources; (c) that
it entails significant _____
which are not paid by advertisers; (d) that it
does not lower _____;

(e) that it does not really increase _____

_____ in the economy;
and (f) that advertising expenditures are a significant _____
into many industries.

12. In attempting to maximize his profits the
monopolistic competitor will vary his price,

his _____,

and the _____
of his product until he feels that no further
change in these three variables will result in
greater profits.

■ PROBLEMS AND PROJECTS

1. Listed below are several industries. Indicate in the space to the right of each whether
you believe it is monopolistically competitive
(MC) or not monopolistically competitive (N).
If you indicate the latter, explain why you
think the industry is not a monopolistically
competitive one.

a. The production of automobiles in the

United States. _____

_____

b. The retail distribution of automobiles in
the United States. _____

c. Grocery supermarkets in a city of 500,000

people. _____

_____

d. The retail sale of gasoline in a city of
500,000 people. _____

_____

e. The production of low-priced shoes in the
United States. _____

_____

f. The mail-order sale of men's clothes.

_____

_____

2. Assume that the short-run cost and demand data given in the table below confront a
monopolistic competitor selling a given product and engaged in a given amount of product
promotion.

a. Compute the marginal cost and marginal
revenue of each unit of output and enter these
figures in the table.

b. In the short run the firm will (1) pro-

duce _____ units of output, (2)

sell its product at a price of $_____,

and (3) have a total profit of $_____

c. In the long run, (1) the demand for the

firm's product will _____,

(2) until the price of the product equals _____

_____

and (3) the total profits of the firm are _____

Output	Total cost	Marginal cost	Quantity demanded	Price	Marginal revenue
0	$ 50		0	$120	
1	80	$_____	1	110	$_____
2	90	_____	2	100	_____
3	110	_____	3	90	_____
4	140	_____	4	80	_____
5	180	_____	5	70	_____
6	230	_____	6	60	_____
7	290	_____	7	50	_____
8	360	_____	8	40	_____
9	440	_____	9	30	_____
10	530	_____	10	20	_____

■ SELF-TEST

Circle the T if the statement is true, the F if it is false.

1. Monopolistic competitors have no control over the price of their products.   **T   F**

2. The smaller the number of firms in an industry and the greater the extent of product differentiation, the greater will be the elasticity of the individual seller's demand curve. **T   F**

3. One reason why monopolistic competition is wasteful, given the products the firms are producing and the extent to which they are promoting them, is that the average cost of producing the product is greater than the minimum average cost at which the product could be produced.   **T   F**

4. If advertising expenditures fluctuate directly (or positively) with total spending in the economy, they will be countercyclical and lead to greater stability in employment and the price level.   **T   F**

5. Those who contend that advertising contributes to "social imbalance" argue that there is an overproduction of private goods partly as a result of persuasive advertising.
                                  T   F

6. A firm will improve the quality of its product only if it expects that the additional revenue which it will receive will be greater than the extra costs involved.   **T   F**

7. There tends to be rather general agreement among both critics and defenders of advertising that advertising increases the average cost of producing and promoting the product.   **T   F**

8. Empirical evidence clearly indicates that advertising reduces competition and makes entry into an industry more difficult.   **T   F**

Underscore the letter that corresponds to the best answer.

1. Which of the following is *not* characteristic of monopolistic competition? *(a)* product differentiation; *(b)* a relatively large number of firms; *(c)* a feeling of interdependence among the firms; *(d)* relatively easy entry in the long run.

2. Given the following short-run demand and cost schedules for a monopolistic competitor, what output will the firm produce? *(a)* 2; *(b)* 3; *(c)* 4; *(d)* 5.

Price	Quantity demanded	Total cost	Output
$10	1	$14	1
9	2	17	2
8	3	22	3
7	4	29	4
6	5	38	5
5	6	49	6

3. Assuming the short-run demand and cost data in question 2 above, *in the long run* the number of firms in the industry: *(a)* will be less than in the short run; *(b)* will be the same as in the short run; *(c)* will be greater than in the short run; *(d)* cannot be determined from the available information.

4. Given the product the firm is producing and the extent to which the firm is promoting it, *in the long run:* *(a)* the firm will produce that output at which marginal cost and price are equal; *(b)* the elasticity of demand for the firm's product will be less than it was in the short run; *(c)* the number of firms in the industry will be greater than it was in the short run; *(d)* the profits being earned by the firms in the industry will tend to equal zero.

5. Which of the following is *not* one of the features of monopolistic competition which may offset the wastes associated with such a market structure? *(a)* a wider variety of products is offered to consumers; *(b)* advertising tends to be of the competitive type; *(c)* the quality of products improves over time; *(d)* consumers are better informed of the availability and prices of products.

6. Which of the following would probably be the best example of "competitive advertising"? *(a)* a "for sale" ad in the classified section of a newspaper; *(b)* one of the twice-weekly full-page advertisements of a grocery supermarket in a newspaper; *(c)* the advertisement for a particular brand of aspirin in a monthly magazine; *(d)* the national television advertisement of a drugstore chain announcing a "one-cent sale."

7. Which of the following would *not* be characteristic of a monopolistically competitive firm when it is in long-run equilibrium? *(a)* no further increase in the firm's output will decrease the firm's average revenue more than it decreases average cost; *(b)* no further decrease in the firm's price will increase the firm's total revenue more than it increases total costs; *(c)* no further variation in the firm's product will reduce total costs less than it reduces total revenue; *(d)* no further change in the firm's advertising campaign will increase total revenue more than it increases total costs.

8. Which of the following can be fairly concluded with respect to the economic effects of advertising? *(a)* advertising helps to maintain a high level of aggregate demand in the economy; *(b)* consumers benefit less from advertising expenditures than they do from expenditures for product development; *(c)* advertising in the American economy is more informative than competitive; *(d)* lower unit costs and lower prices result when a firm advertises because advertising increases the size of the firm's market and promotes economies of scale.

■ DISCUSSION QUESTIONS

1. What are the chief characteristics of a monopolistically competitive market? In what sense is there competition and in what sense is there monopoly in such a market?

2. What is meant by product differentiation? By what methods can products be differentiated? How does product differentiation affect the kind of competition in and inject an element of monopoly into markets?

3. Comment on the elasticity of the demand curve faced by the monopolistically competitive firm in the short run, assuming that the firm is producing a given product and is en-

gaged in a given amount of promotional activity. What two factors determine just how elastic that demand curve will be?

4. What output will the monopolistic competitor produce in the short run, and what price will he charge for his product? What determines whether the firm will earn profits or suffer losses in the short run?

5. In the long run what level of profits will the individual monopolistically competitive firm *tend* to receive? Why is this just a tendency? What forces profits toward this level, and why will the firm produce a long-run output which is smaller than the most "efficient" output? (Again assume, in answering this question, that the firm is producing a given product and selling it with a given amount of promotional activity.)

6. In what two senses is monopolistic competition wasteful or a misallocation of resources?

7. What methods, other than price cutting, can an individual monopolistic competitor employ to attempt to protect and increase his profits in the long run?

8. To what extent and how do product differentiation and product development offset the "wastes" associated with monopolistic competition?

9. Does advertising result in a waste of resources, or does it promote a more efficient utilization of resources? What arguments can be presented to support the contention that it is wasteful and detrimental, and what claims are made to support the view that it is beneficial to the economy? What empirical evidence is there?

10. When is a monopolistic competitor in long-run equilibrium not only with respect to the price he is charging but also with respect to the product he is producing and the extent to which he is promoting his product?

PRICE AND OUTPUT
DETERMINATION:
OLIGOPOLY

This last of the four chapters dealing with specific market situations is in a way the most difficult. Oligopoly is one of those areas of economic study where economists have found it impossible to reach definite conclusions. Under conditions of pure competition, pure monopoly, and monopolistic competition fairly definite conclusions regarding market prices and the outputs of individual firms are reached, but such conclusions are not easily drawn from an analysis of oligopoly. This is why the study of oligopoly is difficult—the generalizations are few in number—and this is unfortunate but also unavoidable.

Oligopoly is probably the most realistic market situation which the student will examine, and many economists believe it is the type of market most prevalent—or at least, most important—in the American economy. Because it is so realistic its study is all the more difficult. Chapter 29 is little more than an introduction to this very complex market situation. There are, however, certain things the student can and should learn about it.

What oligopoly *is* is fairly simple to understand. The *consequences* of "fewness" and the "mutual interdependence" and feeling of uncertainty to which it gives rise are not quite so easy to grasp, but they are of the greatest importance. For these reasons the student should make every attempt to learn exactly what is meant by mutual interdependence and uncertainty and why they exist in an oligopoly. If he can do this, he is well on the road to understanding why specific and definite conclusions cannot be reached concerning market prices and the outputs of individual firms. He will also see why oligopolists are loath to engage in price competition and why they frequently resort to collusion to set prices and to nonprice competition to determine market shares.

Chapter 29 employs several devices to explain the two major behavioral characteristics of oligopoly: the tendency for the prices charged by oligopolists to be rigid, and the tendency for oligopolists to determine what price to charge by collusion. The kinked demand curve is one of these devices. It explains why, in the absence of collusion, oligopolists will not raise or lower their prices even when their costs change. But the kinked demand curve does not explain what price oligopolists will set; it only explains why price, once set, will be relatively inflexible. To set price, oligopolists often resort to some form of collusion (such as a cartel, gentlemen's agreement, or price leadership). Collusion reduces the uncertainty each firm has about the prices rivals will charge and enables it to increase its profits. It also enables the industry as a whole to increase its joint profit. The results of collusion are a price and output which are about the same as would prevail if the industry were a pure monopoly. But collusion is seldom perfect because there are so many obstacles to collusion. As a result of these obstacles, price may be somewhat less and output somewhat greater than those which would be set by a monopolist.

Another device used to explain the behavior of oligopolists is the theory of games and the profits-payoff table. Using this table, we can again understand why noncolluding oligopolists will tend to keep their price unchanged. The table also helps us see why oligopolists will find it more profitable either to set price collusively or to merge their firms.

The final section of the chapter poses the question of whether oligopolies efficiently allocate resources. As with the same question with respect to monopolistic competition, there is only a tentative answer. There are, however, several reasons to believe that over the years oligopoly may have beneficial results for society as a whole, even though it may not appear at any given moment to be allocating resources efficiently.

■ CHAPTER OUTLINE

1. An oligopoly is an industry composed of a few mutually interdependent firms selling either a standardized or a differentiated product. The existence of such industries is usually the result of economies of scale and the advantages of merger.

2. The economic analysis of oligopoly is difficult for two reasons: The term "oligopoly" actually covers many different market situations; and the individual oligopolist, because of the uncertainty which accompanies mutual interdependence, is seldom able to estimate his own demand curve. Important characteristics of oligopoly are inflexible prices and simultaneous price changes.

3. An examination of two oligopoly models helps to explain price rigidity and the price-output behavior of oligopolists.

a. Under conditions of noncollusive oligopoly, an oligopolist believes that when he lowers his price his rivals will lower their prices, and that when he increases his price his rivals will not increase their prices. He is therefore reluctant to change his price at all for fear of decreasing his profits and beginning a price war.

b. Because of the uncertainties of noncollusive oligopoly, oligopolists may collude to maximize their joint profit by setting their price and joint output at the same levels at which a pure monopolist would set them.

c. Joint-profit maximization by collusive oligopolists is only a tendency because of several obstacles to collusion.

4. The theory of games and a profits-payoff table help us understand the behavior of oligopolists. A profits-payoff table:

a. Shows the different prices two oligopolists might charge and their profits for every combination of prices.

b. Demonstrates their mutual interdependence: the price one firm should set to maximize its profits depends upon the price charged by the other firm.

c. Illustrates price rigidity and explains why each firm is reluctant either to raise or to lower its price.

d. Indicates how both firms may gain by setting a collusive price or may increase their joint profits by merging.

5. Oligopolistic firms avoid price competition but engage in nonprice competition to determine each firm's market share (sales).

6. Whether oligopoly is economically efficient is almost impossible to determine.

a. At a given moment of time oligopoly probably results in restricted outputs, economic profits, and higher costs and prices.

b. Over a period of time, oligopoly may be progressive and result in larger outputs, lower costs, and technological progress.

(1) Technological competition among firms that have both the means and the incentives to improve their products and production techniques will result in economic progress.

(2) The evidence suggests that while many oligopolies have been progressive, many others have not engaged in any significant research and have failed to develop products and processes.

c. Countervailing power may also limit the restrictive power of oligopolies.

d. Oligopoly, *if* it results in technological progress or in economies of scale or *if* it is curbed by countervailing power, may be as efficient in allocating resources as competition.

■ IMPORTANT TERMS

Oligopoly

Fewness

Mutual inter-
dependence

Price rigidity

Noncollusive oligopoly

Collusive oligopoly

Kinked demand curve

Joint-profit
maximization

Cartel

Gentlemen's
agreement

Price leadership

Price break

Theory of games

Profits-payoff (price-
profits) table

Duopoly

Restrictive oligopoly

Progressive oligopoly

Countervailing power

■ FILL-IN QUESTIONS

1. In an oligopoly a _____
firms produce either a _____
or a _____
product, and entry into such an industry is
_____

2. Because oligopoly consists of a small number of firms, they are necessarily _____
_____ ;
this means that each firm must consider ____
_____
when setting the price of its product; the monopolist does not face this problem because
he has _____ rivals, and
the pure competitor does not face it because
he has _____ rivals.

3. The two major underlying causes of oligopoly are _____
and _____

4. Formal economic analysis cannot be easily
used to explain the prices and outputs of
oligopolists because _____
and _____

5. Oligopoly prices tend to be _____
and oligopolists tend to change their prices
_____
when they change them.

6. There tends to be very little _____
competition and a great deal of _____
_____
competition in oligopolies.

7. The kinked demand curve which the individual oligopolist sees for his product is
highly _____
at prices above the current or going price and
tends to be only slightly _____
or _____
below that price.

8. The kinked demand curve for an oligopolist
is drawn on the assumption that if the oligopolist raises his price his rivals will _____
_____
and if he lowers his price his rivals will _____
_____

9. Because the oligopolist who confronts a
kinked demand curve finds that there is a ____
_____ in his marginal-
revenue curve, small changes in the marginal-
cost curve do not change the _____
_____

10. When oligopolists collude to maximize
joint profits, the price they set and their combined output tend to be the same as _____

11. Four obstacles to the tendency of collusive oligopolists to maximize joint profits
are:

a. _____

b. _____

c. _____

d. _____

12. A cartel is a written or oral agreement
either to _____
or to _____

13. A gentlemen's agreement is a _____
agreement on _____ ;

each firm's share of the market is determined

by _____

_____

The firm that sets the price which the other

firms in the industry follow is the _____

14. In a profits-payoff (or price-profits) table

the _____ are

along the top and the _____
are along the left side. The two figures in each

box (or cell) in the table are the _____

_____

15. The profits-payoff table demonstrates that:
  a. The most profitable price for one firm to

charge depends upon _____
  b. In most cases either a price increase or a

decrease by one firm will _____
that firm's profit, because when it raises price

its rival will _____

and when it lowers price its rival will _____

_____

  c. The two firms can increase their joint

profit either by _____ or _____

16. Oligopolists use nonprice competition to
determine each firm's share of the market be-

cause _____

and _____

17. Oligopolists typically have both the means
and the incentives to effect technological ad-

vances; the means are _____

_____

and the incentives are:

  a. _____

  b. _____

  c. _____

  d. _____

18. Such evidence as is available makes it
clear that most oligopolies (have, have not)

_____ been progres-

sive in developing new products and techniques; their expenditures for research and

development have been _____
and a large percentage of such expenditures

of oligopolists have been _____

_____

19. Countervailing power tends to develop for
both defensive and offensive reasons. The

defensive reason is the desire of _____

and _____

to protect themselves from _____

_____

and the offensive reason is the desire to _____

_____

20. Oligopoly may be more efficient in allocating resources than competition if it has

lower _____, produces

a _____ product, or is curbed

by _____; in the
absence of these conditions it will produce

_____ outputs and charge

_____ prices than a competitive industry.

■ PROBLEMS AND PROJECTS

1. The kinked demand schedule which an oligopolist believes confronts him is given in the
table on page 216.
  a. Compute the oligopolist's total revenue at
each of the nine prices, and enter these figures in the table.
  b. Also compute marginal revenue and the
coefficient (arc) of elasticity of demand between the nine prices, and enter these figures
in the table.
  c. What is the current, or going, price for

the oligopolist's product? $_____

How much is he selling? _____
  d. On the graph on page 216 plot the oligopolist's demand curve and marginal-revenue
curve. Connect the demand points and the

Price	Quality demanded	Total revenue	Marginal revenue	Elasticity of demand
$2.90	100	$_____		
2.80	200	_____	$_____	$_____
2.70	300	_____	_____	_____
2.60	400	_____	_____	_____
2.50	500	_____	_____	_____
2.40	525	_____	_____	_____
2.30	550	_____	_____	_____
2.20	575	_____	_____	_____
2.10	600	_____	_____	_____

marginal-revenue points with as straight a line as possible. *Be sure* to plot the marginal-revenue figures at the average of the two quantities involved, that is, at 150, 250, 350, 450, 512½, 537½, 562½, and 587½.

e. Assume that the marginal-cost schedule of the oligopolist is given in columns (1) and (2) of the table on page 217. Plot the mar-ginal-cost curve on the graph on which demand and marginal revenue are plotted.

(1) Given demand and marginal cost, what price should the oligopolist charge to maximize his profits? $_____

How many units of product will he sell at this price? _____

Dollars

0   Quantity

(1) Output	(2) MC	(3) MC′	(4) MC″
150	$1.40	$1.90	$.40
250	1.30	1.80	.30
350	1.40	1.90	.40
450	1.50	2.00	.50
512½	1.60	2.10	.60
537½	1.70	2.20	.70
562½	1.80	2.30	.80
587½	1.90	2.40	.90

(2) If the marginal-cost schedule changed from that shown in columns (1) and (2) to that shown in columns (1) and (3), what price should he charge? $_____ What level of output will he produce? _____ How have his profits changed as a result of the change in costs? _____ Plot the new marginal-cost curve on the graph.

(3) If the marginal-cost schedule changed from that shown in columns (1) and (2) to that shown in columns (1) and (4), what price should he charge? $_____ What level of output will he produce? _____ How have his profits changed as a result of the change in costs? _____ Plot the new marginal-cost curve on the graph.

2. An oligopoly producing a homogeneous product is composed of three firms. Assume that these three firms have identical cost schedules. Assume also that if any one of these firms sets a price for the product, the other two firms will follow and charge the same price. As long as they all charge the same price they will share the market equally: the quantity demanded of each will be the same.

Below is the total-cost schedule of one of these firms and the demand schedule that confronts it when the other two firms charge the same price as this firm.

a. Complete the marginal-cost and marginal-revenue schedules facing the firm.

b. What price would this firm set if it wished to maximize its profits? $_____

c. How much would:

(1) It sell at this price? _____

(2) Its profits be at this price? $_____

d. What would be the industry's:

(1) Total output at this price? _____

(2) Joint profits at this price? $_____

e. Is there any other price this firm can set, assuming that the other two firms will charge the same price, which would result in a greater joint profit for them? _____ If so, what is that price? $_____

f. If these three firms colluded (or merged) in order to maximize their joint profit, what price would they charge? $_____

3. On page 218 is a profits-payoff (or price-profits) table.

Output	Total cost	Marginal cost	Price	Quantity demanded	Marginal revenue
0	$ 0		$140	0	
1	30	$_____	130	1	$_____
2	50	_____	120	2	_____
3	80	_____	110	3	_____
4	120	_____	100	4	_____
5	170	_____	90	5	_____
6	230	_____	80	6	_____
7	300	_____	70	7	_____
8	380	_____	60	8	_____

Firm Y's prices

X \ Y	$4	$3	$2
$4	$49 / $50	$40 / $57	$32 / $60
$3	$50 / $39	$44 / $44	$38 / $42
$2	$48 / $30	$46 / $35	$42 / $40

Firm X's prices

a. If firm X charges a price of $3, for Y to maximize its profits it should charge a price of

$_____. But if firm Y sets a price of $3, the most profitable price for X to charge is

$_____. And if X charges $2, the most

profitable price for Y is $_____.

b. Assume both firm X and firm Y are initially charging a price of $3.

(1) If X increased its price from $3 to $4,

Y (would or would not) _____

increase its price to $4 because _____

_____

(2) Knowing that Y would not follow a price increase from $3 to $4, X (would, would not)

_____ increase its price to

$4 because _____

_____

(3) If X decreased its price from $3 to $2,

Y (would, would not) _____ decrease its price to $2 because _____

(4) Knowing that Y would follow a price decrease from $3 to $2, X (would, would not)

_____ decrease its price to $2

because _____

c. If X and Y colluded to maximize their joint profit:

(1) Firm X would set a price of $_____

and have a profit of $_____

(2) Firm Y would set a price of $_____

and have a profit of $_____

(3) Firms X and Y would have a joint profit

of $_____

■ SELF-TEST

Circle the T if the statement is true, the F if it is false.

1. The element of "uncertainty" which exists in oligopolies is the uncertainty faced by each firm on how its rivals will react if it changes its price.   **T   F**

2. Price competition between firms is an important characteristic of oligopoly.   **T   F**

3. The kinked demand curve is an economic tool which can be used to explain how the current market price of a product is determined.   **T   F**

4. A cartel is usually a written agreement among firms which sets the price of the product and determines each firm's share of the market.   **T   F**

5. The practice of price leadership is almost always based on a formal written or oral agreement.   **T   F**

6. Whenever oligopoly exists, firms will collude to maximize their joint profit. **T F**

7. Nonprice competition is the typical method of determining each oligopolist's share of the total market. **T F**

8. It is often argued that oligopolists typically possess both the means and the incentives to technological progress, and that the means are the substantial profits received by them. **T F**

9. Almost all the important technological advances in the United States since 1900 can be attributed to the research and development activities of large business firms. **T F**

10. Oligopoly may be socially desirable if it results in lower production costs or in better products than would be obtainable under more competitive conditions. **T F**

Underscore the letter that corresponds to the best answer.

1. "Mutual interdependence" means that: (a) each firm produces a product similar but not identical to the products produced by its rivals; (b) each firm produces a product identical to the products produced by its rivals; (c) each firm must consider the reactions of its rivals when it determines its price policy; (d) each firm faces a perfectly elastic demand for its product.

2. The demand curve confronting an oligopolist tends to be: (a) elastic; (b) of unitary elasticity; (c) inelastic; (d) one which depends upon the prices charged by his rivals.

3. If an individual oligopolist's demand curve is "kinked," it is necessarily: (a) inelastic below the going price; (b) inelastic above the going price; (c) elastic above the going price; (d) of unitary elasticity at the going price.

4. In the next column is the demand schedule confronting an oligopolist. Which one of the eight prices seems to be the "going" price of the product produced by the firm? (a) $4.50; (b) $4; (c) $3.50; (d) $3.

5. When oligopolists collude to maximize their joint profit, the results are generally: (a) greater output and higher price; (b) greater output and lower price; (c) smaller output and lower price; (d) smaller output and higher price

Price	Quantity demanded
$5.00	10
4.50	20
4.00	30
3.50	40
3.00	42
2.50	44
2.00	46
1.00	48

6. Which of the following constitutes an obstacle to collusion among oligopolists? (a) a general business recession; (b) a small number of firms in the industry; (c) a homogeneous product; (d) the patent laws.

7. Which of the following is *not* a means of colluding? (a) a cartel; (b) a price break; (c) a gentlemen's agreement; (d) price leadership.

8. Which of the following does *not* contribute to the existence of oligopoly? (a) the economies of large-scale production; (b) the gains in profits that result from mergers; (c) low barriers to entry into an industry; (d) extensive sales promotion activities by the established firms in an industry.

9. A profits-payoff (or price-profits) table is used to explain all but one of the following: (a) mutual interdependence; (b) the advantages of collusion; (c) price rigidity; (d) product differentiation.

10. Countervailing power means that: (a) new firms enter oligopolistic industries to compete with and lower the profits of the firms in the industry; (b) oligopolists restrict their profits for fear the government will investigate their pricing policy and for fear of adverse public opinion; (c) technological advance results over time in lower prices, improved products, and larger outputs in oligopolies; (d) resource suppliers and customers of oligopolists tend to become oligopolists themselves in order to protect themselves and to share in the oligopolists' profits.

■ DISCUSSION QUESTIONS

1. What are the essential characteristics of an oligopoly? How does it differ from monopolistic competition?

2. How prevalent is oligopoly in the American economy? Is it more or less prevalent than monopolistic competition?

3. What do "mutual interdependence" and "uncertainty" mean with respect to oligopoly? Why are they special characteristics of oligopoly?

4. What are the underlying causes of oligopoly?

5. Why is it difficult to employ formal economic analysis to explain the prices charged by and the outputs of oligopolists?

6. To what extent are oligopoly prices flexible and to what extent is there price competition among oligopolistic firms?

7. Explain what the kinked demand curve is, its most important characteristics, the assumptions upon which it is based, and the kind of marginal-revenue curve to which it gives rise. How can the kinked demand curve be used to explain why oligopoly prices are relatively inflexible? Under what conditions will oligopolists acting independently raise or lower their prices even though their demand curves may be kinked?

8. Explain the difference between (a) collusive and noncollusive oligopoly, (b) restric-tive and progressive oligopoly, and (c) homogeneous and differentiated oligopoly.

9. Why do oligopolists find it advantageous to collude? What are the obstacles to collusion?

10. Explain (a) a cartel, (b) a gentlemen's agreement, and (c) price leadership.

11. Why do oligopolists engage in extensive nonprice competition?

12. Explain what a profits-payoff (or price-profits) table is and how it is used to demonstrate (a) mutual interdependence, (b) price rigidity, and (c) the advantages of collusion and merger.

13. Is oligopoly economically efficient and beneficial to society? Explain why your answer depends upon whether a short-run or a long-run view is taken.

14. What is meant when it is said that oligopolists have both the means and the incentives for technological improvements?

15. Explain precisely what is meant by countervailing power. How does it differ from the more traditional view that the self-interest of firms is regulated by "same-side-of-the-market" competition? What shortcomings does it have as a regulatory force?

30

PRODUCTION AND THE DEMAND
FOR ECONOMIC RESOURCES

Chapter 30 is the first of a group of three chapters which examine the markets for resources. A resource market is simply a market in which demand and supply determine the prices (called wages, rent, interest, and profit) of resources and the quantities of these resources that will be hired. Just as Chapters 22 through 29 have looked behind demand and supply in product markets, Chapters 30 through 32 look behind demand and supply in resource markets.

The demanders of resources are business firms who employ resources to produce their products. Chapter 30 begins the examination of resource markets by looking at the business firm and the demand side of the resource market. The material in this chapter is *not* an explanation of what determines the demand for a *particular* resource—such as labor, land, capital, or entrepreneurial ability—but is rather an explanation of what determines the demand for *any* resource. In Chapters 31 and 32 the supply sides of the resource market and particular resources are examined in detail.

The list of important terms for Chapter 30 is relatively short, but included in the list are two very important concepts—marginal revenue product and marginal resource cost—which the student must grasp if he is to un-

derstand how much of a resource a firm will hire. These two concepts are similar to but not identical with the marginal-revenue and marginal-cost concepts employed in the study of product markets and in the explanation of how large an output a firm will produce. Marginal revenue and marginal cost are, respectively, the change in the firm's total revenue and the change in the firm's total cost when it produces and sells an additional unit of *output;* marginal revenue product and marginal resource cost are, respectively, the change in the firm's total revenue and the change in the firm's total cost when it hires an additional unit of an *input*. (*Note:* The two new concepts deal with changes in revenue and costs as a consequence of hiring more of a *resource*.)

When a firm wishes to maximize its profits, it produces that *output* at which marginal revenue and marginal cost are equal. But how much of each resource does it hire if it wishes to maximize its profits? It hires that amount of each *resource* at which the marginal revenue product and the marginal resource cost of that resource are equal.

There is still another similarity between the output and the input markets insofar as the firm is concerned. You will recall that the competitive firm's *supply* curve is a portion of its *marginal-cost* curve. The competitive firm's *demand* curve for a resource is its *marginal-revenue-product* curve. Just as cost is the important determinant of supply, the revenue derived from the use of a resource is the important factor determining the demand for that resource.

■ CHAPTER OUTLINE

1. The study of what determines the prices of resources is important because resource prices influence the size of individual incomes and the distribution of income; and they ration scarce resources.

2. Economists generally agree upon the basic principles of resource pricing, but the complexities of different resources markets make these general principles difficult to apply.

3. The demand for a single resource depends upon (or is derived from) the demand for the goods and services it can produce.
   a. Because resource demand is a derived demand, the demand for a single resource depends upon the marginal productivity of the resource and the market price of the good or service it is used to produce.
   b. Marginal revenue product combines these two factors—the marginal physical product of a resource and the market value of the product it produces—into a single useful tool.
   c. A firm will hire a resource up to the point where the marginal revenue product of the resource is equal to the marginal resource cost.
   d. The firm's marginal-revenue-product schedule for a resource is that firm's demand schedule for the resource.
   e. If a firm sells its output in an imperfectly competitive market, the more the firm sells the lower becomes the price of the product. This causes the firm's marginal-revenue-product (resource demand) schedule to be less elastic than it would be if the firm sold its output in a purely competitive market.
   f. The market (or total) demand for a resource is the sum of the demand schedules of all firms employing the resource.

4. Changes in the demand for the product being produced, changes in the productivity of the resource, and changes in the prices of other resources will tend to change the demand for a resource.

5. The elasticity of the demand for a particular resource depends upon the rate at which the marginal physical product of that resource declines, the extent to which other resources can be substituted for the particular resource, the elasticity of demand for the product being produced, and the importance of the total cost of the resource relative to the total costs of the firm.

6. Firms typically employ more than one resource in producing a product.
   a. The firm is hiring resources in the most profitable combination, if it hires resources in a competitive market, when the marginal revenue product of each resource is equal to the price of the resource.
   b. The firm employing resources in perfectly competitive markets is hiring resources in the least-cost combination when the ratio of the marginal physical product of a resource to its price is the same for all the resources the firm hires.
   c. If the firm employs resources in imperfectly competitive markets it is hiring resources in the most profitable combination when the marginal revenue product of each resource is equal to its marginal resource cost; and it is hiring resources in the least-cost combination when the ratio of the marginal physical product of a resource to its marginal resource cost is the same for all resources.

■ IMPORTANT TERMS

Derived demand	**Output effect**
Marginal revenue product	**Profit-maximizing combination of resources**
Marginal resource cost	
MRP = MRC rule	**Least-cost combination of resources**
Substitution effect	

■ FILL-IN QUESTIONS

1. Resource prices ration _____ and are one of the factors that determine the

_____

of households; they are also one of the determinants of the _____ of business firms.

2. The demand for a resource is a _____

_____

demand and depends upon the _____

_____

and the _____

3. A firm will find it profitable to hire additional units of a resource up to the point at

which the _____

and the _____
of the resource are equal; if the firm hires the resource in a purely competitive market, the

_____

and the _____
of the resource are necessarily equal.

4. A firm's demand schedule for a resource

is the firm's _____
schedule for that resource because both indi-

cate the _____
of the resource the firm will hire at various

resource _____

5. A producer who sells his product in an imperfectly competitive market finds that the more of a resource he hires, the _____

_____

becomes the price at which he can sell his product. As a consequence the marginal-revenue-product (or demand) schedule for the re-

source is _____
elastic than it would be if the output were sold in a purely competitive market.

6. A firm can hire 4 units of a resource and produce 20 units of a product which sells for $6 per unit; if it were to hire 5 units of the resource, it would be able to produce 27 units of product which would sell for $5 per unit. The marginal revenue product of the 5th unit

of the resource is $_____, which is equal

to _____ $\times$ $_____

minus _____ $\times$ $_____

7. The market demand curve for a resource

is obtained by _____

_____

8. The demand for a resource will change if

the demand for the _____

changes, if the _____

of the resource changes, or if the _____

_____

of other resources change.

9. In the space to the right of each of the following, indicate whether the change would tend to increase (+), decrease (−), or have no effect (0) upon a firm's demand for a particular resource:

a. An increase in the price of the firm's

product _____

b. A decrease in the amounts of all other

resources the firm employs _____

c. An increase in the efficiency of the re-

source _____

d. An increase in the price of a substitute

resource _____

e. A decrease in the price of a complemen-

tary resource _____

10. Other things being equal, a decrease in the price of resource A will induce the firm

to hire _____ of resource

A and _____ of other resources;

this is called the _____ effect.
But if the decrease in the price of A results in lower total costs and an increase in output,

the firm may hire _____

of other resources; this is called the _____

_____ effect.

11. Four determinants of the elasticity of demand for a resource are the rate at which

the _____
of the resource decreases, the degree to which

other resources can be _____

for the resource, the _____
for the product which it is used to produce,

and the _____

_____

12. A firm that hires resources in purely competitive markets is employing the combination of resources which will result in maximum profits for the firm when the _____

of every resource is equal to its _____

13. Suppose a firm employs resources in purely competitive markets. If the firm wishes to produce any given amount of its product in

the least costly way, the ratio of the _____

_____ of each resource to its

_____ must be the same for all resources.

14. When the marginal revenue product of a resource is equal to the price of that resource, the marginal revenue product of the

resource divided by its price is equal to _____

_____

15. Assume that a firm employs resources in imperfectly competitive markets. The firm is:
   a. Employing the combination of resources

that maximizes its profits when the _____

of every resource is equal to its _____

(or when the _____

each resource divided by its _____

is equal to _____).
   b. Employing the combination of resources that enables it to produce any given output in

the least costly way when the _____

of every resource divided by its _____
is the same for all resources.

■ **PROBLEMS AND PROJECTS**

1. The bottom table shows the total product a firm will be able to obtain if it employs varying amounts of resource A, the amounts of the other resources the firm employs remaining constant.
   a. Compute the marginal physical product of each of the seven units of resource A and enter these figures in the table.
   b. Assume the product the firm produces sells in the market for $1.50 per unit. Compute the total revenue of the firm at each of the eight levels of output and the marginal revenue product of each of the seven units of resource A. Enter these figures in the table.
   c. On the basis of your computations complete the firm's demand schedule for resource A in the table below by indicating how many units of resource A the firm would employ at the given prices.

Price of A	Quantity of A demanded
$21	_____
18	_____
15	_____
12	_____
9	_____
6	_____
3	_____
1	_____

Quantity of resource A employed	Total product	Marginal physical product of A	Total revenue	Marginal revenue product of A
0	0		$_____	
1	12	_____	_____	$_____
2	22	_____	_____	_____
3	30	_____	_____	_____
4	36	_____	_____	_____
5	40	_____	_____	_____
6	42	_____	_____	_____
7	43	_____	_____	_____

Quantity of resource B employed	Marginal physical product of B	Total product	Product price	Total revenue	Marginal revenue product of B
0		_____	$ 0.00		
1	22	_____	$1.00	_____	$_____
2	21	_____	.90	_____	_____
3	19	_____	.80	_____	_____
4	16	_____	.70	_____	_____
5	12	_____	.60	_____	_____
6	7	_____	.50	_____	_____
7	1	_____	.40	_____	_____

2. In the table at the top of this page you will find the marginal-physical-product data for resource B. Assume that the quantities of other resources employed by the firm remain constant.

a. Compute the total product (output) of the firm for each of the eight quantities of resource B employed and enter these figures in the table.

b. Assume that the firm sells its output in an imperfectly competitive market and that the prices at which it can sell its product are those given in the table. Compute and enter in the table:

(1) Total revenue for each of eight quantities of B employed.

(2) The marginal revenue product of each of the seven units of resource B.

c. How many units of B would the firm employ if the market price of B were:

(1) $25: _____
(2) $20: _____
(3) $15: _____
(4) $9: _____
(5) $5: _____
(6) $1: _____

3. In the table below are the marginal-physical- and marginal-revenue-product schedules for resource C and resource D. Both resources are variable and are employed in purely competitive markets. The price of C is $2 and the price of D is $3.

a. The least-cost combination of C and D that would enable the firm to produce:

(1) 64 units of its product is _____ C

and _____ D.

Quantity of resource C employed	Marginal physical product of C	Marginal revenue product of C	Quality of resource D employed	Marginal physical product of D	Marginal revenue product of D
1	10	$5.00	1	21	$10.50
2	8	4.00	2	18	9.00
3	6	3.00	3	15	7.50
4	5	2.50	4	12	6.00
5	4	2.00	5	9	4.50
6	3	1.50	6	6	3.00
7	2	1.00	7	3	1.50

(2) 99 units of its product is _____ C

and _____ D.

b. The profit-maximizing combination of C

and D is _____ C and _____ D.

c. When the firm employs the profit-maximizing combination of C and D, it is also employing C and D in the least-cost combination

because _____

equals _____

d. Examination of the figures in the table

reveals that the firm sells its product in a ___

_____ competitive market at

a price of $_____

e. Employing the profit-maximizing combination of C and D, the firm's:

(1) Total output is _____

(2) Total revenue is $_____

(3) Total cost is $_____

(4) Total profit is $_____

*Circle the T if the statement is true, the F if it
is false.*

1. The prices of resources are an important
factor in the determination of the supply of a
product.   **T   F**

2. A resource which is highly productive will
always be in great demand.   **T   F**

3. A firm's demand schedule for a resource is
the firm's marginal-revenue-product schedule
for the resource.   **T   F**

4. A producer's demand schedule for a resource will be more elastic if he sells his
product in a purely competitive market than
it would be if he sold the product in an imperfectly competitive market.   **T   F**

5. If two resources are "complementary," an
increase in the price of one of them will reduce the demand for the other.   **T   F**

6. An increase in the price of a resource will
cause the demand for the resource to decrease.   **T   F**

Use the following information as the basis
for answering questions 7 and 8. The marginal revenue product and price of resource A
are $12 and a constant $2, respectively, and
the marginal revenue product and price of resource B are $25 and a constant $5, respectively. The firm sells its product at a constant
price of $1.

7. The firm should decrease the amount of
A and increase the amount of B it employs if
it wishes to decrease its total cost without
affecting its total output.   **T   F**

8. If the firm wishes to maximize its profits,
it should increase its employment of both A
and B until their marginal revenue products
fall to $2 and $5, respectively.   **T   F**

*Underscore the letter that corresponds to the
best answer.*

1. The study of the pricing of resources tends
to be complex because: (a) supply and demand do not determine resource prices; (b)
economists do not agree on the basic principles of resource pricing; (c) the basic principles of resource pricing must be varied and
adjusted when applied to particular resource
markets; (d) resource pricing is essentially an
ethical question.

Use the total-product and marginal-physical-
product schedules for a resource found below
to answer questions 2, 3, and 4. Assume that
the quantities of other resources the firm employs remain constant.

Units of resource	Total product	MPP
1	8	8
2	14	6
3	18	4
4	21	3
5	23	2

2. If the product the firm produces sells for
a constant $3 per unit, the marginal revenue
product of the 4th unit of the resource is:
(a) $3; (b) $6; (c) $9; (d) $12.

3. If the firm's product sells for a constant
$3 per unit and the price of the resource is a
constant $15, the firm will employ how many
units of the resource? (a) 2; (b) 3; (c) 4;
(d) 5.

4. If the firm can sell 14 units of output at a price of $1 per unit and 18 units of output at a price of $0.90 per unit, the marginal revenue product of the 3rd unit of the resource is: (a) $4; (b) $3.60; (c) $2.20; (d) $0.40.

5. Which of the following would increase a firm's demand for a particular resource? (a) an increase in the prices of complementary resources used by the firm; (b) a decrease in the demand for the firm's product; (c) an increase in the productivity of the resource; (d) a decrease in the price of the particular resource.

6. Which of the following would result in an increase in the elasticity of demand for a particular resource? (a) an increase in the rate at which the marginal physical product of that resource declines; (b) a decrease in the elasticity of demand for the product which the resource helps to produce; (c) an increase in the percentage of the firm's total costs accounted for by the resource; (d) a decrease in the number of other resources which are good substitutes for the particular resource.

7. A firm is allocating its expenditure for resources in a way that will result in the least total cost of producing any given output when: (a) the amount the firm spends on each resource is the same; (b) the marginal revenue product of each resource is the same; (c) the marginal physical product of each resource is the same; (d) the marginal physical product per dollar spent on the last unit of each resource is the same.

8. A firm that hires resources in competitive markets is *not necessarily* maximizing its profits when: (a) the marginal revenue product of every resource is equal to 1; (b) the marginal revenue product of every resource is equal to its price; (c) the ratio of the marginal revenue product of every resource to its price is equal to 1; (d) the ratio of the price of every resource to its marginal revenue product is equal to 1.

■ DISCUSSION QUESTIONS

1. Why is it important to study resource pricing?

2. Why is resource demand a derived demand, and upon what two factors does the strength of this derived demand depend?

3. Explain why firms that wish to maximize their profits follow the MRP =MRC rule.

4. What constitutes a firm's demand schedule for a resource? Why?

5. Why is the demand schedule for a resource less elastic when the firm sells its product in a noncompetitive market than when it sells it in a purely competitive market?

6. What determines the total, or market, demand for a resource?

7. Explain what will cause the demand for a resource to increase and what will cause it to decrease.

8. Explain the difference between the "substitution effect" and the "output effect."

9. What determines the elasticity of the demand for a resource? Explain the exact relationship between each of these four determinants and elasticity.

10. Assuming a firm employs resources in purely competitive markets, when is it spending money on resources in such a way that it can produce a given output for the least total cost?

11. When is a firm that employs resources in purely competitive markets utilizing these resources in amounts that will maximize the profits of the firm?

12. Were a firm to employ resources in *imperfectly* competitive markets, what would your answers to questions 10 and 11 be?

THE PRICING AND EMPLOYMENT
OF RESOURCES:
WAGE DETERMINATION

In the preceding chapter the text explained what determines the demand for *any* particular resource. Chapter 31 builds upon this explanation and applies it to the study of a very particular resource, labor, and to the price paid for the use of labor, the wage rate.

As was learned in Chapters 26 through 29, it takes more than an understanding of supply and demand to explain prices and the outputs of firms and industries. An understanding of the type of market in which products are bought and sold is also required. For this reason purely competitive, monopolistic, monopolistically competitive, and oligopolistic markets were examined in some detail. The same tends to be true of labor markets: Different types of labor markets must be examined if the factors which determine wage rates are to be understood.

Following some brief comments on the meanings of certain terms, the general level of wages, and the reasons for the high and increasing general wage level in the United States, Chapter 31 explains how supply and demand determine wage rates in particular types of labor markets. Four kinds of labor markets are studied: (1) the competitive market in which the number of employers is large and labor is nonunionized; (2) the monopsony market in which a single employer hires labor

under competitive (nonunion) conditions; (3) markets in which unions control the supply of labor and the number of employers is large; and (4) bilateral monopoly markets, in which a single employer faces a labor supply controlled by a single union.

It is, of course, important for the student to learn the characteristics of and the differences between each of these labor markets. It is also important that he study each of them carefully to see *how* supply and demand are affected by the characteristics of the market and to see what wage rate will tend to be paid in these markets. In the first two types of market the wage rate which will be paid is quite definite, and here the student should learn exactly what level of wages and employment will prevail.

When unions control the supply of labor, wage and employment levels are less definite. If the demand for labor is competitive, the wage rate and the amount of employment will depend upon how successful the union is in increasing the demand for labor, in restricting the supply of labor, or in setting a wage rate which employers will accept. If there is but a single employer, wages and employment will fall within certain limits; exactly where they occur within these limits will depend upon the bargaining strength of the union and of the firm. The student should, however, know what the limits are.

The sections explaining wages in particular labor markets are probably the most important parts of the chapter. But the sections which examine the effects of minimum wage laws on employment and wage rates, the effect of unionization upon wage rates in the United States, the reasons why different workers receive different wage rates, and the effect of investment in human capital are also important. The minimum wage laws, the author concludes, tend to reduce the level of employment in labor markets affected by the law; and so workers who lose their jobs because of minimum wage legislation are hurt. But those workers who retain their jobs at an increased wage are helped. The organization of workers into unions has resulted in higher wages for and has benefited these workers; but has decreased the wages of and has hurt the unorganized workers in the economy. Overall, the average wage of workers, organized and unorganized, has not been increased by unionization.

Aside from the unionization of workers, workers receive different wage rates because the workers are different, the jobs they do are different, and workers do not and cannot always move from one job to another even if there is a strong economic motive to do so. The differences among workers and the differences in their mobility, the author explains in the last section of the chapter, are largely the result of the different amounts spent by the worker, by his family, and by society to educate him, to improve his health, and to increase his mobility. Each of these three kinds of expenditure is an investment in human capital. The amounts invested in human capital explain wage differentials among the races, between the sexes, among geographic regions, and among individual workers; they also explain the historic increases in the average level of real wages in the American economy.

■ CHAPTER OUTLINE

1. A wage (or wage rate) is the price paid per unit of time for any type of labor and can be measured either in money or in real terms. Earnings are equal to the wage multiplied by the amount of time worked.

2. The general level of wages in the United States is the highest in the world. This is due to the high productivity of American labor and, therefore, the strong demand for labor relative to the supply of labor.

3. The wage rate received by a specific type of labor depends upon the demand for and the supply of that labor and upon the characteristics of the market in which labor is hired.

a. In a purely competitive and nonunionized labor market the total demand for and the total supply of labor determine the wage rate; from the point of view of the individual firm the supply of labor is perfectly elastic at this wage rate (that is, the marginal labor cost is equal to the wage rate) and the firm will hire that amount of labor at which the marginal revenue product of labor is equal to the marginal labor cost.

b. In a monopsonistic and nonunionized labor market the firm's marginal labor costs are greater than the wage rates it must pay to obtain various amounts of labor; and it hires that amount of labor at which marginal labor cost and the marginal revenue product of labor are equal. Both the wage rate and the level of employment are less than they would be under purely competitive conditions.

c. In labor markets in which unions control the supply of labor, they attempt to increase wage rates by increasing the demand for labor, by limiting the supply of labor, or by imposing upon employers wage rates in excess of the equilibrium wage rate which would prevail in a purely competitive market.

d. In a labor market characterized by bilateral monopoly, the wage rate depends, within certain limits, on the relative bargaining power of the union and of the employer.

e. Whether minimum wage laws reduce poverty is a debatable question; but the evidence suggests that while they increase the incomes of employed workers they also reduce the number of workers employed.

f. The unionization of workers has increased the wages received by union members slightly above what they would have received in the absence of unionization; but these wage increases have been at the expense of unorganized workers and unionization has not increased the average real wages of all workers.

4. Not all labor receives the same wage. Wage differentials exist because the labor force consists of noncompeting groups, because jobs vary in difficulty and attractiveness, and because laborers are not perfectly mobile.

5. Differences in wages received are to a great extent the result of differences in the amounts invested in human capital: the amounts expended to improve the education, the health, and the mobility of workers. Investment in human capital increases the productivity of a worker and, as a consequence, the wage and income he receives.

■ IMPORTANT TERMS

Wage
Wage rate
Earnings
Money wage
Real wage
Marginal labor cost
Monopsony
Oligopsony
Exclusive unionism
Craft union

Inclusive unionism
Industrial union
Bilateral monopoly
Wage differential
Noncompeting groups
Equalizing differences
Immobility
Investment in human capital

■ FILL-IN QUESTIONS

1. A wage rate is the price paid for labor per _____ and the earnings of labor are equal to _____ _____; money wages are an amount of money, while real wages are _____

2. American labor tends to be highly productive, among other reasons, because of the large amounts of _____ and _____ in the economy relative to the size of the labor force and because of the _____ _____ and _____ methods employed.

3. In a competitive market the supply curve for a particular type of labor tends to slope upward from left to right because _____ _____; the wage rate in the market will equal the rate

at which the _____ and the _____ are equal. Demand here is the sum of the _____ of all firms hiring this type of labor.

4. Insofar as an individual firm hiring labor in a competitive market is concerned, the supply of labor is _____ elastic because _____

5. The individual employer who hires his labor in a competitive market hires that quantity of labor at which the _____ of labor is equal to the _____ or the _____

6. A monopsonist employing labor in a market which is competitive on the supply side will hire that amount of labor at which _____ _____ and _____ are equal; because _____ is always greater than _____ in such a market, he will pay a wage which is less than _____ and _____

7. When compared with a competitive labor market, a market dominated by a monopsonist results in _____ wage rates and _____ employment.

8. The basic objective of labor unions is to _____; they attempt to accomplish this goal either by _____, by _____, or by _____

9. Craft unions typically try to increase wages by _____ while industrial unions try to increase wages by _____; if they are successful, employment in the craft or industry affected is _____

0   Quantity of labor

ginal-labor-cost curve on the graph below; indicate the quantity of labor the firm will employ and the wage it will pay.

0   Quantity of labor

d. If this firm hired labor in a competitive

labor market, it would hire at least _____

units and pay a wage of at least $_____

3. Assume that the employees of the monopsonist in problem 2 organize a strong industrial union. The union demands a wage rate
of $16 for its members, and the monopsonist
decides to pay this wage because a strike
would be too costly for him.

a. In the table below compute the supply
schedule for labor which now confronts the
monopsonist by completing column 2.

(1) Number of labor units	(2) Wage rate	(3) Total labor cost	(4) Marginal labor cost
1	$_____	$_____	$_____
2	_____	_____	_____
3	_____	_____	_____
4	_____	_____	_____
5	_____	_____	_____
6	_____	_____	_____
7	_____	_____	_____
8	_____	_____	_____

b. Compute the total labor cost and the
marginal labor cost at each level of employment, and enter these figures in columns 3
and 4.

c. The firm will:

(1) hire _____ units of labor.

(2) pay a wage of $_____

(3) pay total wages of $_____

d. As a result of unionization the wage rate

has _____,

the level of employment has _____,

and the earnings of labor have _____

e. On the graph below plot the firm's mar-

0   Quantity of labor

ginal revenue product of labor schedule, the labor supply schedule, and the marginal-labor-cost schedule. Indicate also the wage rate the firm will pay and the number of workers it will hire.

■ SELF-TEST

Circle the T if the statement is true, the F if it is false.

1. The general level of real wages is higher in the United States than in foreign countries because the supply of labor is great relative to the demand for it. **T F**

2. If an individual firm employs labor in a competitive market, it finds that its marginal labor cost is equal to the wage rate in that market. **T F**

3. Both monopsonists and firms hiring labor in competitive markets hire labor up to the point where the marginal revenue product of labor and marginal labor cost are equal. **T F**

4. A monopsonist is also a monopolist in the product market. **T F**

5. Restricting the supply of labor is a means of increasing wage rates more commonly used by craft unions than by industrial unions. **T F**

6. The imposition of an above-equilibrium wage rate will cause employment to fall off more when the demand for labor is inelastic than it will when the demand is elastic. **T F**

7. If a labor market is competitive, the imposition of an effective minimum wage will increase the wage rate paid and decrease employment in that market. **T F**

8. Actual wage rates received in different labor markets tends to differ because the demands for particular types of labor relative to their supply differ. **T F**

9. "Ben Robbins is a skilled artisan of a particular type, is unable to obtain membership in the union representing that group of artisans, and is, therefore, unable to practice his trade." This is an example of labor immobility. **T F**

10. Given a firm's demand for labor the lower the wage it must pay the more workers it will hire. **T F**

Underscore the letter that corresponds to the best answer.

1. Real wages would decline if the: *(a)* prices of goods and services rose more rapidly than money wage rates; *(b)* prices of goods and services rose less rapidly than money wage rates; *(c)* prices of goods and services and wage rates both rose; *(d)* prices of goods and services and wage rates both fell.

2. The individual firm which hires labor under competitive conditions faces a supply curve for labor which: *(a)* is perfectly inelastic; *(b)* is of unitary elasticity; *(c)* is perfectly elastic; *(d)* slopes upward from left to right.

3. A monopsonist pays a wage rate which is: *(a)* greater than the marginal revenue product of labor; *(b)* equal to the marginal revenue product of labor; *(c)* equal to the firm's marginal labor cost; *(d)* less than the marginal revenue product of labor.

4. Compared with a competitive labor market, a monopsonistic market will result in: *(a)* higher wage rates and a higher level of employment; *(b)* higher wage rates and a lower level of employment; *(c)* lower wage rates and a higher level of employment; *(d)* lower wage rates and a lower level of employment.

5. Higher wage rates and a higher level of employment are the usual consequences of: *(a)* inclusive unionism; *(b)* exclusive unionism; *(c)* an above-equilibrium wage rate; *(d)* an increase in the productivity of labor.

6. Which of the following has been a consequence of unionization? *(a)* higher wage rates for unionized workers; *(b)* greater employment of unionized workers; *(c)* greater employment of the workers in the labor force; *(d)* a higher level of real wages in the economy.

7. Industrial unions typically attempt to increase wage rates by: *(a)* imposing an above-equilibrium wage rate upon employers; *(b)* increasing the demand for labor; *(c)* decreasing the supply of labor; *(d)* forming a bilateral monopoly.

8. The fact that a star baseball player receives a wage of $125,000 a year can *best* be explained in terms of: *(a)* noncompeting labor groups; *(b)* equalizing differences; *(c)* labor immobility; *(d)* imperfections in the labor market.

9. The fact that unskilled construction workers received higher wages than gas station attendants is *best* explained in terms of: *(a)* noncompeting labor groups; *(b)* equalizing differences; *(c)* labor immobility; *(d)* imperfections in the labor market.

10. Which of the following is *not* true? *(a)* investment in human capital increases the productivity of workers; *(b)* expenditures for health, education, and mobility are investments in human capital; *(c)* whether to invest in real capital is a decision similar to the decision of whether to invest in human capital; *(d)* differences in the amounts invested in human capital explain the equalizing differences in wage rates.

■ DISCUSSION QUESTIONS

1. Why is the general level of real wages higher in the United States than in foreign nations? Why has the level of real wages continued to increase even though the supply of labor has continually increased?

2. Explain why the productivity of the American labor force is so high. In what way has the labor force itself contributed to this high productivity?

3. In the competitive model what determines the market demand for labor and the wage rate? What kind of supply situation do all firms as a group confront? Why? Under what economic conditions would a group of firms in a competitive market not confront such a supply schedule? What kind of supply situation does the individual firm confront? Why?

4. In the monopsony model what determines the market demand for labor and the wage rate? What kind of supply situation does the monopsonist face? Why? How does the wage rate paid and the level of employment compare with what would result if the market were competitive?

5. In what sense is a worker who is hired by a monopsonist "exploited" and one who is employed in a competitive labor market "justly" rewarded for his labor? *Why* do monopsonists wish to restrict employment?

6. When supply is less than perfectly elastic, marginal labor cost is greater than the wage rate. Why?

7. What basic methods do labor unions employ to try to increase the wages received by their members? If these methods are successful in raising wages, what effect do they have upon employment?

8. When labor unions attempt to restrict the supply of labor to increase wage rates, what devices do they employ to do this for the economy as a whole and what means do they use to restrict the supply of a given type of worker?

9. How do industrial unions attempt to increase wage rates, and what effect does this method of increasing wages have upon employment in the industry affected?

10. What is bilateral monopoly? What determines wage rates in a labor market of this type?

11. What is the effect of minimum wage laws upon wage rates and employment in *(a)* competitive labor markets; *(b)* monopsony labor markets; *(c)* the economy as a whole?

12. How has the unionization of workers affected the wage rates and the employment of *(a)* unionized workers; *(b)* nonunionized workers; *(c)* workers in general?

13. Why are the wage rates received by workers in different occupations, by workers in the same occupations, and by workers in different localities different?

14. Explain what is meant by investment in human capital and why the decision to invest in human capital is like the decision to invest in real capital. What is the effect of investment in human capital upon the productivity, the wage rate, and the income of workers?

15. Using the concept of investment in human capital, explain *(a)* the differences in wage rates among the races and geographic regions and the differences between the sexes; and *(b)* the historic rise in real wages in the American economy.

THE PRICING AND EMPLOYMENT
OF RESOURCES:
RENT, INTEREST, AND PROFITS

Chapter 32 concludes the study of the prices of resources by examining rent, interest, and profits. Compared with the study of wage rates in Chapter 31, each of the three major sections in Chapter 32 is considerably briefer and a good deal simpler. The student might do well to treat this chapter as if it were actually three very short chapters.

There is nothing especially difficult about Chapter 32. By now the student should understand that the marginal revenue product of a resource determines the demand for that resource and that this understanding can be applied to the demand for land and capital. It will be on the supply side of the land and capital markets that the student will encounter whatever difficulties there are. The supply of land is unique because it is perfectly *inelastic:* changes in rent do not change the quantity of land which will be supplied. Demand, given the quantity of land available, is thus the sole determinant of rent. Of course land varies in productivity and can be used for different purposes, but these are merely the factors which explain why the rent on all land is not the same.

Capital, as the economist defines it, means capital goods. Is the rate of interest, then, the price paid for the use of capital goods? No, not quite. Capital is not one kind of good; it

is many different kinds. In order to be able to talk about the price paid for the use of capital goods there must be a common denominator, a simple way of adding up different kinds of capital goods. The common denominator is money. Interest (or the rate of interest) is the price paid for the use of money. *Businessmen* hire money in order to purchase capital goods, but households and governments also hire money, and for different purposes. The total demand for money is derived, therefore, not only from the *expected* marginal revenue product of additional capital goods but also from the demands of households and governments for money.

On the supply side of the money (or loanable funds) market it is sufficient to determine who has money to loan, to determine how much money they *could* loan, and to determine how much they *will* loan. Here it is particularly important to note that savers are the principal suppliers of loanable funds, that they have motives for *not* loaning their money, and that the supply of loanable funds depends upon the strength of these motives. Interest is the reward which must be paid to overcome their desire not to lend their money.

When it comes to profits, supply and demand analysis fails the economist. Profits are not merely a wage for a particular type of labor;

rather they are rewards for taking risks and the gains of the monopolist. Such things as "the quantity of risk taken" or "the quantity of effort required to establish a monopoly" simply can't be measured; consequently it is impossible to talk about the demand for or the supply of them. Nevertheless, profits are important in the economy. They are largely rewards for doing things that have to be done if the economy is to allocate resources efficiently and to progress and develop; they are the lure or the bait which makes men willing to take the risks that result in efficiency and progress.

The final section of Chapter 32 answers two questions about the American economy. What part of the national income goes to workers and what part goes to capitalists—those who provide the economy with land, capital goods, and entrepreneurial ability? And have the shares going to workers and to capitalists changed in the past seventy-five or so years? The student may be surprised to learn that the lion's share—about 80%—of the national income goes to workers today and went to workers at the beginning of the century; and that capitalists today and in 1900 got about 20%. There is, in short, no evidence to support the belief that workers get less and capitalists more or the opposite belief that workers obtain a greater part and capitalists a smaller part of the national income today than they did three-quarters of a century ago in the United States.

■ CHAPTER OUTLINE

1. Economic rent is the price paid for the use of land or natural resources whose supply is perfectly inelastic.

   a. Demand is the active determinant of economic rent because changes in the level of economic rent do not change in the quantity of land supplied; economic rent is, therefore, a payment which in the aggregate need not be paid to ensure that the land will be available.

   b. Some people have argued that land rents are unearned incomes and that either land should be nationalized or rents should be taxed away. The single tax advocated by Henry George would have no effect upon resource allocation. While critics have pointed out the disadvantages of such a tax, there is a renewed interest in taxing land values to improve the equity and efficiency of local tax systems.

   c. Economic rents on different types of land vary because land differs in its productivity and because it has alternative uses; hence rent is a cost to a firm because it must compete to lure superior land away from alternative employments.

2. Interest is the price paid for the use of money (loanable funds), and the rate of interest is determined by the demand for and the supply of loanable funds.

   a. Businesses, households, and governments are the demanders, while the potential suppliers of loanable funds are households, businesses, and commercial banks; the actual supply of loanable funds may be less than the potential supply because households and businesses have motives for liquidity.

   b. The rate of interest tends to be an administered price because government is both a large demander and a large supplier (through the bank system) of loanable funds relative to the size of the market.

   c. The interest rate performs two important functions: It determines the total amount of investment in the economy, and it rations the investment among different firms and industries.

3. Economic profit is what remains for the firm after all its explicit and implicit opportunity costs have been paid.

   a. Profit is a payment for entrepreneurial ability, which involves combining and directing the use of resources in an uncertain and innovating world.

   b. Profits are rewards for assuming the risks in an economy in which the future is uncertain and subject to change and for assuming the risks and the uncertainties inherent in innovation. They are also surpluses which business firms obtain from the exploitation of monopoly power.

   c. The expectation of profits motivates business firms to innovate, and profits (and losses) guide business firms to produce products and to use resources in the way desired by society.

4. National income data for the American economy indicate that:

   a. in the period 1963–1970 wages and salaries were 72% of the national income; but, using a broader definition of labor income

(wages and salaries plus proprietors' income
—which is mostly a payment for labor),
labor's share was 81% and capital's share
(rent, interest, and corporate profits) was
19% of national income.

b. since the years 1900–1909 wages and
salaries have increased from 55 to 72%;
but labor's share, employing the broader definition of labor income, has remained at about
80% and capital's share at about 20% of
the national income.

■ IMPORTANT TERMS

Economic rent

Incentive function

Single-tax movement

Loanable funds

The (or pure)
rate of interest

Liquidity preference

Transactions motive

Precautionary motive

Speculative motive

Economic (pure)
profit

Static economy

Insurable risk

Uninsurable risk

Pursuit and escape
theory

■ FILL-IN QUESTIONS

1. Rent is the price paid for the use of _____

and _____
and their total supply is _____

2. _____
is the active determinant of rent, while _____

is passive. Because rent does not perform an

function, economists consider it to be a _____

a payment that need not be made to ensure
that the land will be made available to the
economy.

3. Socialists argue that land rents are _____

incomes and that land should be _____

so that these incomes can be used for the
good of society as a whole. Proponents of ___

argue that economic rent could be completely
taxed away without affecting the amount of
land available for productive purposes.

4. Rents on different pieces of land are not
the same because _____

And while rent from the viewpoint of the
economy as a whole is a surplus, rent is a

cost to _____
users of land which must be paid because

land has _____
5. Interest is the price paid for the use of

or _____
which are not economic resources but which

business firms are willing to hire because ___

6. Interest rates on different loans tend to
differ because of differences in _____,

_____,
and _____,
and because of _____
7. The greatest percentage of loanable funds

is borrowed by _____
and the amount they are willing to borrow

depends basically upon _____
8. The relationship between the quantity of
loanable funds demanded and the rate of in-

terest is a _____
one, but the demand for loanable funds tends

to be _____
9. The potential sources of loanable funds

are the _____
and _____
saving of _____
and _____

and the money _____

by _____

and _____

10. Savers have three principal motives for holding money rather than securities; these

are the _____,

_____,

and _____

motives.

11. The rate of interest tends to be an _____

_____

price, yet it performs two important functions for the economy: The rate of interest helps to

determine how much _____ will occur in

the economy and then _____

_____ it among various firms and industries in the economy.

12. Economic profits are a payment for the

resource called _____,

which involves combining _____

and making _____

with regard to their use and _____

in an _____

environment.

13. When the future is _____,

businessmen necessarily assume risks, some

of which are _____

and some of which are _____.

The risks which businessmen cannot avoid

arise either because the _____

_____

is changing or because the firm itself delib-

erately engages in _____

14. Profits:

a. are important in the American economy because the expectation of profits stimulates firms to innovate, and the more innovation there is, the higher will be the levels of

_____,

_____,

and _____

in the economy;

b. and losses promote the efficient _____

of resources in the economy unless the profits

are _____ profits.

15. Defining labor income broadly to include both wages and salaries and proprietors' income:

a. Labor's share of the national income is

today about _____%;

b. The capitalists' share is the sum of

_____, _____, and

_____; and is today about _____% of the national income;

c. Since the beginning of the twentieth century:

(1) Labor's share has (increased, decreased,

remained constant) _____

(2) Capital's share has _____

16. The pursuit and escape theory suggests that:

a. when laborers increase their money

wages they are in pursuit of the _____ of business firms;

b. businesses escape by raising _____

and _____;

c. and that as a result _____ remains constant.

■ PROBLEMS AND PROJECTS

1. Assume that the quantity of a certain type of land available is 300,000 acres and the demand for this land is that given in the table below.

Pure land rent, per acre	Land demanded, acres
$350	100,000
300	200,000
250	300,000
200	400,000
150	500,000
100	600,000
50	700,000

a. The pure rent on this land will be $_____

b. The total quantity of land rented will be

_____ acres.

c. On the graph below plot the supply and demand curves for this land and indicate the pure rent for land and the quantity of land rented.

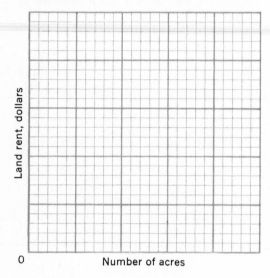

Land rent, dollars

0   Number of acres

d. If landowners were taxed at a rate of $250 per acre for their land, the pure rent on

this land after taxes would be $_____

and the number of acres rented would be ___

_____

2. What effect—increase (+), decrease (−), or indeterminate (?)—will each of the following have upon the rate of interest in the economy?

a. Increases in the amounts of money commercial banks are willing to lend at any given

rate of interest.   _____

b. An increase in the economy's NNP. _____

c. An increase in the amount of all business done on a "charge it until the first of the

month" basis.   _____

d. The belief that interest rates will decline

in the near future.   _____

e. A deficit in the budget of the Federal

government.   _____

f. An increase in the profits which business

firms expect to realize from the purchase of

new capital goods.   _____

g. A technological breakthrough which makes much of the capital equipment in the economy

obsolete.   _____

h. A belief on the part of households *only* that a depression is over and prosperity is

"just around the corner."   _____

■ SELF-TEST

Circle the T if the statement is true, the F if it is false.

1. Rent is the price paid for the use of land and other property resources.   **T   F**

2. Rent is a surplus because it does not perform an incentive function.   **T   F**

3. The demand for loanable funds is inelastic.
T   F

4. The rate of interest tends to be an administered price because government is both a heavy demander of and an important supplier of loanable funds.   **T   F**

5. The potential supply of loanable funds is usually greater than the actual supply because savers often prefer to have demand deposits or cash rather than securities which pay interest.   **T   F**

6. If the economists' definition of profits were used, total profits in the economy would be greater than they would be if the businessman's definition were used.   **T   F**

7. The expectation of profits is the basic motive for innovation, while actual profits and losses aid in the efficient allocation of resources.   **T   F**

8. The increasing importance of the corporation in the American economy is a part of the explanation of why wages and salaries have increased and proprietors' incomes have decreased as shares of the national income.
T   F

9. The growth of labor unions is the main cause of the expansion of wages and salaries as a share of the national income.   **T   F**

10. Over the past seventy-five years there has

been a shift from labor-intensive to capital- and land-intensive production.   **T F**

Underscore the letter that corresponds to the best answer.

1. The supply of land is: *(a)* perfectly in- elastic; *(b)* of unitary elasticity; *(c)* perfectly elastic; *(d)* elastic but not perfectly elastic.

2. Which of the following is *not* characteris- tic of the tax proposed by Henry George? *(a)* it would be equal to 100 percent of all land rent; *(b)* it would be the only tax levied by government; *(c)* it would not affect the supply of land; *(d)* it would reduce rents paid by the amount of the tax.

3. The smaller the *rate* of interest on a loan: *(a)* the greater the risk involved; *(b)* the shorter the length of the loan; *(c)* the smaller the amount of the loan; *(d)* the greater the imperfections in the money market.

4. Given the demand for loanable funds, the higher will be the rate of interest: *(a)* the more new money commercial banks are creat- ing; *(b)* the less the economy needs money for transaction purposes; *(c)* the greater the number of savers who expect the rate of in- terest to rise in the future; *(d)* the fewer the number of savers who find it necessary to take precautions against unfavorable financial con- tingencies in the future.

5. Changes in the rate of interest do *not*: *(a)* affect the total amount of investment in the economy; *(b)* affect the amount of invest- ment occurring in particular industries; *(c)* guarantee that the demand for and the sup- ply of loanable funds will be equal; *(d)* guar- antee that there will be full employment in the economy.

6. Which of the following would *not* be a function of the entrepreneur? *(a)* the intro- duction of a new product on the market; *(b)* the making of decisions in a static economy; *(c)* the incurring of unavoidable risks; *(d)* the combination and direction of resources in an uncertain environment.

7. The monopolist who earns an economic profit is able to do so because: *(a)* he is an innovator; *(b)* all his risks are insurable; *(c)* uncertainty has been reduced to the minimum; *(d)* most of his decisions are nonroutine.

8. Since around 1900: *(a)* capital's share of national income has increased; *(b)* labor's share has increased; *(c)* labor's share has decreased; *(d)* capital's share has been al- most constant.

■ DISCUSSION QUESTIONS

1. Explain what determines the economic rent paid for the use of land. What is unique about the supply of land?

2. Why is land rent a "surplus"? What eco- nomic difficulties would be encountered if the government adopted Henry George's single-tax proposal as a means of confiscating this sur- plus? What arguments are used to support the renewed interest in the heavy taxation of land values?

3. Even though land rent is an economic sur- plus it is also an economic cost for the in- dividual user of land. Why and how can it be both an economic surplus and an economic cost?

4. What is interest? What determines the rate of interest in the economy?

5. Why are there actually many different rates in the economy at any given time?

6. Who are the demanders of loanable funds? Why do they wish to borrow? Who are the potential suppliers, and what motives do po- tential suppliers have for remaining liquid (that is, for retaining possession of their money rather than exchanging it for interest- bearing securities)?

7. Upon what does the amount of loanable funds which business firms wish to borrow primarily depend?

8. What two important functions does the rate of interest perform in the economy? How well does it perform these functions?

9. What are economic profits? For what re- source are they a payment, and what tasks does this resource perform?

10. Why would there be no economic profits in a purely competitive static economy?

11. "The risks which an entrepreneur as- sumes arise because of uncertainties which are external to the firm and because of uncertainties which are developed by the initiative of the firm itself." Explain.

12. What two important functions do profits or the expectation of profits perform in the economy? How does monopoly impede the effective performance of these functions?

13. Monopoly results in profits and reduces uncertainty. Is it possible that monopolists may undertake more innovation as a result? Why?

14. What part of the American national income is wages and salaries and what part is labor income? Why do your answers to these two questions differ? What part of the national income is the income of capitalists? What kinds of income are capitalist income?

15. What have been the historical trends in the shares of national income that are wages and salaries, labor income, and capitalist income? What changes in the American economy can account for these trends?

16. Explain (a) why the growth of labor unions is not a good explanation of the expanding share of the national income going for wages and salaries; (b) the pursuit and escape theory.

GENERAL EQUILIBRIUM: THE PRICE SYSTEM AND ITS OPERATION

Chapter 33 provides a conclusion to the previous eleven chapters, tying together many of the things the student has already learned about microeconomics. By this time he has read a large amount of material concerning the operation of supply and demand in product and resource markets under different market conditions. He may have lost sight of the fact—emphasized in Chapter 5—that the American economy is a *system* of markets and prices. This means that *all* prices and *all* markets are linked together.

The chief purpose of Chapter 33 is to help the student understand why and how these markets are linked together, connected, and interrelated. The theory which explains the relationships between different markets and different prices is called *general* equilibrium analysis. (By way of contrast, the theory which explains a single product or resource market and the price of the one good or service bought and sold in that market is called *partial* equilibrium analysis.) An understanding of general equilibrium is necessary in order to understand how the price system as a whole operates to allocate its scarce resources.

The author employs three approaches to enable the student to grasp the essentials and the importance of general equilibrium analysis. He first explains in words the effects of an increase in the demand for automobiles. Then, using graphs and curves, he explains in more detail the effects of an increase in the demand for a hypothetical product X accompanied by a decrease in the demand for product Y. Both of these explanations include not only the short- and long-run effects upon the products involved but also the effects upon the markets in which the producers employ resources, upon the markets for complementary and substitute products, upon the markets in which the resources used to produce these other products are employed, and upon the distribution of income in the economy. Finally, to help the student understand the interrelationships between the different sectors of the economy, the author employs an input-output table.

Having examined these market and price interrelationships, the student next should note this. Given the distribution of income among consumers, and subject to several important exceptions, a price system in which all markets are purely competitive will bring about an ideal allocation of the economy's resources. It will maximize the satisfaction of consumer wants and thereby maximize economic welfare in the economy. The American economy, of course, is *not* made up of purely competitive markets. And because of these imperfectly

competitive markets, the allocation of resources is actually less than ideal and economic welfare is somewhat less than a maximum.

In addition—and these are important exceptions—even a purely competitive price system
does not allocate resources to allow for the
spillover costs and the spillover benefits of
the products it produces; and it does not produce social goods in sufficient quantities.
Hence government seems to be needed (remember the fourth economic function of government in Chapter 6) to adjust output for
spillover costs and benefits and to provide
society with social goods.

Also, a price system that allocates resources
ideally does not necessarily distribute its total
output (or income) in accordance with our
ethical standards. Economists don't and probably never will know which of the many possible distributions of income is ideal. But according to society's notions of what is right
and wrong (just and unjust), it is wrong to
have highly unequal distributions of incomes,
or incomes below a certain minimum level.
Hence the third economic function of government: the redistribution of income and wealth.

Chapter 33 ends by reemphasizing the importance of general equilibrium analysis. Interrelations between markets and prices do
exist, and they can be extremely important
in tracing through the economy the *total effect*
of an economic policy or the *full consequences*
of changes in consumers' tastes, the availability of resources, oil, for example, and technology. At the conclusion of this chapter the
student should be ready to examine several
of the trouble spots that concern the operation
of the price system and the way in which we
allocate our scarce resources. These trouble
spots are examined in the next seven chapters which make up Part 6 of the text.

■ CHAPTER OUTLINE

1. Partial equilibrium analysis is the study
of equilibrium prices and quantities in the
specific product and resource markets which
form the price-market system. General equilibrium analysis is the study of the interrelations between these markets.

2. Any change in tastes, in the supply of resources, or in technology will not only have an
immediate effect upon equilibrium price and
quantity in a specific market, but will also
have secondary effects in other markets and
upon other equilibrium prices and quantities.

3. To understand the effects of an increase
in consumer demand for product X accompanied by a decrease in consumer demand for
product Y, imagine that the industry producing X uses only type A labor and that the industry producing Y uses only type B labor.

a. Assume also that the demand curve for
each product has a negative slope because of
diminishing marginal utility and the supply
curve has a positive slope because of increasing marginal cost; and assume that the demand curve for each type of labor has a
negative slope because of diminishing marginal product and the supply curve has a
positive slope because of the work-leisure
preferences of workers.

b. Beginning with all markets in long-run
equilibrium, the short-run effects are an increased (decreased) output and price and
economic profits (losses) in industry X (Y), an
increased (decreased) derived demand for
type A (type B) labor, and increased (decreased) wage rates and employment for type
A (type B) labor.

c. The long-run adjustments are the entry
(exit) of firms in industry X (Y); an increase
(decrease) in the supply of X (Y); a higher
(lower) price than existed initially in industry
X (Y), assuming increasing-cost industries; an
increase (decrease) in the supply of A (B);
and higher (lower) wage rates for A (B) than
initially existed.

d. In addition to these adjustments there
will also be:

(1) An increase (decrease) in the demand
for and the prices and outputs of products
which are substitutes (complements) for X or
complements (substitutes) for Y; and an increased (decreased) demand for the resources
used to produce those products whose output
increases.

(2) An increase (decrease) in the demand
for the other resources used along with A (B).

(3) A redistribution of income from workers
and entrepreneurs in industry Y to those in
industry X.

4. Given the distribution of consumer income, purely competitive product and resource
markets result in an allocation of an econ-

omy's resources and the output of those goods and services which maximize the satisfaction of wants.

5. To the extent that product and resource markets in the real world are imperfectly competitive, the satisfaction of wants will be less than a maximum, and adjustments to changes will be less complete and slower. But this may be offset by more rapid technological progress and greater product variety.

6. For two reasons, even an economy in which all markets are perfectly competitive may not allocate resources efficiently.
  a. The price system does not take spillover costs and spillover benefits into account and does not automatically produce social goods.
  b. The price system may not distribute the economy's income ideally or optimally.

7. The input-output table indicates the specific relationships that exist between the outputs of the various sectors of the economy.
  a. Any change in the output of a particular sector alters the quantities of inputs it employs; and these inputs are the outputs of other sectors.
  b. A change in a particular sector's output will, therefore, initiate a series of changes in output in many other sectors of the economy.

8. General equilibrium analysis is important because it provides a wider understanding of the effects of any economic change or policy upon the economy.

■ IMPORTANT TERMS

Price system
Partial equilibrium analysis
General equilibrium analysis
Input-output analysis
Input-output table

■ FILL-IN QUESTIONS

1. Partial equilibrium analysis is concerned with prices and outputs in _____ markets in the economy, and general equilibrium analysis is concerned with the _____

_____ between markets and prices.

2. A change in the demand for product Z will affect not only the equilibrium price and quantity of product Z but may also affect the equilibrium price and quantity of:
  a. _____
  b. _____
  c. _____
  d. _____

3. General equilibrium exists in an economy where there is _____ in all the _____ and _____ markets in the economy.

4. Economic changes or disturbances which may result not only in "big splashes" but also in little waves and ripples are of three basic types: changes in _____, changes in _____, and changes in _____

5. When studying the markets for products and for resources, we assume that the demand curves slope _____ and the supply curves slope _____
  a. The slope of the demand curve for:
  (1) Products is due to _____
  (2) Resources is due to _____
  b. The slope of the supply curve for:
  (1) Products is due to _____
  (2) Resources is due to _____

6. Assume the demand for consumer good P increases while the demand for consumer good Q decreases. In the short run:
  a. The price and output of P will _____ and the price and output of Q will _____
  b. Profits in industry _____ will increase and profits in industry _____ will decrease.
  c. If the only resource used in industry P is type C labor and the only resource used in industry Q is type D labor, the demand for C will _____ and the demand for D will _____
  d. Wage rates and the quantity of labor em-

ployed in the market for _____ will increase while those in the market for _____ will decrease.

7. Using the same assumptions made in 6 above, if the two industries are increasing-cost industries, the increase in the demand for P along with the decrease in the demand for Q will in the long run:

a. Cause firms to enter industry _____ and to leave industry _____

b. _____ the supply of P and _____ the supply of Q.

c. _____ the price of P and _____ the price of Q from what they were originally.

d. Increase the supply of type _____ labor and decrease the supply of type _____ labor.

e. _____ the employment of type C labor and _____ the employment of type D labor.

8. Still using the assumptions made in 6 and 7 above, the increase in the demand for P and the decrease in the demand for Q will:

a. Increase the demand for products which are (substitutes, complements) _____ for P and decrease the demand for _____

b. _____ the demand for those resources used along with type C labor and _____ the demand for those resources used along with type D labor.

c. Redistribute income from workers and entrepreneurs in industry _____ to those in industry _____

9. Given the distribution of income, purely competitive product and resource markets bring about the production of a combination of goods and services which _____ of consumers because:

a. The _____ of each good or service is equal to its _____

b. The average cost of each product is a ___

c. The utility of the last dollar spent by a consumer on each good or service is _____

for all goods and services.

10. Product and resource markets in the real world are actually _____ competitive. As a result the allocation of resources is _____ and adjustments to changes in tastes, technology, and the availability of resources are _____ _____ and _____

11. Two potential offsets to imperfectly competitive markets are more rapid _____ _____ and greater _____

12. The ability of a purely competitive price system to allocate resources efficiently is open to question for two reasons.

a. It fails to take into account the _____ _____ and the _____ of the goods and services produced and it neglects or ignores the production of _____

b. It does not necessarily result in an ideal _____ of _____

13. The _____ sectors of the economy are listed down the left side of an input-output table and the _____ sectors across the top of the table. The _____ _____ of any sector in the table is a(n) _____ of other sectors of the economy.

14. Assuming constant returns to scale, if industry X sells 30% of its product to industry Y and if industry Y decides to increase its production by 25%, then industry X will have to increase its production by _____ %.

15. An understanding of general equilibrium analysis is important if one is to evaluate the overall _____, to understand specific _____, and to formulate good _____

■ PROBLEMS AND PROJECTS

1. Listed below are three types of economic change which can occur in the economy. In the spaces allotted following each change, indicate what you think the effect will be—increase (+), decrease (−), no change (0), or an indeterminate change (?)—on demand or supply, price, and output or employment in the markets affected by the initial change.

No answers to this problem will be found in the "Answers" section because the answer to each question depends upon such things as whether the short run or the long run is considered, whether the industry is an increasing- or constant-cost industry, and whether the student considers only the "immediate-secondary effect" or considers also the "secondary-secondary effect" of the initial change. The purpose of this exercise is simply to get the student to *attempt* to trace through the economy the full effect of an initial change and to see the extent and complexity of price-market interrelations.

a. Decrease in the demand for consumer good X but no *initial* change in the demand for other consumer goods.

(1) Effect on the price of and the quantity of good X produced. _____

(2) Effect on the demand for, the price of, and the output of goods which are substitutes for good X. _____

(3) Effect on the demand for, the price of, and the output of goods which are complements for good X. _____

(4) Effect on the demand for, the price of, and the employment of resources used in the production of good X. _____

(5) Effect on the supply of, the price of, and the output of goods which employ the same resources used in the production of good X. _____

(6) Effect on the demand for, the price of, and the employment of resources which are substitutes for the resources used to produce good X. _____

b. Increase in the supply of resource Y.

(1) Effect on the price of and the employment of resource Y. _____

(2) Effect on the supply of, the price of, and the output of goods which employ resource Y in the production process. _____

(3) Effect on the demand for, the price of, and the employment of resources which are complementary to resource Y. _____

(4) Effect on the demand for, the price of, and the output of those goods which are substitutes for the goods produced with resource Y. _____

(5) Effect on the demand for, the price of, and the output of those goods which are complements for the goods produced with resource Y. _____

(6) Effect on the demand for, the price of, and the employment of resources which are substitutes for resource Y. _____

c. Improvement in the technology of producing good Z.

(1) Effect on the supply of, the price of, and the output of good Z. _____

(2) Effect on the demand for, the price of, and the output of goods which are substitutes for good Z. _____

(3) Effect on the demand for, the price of, and the output of goods which are complements for good Z. _____

(4) Effect on the demand for, the price of, and the employment of resources used to produce good Z. _____

(5) Effect on the supply of, the price of, and the output of those goods which also employ the resources used to produce good Z.

2. Below is an incomplete input-output table for an economy with five sectors. All the figures in the table are physical units rather than dollars.

| Producing sectors | Using sectors | | | | | Total outputs |
	A	B	C	D	E	
A	100	150	75	___	25	425
B	30	20	70	80	200	___
C	10	60	___	20	20	110
D	205	35	40	10	___	300
E	___	140	60	35	80	390

a. Complete the table by computing (by addition or subtraction) the missing input-output figures.

b. Assume that sector B wishes to expand its output by 100 units. By what percentage does sector B wish to expand its output?

_____%

c. Assuming constant returns to scale in all sectors of the economy, by how many *units* will each of the following sectors of the economy have to expand their outputs if sector B is to expand its output by 100 units?

(1) Sector A: _____

(2) Sector C: _____

(3) Sector D: _____

(4) Sector E: _____

d. By what *percentage* will each of these sectors have to expand their outputs?

(1) Sector A: _____%

(2) Sector C: _____%

(3) Sector D: _____%

(4) Sector E: _____%

e. What further adjustments in the outputs of the various sectors of the economy will follow those given in (c) and (d) above?

_____

_____

■ SELF-TEST

Circle the T if the statement is true, the F if it is false.

1. General equilibrium analysis is the same thing as macroeconomics.　　**T　F**

2. The study of the effect of an increase in the demand for product C, other things remaining equal, upon the price and the output of product C is an example of partial equilibrium analysis.　　**T　F**

3. The supply curve for a product slopes upward in the short run because of the diminishing marginal productivity of variable resources.　　**T　F**

Use the following data for the three questions below and for multiple choice questions 6 and 7. Initially there is general equilibrium, and then the demand for consumer good W increases and the demand for consumer good Z decreases. Both industries are increasing-cost industries in the long run. Industry W employs only type G labor, and Z employs only type H labor.

4. In the short run, price, output, and profits will increase in industry Z and decrease in industry W.　　**T　F**

5. In the long run, the quantity of type G labor employed will increase and the quantity of type H labor employed will decrease. **T　F**

6. Income will be redistributed from workers and entrepreneurs in industry Z to those in industry W.　　**T　F**

7. Given the distribution of income in the economy, purely competitive product and resource markets lead to the production of a collection of products which maximizes the satisfaction of consumer wants.　　**T　F**

8. In the real world, product and resource markets tend to be purely competitive. **T　F**

9. A purely competitive price system results in an ideal or optimal distribution of income.　　**T　F**

10. General equilibrium analysis gives a broader picture of the economic consequences of economic changes and economic policies than partial equilibrium analysis even though some of these consequences turn out to be insignificant.　　**T　F**

Underscore the letter that corresponds to the best answer.

1. If the demand for consumer good A increased, which one of the following would *not* be a possible consequence? (*a*) increase in the price of A; (*b*) increase in the demand for resources used to produce A; (*c*) increase in the supply of those goods which are substitutes for A; (*d*) increase in the prices of other goods which employ the same resources used to produce A.

2. If the supply of resource B increased, which one of the following would *not* be a possible consequence? (*a*) decrease in the price of B; (*b*) decrease in the demand for those goods produced from B; (*c*) decrease in the demand for those resources which are substitutes for resource B; (d) decrease in the demand for those goods which are substitutes for the goods produced with resource B.

3. The price system produces approximately what percentage of the output and employs about what percentage of the resources of the American economy? (a) 70%; (b) 80%; (c) 90%; (d) 100%.

4. The downward slope of the demand curve for a product is the result of: (a) diminishing marginal utility; (b) diminishing marginal productivity; (c) increasing marginal cost; (d) the work-leisure preferences of workers.

5. The upward slope of the supply curve of labor is the result of: (a) diminishing marginal utility; (b) diminishing marginal productivity; (c) increasing marginal cost; (d) the work-leisure preferences of workers.

Use the data preceding True-False question 4 to answer the following two questions.

6. When the new long-run general equilibrium is reached: (a) the wage rate for type G labor will be higher than it was originally; (b) the wage rate for type G labor will be lower than it was originally; (c) wage rates in both labor markets will be the same as they were originally; (d) it is impossible to tell what will have happened to wage rates.

7. As a result of the changes in the demands for W and Z: (a) the demand for products which are substitutes for Z will have increased; (b) the demand for products which are complements for W will have decreased; (c) the demand for products which are substitutes for Z will have decreased; (d) the demand for products which are complements for Z will have decreased.

8. Which of the following is *not* the result of purely competitive product and resource markets? (a) the distribution of income among consumers maximizes the satisfaction of wants in the economy; (b) the average cost of producing each product is a minimum; (c) the price of each product is equal to its marginal cost; (d) the marginal utility of every product divided by its price is the same for all products purchased by an individual consumer.

9. All but one of the following is the result of imperfectly competitive product and re-

source markets. Which one? (a) resources are allocated less efficiently than under purely competitive conditions; (b) the price system is less responsive to changes in tastes, technology, and the availability of resources than a purely competitive price system; (c) there is a smaller variety of products than in a purely competitive system; (d) monopoly drives prices above and monopsony drives them below their competitive levels.

10. Which of the following is a disadvantage of a purely competitive price system? (a) underallocates resources to those products whose production entails a spillover cost; (b) overallocates resources to those products whose consumption entails spillover benefits; (c) underallocates resources to the production of social goods and services; (d) fails to distribute income optimally.

Use the following input-output table to answer questions 11 and 12 below.

Producing sectors	Using sectors					Total outputs
	A	B	C	D	E	
A	20	15	35	25	60	155
B	45	55	90	10	20	220
C	40	15	80	10	5	150
D	65	10	25	20	40	160
E	100	75	80	45	10	310

11. If sector C were to decrease its output by 50 units, and assuming constant returns to scale in all sectors, the *initial* impact on sector B would be a decrease in its output of: (a) 5 units; (b) 13⅓ units; (c) 26⅔ units; (d) 30 units.

12. If sector C is to increase its output by 20%, and assuming constant returns to scale, sector E's output will have to increase initially by: (a) 5.2%; (b) 19.4%; (c) 20%; (d) 37.5%.

■ DISCUSSION QUESTIONS

1. Explain the difference between partial equilibrium and general equilibrium analysis.

2. Why is general equilibrium analysis so important?

3. Suppose the demand for television sets decreases at the same time that the demand for airline travel increases. What would be (a) the short-run effects of these changes in the markets for television sets and airline travel and in the markets for television-set production workers and airline workers; (b) the long-run effects in these markets; (c) the long-run effects in the markets for complementary and substitute products and in the markets for other resources; and (d) the effect upon the distribution of income?

4. Imagine that the availability of iron ore used to produce steel increased or the technology of steel making improved. What would be the short- and long-run effects upon (a) the steel industry; (b) steelworkers; (c) the automobile industry; (d) the aluminum industry; (e) the machine tool industry; and (f) the coal industry?

5. Why is a purely competitive price system

"conducive to an efficient allocation of resources"?

6. When a price system is less than purely competitive, what are the economic consequences?

7. What costs, benefits, and goods does even a purely competitive price system neglect or ignore? What are the economic results of this neglect?

8. What is meant by an ideal or optimal distribution of income? Why can't economists determine what the optimal distribution of income is?

9. Explain precisely what an input-output table is and the kind of information it contains.

10. In addition to indicating the interrelationships between the various sectors of the economy, an input-output table can be used for what other purposes?

THE MONOPOLY PROBLEM:
THE SOCIAL CONTROL
OF INDUSTRY

This is the first of seven chapters which deal with specific trouble spots in the American economy and is one of the two chapters which concern the monopoly problem. Chapter 34 examines the monopoly problem in output markets, and Chapter 38 examines the monopoly problem in the labor market. It should be noted that the term "monopoly" as used here does *not* mean pure or absolute monopoly; it means, instead, control of a large percentage of total supply by one or a few suppliers. Actually there is no such thing as pure monopoly.

Whether big business and industrial monopolies are a real threat to efficient resource allocation and technological progress in the United States is certainly a debatable question. It is a question that will be argued from time to time by the American people and their representatives in Congress. Chapter 34 does not attempt to answer the question. It is important, however, for students to see that it is a debatable question, to see that there are good and plausible arguments on both sides of the question, and to see that the empirical evidence is very tentative.

A part of Chapter 34 is devoted to an examination of the ways in which the Federal government has attempted to prevent the formation of business monopolies and to limit the use of monopoly power. In addition, the chapter examines the ways in which this same government has—either intentionally or unintentionally—promoted and fostered monopoly. In these sections the student will find a discussion of a rather large number of Federal laws, and the question which the student almost always raises is, "Am I expected to know all these laws?" The answer is yes, he should have a general knowledge of these laws. If the student is to understand how government has restricted and promoted monopoly, he should know (1) what the major pieces of Federal legislation with these aims and/or results have been; (2) what the main provisions of each of these laws were; and (3) how successful each of these laws was in accomplishing its aims.

Another question which the student often raises with respect to these laws is, "What good is there in knowing them anyway?" In examining any important current problem it is important to know how the problem arose, what steps have already been taken to solve it, how successful the attempts were, and why the problem is still not solved. A more general answer to the same question is that an informed citizenry is necessary if a democracy is to solve its problems. And most of these laws continue in force and are enforced; many students will work for business firms which are subject to their provisions.

Two final points: In studying the ways in which government has promoted business monopoly, the student should again note specific laws. In addition, three possible future policies which the government might adopt with respect to business monopoly are listed, and the student should learn what arguments proponents of these policies advance to support their proposals.

■ CHAPTER OUTLINE

1. The term "monopoly," as used in this chapter, means a situation in which a small number of firms control all or a substantial percentage of the total output of a major industry. Business firms may be large in either an absolute or a relative sense, and in many cases they are large in both senses. Chapter 34 is concerned with firms large in both senses.

2. Whether business monopoly is beneficial or detrimental to the American economy is debatable. A case can be made *against* business monopoly and *for* it.

3. Many argue that while competition is not perfect in many industries it is "workable"; that big business is able to realize the economies of mass production; that it is conducive to a rapid rate of technological change; that business investment and pricing policies are a stabilizing influence in the economy; and that socially responsible business leaders do not abuse their monopoly power.

4. Others argue, however, that monopoly power results in restricted outputs, higher prices, misallocation of resources, greater income inequality, a slow rate of technological progress, economic instability, and less political freedom.

5. Government policies toward business monopoly have not been clear and consistent; legislation and policy have at various times both restricted and promoted monopoly power.
a. Following the Civil War, the expansion of the American economy brought with it the creation of trusts (or business monopolies) in many industries; and the fear of the trusts resulted in the establishment of regulatory agencies and the enactment of antitrust legislation.

b. Where natural monopoly existed and competition was not economical (as in the railroad industry) regulatory agencies were empowered to control and limit monopoly power.
c. Such antitrust legislation as the Sherman Act, the Clayton Act, the Federal Trade Commission Act, and other laws have attempted to restrain the growth and use of monopoly power.
d. Yet numerous exceptions to and suspensions of the antitrust laws have been made and various pieces of legislation have directly promoted monopoly.

6. There are at least three proposals (with supporting arguments) which have been suggested as future government policies for dealing with business monopoly: maintenance of the present policy, direct government ownership or regulation of business monopoly, and the restoration of effective competition in monopolistic industries.

■ IMPORTANT TERMS

Monopoly	Tying agreement
Big business	Cease-and-desist order
Absolute bigness	
Relative bigness	Wheeler-Lea Act
Workable competition	Robinson-Patman Act
Regulatory agency	Celler-Kefauver Act
Natural monopoly	Conglomerate
Interstate Commerce Act	Reciprocal selling
	Webb-Pomerene Act
Sherman Act	Resale price maintenance
Clayton Act	
Federal Trade Commission Act	Miller-Tydings Act
	Technological determinism
Interlocking directorate	Effective competition

■ FILL-IN QUESTIONS

1. As used in this chapter, monopoly means that a _____ firms control _____ of the output of a _____ industry; and this chapter is concerned with firms that are large in both a _____ _____

and an _____
sense.

2. Those who argue the case *for* business monopoly contend that _____ competition regulates big business; that big firms are able to realize _____; that big business leads to a _____ of technological change; that the _____

_____

and _____
policies of large firms contribute to economic stability; and that business leaders have a ___

_____

which prevents abuses of monopoly power.

3. Workable competition includes at least five varieties of competition other than price competition; these are:

a. _____

b. _____

c. _____

d. _____

e. _____

4. Galbraith argues that:
a. the dominant role of the giant corporation is dictated by _____: efficient production requires large amounts of _____, highly sophisticated _____, and detailed _____
b. the goals of a mature corporation are _____ and _____; and to achieve these goals the corporation integrates _____, finances its expansion _____ _____, controls consumers by _____ and _____, and allies itself with _____ to manage the economy.

5. Those who argue the case *against* business monopoly assert that monopolists _____ output; _____ prices; _____ resources; contribute to _____ in the distribution of income, to a _____

of technological progress, and to _____

_____

in the economy; and pose serious _____
dangers.

6. Federal legislation and policies have at times attempted to maintain _____ while at other times they have fostered _____

_____

7. When a single firm is able to supply the entire market at a lower average cost than a number of competing firms, there is a _____ _____ monopoly. In the United States many of these monopolies are controlled by regulatory _____ or _____ whose function is to prevent the abuse of monopoly power.

8. The Sherman Antitrust Act of 1890 made

_____

and _____
illegal.

9. The Clayton Act of 1914 prohibited such practices as _____.

_____,

_____,

and _____

10. The Federal Trade Commission was set up under the act of that name in 1914; the commission was given the power to _____

_____,

hold _____,

and to issue _____,
but the power of the commission has been limited by the ruling of _____ that they hold the final authority to _____

_____

11. The _____
Act banned the acquisition of the assets of one firm by another, and the _____
Act prohibited the acquisition of the stock of

one firm by another when the result would be reduced competition.

12. The _____
Act had the effect of prohibiting false and mis-

leading advertising, and the _____

_____

Act was aimed at eliminating the _____

_____

which large chain stores were able to obtain from their suppliers.

13. Most of the mergers of business firms

within the last ten years have been _____

_____ mergers in which a firm

in one industry merges with firms in _____

_____

14. Government promotes the growth of mo-

nopoly when it _____
certain industries or practices from antitrust

prosecution, when it grants _____,

and when it enacts _____

15. Export trade associations and resale price maintenance contracts were exempted from the provisions of the antitrust laws by, re-spectively, the _____

Act and the _____

Act; in addition, _____

and _____
have been made exempt from the antitrust laws by other Federal legislation.

16. The _____
have the effect of granting inventors legal mo-

nopolies on their products, while _____

_____

shelter American producers from foreign com-petition.

17. Three possible future policy alternatives for dealing with business monopoly are:

a. _____

b. _____

c. _____

18. Effective competition means that the

number of producers is large enough that ___

_____,

the absence of _____,

and _____

■ PROBLEMS AND PROJECTS

Below is a list of Federal laws. Following this list is a series of provisions found in Fed-eral laws. Match each of the laws with the appropriate provision by placing the appro-priate letter after each of the provisions.
  A. Sherman Act
  B. Clayton Act
  C. Federal Trade Commission Act
  D. Wheeler-Lea Act
  E. Robinson-Patman Act
  F. Celler-Kefauver Act
  G. Webb-Pomerene Act
  H. Miller-Tydings Act
  I. Interstate Commerce Act

1. Exempted American exporters from the antitrust laws by permitting them to form ex-port trade associations. _____

2. Established a commission to investigate and prevent unfair methods of competition. _____

3. Established a commission to regulate the railroads, their rates, and their services. _____

4. Made monopoly and restraint of trade illegal and criminal. _____

5. Outlawed quantity discounts and unrea-sonably low prices where their effect is to eliminate competition. _____

6. Prohibited the acquisition of the assets of a firm by another firm when such an acquisi-tion will lessen competition. _____

7. Had the effect of prohibiting false and misleading advertising and the misrepresenta-tion of products. _____

8. Clarified the Sherman Act and outlawed specific techniques or devices used to create monopolies and restrain trade. _____

9. Exempted resale price maintenance con-tracts from the provisions of the Sherman Act in those states in which state law allows such contracts. _____

■ SELF-TEST

Circle the T if the statement is true, the F if it is false.

1. The term "monopoly" in this chapter is taken to mean a situation in which a single firm produces a unique product and entry into the industry is blocked.   **T   F**

2. It is clear that on balance, business monopoly is detrimental to the functioning of the American economy.   **T   F**

3. Those who support the case for business monopoly contend that only big business is able to achieve significant economies of scale.   **T   F**

4. Those who emphasize the importance of workable competition as a device for the regulation of big business contend that the competitiveness of any industry should be judged almost solely on the basis of the number of firms in it and the barriers to entry.   **T   F**

5. The Federal government has consistently passed legislation and pursued policies designed to maintain competition.   **T   F**

6. The Federal courts are the final authority in interpreting the antitrust laws.   **T   F**

7. The Robinson-Patman Act was aimed at preventing firms from acquiring the *assets* of other firms where the effect would be to reduce competition.   **T   F**

8. The doctrine of technological determinism is one of the arguments advanced to support the view of those who advocate the restoration of vigorous and effective competition.   **T   F**

9. Those who propose the maintenance of the *status quo* as a policy for dealing with business monopoly argue that workable competition regulates big business.   **T   F**

10. Proponents of public regulation and ownership as a means of controlling business monopoly point to the success of the antitrust laws in limiting the growth of monopoly power.   **T   F**

Underscore the letter that corresponds to the best answer.

1. "Big business" in this chapter refers to which one of the following? (a) firms that are absolutely large; (b) firms that are relatively large; (c) firms that are either absolutely or relatively large; (d) firms that are both absolutely and relatively large.

2. Which of the following is *not* a part of the case *against* business monopoly? (a) monopolists charge higher prices than competitive firms would charge; (b) monopolists earn economic profits which they use for research and technological development; (c) monopoly leads to the misallocation of resources; (d) monopoly leads to greater income inequality.

3. An essential part of the case *for* business monopoly is that the operations of big business are regulated by: (a) pure competition; (b) monopolistic competition; (c) workable competition; (d) effective competition.

4. Which one of the following is *not* a part of the case *for* big business? (a) large firms have lower unit costs because they are able to use their power to depress resource prices; (b) large firms are led by socially responsible business executives who refuse to use their economic power in a way detrimental to the public; (c) large firms result in a more rapid rate of technological progress because they have both the resources and the incentives for research; (d) large firms are effectively regulated by interproduct, technological, and potential competition.

5. Which one of the following laws stated that contracts and conspiracies in restraint of trade, monopolies, attempts to monopolize, and conspiracies to monopolize were illegal? (a) Sherman Act; (b) Clayton Act; (c) Federal Trade Commission Act; (d) Robinson-Patman Act.

6. Insofar as its effect upon competition and monopoly is concerned, which one of the following acts has the least in common with the other three acts? (a) Wheeler-Lea Act; (b) Miller-Tydings Act; (c) Celler-Kefauver Act; (d) Clayton Act.

7. Which one of the following acts specifically outlawed tying contracts and interlocking directorates? (a) Sherman Act; (b) Clayton Act;

(c) Federal Trade Commission Act; (d) Wheeler-Lea Act.

8. Which one of the following acts has given the Federal Trade Commission the task of preventing false and misleading advertising and the misrepresentation of products? (a) Clayton Act; (b) Federal Trade Commission Act; (c) Robinson-Patman Act; (d) Wheeler-Lea Act.

9. Which one of the following is not characteristic of the Interstate Commerce Act of 1887? (a) it was based on the supposition that competition was unworkable in the railroad industry; (b) transportation was deemed essential to many individuals, firms, and industries; (c) it substituted government management and operation of the railroads for private management and operation; (d) the Interstate Commerce Commission was established to regulate railroad rates and services.

10. Which one of the following acts amended the Sherman Act to exempt resale price maintenance contracts from the antitrust laws? (a) Webb-Pomerene Act; (b) Miller-Tydings Act; (c) Robinson-Patman Act; (d) Celler-Kefauver Act.

■ DISCUSSION QUESTIONS

1. Explain the difference between the way the term "monopoly" is used in this chapter and the way it is used in Chapter 27. How can "big business" be defined? How is the expression used in this chapter?

2. What are the chief arguments in the case for business monopoly?

3. What are the chief arguments in the case against business monopoly? What empirical evidence is there to support this case?

4. Explain what is meant by "workable competition." How does it differ from pure competition, and what forms of competition does it include?

5. Against the argument that big business results in economies of scale (that is, mass-production economies) three counterarguments are often presented. What are they?

6. What are the "technological imperatives" that "have brought the corporate giant to a dominant role in the American economy"? What are the goals of the mature corporation and how does it attempt to achieve these goals, according to Galbraith?

7. In what way is the approach of the Interstate Commerce Act to the problem of monopoly different from the approach of the other antitrust laws? Why were the railroads (and later, other industries) subject to this approach?

8. What are the essential provisions of the Sherman Act?

9. The Clayton Act and the Federal Trade Commission Act amended or elaborated the provisions of the Sherman Act, and both aimed at preventing rather than punishing monopoly. What were the chief provisions of each of these acts, and how did they attempt to prevent monopoly? How has the power of the FTC been subsequently limited by the Federal courts?

10. What are the main provisions of each of the following acts? (a) Wheeler-Lea Act; (b) Robinson-Patman Act; (c) Celler-Kefauver Act.

11. How effective has antitrust legislation been in preventing monopoly and in restoring competition?

12. In what ways has the Federal government fostered the growth of monopoly? How did each of the following acts contribute to such growth? (a) Webb-Pomerene Act; (b) Miller-Tydings Act; (c) Robinson-Patman Act; (d) the various protective tariffs.

13. How do patent laws contribute to the growth of monopoly power? (In your answer, mention patent pools and tying agreements.)

14. What are the three alternatives which are often suggested as future policies for dealing with business monopoly? What arguments can you present to support each of these policies?

15. Explain the difference between "workable" and "effective" competition.

RURAL ECONOMICS:
THE FARM PROBLEM

Probably no economic problem has aroused public interest to the extent and for the number of years that the farm problem has. It has concerned not only those directly engaged in agriculture or living and working in agricultural areas but also every American consumer and taxpayer. Other problems seem to come and go; the farm problem seems always to have been with us.

Chapter 35 is devoted exclusively to an examination of rural poverty and the farm problem—the second of the seven specific trouble spots studied in this part of the book. The chapter opens with a brief history of the experiences of American farmers. The *symptoms* of the farm problem are declining farm prices, declining farm incomes, farm incomes which are low relative to the incomes of nonfarm families, and a highly unequal distribution of farm income among farm families.

The symptoms of the farm problem, however, are not the same thing as the *causes* of the farm problem. If the problem is to be solved, it is necessary to understand what has occasioned the straits in which agriculture finds itself. In fact, as the author points out, the failure to solve the problem has been brought about by the failure to understand and treat its causes. Actually there are two farm problems, a long-run problem and a short-run problem. Each problem has its own particular causes, and the next major section of the chapter deals with the two problems.

The long-run problem is that farm prices and farm incomes have tended to decline relatively over the years. To understand the causes of this problem, the student is asked to make use of his knowledge of the concept of inelasticity of demand and his knowledge of the effect upon price and total receipts of a large increase in supply and a small increase in demand. Why demand tends to be inelastic for agriculture products and why supply has increased so much more than demand is explained, but it is up to the student to see how these two causes, plus the relative immobility of agricultural resources, give rise to the symptoms of the long-run farm problem.

The short-run farm problem is that farm prices and farm incomes tend to fluctuate sharply from year to year. The cause of this problem is again the inelasticity of demand for agricultural products. Under such conditions relatively small year-to-year changes in either demand or supply will result in relatively large changes in the prices and total income received by farmers. To understand the short-run farm problem, the student is required again to make use of his knowledge of supply and demand.

The policies of the Federal government in dealing with the farm problem (the farm program) have been directed at raising farm incomes by supporting farm prices. In connection with the support of farm prices the student is introduced to the concept of parity. Once the student understands parity and recognizes that the parity price has in the past been above what the purely competitive price would have been, he will come to some fairly obvious conclusions. Not only did consumers pay a higher price and consume less but at the parity price there was a surplus of the commodity. The Federal government bought this surplus in order to keep the actual market price above the competitive market price. To eliminate these surpluses, government had to find ways to increase the demand for or to decrease the supply of these commodities. Programs to increase demand and to decrease supply were put into effect; but they did not succeed in eliminating the annual surpluses of farm products. Until 1973 agriculture in the United States had a problem which the farm program, for reasons explained by the author, had not been able to solve.

But in 1973 an economic boom came to American agriculture. No one can yet say whether this boom is temporary (and agriculture will in the near future again face the same old problem) or permanent (and agriculture in the years to come will feature rising prices, increasing farm incomes, and shortages). The causes of the boom are explained and its consequences are spelled out. During 1973 Congress also enacted a new farm program designed to increase farm production, reduce the extent of government involvement in agriculture, and decrease the importance of subsidies and price supports. The student should be warned that should this boom prove to be permanent the economic welfare of farmers may improve but American households may have to pay higher prices for and consume less food than they have in the years when agriculture was a sick industry.

■ CHAPTER OUTLINE

1. A history of American agriculture in the twentieth century makes it clear that agricultural prices and farm incomes have fluctuated with changes in demand; and that there has been a general tendency for the prices received by farmers and their incomes to decline.

2. The evidence also makes it clear that farmers are, on the average, poorer than people not engaged in farming; that the distribution of income among farmers is highly unequal; and that rural poverty is exceedingly common.

3. The farm problem is both a long-run and a short-run problem. The symptoms of the former are the relative decreases in farm incomes and prices which have occurred over the years; and the symptoms of the latter are the sharp changes in farmers' incomes from year to year.

  a. The causes of the long-run problem are the inelastic demand for farm products, the large increases in the supply of these products which have taken place relative to modest increases in the demand for them, and the relative immobility of agricultural resources.

  b. The cause of the short-run problem is the inelastic demand for agricultural products: relatively small changes in demand or supply result in relatively large changes in agricultural prices and farm incomes.

  c. The long-run problem is, therefore, the result of four factors, and the short-run problem is the result of inelastic demand.

  d. Another explanation of the long-run problem is that as the American economy grew and improved its agricultural technology, it reallocated too small an amount of its resources away from agriculture and into the nonagricultural sectors of the economy.

4. Those who represent the farmer claim that he has a special right to assistance from the government.

  a. Farmers have been successful in obtaining various forms of public aid, and the policy of the Federal government toward agriculture has included programs designed to raise farm prices and incomes.

  b. The parity price of any agricultural product would give the farmer the same real income per unit of output year after year.

  c. The farm program of the government has supported farm prices at some percentage of the parity price. But because the parity price has almost always been above the purely competitive market price, government has had to support the parity price by purchasing and accumulating expensive surpluses of these agricultural commodities.

d. To reduce the annual and accumulated surpluses, government has attempted to reduce supply by means of acreage-allotment and soil bank programs and to expand demand by means of a variety of programs.

5. The farm program has been largely unsuccessful in raising farm prices and incomes because it has failed to move resources out of agriculture and because the major benefits have not been directed toward the low-income families.

6. Economic conditions in American agriculture changed substantially during the early 1970s.

a. Increased foreign demand, poor harvests abroad, devaluation of the dollar, the opening of markets in Communist nations, and increased incomes in the United States all worked to expand the total demand for the output of American farmers.

b. The immediate consequences were higher farm prices, the disappearance of excess productive capacity and reserve stockpiles, and some increase in net farm incomes.

c. New farm legislation was passed in 1973 to lessen government involvement and to make agricultural markets more nearly free markets by replacing price supports with target prices, by encouraging production, and by limiting the size of the subsidy any one farmer might receive.

■ IMPORTANT TERMS

Farm problem
Long-run farm problem
Short-run farm problem
Farm program
Agricultural Adjustment Act
Parity
Price support
Parity price

Public Law 480
Food for Peace program
Acreage-allotment program
Acreage-reserve (soil bank) program
Agricultural and Consumer Protection Act
Target price

■ FILL-IN QUESTIONS

1. What was the economic condition—prosperity or depression—of American agriculture in each of the following periods?

a. 1894 to 1914: _____

b. 1914 to 1920: _____

c. 1920 to 1940: _____

d. 1940 to 1950: _____

e. 1950 to 1973: _____

2. The per capita farm income tends to be _____ than per capita nonfarm income, and the distribution of farm income is _____

3. The long-run farm problem is one of _____ and the short-run farm problem is one of _____

4. The basic causes of the long-run farm problem are _____, _____, and _____

5. The demand for farm products tends to be inelastic because _____

6. The supply of farm products has increased rapidly since about the time of World War I because of _____

7. The demand for agricultural products in the United States has not increased as rapidly as the supply of these products because _____ and _____

8. The price system has failed to reallocate farmers into occupations earning higher incomes because as resources, farmers, their land, and their capital are highly _____

9. The basic cause of the short-run farm problem is the _____ demand for agricultural commodities, and this contributes to unstable farm prices and incomes in two ways. Relatively _____ changes in the output of farm products result in relatively _____ changes in farm prices and incomes, and relatively _____ changes in demand result in relatively _____ changes in prices and incomes.

10. As the American economy has grown and improved its agricultural technology, it has failed to reallocate _____ from _____ to _____

11. Two of the reasons advanced to support the farmers' claim to assistance from the Federal government are the contentions that agriculture:

a. Has borne too large a share of the _____
_____
of _____ in the U.S.

b. Sells its products in _____ markets and is unable to control the _____ _____ of these products.

12. The "farm program" is actually a series of programs concerned with (*a*) farm _____
_____,
_____,
and _____;
(*b*) _____; (*c*) _____;
(*d*) _____; (*e*) _____;
etc. In practice the principal aim of the farm program has been to _____

13. If a farmer receives a parity price for his product, he is guaranteed that year after year a _____
output will enable him to acquire _____
_____

14. If the government supports farm prices at an above-equilibrium level, the result will be _____ which the government must _____ in order to maintain prices at their support levels.

15. To bring the equilibrium level of prices in the market up to their support level, government has attempted to _____
the demand for and to _____
the supply of farm products.

16. Two programs employed by the government to reduce agricultural production are the
_____

and the _____
programs. To increase demand it has attempted to find _____
for agricultural commodities, to increase ____
_____,
and to _____
more agricultural products.

17. The farm program has not been successful in solving the farm problem because it has not _____
resources and it has most benefited those farmers who _____
_____

18. List five causes of the recent sharp increase in the demand for the products of American farms.

a. _____
b. _____
c. _____
d. _____
e. _____

19. This sharp increase in demand has increased the _____ of farm products in the United States, reduced excess productive _____ and the _____ of grain, and increased the net _____ of farmers.

20. The new farm program of 1973 will tend to (increase, decrease, leave unchanged) ____
_____ the extent of government involvement with agriculture; and resulted in the
_____
Act of 1973 which replaces price supports with _____ prices and limits the total subsidy that may be paid to an individual farmer to $_____ a year.

■ PROBLEMS AND PROJECTS

1. The following table gives the index of prices farmers paid in three different years. The price farmers received in year 1, the base year, for a certain agricultural product was $.35 per bushel. Complete the table by computing the parity prices of the product in years 2 and 3.

Year	Index of prices farmers paid	Parity price of product
1	100	$.35
2	120	_____
3	200	_____

2. In columns 1 and 2 in the table below is a demand schedule for agricultural product X.

(1) Price	(2) Bushels of X demanded	(3) Bushels of X demanded
$2.00	600	580
1.80	620	600
1.60	640	620
1.40	660	640
1.20	680	660
1.00	700	680
.80	720	700
.60	740	720

a. Is demand elastic or inelastic in the price range given? _____

b. If the amount of X produced should increase from 600 to 700 bushels, the income of producers of X would _____

from $_____ to $_____;

an increase of _____% in the amount of X produced would cause income to _____

_____ by _____%.

c. If the amount of X produced were 700 bushels and the demand for X changed from that shown in columns 1 and 2 to that shown in columns 1 and 3, the price of X would

_____

from $_____ to $_____;

the income of farmers would _____

from $_____ to $_____

d. Assume that the government supports a price of $1.80, that the demand for X is that shown in columns 1 and 2, and that farmers grow 720 bushels of X. There will be a surplus

of _____

bushels of X, and if the government buys this surplus at the support price, the cost to the government will be $_____

e. Assume that instead of supporting a price of $1.80 as it did in (*d*), the government pays farmers the difference between $1.80 and the price they would receive in a free market. If demand and the output of farmers are the same:

(1) The free-market price will be $_____

and the government will pay farmers $_____ per bushel

(2) The total cost to the government of this program will be $_____

(3) The total cost of this program will be (greater, less) _____ than the cost of the program in (*d*), but the government will

have no problem of _____

(4) The total cost of this program will be greater than the cost of the program in (*d*)

because the demand for the product is _____

_____

3. The demand schedule for agricultural product Y is given in columns 1 and 2 of the following table.

(1) Price	(2) Bales of Y demanded	(3) Bales of Y demanded
$5.00	40,000	41,000
4.75	40,200	41,200
4.50	40,400	41,400
4.25	40,600	41,600
4.00	40,800	41,800
3.75	41,000	42,000
3.50	41,200	42,200

a. If farmers were persuaded by the government to reduce the size of their crop from 41,000 to 40,000 bales, the income of farmers would _____

from $_____ to $_____

b. If the crop remained constant at 41,000 bales and the demand for Y increased to that shown in columns 1 and 3, the income of

farmers would _____

from $_____ to $_____

■ SELF-TEST

Circle the T if the statement is true, the F if it is false.

1. The distribution of the total farm income among farmers in the American economy can be said to be a highly unequal one.   T F

2. Per capita nonfarm income is greater than per capita farm income.   T F

3. Most of the recent technological advances in agriculture have been initiated by farmers.   T F

4. The supply of agricultural products has tended to increase more rapidly than the demand for these products in the United States.   T F

5. The size of the farm population of the United States has declined at a more rapid rate than the rate at which agriculture's share of national income has declined.   T F

6. The size of the farm population in the United States has declined in both relative and absolute terms since about 1935.   T F

7. The quantities of agricultural commodities produced tend to be fairly *insensitive* to changes in agricultural prices because a large percentage of farmers' total costs are variable.   T F

8. Application of the parity concept to farm prices causes farm prices to decline and results in agricultural surpluses.   T F

9. The acreage-allotment and acreage-reserve programs are designed to decrease the supply of farm products.   T F

10. Restricting the number of acres which farmers employ to grow agricultural products has not been a very successful method of reducing surpluses because farmers tend to cultivate their land more intensively when the acreage is reduced.   T F

Underscore the letter that corresponds to the best answer.

1. Which one of the following periods has little or nothing in common with the other three insofar as the economic condition of American agriculture in the period is concerned? (a) 1900 to 1914; (b) 1914 to 1920; (c) 1920 to 1940; (d) 1940 to 1950.

2. Which of the following is *not* characteristic of American agriculture? (a) farmers sell their products in highly competitive markets; (b) farmers buy in markets which are largely noncompetitive; (c) the demand for agricultural products tends to be inelastic; (d) agricultural resources tend to be highly mobile.

3. If both the demand for and the supply of a product increase: (a) the quantity of the product bought and sold will increase; (b) the quantity of the product bought and sold will decrease; (c) the price of the product will increase; (d) the price of the product will decrease.

4. Which one of the following is *not* a reason why the increases in the demand for agricultural commodities have been relatively small? (a) the population of the United States has not increased as rapidly as the productivity of agriculture; (b) the increased per capita incomes of American consumers have resulted in less than proportionate increases in their expenditures for farm products; (c) the demand for agricultural products is inelastic; (d) the standard of living in the United States is well above the level of bare subsistence.

5. The price system has failed to solve the problem of low farm incomes because: (a) the demand for agricultural products is relatively inelastic; (b) the supply of agricultural products is relatively elastic; (c) agricultural products have relatively few good substitutes; (d) agricultural resources are relatively immobile.

6. If the demand for agricultural products is inelastic, a relatively small increase in supply will result in: (a) a relatively small increase in farm prices and incomes; (b) a relatively small decrease in farm prices and a relatively large increase in farm incomes; (c) a relatively large decrease in farm prices and incomes; (d) a relatively large increase in farm prices and a relatively small decrease in farm incomes.

7. Farm parity means that: (a) the real income of the farmer remains constant; (b) a given output will furnish the farmer with a constant amount of real income; (c) the purchasing power of the farmer's money income remains constant; (d) the money income of the farmer will buy a constant amount of goods and services.

8. If the price of a certain farm product were

$.75 in the base period when the index of prices paid by farmers was 90, and if the present index of prices paid by the farmer is 150, then the parity price of the farm product today is: (a) $.90; (b) $1.12½; (c) $1.25; (d) $1.50.

9. The necessary consequence of the government's supporting farm prices at an above-equilibrium level is: (a) a surplus of agricultural products; (b) increased consumption of agricultural products; (c) reduced production of agricultural products; (d) the dumping of agricultural products.

10. Which one of the following is not a reason why the farm program has been generally unsuccessful in accomplishing its aims? (a) the farm programs have not eliminated the basic cause of the problem; (b) restricting agricultural output increases farm prices but reduces farm income when demand is inelastic; (c) the human and nonhuman resources employed in agriculture have not been reduced and reallocated; (d) the principal beneficiaries of government aid have been farmers with high, not low, incomes.

■ DISCUSSION QUESTIONS

1. What was the economic condition of American agriculture: (a) prior to World War I; (b) during World War I; (c) from 1920 to 1940; (d) during World War II; (e) since 1950? Explain the fundamental causes of the condition of agriculture in each of these periods.

2. Comment on (a) the size of farm incomes relative to nonfarm incomes; (b) the trend of farm incomes relative to nonfarm incomes; (c) the distribution of total farm income among farmers.

3. What is the long-run farm problem and its specific causes? What is the short-run farm problem and its causes?

4. Why does the demand for agricultural products tend to be inelastic?

5. What have been the specific causes of the large increases in the supply of agricultural products since World War I?

6. Why has the demand for agricultural products failed to increase at the same rate as the supply of these products?

7. Explain why the farm population tends to be relatively immobile. If farmers were more mobile, how would the price system reallocate their labor away from agriculture and into more prosperous occupations?

8. Explain why the inelastic nature of the demand for and the supply of agricultural products results in prices and incomes which change by large amounts as a consequence of small changes in either demand or supply.

9. Why do agricultural interests claim that farmers have a special right to aid from the Federal government?

10. What is meant by "the farm program" in the broad sense? What particular aspect of the farm problem has received the major attention of farmers and their representatives in Congress?

11. Explain the concept of parity and what a parity price is.

12. What device does the government employ to support above-equilibrium agricultural prices? Why is the result of government-supported prices invariably a surplus of farm commodities?

13. What programs has the government used to try to restrict farm production? Why have these programs been relatively unsuccessful in limiting agricultural production?

14. How has the Federal government tried to increase the demand for farm products?

15. Why has the farm program not been successful in preventing falling farm prices and incomes, surpluses, and an unequal distribution of farm income?

16. Explain why American agriculture began to boom in 1973 and the consequences of this boom for the farmer and for the American economy.

17. In what ways does the new farm program initiated in 1973 differ from previous farm programs?

18. Was the agricultural boom of 1973 the result of a "peculiar combination of circumstances"—a windfall—or has American agriculture moved permanently to "an environment of full capacity and scarcity"—a watershed?

URBAN ECONOMICS:
THE PROBLEMS OF THE CITIES

The farmers whose economic problems were examined in the last chapter have tilled the soil since before the beginning of recorded history. Cities and the problems of city living are nearly as old. Cities have been plagued by crowded conditions, crime, disease, poverty, and pollution for as long as cities have existed. Like the problems of the farmers, the problems of the city are not entirely new. What makes the problems of the cities especially important in the United States today is the simple statistic that over two-thirds of the American population now reside in cities. (By way of contrast, only about one-twentieth of the population is engaged in farming.)

While the problems of cities may not be completely new, some of these problems have become more pressing than ever before. Other city problems are new and did not exist in the large cities of early recorded history. It is not possible in a single chapter to examine all the contemporary problems confronting American cities. The author, therefore, focuses his attention on the more crucial of these problems, their causes, and their potential solutions.

Economics is not the only discipline interested in the development of cities and their problems. Other social scientists and natural and physical scientists are concerned and contribute to the analysis of these problems and to their solutions. This is to say that city problems and solutions go well beyond economics. But economics is an essential part of the explanation of the development of cities, their current plight, and the steps necessary to the improvement of city living. And this is the subject matter of this chaper: the economic aspects of urban problems.

The organization of Chapter 36 is relatively simple. Professor McConnell first explains the economic reasons why cities emerge and grow by examining the economies of agglomeration. But as cities grow larger the disadvantages of agglomeration eventually appear. These deglomerative forces lead firms and families to the suburbs where they can enjoy the benefits of urban life without having to contend with its increasing problems. With this flight to suburbia comes political fragmentation and an economic imbalance between the central city and the suburbs. This historical development is the source of many of our current urban problems. The three problems given special attention by the author are transportation, pollution, and the ghetto. Each is examined in some detail and the possible solutions to each problem are considered. The final section of the chapter looks at the financial and institutional changes which may have to be made before any improvement in city living is possible. These changes include the political consolidation of the fragmented local governments, the employment of new methods of financing metropolitan governments, and the creation of entirely new cities.

The problem of the inadequate income of many of those who live in cities, especially in the ghettos, is not examined in great detail in this chapter. Poverty and the economics of inequality in the American economy is the trouble spot examined in Chapter 37.

■ CHAPTER OUTLINE

1. Today over two-thirds of the American population live in urban areas.

2. Economic forces have lead to the development and expansion of cities.

a. Firms can lower the cost of transporting resources and products by locating near their markets and other firms.

b. The increased productivity of agriculture has reduced the number of workers in farming. These excess workers have been drawn to cities where, because of the economies of agglomeration, business firms and jobs are located.

c. Only the large populations of urban centers have a demand for the amenities of life that is sufficient to warrant their production; and, as a result, consumers in cities find a wider variety of products available.

d. Deglomerative forces, sooner or later, limit the growth of central cities and the concentration of firms, and lead to the expansion of the suburbs and to business decentralization.

3. To reap the advantages of urban life and to avoid its disadvantages, firms and households have moved to the suburbs. This flight to suburbia and the resulting suburban sprawl have had at least two important consequences.

a. A large number of separate political units surround the central city.

b. Wealth and income have increased in the suburbs and decreased in the central city; and the central city has experienced a decline in its tax base while its problems and need for public revenue have expanded.

4. The flight to the suburbs has led to a locational mismatch of jobs and the labor force, automobile congestion and pollution, and the need for a more efficient transportation system.

5. The improvement of urban transportation requires solutions to both a short-run and a long-run problem.

a. To utilize the existing transport facilities more effectively entails the adoption of user charges and peak pricing policies.

b. To build a better transport system entails the development of public mass-transit systems.

6. Because of their high concentrations of population and industry, urban areas have a pollution problem.

a. The dimensions of the problem are well known and the long-run consequences are little short of terrifying.

b. The cause of the pollution problem is the material imbalance between the wastes that result from production and consumption and the ability of the environment to reabsorb these wastes.

c. To reduce pollution requires that the costs of pollution be made private instead of social costs (be transferred from society to the polluter); and this may be accomplished by legislating standards, levying special taxes on polluters, or by creating a market for pollution rights.

7. Another problem characteristic of cities is the central city ghetto of low income, nonwhite, inadequately housed, and poorly educated inhabitants.

a. The poverty of the ghetto can be reduced by providing more and better jobs, income maintenance, and better education and training for those who live there.

b. For a variety of reasons the environment of the ghetto has not yet been improved by subsidized housing and urban renewal.

8. Solutions to the various urban problems require that sufficient financial resources be allocated and that certain institutional changes be made.

a. Consolidation of the many political units would increase the efficiency of decision making and improve equity by putting the needs and the resources within the same governmental unit.

b. To obtain sufficient resources to deal with urban problems may also require Federal revenue sharing, the shifting of some of the burden to the Federal government, and a restructuring of the property tax.

c. Because of the problems currently facing cities and the expected 100 million expansion in the urban population within the next 30 years, entirely new cities may need to be built.

■ IMPORTANT TERMS

Economies of agglomeration	Peak pricing
Internal economies	Materials balance approach
External economies	Emission fees
Infrastructure	Political fragmentation
Deglomerative forces	
User charge	Black capitalism

■ FILL-IN QUESTIONS

1. About _____ million people and _____% of the American population live in cities today; and both these figures will probably _____ during the next 30 years.

2. Deciding how to produce goods and services includes the decision of _____ to produce them. This latter decision is an important one because there are _____ costs involved in moving _____ to the firm and in moving the finished products to _____.

3. Before cities can develop agriculture must be able to produce _____ food and fiber so that _____ is available to produce nonagricultural goods and services.

4. The economies of agglomeration refer to the lower production and marketing costs which firms realize when they locate _____ _____
The three such principal economies are:

a. _____

b. _____

c. _____

5. The deglomerative forces include all those forces which result in _____ production costs. Some of these are _____ to the firm; and others are _____,

are shifted to _____, and are called _____ costs.

6. The flight of people and firms to the suburbs enables them to obtain _____

_____

and to avoid _____.
The chief consequences of this movement have been political _____ and economic _____ between the central city and the suburbs.

7. The movement of the higher-income families and the wealthier firms to new political units in suburbia has:

a. eroded the _____ tax _____ and brought about increases in tax _____ in the central city;

b. left behind a central city of poor families, many of whom are _____ and on _____, living in _____ populated areas for which the cost of providing social facilities and services is _____.

8. The flight to the suburbs has also resulted in:

a. a locational mismatch because the _____ of those who live in suburbia are in the central city and of those who live in the central city are in suburbia;

b. the need for a more efficient _____ system;

c. expanded use of the _____, traffic _____, and air _____

d. the construction of still more _____ _____, the development of more distant _____, and still more _____ and _____

e. the general deterioration of the _____ _____ systems of the cities

9. It has been suggested that:

a. to relieve highway congestion there be _____ on drivers and that _____ _____ policies should be used on highways and mass transit systems;

b. in the long run it will be necessary to rebuild the _____ in urban areas.

10. The materials balance approach to pollution is that the _____ of the residual _____ produced by society has come to exceed the ability of _____ to _____ them. This imbalance is the result of increases in the nation's _____ and _____, changes in _____ and the absence of economic _____ to refrain from pollution.

11. The central city ghetto has developed in major American cities because:

a. the more _____ and better _____ whites have moved to the _____ and left behind obsolete _____

b. their places have been taken by poorly _____, unskilled, and _____-income Negroes from the rural _____

c. job opportunities for the ghetto inhabitants have shifted from the _____ to the _____; and access to these opportunities has been limited by the deterioration of the _____ system and racial _____

12. To alleviate poverty in the ghettos requires that their residents be provided with more and better _____, improved _____ and _____; and that a program of income _____ be instituted.

13. Bringing ghetto residents to the job opportunities in the suburbs will necessitate an improved _____. One way of creating new job opportunities in the central city is _____

14. The institutional and financial prerequisites to the solution of urban problems are political _____ and an increase in the _____ of urban governments.

15. Political consolidation will result in more efficient _____ making and reduce the disparity between _____ and _____ within urban areas.

16. The larger financial problem of urban areas will be reduced by political consolidation, Federal revenue _____, the shifting of some of the financial burden of cities to _____, and by overhauling the _____ tax so that _____ is taxed more heavily and _____ less heavily.

■ **PROBLEMS AND PROJECTS**

1. Below is a table showing the average number of motor vehicles traveling each mile of highway in a hypothetical metropolitan area and the estimated cost to society of each vehicle-mile traveled during various periods of the day. Compute the total cost per mile of highway in each of the seven periods of the day.

Period of the day	Vehicles per high-way-mile	Cost per vehicle-mile	Total cost
7am–9am	500	$ .60	$_____
9am–12n	150	.10	_____
12n–2pm	200	.15	_____
2pm–4pm	100	.10	_____
4pm–6pm	600	.85	_____
6pm–10pm	200	.15	_____
10pm–7am	50	.10	_____

a. In every twenty-four hour period the total number of vehicles traveling each mile of highway is _____ and the total cost for each mile of highway traveled is $_____

b. The average cost to society for a vehicle to travel one mile is $_____

c. Assuming that the number of vehicles per highway-mile is not affected by the imposition of a user charge and that the user charge is the same during all periods, the user charge that would enable society to recover the full

cost of the highway system would be $_____ per vehicle-mile

d. Imagine now that the imposition of this user charge results in the following change in vehicular traffic during the various periods of the day. The cost per vehicle-mile remains the same in each period; and the total cost in each period is shown in the table below.

Period of the day	Vehicles per high-way-mile	Total cost	Total revenue
7am–9am	450	$270.00	$_____
9am–12n	135	13.50	_____
12n–2pm	180	27.00	_____
2pm–4pm	90	9.00	_____
4pm–6pm	540	459.00	_____
6pm–10pm	180	27.00	_____
10pm–7am	45	4.50	_____

(1) The total cost per day of each mile of highway is $_____

(2) Compute the total revenue in each period when a 50 cents per mile user charge is made. The total revenue per day on each mile of highway is $_____

(3) In what two periods are the revenues received less than the cost in that period?

_____ and _____

e. If it is desired to reduce the number of vehicles per mile of highway in these two periods to 400; and if each 1 cent increase in the user charge decreases the number of vehicles per mile by 10 vehicles, the user charge in the:

(1) 7am–9pm period should be increased to

_____ cents per mile

(2) 4pm–6pm period should be increased to

_____ cents per mile

2. Assume the atmosphere of Cuyahoga County, Ohio (the Cleveland metropolitan

area), is able to reabsorb 1,500 tons of pollutants per year. The schedule below shows the price polluters would be willing to pay for the right to dispose of 1 ton of pollutants per year and the total quantity of pollutants they would wish to dispose of at each price.

Price (per ton of pollutant rights)	Total quantity of pollutant rights demanded (tons)
$ 0	4,000
1,000	3,500
2,000	3,000
3,000	2,500
4,000	2,000
5,000	1,500
6,000	1,000
7,000	500

a. If there were no emission fee, polluters would put _____ tons of pollutants in the air each year; and this quantity of pollutants would exceed the ability of nature to reabsorb them by _____ tons.

b. To reduce pollution to the capacity of the atmosphere to recycle pollutants, an emission fee of $_____ per ton should be set.

c. Were this emission fee set, the total emission fees collected would be $_____

d. Were the quantity of pollution rights demanded at each price to increase by 500 tons, the emission fee could be increased by $_____ and total emission fees collected would increase by $_____

3. Describe conditions in the central city ghetto by placing one or more of the adjectives in the list below after each of the following indicators of well-being.

high   crowded
low   grossly inadequate
inadequate   deteriorated
old   deplorable
poor

a. Schools: _____

b. Mortality rates: _____

c. Income levels: _____

d. Medical care: _____

e. Housing: _____

f. Crime rates: _____

g. Sanitation: _____

h. Disease incidence: _____

■ SELF-TEST

Circle the T if the statement is true, the F if it is false.

1. About 150 million Americans live in cities.
T F

2. External economies of scale shift a firm's average-cost curve downward.
T F

3. A deglomerative force increases the cost of producing a product and may be either internal or external to the firm.
T F

4. Since 1900 the percentage of the American population living in central cities has increased.
T F

5. The flight to the suburbs has involved the migration of families but has not resulted in the movement of business firms.
T F

6. The flight to the suburbs has brought about a general improvement in the public mass-transit systems of cities.
T F

7. Pollution is caused almost exclusively by profit-seeking business firms.
T F

8. An effective antipollution policy requires that the social costs of pollution be turned into private costs.
T F

9. Black capitalism entails the development of business firms in ghetto areas which are owned and operated by blacks.
T F

10. It has been estimated that improved employment opportunities for its residents will eliminate 90% of the ghetto poverty.
T F

Underscore the letter that corresponds to the best answer.

1. About what percentage of the American population lives in cities? (a) 85%; (b) 75%; (c) 55%; (d) 45%.

2. Deciding where to produce a product is a part of the decision a firm makes when it decides (a) what to produce; (b) how much to produce; (c) how to produce; (d) for whom to produce.

3. Which of the following will result in an internal economy of scale for firm A? (a) the growth of the market for firm A's product; (b) the development of other firms who are able to perform specialized services for firm A; (c) the expansion and improvement of the infrastructure; (d) the improvement of the transportation facilities employed by firm A.

4. The flight to the suburbs has had all but one of the following consequences. Which one? (a) political consolidation; (b) an economic imbalance between the central city and the suburbs; (c) an erosion of the property tax base in the central city; (d) a mismatch between the location of the labor force and the location of job opportunities.

5. Which of the following is *not* generally considered to be a step that would lead to the solution of the urban transportation problem? (a) the imposition of user charges on the highway system; (b) following a peak pricing policy on the public mass-transit systems; (c) the reconstruction and expansion of the mass-transit systems; (d) the construction of more and the expansion of existing highways to connect the central city with the suburbs.

6. Which of the following would do little or nothing to reduce pollution? (a) create a market for pollution rights; (b) charge polluters an emission fee; (c) enact legislation that prohibits pollution and fines polluters; (d) redesign and reconstruct the infrastructure.

7. Which of the following has probably been the most important cause of the emergence of black ghettos? (a) racial discrimination; (b) the flight to the suburbs; (c) the deterioration of public mass-transit systems; (d) high crime rates in the central cities.

8. The unemployment rate among blacks is (a) less than; (b) about the same as; (c) double; (d) triple the rate for whites.

9. Which of the following would do little by itself to solve the problems of the central city? (a) political consolidation; (b) increased use of local income taxes; (c) Federal revenue sharing with the cities; (d) reduced taxation of buildings.

10. The suggestion to overhaul the property tax system has been made (a) because the property tax is proportional; (b) to reduce land values; (c) as an incentive for the construction and improvement of buildings; (d) to increase the supply of land.

■ DISCUSSION QUESTIONS

1. Explain why firms must decide where to produce and why they tend to agglomerate.

2. What is the difference between an internal and an external economy? What are the principal economies which induce firms to locate near other firms?

3. What is a deglomerative force? What are the principal deglomerative forces internal to the firm? What deglomerative forces are external to the firm?

4. Explain the reasons for the flight of families and business firms to the suburbs. What families and kinds of firms have remained in the central city?

5. Explain in detail the two most important consequences of the flight to suburbia.

6. What are the causes of the urban transportation problem and what might be done to improve urban transportation systems? Include in your answer the user charge and peak pricing concepts.

7. Employing the materials balance approach, explain the causes of the pollution problem. What are the three major policies that might be adopted to reduce pollution and what problems would be encountered in applying these policies?

8. Explain why ghettos developed in central cities and describe living conditions in and the characteristics of the typical ghetto. What can be done to change these conditions?

9. What steps has government taken to stimulate the construction of new housing? Why have these programs failed to help low-income families in the central city?

10. What are the institutional and financial requisites to the solution of urban problems? Why are these changes necessary and how might they be accomplished?

THE ECONOMICS
OF INEQUALITY AND POVERTY

Chapter 37 examines the fourth of the so-called trouble spots in the American economy—the unequal distribution of the total income of the economy among its families and the poverty of many of its families.

The things which the student will learn are (1) the extent and the causes of income inequality in the United States; (2) the degree to which income inequality has changed in the past thirty-five years and since World War II; (3) why some people contend that income inequality is bad and should be reduced and why others argue that it is beneficial and should not be reduced; (4) how poverty is defined, how many poor there are, and where the greatest concentrations of poverty are in the American economy; (5) how racial discrimination contributes to poverty and income-inequality and the cost to the economy of this discrimination; (6) why the poor are "invisible" and caught in a "vicious circle"; (7) the two fundamental and opposing views of the cause of poverty; (8) the types of programs that are included within the American social security system and why this system is a "paradox"; (9) how the market approach to the problem of poverty would increase the economic opportunities of the poor; and (10) how the tax-transfer approach would employ the negative income tax to guarantee a minimum income to all citizens.

Several ideas are worth repeating here because of their importance to the whole discussion of inequality and poverty. First, the student will recall from Chapter 6 that one of the functions of government in the American economy is to modify the economic results which a *pure* price-market system would yield: it is the price-market system and the institutions of capitalism which bring about an unequal distribution of income, and government in the United States has worked to reduce—but not eliminate—this unequal distribution.

Second, the critics of the price-market system (see Chapter 5), including the socialists and communists, have attacked the system because of the inequality and poverty that it breeds; but capitalism has replied to its critics by reducing these faults and in so doing has maintained the faith of the American people in the price-market system as an efficient method of resource allocation. It is for this reason that the Socialist Party and other groups advocating drastically different economic systems have met with so little success in the United States.

Third, the single most effective method of reducing the importance of income inequality and the extent of poverty in the United States has been the maintenance of full employment and an expanding average standard of living.

Other programs have aided in the achievement of this goal, but the best cure has been the high and ever-increasing output of the American economy.

Fourth, very few people advocate an absolutely equal distribution of income; the question to be decided is not one of inequality or equality, but of how much or how little inequality there should be. The question can be looked at either ethically or economically, and the economist has nothing to offer on the ethical question but his own personal value judgment. From the economic point of view the question is what *degree* of income inequality will result in the most efficient allocation and the highest level of employment of resources. The pros and cons of the income-inequality issue represent no more than different opinions on what degree of inequality will bring about full employment and full production.

Finally, while poverty is caused by many forces, it is essentially an economic problem. Any attack on poverty will have to be basically an economic attack. There are reasons why the problem of poverty may not be solved in the United States; but one of these reasons is not that the American economy cannot afford to abolish poverty. The costs of poverty far outweigh the costs of eliminating it; and surely the richest nation in the world can afford what it costs to provide the necessities of life for all of its citizens.

■ CHAPTER OUTLINE

1. The facts concerning the extent of income inequality and of poverty in the United States can be seen by examining distribution-of-income tables.

a. The impersonal price system does not necessarily result in a distribution of income which society deems just; at least five specific factors explain why income inequality exists.

b. Since 1929 the real incomes received by all income classes have increased; and between 1929 and 1944 the relative distribution of personal income changed to reduce income inequality. But since 1944 the relative distribution has been almost constant; and the income gap between the richest and the poorest families has widened.

c. The relative distribution of income after

taxes is about the same as it was before taxes were collected; and there is little movement of families from one income class to another class over the years.

d. Whether income equality is desirable or not is open to debate. Those who attack it contend that it results in reduced consumer satisfaction, lower productivity, fewer occupational opportunities for the lower income groups, and social and political inequality.

e. Income inequality is defended primarily on the grounds that it makes a large volume of saving (and, therefore, investment) possible; that it furnishes incentives to work, produce, and innovate; and that it provides the higher incomes which subsidize the development of new products and cultural progress.

f. While equality in the distribution of income does not appear to be desirable, the economy must determine the degree of inequality that is desirable.

2. Using the generally accepted definition of poverty, over one-tenth of the people in the American economy live in poverty. These poor tend to be concentrated among poorly educated and trained, aged, agricultural, manless, physically unhealthy, nonwhite, and unemployed families in which there are many children.

3. The greater incidence of poverty among nonwhites is in part the result of racial discrimination.

a. This racial discrimination is found in the wage, employment, occupation, human-capital, and other forms of discrimination to which nonwhites are subject.

b. The costs of this discrimination to the economy are estimated at 4% of the GNP.

4. Poverty in the United States tends to be both invisible and self-perpetuating.

a. American poverty is obscured by the general affluence of the economy as a whole and by the fact that much of the poverty is hidden from the eyes of the remainder of society.

b. Poverty also tends to be self-perpetuating: The children of the poor in one generation become the poor families of the next generation.

5. There are two fundamental and opposing philosophies regarding the cause of poverty and the policies to deal with it.

a. One view is that the poor are responsible for their own plight and government should not help them.

b. The opposing view is that poverty is the result of social forces beyond the control of the individual and that society as a whole must assist the poor.

c. The evidence indicates that most of those who are poor are unable to help themselves.

6. The social security system of the United States has three principal programs.

a. OASDI is the national social insurance program financed by taxes levied on employers and employees.

b. The fifty state governments have unemployment insurance programs.

c. A variety of public assistance programs provide aid for the aged and blind, the disabled, and dependent children.

d. It is paradoxical that while the United States has various welfare programs to assist the poor, these programs tend to benefit least those who most need help.

7. Two basic techniques or approaches may be utilized to reduce poverty and income inequality in the United States.

a. The market approach would expand the economic opportunities of low-income workers by improving their education and skills.

b. The tax-transfer approach would guarantee a minimum income to all citizens by instituting a negative income tax.

■ IMPORTANT TERMS

Income inequality

Poverty

Old age, survivors, disability, and health insurance

Medicare

Unemployment insurance

Guaranteed income

Negative income tax

■ FILL-IN QUESTIONS

1. It can fairly be said that the extent of income inequality in the United States is ___

_____

2. The important factors which explain income inequality are differences in _____

_____,

_____,

and _____,

the unequal distribution of _____,

and the unequal distribution of _____, among the population.

3. The percentage of total personal income received by the highest quintile has _____

_____

since 1929 and these changes can fairly be

said to have been _____; but since the close of World War II the distribution of personal income in the United

States has _____

4. In the United States:

a. The _____ and the _____ distributions of income are not noticeably different.

b. There is not much _____ of income receivers between different income classes.

5. Those who condemn income inequality contend that it reduces _____,

_____,

and _____;

and that it fosters _____ inequality.

6. The defenders of income inequality argue

that it results in _____,

_____,

and _____

7. Using the more or less official definition of poverty,

a. The poor includes any family of four with

less than _____ and any individual with

less than _____ a year to spend.

b. Approximately _____% of the

population and about _____ million people are poor.

8. While there is no "typical" poor family, the families of the nation living in poverty tend to be concentrated among certain groups. These groups are:

a. _____

b. _____

c. _____

d. _____

e. _____

f. _____

g. _____

h. _____

9. The median income of nonwhites is only about _____% of the median income of whites because of _____ which has the following four principal economic dimensions.

a. _____

b. _____

c. _____

d. _____

10. What four reasons explain why in the affluent American economy those living in poverty remain hidden or invisible?

a. _____

b. _____

c. _____

d. _____

11. There are two conflicting philosophies regarding the source of poverty. One philosophy contends that poverty is due to _____

_____

and that government should not help the poor; the other argues that the cause of poverty is

_____

and that the poor must be helped by the government.

12. The three parts of the social security

system in the United States are _____

_____

insurance, _____

insurance, and _____

13. The paradox of the welfare programs of the United States is that these programs tend to be of _____ benefit to those who need economic assistance the _____

14. The market approach to the reduction of poverty entails increasing the economic _____ _____ of the low-income workers by improving their _____ and _____

15. The tax-transfer approach to poverty would guarantee the poor a _____ by making provisions in the Federal tax laws for a _____ tax.

■ PROBLEMS AND PROJECTS

1. The distribution of personal income among consumer units in a hypothetical economy is shown in the table at the top of page 275.
a. Complete the table by computing:
(1) The percentage of all consumer units in each income class and all lower classes; enter these figures in column 4.
(2) The percentage of total income received by each income class and all lower classes; enter these figures in column 5.
b. From the distribution of income data in columns 4 and 5 it can be seen that:
(1) Consumer units with less than $3,000 a year income constitute the lowest _____%
of all consumer units and receive _____% of the total personal income.
(2) Consumer units with incomes of $7,500 a year or more constitute the highest _____%
of all consumer units and receive _____% of the total personal income.

2. On page 275 is a table containing different possible earned incomes for a family of a certain size.

(1) Personal income class	(2) Percentage of all consumer units in this class	(3) Percentage of total income received by this class	(4) Percentage of all consumer units in this and all lower classes	(5) Percentage of total income received by this and all lower classes
Under $2,000	18	4	_____	_____
2,000–2,999	12	6	_____	_____
3,000–3,999	14	12	_____	_____
4,000–4,999	17	14	_____	_____
5,000–7,499	19	15	_____	_____
7,500–9,999	11	20	_____	_____
10,000 and over	9	29	_____	_____

Earned income	Income deficit	Income subsidy	Total income
$ 0	$_____	$_____	$_____
1,000	_____	_____	_____
2,000	_____	_____	_____
3,000	_____	_____	_____
4,000	_____	_____	_____
5,000	_____	_____	_____

a. Assume that $5,000 is the minimum income desirable for a family of this size. Compute the income deficit at each earned income level and enter them in the table.

b. Assume the negative income tax rate is 60%. Enter the income subsidy and the total income at each level of earned income in the table.

c. This negative income tax program retains incentives to work because whenever the family earns an additional $1,000 the income subsidy decreases by only $_____ and total income increases by $ _____

d. But this program does not result in a total income of $5,000 for the family unless its earned income is $_____

e. Complete the table in next column to show the amount of income subsidy the family would have to receive in order to make its total income $5,000. Income subsidies of this size would ensure the family a minimum income of $5,000; but would destroy incentives to work because whenever the family earns an addi-

Earned income	Income subsidy	Total income
$ 0	$_____	$5,000
1,000	_____	$5,000
2,000	_____	$5,000
3,000	_____	$5,000
4,000	_____	$5,000
5,000	_____	$5,000

tional $1,000 its income subsidy would decrease by $_____ and its total income would increase by $_____

f. Below is another table showing the different possible earned income levels for a family of a certain size.

Earned income	Income deficit	Income subsidy	Total income
$ 0	$_____	$_____	$_____
1,000	_____	_____	_____
2,000	_____	_____	_____
3,000	_____	_____	_____
4,000	_____	_____	_____
5,000	_____	_____	_____

(1) Assume that $5,000 is still the minimum income desirable for a family of this size; but that the income deficit is found by subtracting earned income from $8,333⅓. Compute the income deficit at each level of earned income and enter them in the table.

(2) Assume the negative income tax rate is still 60% of the income deficit. Compute the income subsidy at each earned income level; and the total income. Enter these amounts in the table.

(3) This negative income tax program maintains incentives to work because whenever earned income increases by $1,000 the subsidy decreases by $_____ and total income increases by $_____

(4) It also ensures that the family, no matter what its earned income is, receives a total income of $_____ or more; but results in total incomes in excess of $5,000 if the family has an earned income greater than

$_____

■ SELF-TEST

Circle the T if the statement is true, the F if it is false.

1. According to the author of the text, there is considerable income inequality in the United States.   **T   F**

2. Since 1929 the percentage of total personal income received by consumer units in the highest income quintile has decreased.
                                                    T   F

3. The greater incidence of poverty among nonwhites is, for the most part, attributable to racial discrimination.   **T   F**

4. Those who defend income inequality contend that it results in a higher level of consumption spending and thereby promotes a higher level of aggregate demand, output, and employment in the economy.   **T   F**

5. Using the semiofficial definition of poverty, some 12% of the population of the United States is poor.   **T   F**

6. The incidence of poverty tends to be greater among the unhealthy than the healthy segments of the population.   **T   F**

7. In percentage or relative terms the before-tax and after-tax distributions of income in the United States are approximately the same.

8. The paradox of the welfare state is that the United States has a higher per capita income than all other nations, but a less developed social security system than most other countries in the world.   **T   F**

9. The "vicious circle of poverty" refers to the fact that poverty tends to be passed on from generation to generation.   **T   F**

10. Of the two philosophies of poverty, one contends that poverty is caused by social forces beyond the control of the individual and the other believes that poverty is due to government interferences with the price-market system.   **T   F**

Underscore the letter that corresponds to the best answer.

1. Approximately what percentage of all American families have personal incomes of over $15,000 annually? (a) 5%; (b) 10%; (c) 15%; (d) 20%.

2. Approximately what percentage of all American families have personal incomes of less than $3,000 a year? (a) 5%; (b) 10%; (c) 15%; (d) 20%.

3. Which of the following would be evidence of a decrease in income inequality in the United States? (a) a decrease in the percentage of total personal income received by the lowest quintile; (b) an increase in the percentage of total personal income received by the highest quintile; (c) an increase in the percentage of total personal income received by the four lowest quintiles; (d) a decrease in the percentage of total personal income received by the four lowest quintiles.

4. In the post-World War II period there has been: (a) a significant decrease in the percentage of total personal income received by the highest quintile; (b) a significant increase in the percentage of total personal income received by the lowest quintile; (c) a significant increase in the percentage of total personal income received by the middle three quintiles; (d) no significant change in the percentage of total personal income received by any of the five quintiles.

5. Which of the following is *not* one of the contentions of those who condemn income inequality? (a) it is an obstacle to the maximization of consumer satisfactions; (b) it leads to social and political inequality; (c) it results in insufficient saving in the economy and thereby causes insufficient investment and an inadequate level of aggregate demand and unemployment; (d) it reduces the productivity of the economy's resources.

6. Poverty does not have a precise definition, but the more or less official definition of "poor" is any family of four and any individual with less to spend annually, respectively, than: (a) $3,700 and $1,800; (b) $4,000 and $2,000; (c) $4,000 and $1,500; (d) $3,000 and $2,000.

7. Which of the following groups is *least* apt to suffer from poverty? (a) farmers living in the South; (b) urban families in the North; (c) nonwhites with little education; (d) families headed either by a woman or an aged person.

8. Which of the following is *not* a cause of the invisibility of the American poor? (a) poverty in the cities is not easily seen from the more common means of transportation; (b) poverty in rural areas is not easily seen from the more common means of transportation; (c) poverty among the old and sick is not easily seen because these people seldom emerge from their dwelling places; (d) poverty among the unemployed is more than offset by unemployment compensation.

9. Which of the following is one of the three parts of the American social security system? (a) public housing; (b) agricultural subsidies; (c) unemployment insurance; (d) minimum wage laws.

10. A negative income tax would (a) reduce incentives to work; (b) fail to guarantee a minimum income to all people; (c) subsidize people who are not poor; (d) result in at least one but not necessarily all of the above.

■ DISCUSSION QUESTIONS

1. How much income inequality is there in the American economy? Cite figures to support your conclusion. What causes income inequality in American capitalism?

2. Has the distribution of income changed in the United States during the past 45 years? If it has, in what way, to what extent, and

why has it changed? Has income distribution changed in the past 25 or so years?

3. How do taxes affect the relative distribution of income in the United States? Does the passage of time tend to change the income class in which a family is located?

4. Is income inequality desirable? What are the arguments on both sides of this question? What does it mean to say that the "real problem is to find the optimum degree of income inequality"?

5. What characteristics—other than the small amounts of money they have to spend—do the greatest concentrations of the poor families of the nation *tend* to have?

6. In what ways does racial discrimination lead to a greater incidence of poverty among nonwhites than among whites? What is the economic cost to the nation of this discrimination?

7. What is the currently accepted and more or less official definition of poverty? How many people and what percentage of the American population are poor if we use this definition of poverty?

8. Why does poverty in the United States tend to be invisible or hidden?

9. What is meant by the "vicious circle of poverty"?

10. Is the problem of poverty primarily a problem to be solved by government or by individuals? What are the two opposing philosophies or viewpoints that would underlie the answer to this question? Which philosophy do you accept and why?

11. What is the "paradox of the welfare state" in the American economy? What are the three programs embodied in the social security system of the United States? In what ways do these programs contribute to the paradox?

12. What are the two approaches government may employ to attack the problem of poverty in the United States? Explain the difference between the two approaches and the kind of programs each approach requires. (Include in your explanation the notions of a guaranteed annual income and a negative income tax.)

UNIONISM, COLLECTIVE BARGAINING, AND WOMEN AT WORK

Another trouble spot in the American economy is in the area of labor-management relations. It is an area that is almost always in the news for one reason or another—strikes, new legislation, wage increases, union demands, and charges and countercharges by both employers and unions.

The labor union has become an important institution in American capitalism. Labor unions did not always occupy the position in the economy that they now do. The first part of Chapter 38 is devoted to a historical review of their development in the United States and is separated into three periods. The important thing for the student to see is that the growth and power of unions in each of these periods clearly depended upon the rights and recognition given to them by Federal law. At first the law repressed them, then it encouraged them, and finally it has sought to curb and control their greatly increased power.

In Chapter 31 the student learned how unions directly and indirectly seek to influence wage rates. The impact of the union upon its own membership, upon employers, and upon the rest of the economy is more than just a matter of wages, however. The third major section of Chapter 38 examines the contents of a typical contract between a union and an employer. The purpose of this examination is to give the student some idea of the goals which unions seek and other issues over which employers and employees bargain and upon which they must reach an agreement. Another extremely important idea which the student will find in the section is this: labor-management relations mean more than the periodic signing of a contract; they also mean the day-to-day working relations between the union and the employer and the new problems and issues not specifically settled in the contract which must be resolved under the general provisions of that contract.

The final section of the chapter examines the role of women in the labor force and in the labor markets of the American economy. This section explains why the percentage of American women who are members of the labor force is greater today than ever before; and why, therefore, the percentage of the labor force that is female is larger than it has ever been. It also explains why the average working woman earns less than the average working man. Part of this difference in earnings is the result of sexual discrimination; but another part is the consequence of rates of absenteeism and of labor force and job turnover which are higher among women than among men.

A final word of advice. The list of important

terms is long, but the student will find it worthwhile to master it. An understanding of the terms leads to a better understanding of the history and many of the issues and problems of labor-management relations.

4. In the last ten years the participation of women in the labor force has expanded significantly. But both because of discrimination and for sound economic reasons the average income of women is less than the average income of men workers.

■ CHAPTER OUTLINE

1. The history of labor unions in the United States can be divided into three periods or phases.

a. During the repression phase, between 1790 and 1930, the growth of unions was severely limited by the judicial application of the criminal conspiracy doctrine and by the refusal of many firms to recognize and bargain with unions; between 1886 and 1930 the AFL, following the union philosophy of Samuel Gompers, was able to organize many crafts and expand its membership.

b. Between 1930 and 1947, the encouragement phase, labor union membership grew rapidly, encouraged by prolabor legislation; and the CIO was formed to unionize industrial workers.

c. In the intervention phase from 1947 onward, government regulation and control of labor-management relations increased with the passage of the Taft-Hartley and Landrum-Griffin Acts.

d. The merger of the AFL and CIO in 1955 reunited the American labor movement.

e. Since the achievement of labor unity, the labor movement, facing both internal and external obstacles, has been unable to increase its membership by any substantial amount; but the number of unionized public employees has increased by a substantial amount since 1965.

2. Collective bargaining and the resulting work agreements are more often than not the result of compromise between labor and management; strikes and violence are actually quite rare.

3. The typical agreement between the employer and the union covers four basic areas. But collective bargaining is more than the periodic negotiation of an agreement; it also involves union and workers' security and day-to-day labor-management relations in an economy which is continually changing.

■ IMPORTANT TERMS

Criminal-conspiracy doctrine
Injunction
Discriminatory discharge
Blacklist
Lockout
Yellow-dog contract
Company union
Business unionism
Norris-La Guardia Act
Wagner (National Labor Relations) Act
National Labor Relations Board
Taft-Hartley (Labor-Management Relations) Act
Jurisdictional strike
Sympathy strike
Secondary boycott
Featherbedding
Closed shop

Union shop
Open shop
Nonunion shop
Right-to-work law
Checkoff
Reopening clause
Landrum-Griffin (Labor-Management Reporting and Disclosure) Act
Preferential hiring
Seniority
Arbitration
American Federation of Labor
Congress of Industrial Organizations
Two terms for review:
Craft unionism
Industrial unionism

■ FILL-IN QUESTIONS

1. Over _____ million workers belong to labor unions in the United States. This is approximately what percentage of the nonagricultural labor force? _____

2. During the repression phase of labor union history, union growth was slow because

_____

and _____

3. Unions were limited in their growth between 1790 and 1930 by courts which applied

the _____

doctrine to labor units and issued _____

_____
to prevent strikes, picketing, and boycotts.

4. Employers used the following nonjudicial means of retarding the growth of labor unions in the repression phase: _____

_____,

_____,

_____,

_____,

_____,

_____,

and _____

5. The philosophy of the AFL under the leadership of Samuel Gompers was _____

_____,

_____,

and _____

6. In the encouragement phase of labor union history, unions grew as a consequence of such favorable legislation as the _____

_____

and _____

Acts; and the _____,

based on the principle of _____

unions, was formed to organize the _____

_____

workers.

7. The National Labor Relations Act of 1935 guaranteed the "twin rights" of labor: the

right to _____

and the right to _____;

in addition it established the _____

and listed a number of _____

8. Three important events that occurred in the history of labor unions after 1946 were

the passage of the _____

and _____

Acts and the _____.
Some economists contend that in the 1955–1965 period union membership was almost

_____ and that the labor movement

was characterized by _____;

but since 1965 a large number of _____
employees have joined unions.

9. The four principal sections of the Labor-Management Relations Act of 1947 are:

a. _____

b. _____

c. _____

d. _____

10. The Landrum-Griffin Act of 1959 regu-

lates union _____

and _____

and lists the rights of _____

upon which _____
may not infringe.

11. A typical work agreement between a union and an employer covers four basic areas:

a. _____

b. _____

c. _____

d. _____

12. Labor and management tend to base their arguments for and against higher wages on

four points, namely, _____

_____,

_____,

_____,

and _____

13. Collective bargaining is concerned not

only with wage rates but also with the _____

_____

and _____
of unions and their numbers; and while negotiation of a work agreement is important __

and _____
the agreement are equally important.

14. The rate at which women participate in the labor force has _____ since World War II because of:

a. _____

b. _____

c. _____

d. _____

e. _____

15. The average earnings of a full-time female worker is only about _____% of the average earnings of a full-time male worker because of

_____

and _____

■ PROBLEMS AND PROJECTS

1. Below is a list of frequently employed terms, and following the terms is a series of identifying phrases. Match the term with the phrase by placing the appropriate letter after each of the phrases. (*Note:* All the terms will not be needed.)

A. Injunction
B. Blacklist
C. Lockout
D. Yellow-dog contract
E. Company union
F. Business union
G. Jurisdictional strike
H. Sympathy strike
I. Secondary boycott
J. Featherbedding
K. Closed shop
L. Union shop
M. Open shop
N. Nonunion shop
O. Checkoff
P. Craft union
Q. Industrial union

1. A worker must be a member of the union before he is eligible for employment. _____

2. A worker agrees when employed not to join a union. _____

3. A union open to all workers employed by a given firm or in a given industry. _____

4. A union organized and encouraged by an employer to prevent the formation of a union which might make "unreasonable" demands. _____

5. The deduction by an employer on behalf of the union of a worker's union dues from his wages. _____

6. A dispute between two unions over whose members are to perform a certain job. _____

7. A court order which forbids a person or group of persons to perform some act. _____

8. The closing of the place of employment by the employer as a means of preventing the formation of a union. _____

9. Concern of unions with better pay, hours, and working conditions rather than with plans for social and economic reform. _____

10. Payment of workers for work not actually performed. _____

2. Below is a list of provisions found in four important pieces of labor legislation. Identify the act in which the provision is found by putting either (A) for the Norris-La Guardia Act, (B) for the Wagner Act, (C) for the Taft-Hartley Act, or (D) for the Landrum-Griffin Act in the space following each provision.

a. Specified that contracts between a union and an employer must contain a termination or reopening clause. _____

b. Established a board to investigated unfair labor practices and to conduct elections among workers. _____

c. Guaranteed to workers the right to organize unions and to bargain collectively. _____

d. Declared that yellow-dog contracts were unenforceable and limited the use of injunctions against unions. _____

e. Regulated union elections and finances and guaranteed certain rights to union members in their dealings with the union and its officers. _____

f. Outlawed the closed shop, jurisdictional and certain sympathy strikes, secondary boycotts, and featherbedding. _____

g. Provided a procedure whereby strikes affecting the health and safety of the nation might be delayed. _____

h. Outlawed company unions, antiunion discrimination in hiring and discharging workers, and interfering with the rights of workers to form unions. _____

■ SELF-TEST

Circle the T if the statement is true, the F if it is false.

1. An injunction is a court order which declares that combinations of workmen to raise wages are illegal. **T   F**

2. Blacklisting was a device employed by early labor unions to cut off a firm's labor supply. **T   F**

3. Union membership has increased in every year since the end of World War II. **T   F**

4. The CIO was based on the principle of industrial unionism while the AFL was operated on the craft union philosophy. **T   F**

5. The Taft-Hartley Act lists a number of unfair labor practices on the part of management. **T   F**

6. Under the provisions of the Labor-Management Relations Act of 1947 the checkoff and featherbedding are prohibited. **T   F**

7. The Teamsters and the United Mine Workers are important unions not affiliated with the AFL-CIO. **T   F**

8. The four-points criteria employed by unions in arguing for higher wages can also be used by management to resist higher wages and to argue for decreased wages. **T   F**

9. Arbitration means the settlement of a dispute by a third party who renders a decision which the parties to the dispute have agreed in advance to accept. **T   F**

10. The difference between the average earnings of full-time female and male workers is only partly the result of sexual discrimination. **T   F**

Underscore the letter that corresponds to the best answer.

1. About what percertage of all nonagricultural workers are members of unions? (*a*) 23%; (*b*) 28%; (*c*) 33%; (*d*) 38%.

2. Which of the following would not be used by an employer to prevent the organization of a genuine union among his employees? (*a*) lockout; (*b*) featherbedding; (*c*) company union; (*d*) yellow-dog contract.

3. Which one of the following was an essential part of Samuel Gompers' union philosophy? (*a*) industrial unionism; (*b*) support of the Democratic Party at the polls; (*c*) establishment of producer cooperatives operated by labor and management; (*d*) business unionism.

4. The Norris-La Guardia Act outlawed: (*a*) yellow-dog contracts; (*b*) the closed shop; (*c*) company unions; (*d*) blacklisting.

5. The Wagner Act outlawed: (*a*) company unions; (*b*) the closed shop; (*c*) the checkoff; (*d*) injunctions against unions.

6. The Taft-Hartley Act outlawed: (*a*) the nonunion shop; (*b*) the open shop; (*c*) the union shop; (*d*) the closed shop.

7. Which one of the following is *not* a provision of the Landrum-Griffin Act? (*a*) allows a worker to sue his union if the union denies the member certain rights; (*b*) unions are prohibited from making political contributions in elections for Federal offices; (*c*) requires regularly scheduled union elections and the use of secret ballots; (*d*) guarantees union members the right to attend union meetings, to vote and to participate in the meeting, and to nominate union officers.

8. If workers at the time they are hired have a choice of joining the union and paying dues or of not joining the union and paying no dues, there exists: (*a*) a union shop; (*b*) an open shop; (*c*) a nonunion shop; (*d*) a closed shop.

9. Which one of the following is not presently an unfair labor practice? (*a*) the refusal of either unions or companies to bargain in good faith; (*b*) the coercion of employees by unions to join and by companies not to join unions; (*c*) the practices of company and business unionism; (d) both jurisdictional strikes and secondary boycotts.

10. About what percentage of the total labor force are women? (a) 44; (b) 39; (c) 33; (d) 28.

■ DISCUSSION QUESTIONS

1. What are the three phases in the history of labor unions in the United States? What was the law with respect to unions, what was the extent of unionization, and what were the principal events in each of these periods?

2. How were the courts able to retard the growth of unions between 1790 and 1930? How did employers attempt to limit union growth?

3. Explain the union philosophy of Samuel Gompers.

4. What were the chief provisions of the Norris-La Guardia Act and the Wagner Act?

5. Explain how the principles of the CIO differed from those on which the AFL was based.

6. Contrast the philosophy and policy embodied in the Wagner Act with that found in the Taft-Hartley Act.

7. What are the four main sections of the Taft-Hartley Act? What specific practices are outlawed by the act and what specific things are required of unions, union officers, and bargaining agreements?

8. Explain the major provisions of the Landrum-Griffin Act.

9. What were the forces which resulted in the merger of the AFL and CIO in 1955?

10. What do economists mean when they talk of stagnation in the labor movement in the United States? What evidence is there of stagnation? What are the probable causes of it?

11. Explain what usually constitute the "prerogatives of management."

12. What are the four arguments employed by labor (management) in demanding (resisting) higher wages? Why are these arguments "two-edged"?

13. What is meant by grievance procedure? Why is such a procedure so important in labor-management relations? In the typical labor-management contract found in the text, what are the four steps which may be used in settling grievances?

14. What is a right-to-work law? What arguments are presented in support of right-to-work laws by those who favor them? What arguments are advanced by labor unions in opposition to them?

15. Explain why the rate at which women participate in the American labor force has increased substantially in the last thirty-five years.

16. How does the economic status of working women compare with that of working men? How do you explain this difference?

THE ECONOMICS
OF WAR AND DEFENSE

War and national defense require that scarce resources be used to produce military hardware and to staff the armed forces. Because the employment of scarce resources is the subject matter of economics, war and defense are a part of the study of economics.

This chapter is *not* an examination of the case for and against war. It does not debate the issue of whether the United States employs too large or too small a portion of its resources for national defense. Appraising the *benefits* of American defense is beyond the professional competence of economists and the subject matter of economics. All that economists can do is estimate the cost and examine the effects of defending the nation upon the economy. And this is the purpose of Chapter 39: to look at national defense as a user of scarce resources.

There are a variety of things the student should learn from Chapter 39. The more important things he should learn are (1) the size of and the cost to the American economy of the war industry; (2) the ways in which the Department of Defense—the Pentagon—differs from and is like a privately owned business firm; (3) the process employed to procure military hardware in the product markets of the economy; (4) Galbraith's and Melman's criticisms of this process; (5) the reasons for

cost overruns in procuring military goods; (6) the case for and the objections to a volunteer army instead of conscription; (7) the effects of military expenditures on national output and employment and the price level; (8) the problems of obtaining the peace dividend that would be available to the economy if the United States were to disarm; (9) the arguments offered in defense of the war industry; and (10) the nature of the Schultze proposal.

■ CHAPTER OUTLINE

1. Current American military expenditures exceed $80 billion a year; and are about 40% of all Federal expenditures and 10% of the GNP.

2. The opportunity cost of the defense establishment equals the output of civilian goods and services sacrificed and depends upon the level of output the economy would produce if there were no defense expenditures.

3. A military establishment and its expenditures affect the allocation of the economy's resources.

a. Unlike a privately owned business firm, the military establishment does not sell its product in the market and is a nonprofit organization whose existence depends upon the existence of hostile military establishments in other nations.

b. The Department of Defense buys military hardware from private firms; and it has been suggested that they collude to raise the prices of military supplies and the size of the defense budget.

c. It is also contended that the DOD acts like a central-management office and military goods producers like its subsidiaries; and that motivated by the desire to expand, they have made unwise decisions.

d. The actual cost of procuring military goods often grossly exceeds the estimated cost because the DOD seems unable to control the costs of suppliers.

e. Using conscription to obtain military manpower conflicts with freedom of occupational choice.

f. A volunteer army, it is argued, is a means of distributing military manpower costs more equitably, lessening the real cost of the armed forces, and restoring individual freedom of choice.

g. Critics of the volunteer army contend that it increases the cost of maintaining an army and will produce a professional military force to threaten democracy and political freedom.

h. Critics contend that the armed forces make poor use of their manpower and have an excess number of commissioned and noncommissioned officers.

4. A military establishment and its expenditures affect the stability of the economy.

a. Changes in military spending have contributed to economic instability since World War II; and military expenditures have been closely linked historically with inflation.

b. Should disarmament occur, the economy would realize a peace dividend if it adopted proper fiscal and monetary policies and planned reconversion efficiently.

5. In defense of the defense establishment it can be argued that:

a. critics have laid too much of the blame for the problems of American society on the war industry and some of these criticisms seem unjustified.

b. the military establishment preserves the peace which is necessary to the growth of the economy.

6. The extensive size of the military establishment and the uses to which the resources it employs could be put in solving domestic social problems has led to the suggestion that a new method is needed to determine national priorities.

■ IMPORTANT TERMS

War industry   **Pentagon capitalism**
Military–industrial   **Peace dividend**
complex   **Cost overrun**

■ FILL-IN QUESTIONS

1. In 1973 the military expenditures of the United States were about $_____ billion, about _____ percent of the GNP.

2. The opportunity cost of the American defense posture is the _____ the economy foregoes by using resources for military purposes.

3. The military establishment is unlike a private business firm because it:

a. obtains its revenue from _____ and not from _____

b. is a _____ organization rather than a _____ seeking organization

c. depends for its existence upon the existence of _____

4. The methods employed by the Department of Defense to procure military goods from private business firms have been criticized and it is contended that:

a. the military and weapons suppliers have a common interest in increasing the _____

b. the military–industrial complex has become a state-management system in which the Pentagon behaves like a _____ office and military goods producers like its _____; and that the goal of this system is to _____

c. the military is unable to enforce effective _____ controls upon suppliers, extends interest free credit to suppliers in the form of _____, and allows contractors to _____ inventions financed by public money

5. Those who believe in the volunteer army contend that it more equitably _____ the cost of military manpower, that the cost of this manpower is _____ than the real cost of a conscript army, and that it results in greater freedom of _____

6. The objections to the volunteer army are that it has increased the _____ of maintaining an army and may produce an army of _____

7. Defense spending during wartime almost always results in inflation because governments fail to increase _____ by enough to prevent _____ inflation, and finance the war by _____ newly created _____

8. Changes in the amount of military spending since the end of World War II have contributed to the economic _____ of the American economy.

9. A peace dividend is the additional _____ _____ an economy would be able to produce if it decreased its production of ____

_____

10. To offset a large reduction in military expenditures requires that government do at least one of the following: _____ net taxes, _____ expenditures for nonmilitary goods, or follow a(n) _____ money policy.

11. In defense of the American military establishment it can be argued that:
a. in a growing economy it is possible to produce both more _____ goods and more _____ goods
b. expenditures for space and defense have resulted in significant _____ benefits for the civilian economy
c. cost overruns are found both in the _____ _____ sector of the economy and in the nonmilitary agencies of the public sector; and are probably the _____ consequence of the kinds of products and transactions involved.
d. military spending is inflationary only when government fails to employ the proper _____ _____ and _____ policies
e. military expenditures prevent a major military _____ and that this is a prerequisite for economic _____

12. Charles Schultze has proposed that a committee be formed to assess our _____ _____ and to evaluate our _____ and _____ needs.

■ PROBLEMS AND PROJECTS

1. On the graph below is a production possibilities curve showing the different combinations of military and civilian goods and services an economy is capable of producing.

a. If the economy were at point *A* and moved to point *B*, the production of military goods would have increased by _____; and the cost of this increased production of military goods would have been _____ civilian goods.

b. If the economy were at point *B* and moved to point *C*, the production of military goods would have increased by _____; and the cost of this increased production of military goods would have been _____ civilian goods.

c. If the economy were at point *D* and disarmament occurred so that the economy could move to point *E*, the peace dividend would be _____ civilian goods.

d. If the economy were at point *D* and the economy moved to point *A* as a result of disarmament, the peace dividend would be only _____ civilian goods.

■ SELF-TEST

Circle the T if the statement is true, the F if it is false.

1. Economists are better able to estimate the benefits than the costs of defense spending.   T F

2. If the economy fully employed its resources in the absence of any military expenditures, the opportunity cost of military preparedness is zero.   T F

3. To prevent a cutback in defense spending from bringing about a recession it would be appropriate to increase taxes and follow a tight money policy.   T F

4. Most military hardware is not produced in government operated arsenals but by privately operated business firms.   T F

5. Galbraith argues that the relationship of the Department of Defense to the giant corporate suppliers of war goods is bilateral monopoly; and that the prices paid are approximately competitive.   T F

6. A volunteer armed force has shifted a part of the cost of military manpower from draftees and reluctant volunteers to taxpayers.   T F

7. Since the end of World War II changes in military spending have resulted in economic instability in the American economy.   T F

8. It is not possible for an economy to produce both more military and more civilian goods.   T F

9. Defenders of the military argue that without a strong military posture peace is impossible and that without peace economic development and progress are impossible.   T F

10. Now that volunteers have replaced conscripts in the armed forces almost all criticism of the manpower policies of the military establishment has ended.   T F

Underscore the letter that corresponds to the best answer.

1. About what percent of the GNP and labor force of the American economy are used for military purposes? (*a*) 6%; (*b*) 10%; (*c*) 15%; (*d*) 20%.

2. Which of the following results in an overestimation of the size of the war industry? (*a*) failure to include the spillover benefits of military expenditures to the civilian economy; (*b*) the use of volunteer labor to staff the armed forces; (*c*) the exclusion of veterans' benefits from the Department of Defense budget; (*d*) the inclusion of expenditures for space and atomic energy in the budgets of the NASA and the AEC.

3. The military establishment is like a private business firm because they both (*a*) have a problem in selling their product; (*b*) are monopolists; (*c*) are monopsonists; (*d*) employ labor represented by large labor unions.

4. The notion that the Department of Defense acts like a central-management office and producers of military goods like its subsidiaries is referred to as (*a*) the war industry; (*b*) the military–industrial complex; (*c*) Pentagon capitalism; (*d*) mutual deterrance.

5. Which of the following is *not* a part of the case for the volunteer army? (*a*) the monetary cost of a volunteer army is less; (*b*) military manpower costs are more equitably distributed; (*c*) a volunteer army is more consistent with freedom of occupational choice; (*d*) young people make more rational decisions in choosing an occupation.

6. War almost always results in inflation because (a) the production of civilian goods decreases; (b) taxes rise; (c) governments fail to increase taxes; (d) governments borrow newly created money.

7. To prevent unemployment and recession should disarmament take place requires (a) a reduction in net taxes; (b) an increase in government nondefense expenditures; (c) an easy money policy; (d) at least one but not necessarily all of the above.

8. If society wishes to take a peace dividend in the form of more private consumption and investment (a) government nondefense expenditures should be increased; (b) tax rates should be reduced; (c) transfer payments should be reduced; (d) a tight money policy should be followed.

9. Those who would rebut criticism of the military put forth all but one of the following arguments. Which one? (a) military expenditures are always inflationary; (b) military expenditures result in significant spillover benefits for the civilian economy; (c) cost overruns are not peculiar to the military establishment; (d) more military goods and services do not require fewer civilian goods and services.

10. The proposal to establish a committee to assess national priorities came from (a) John Kenneth Galbraith; (b) Seymour Melman; (c) Charles L. Schultze; (d) Robert McNamara.

■ DISCUSSION QUESTIONS

1. Explain why military expenditures have risen from less than 1 percent of national output in the period prior to World War II to about 6 percent today.

2. In what three ways may the dollar-and-cents figures for military expenditures in the United States understate the overall cost of the war industry? What effects have military spending had upon consumption, industrial concentration, geographic concentration, and research and development activities?

3. What is meant by the opportunity cost of national security? When will this cost be zero and when will it be greater than zero? What does foreign experience suggest about the opportunity cost of the military establishment?

4. In what ways is the military establishment unlike a private business firm? Are they alike in any way?

5. Explain how the Department of Defense procures war goods and why this procurement method has been subject to severe criticism.

6. Explain: (a) Pentagon capitalism; (b) change order; (c) "buy in, get well later"; and (d) progress payment.

7. What is the case for the volunteer army? What are the objections to the volunteer army?

8. Explain (a) why conscription results in a large and discriminatory tax on draftees and how a volunteer armed force shifts this tax to society as a whole; and (b) why the real cost of a volunteer army is less than a conscripted army of the same size.

9. What are two criticisms of the manpower policies of the armed forces?

10. Does military spending lead to economic instability? Must it also result in inflation?

11. Explain what is meant by a "peace dividend." What fiscal and monetary policies should be followed if a potential peace dividend is to be realized? How does the mix of fiscal and monetary policies chosen determine the form in which this dividend is taken?

12. What are the structural problems that arise as a consequence of demobilization and disarmament?

13. What arguments can be put forth to defend the war industry and the military establishment against its critics?

14. What is the proposal advanced by Charles Schultze and why did he make this proposal?

THE RADICAL CRITIQUE:
THE ECONOMICS OF DISSENT

Chapter 40 is the last of the seven chapters concerned with the "Current Economic Problems" of the American economy. Unlike the first six chapters in this part of the text, Chapter 40 does not examine a particular trouble spot (such as monopoly, agriculture, the cities, poverty, etc.). Instead it asks if American capitalism is one big trouble spot or problem.

Those who see American capitalism as a giant sore spot are called radical economists, the New Left, or neo-Marxists. Their viewpoint is labeled the radical critique, radical economics, or the economics of dissent. It is their contention that modern capitalism, based on private property, the corporation, and the profit motive, is such a bad system that it ought to be abolished and replaced with a system of socialism. Their contention is essentially an updated or modern version of Marxian economics. Karl Marx argued that capitalism had brought about the tremendous rise in the standard of living in Western Europe; but that capitalism would eventually destroy itself. Its success, he believed, would lead to economic conditions which in turn would lead to the collapse of capitalism, revolution, and the coming of socialism. Chapter 40 begins, therefore, with a detailed examination of the radical economists' Marxian heritage and with an

analysis of the New Left's historical predecessor, the Old Left.

From the Old Left the author turns to an explanation of the two fundamental differences between orthodox economics—the kind of economics accepted by almost all economists, including the author of the text—and radical economics. These two differences are differences in approach or methodology. Orthodox economists, the radical economists argue, don't see what is really going on in the world around them. They either have their eyes closed or are rather simpleminded; and see harmony where there is actually conflict. Moreover, orthodox economists, the New Left contends, have too narrow a viewpoint. They look only at economic matters and disregard the other aspects of modern society; and within economics they devote their efforts to nit-picking while ignoring real and important economic problems.

The most important section of Chapter 40 is a summary of the way in which the radical economists view American capitalism. They see the economy dominated by a relatively few large monopoly corporations in league with the state (that is, the Federal government) and out to exploit workers and consumers. This exploitation leads to inequality in the distribution of income and wealth, alienation (which the student should be sure to define), an economy which irrationally and wastefully uses its resources, and imperialism which exploits underdeveloped nations. The radical economists agree that they don't like what they see in the American economy; and that what is needed is socialism. They don't agree at all on just what socialism is—on what a better economic system would be like.

The chapter concludes with a rebuttal by the orthodox economists. Their critique of radical economics has four parts. The first three parts add up to an attack on the objectivity of the radical economists. They are blinded by their preconceptions and ignore any facts that weaken their case. The fourth part is the most devastating in the view of most of their critics. They don't present any of the details of the better economic system which is to replace the capitalism which they detest. Rejecting both the market system and a bureaucratic government, they don't tell us how they are going to allocate scarce resources to satisfy the unlimited wants of society. The histories of France and Russia suggest that revolution and the elimination of an old system do not always bring about the introduction of a better system. And many, like Hamlet, would

... rather bear those ills we have
Than fly to others we know not of ...

■ CHAPTER OUTLINE

1. Radical economists reject the orthodox explanation of the operation of capitalism and the traditional analysis of the problems of a capitalistic society.

2. The radical explanation of capitalism builds upon the work of Karl Marx who examined the development of capitalism and concluded that capitalism would eventually collapse.

a. Marx argued that as capitalist economies expanded the factory system, improved technology, and increased material well-being, one class of men (capitalists) struggled with another class (workers) to take some of the workers' output from them.

b. The capitalists, fortified by the institution of private property, control the machinery and equipment (the capital) needed to produce goods; and driven by their desire for profits (surplus value), they employ their superior bargaining power to exploit workers and pay them a subsistence wage which is less than the value of their production.

c. Competition forces capitalists to reinvest their profits in more and better capital; and this capital accumulation not only expands the national output but also results in technological unemployment, in a growing Industrial Reserve Army, and in a declining rate of profit.

d. These events work to provide workers with a mere subsistence wage; to ever-increasing unemployment; and, in trying to prevent the profit rate from falling, to still further exploitation of workers.

e. Competition among capitalists in an atmosphere of falling profits and growing unemployment, Marx contended, would lead to the monopolization of industry by a few capitalists; and eventually, searching for cheap foreign labor and foreign markets for their products, to imperialism.

f. The ultimate result of the workings of capitalism is revolution by the workers, the overthrow of capitalism, and the establishment of a socialist state without classes.

3. There are, in the opinion of radical economists, two fundamental shortcomings in orthodox economics.

a. Orthodox economists see a harmony and the reconciliation of opposing interests in capitalism; but radical economists see an irreconcilable conflict between capitalists (and the government which they dominate) and the rest of society.

b. Orthodox economists, according to the radical economists, focus their attention only on the economic aspects of society, ignore the noneconomic aspects of modern capitalism, and fail to understand the real problems of society.

4. The radical economists have a modern version of Marx and see American capitalism in this light.

a. A small group of huge, multiproduct, multinational, monopolistic corporations dominate the American economy.

b. These corporate giants also dominate government and prevent the control of monopoly by government, obtain subsidies from tax revenues, and have government create markets for them.

c. The expansion of capitalism and of the corporate giants requires the expansion of markets and output; and creates new problems while it fails to solve old problems.

d. The first of these problems is the exploitation of laborers and consumers.

e. The second problem is the unequal distribution of income and of wealth.

f. Alienation, or the absence of decision-making power and the inability of individuals to control their lives, is a third problem.

g. A fourth problem is the irrational and wasteful use of resources to produce goods which do not fulfill consumer needs.

h. The last problem is the exploitation of the less developed nations of the world and is the result of imperialism.

i. Radical economists, while agreeing that the socialism which should replace capitalism ought not to be based on private profits and ought to be decent, human, and democratic, cannot agree on the exact nature of the new society.

5. In reply to the radical economists, orthodox economists, contend:

a. that radical economics is nonobjective because it ignores facts and interprets all events in terms of its conception of capitalism;

b. that this radical conception of capitalism is not consistent with reality;

c. that the problems of American capitalism cannot all be the result of ideology because other economies with different ideological bases have the same problems;

d. and that the radical economists have not explained the kind of system with which they would replace modern capitalism.

■ IMPORTANT TERMS

Radical economics
Old Left
Karl Marx
Capital
Class struggle
Bourgeois
Proletariate
Surplus value
Law of capitalist accumulation

Industrial Reserve Army
Monopoly capitalism
Imperialism
Dictatorship of the proletariate
New Left
Exploitation
Alienation
Participatory socialism

■ FILL-IN QUESTIONS

1. Man, according to Marx, is engaged in a perpetual struggle with _____ to obtain material wealth.

a. Simultaneously, some men attempt to improve their own material well-being by wresting output from _____

b. And under the capitalistic system this latter struggle is the struggle of _____ (or the _____) against _____ (or the _____)

2. Because of the institution of _____ _____, capitalists control the _____ and _____ necessary to produce goods and services; workers are dependent upon the capitalists for _____; and the capitalists are driven by their desire for _____ (or _____) to _____ workers by paying them a _____ which is less than the value of their output.

3. The accumulation of capital means that capitalists are forced by _____ to invest their _____ in additional and technologically superior _____ and _____; and capital accumulation results in an expansion of the _____, the substitution of _____ for _____, and a decline in the rate of _____

4. In an effort to offset a decline in the profit rate capitalists will increase their _____ _____ of the working class.

5. As capitalism continues to develop:

a. Marx reasoned that unemployment and falling profits would lead to the _____ of industry;

b. Lenin reasoned that the final stage of this development would be _____

6. Exploitation and unemployment would,

Marx predicted, eventually result in a _____ by the working class, the establishment of a dictatorship of the _____, the socialization of _____, the abolition of the _____ class, and finally in the formation of a _____ society.

7. The radical economists find two major methodological deficiencies in the orthodox approach to economics; and believe:

a. the orthodox economists have an incorrect perception of reality and see _____ where there is actually _____;

b. orthodox economics as a discipline is too _____, is too remote from the real _____ of society, and fails to recognize the importance of _____ in capitalistic societies.

8. In the radical conception of capitalism:

a. the economy is dominated by _____ corporations which also dominate the _____ _____, depend upon finding new _____ for their ever-increasing production, and exploit both _____ and _____;

b. capitalism brings about income _____ _____, the _____ of individuals, the _____ use of society's resources, and _____ beyond the economy's national boundaries;

c. these evils can be eliminated only by replacing capitalism with _____.

9. What are the three ways in which government is alleged by the radical economists to cater to the large corporations?

a. _____

b. _____

c. _____

10. Orthodox economists argue that the wage rate of workers will equal their _____

_____; and that all resources will receive a reward (or income) in proportion to their contribution to the production of the

_____.

But the radical economists challenge this theory by arguing:

a. that these conclusions are true only when markets in the economy are _____;

b. capital goods were created by past _____;

c. and while capital goods are productive, the capitalist is not productive and his income from the ownership of capital is _____

11. Radical economists contend that the causes of inequality in the distribution of income and wealth in the United States are the capitalistic _____; and these include private _____, economic _____, and political _____

12. Alienation:

a. means that individuals have little control over their _____ and are remote from the _____-_____ process;

b. is primarily the result, in the view of radical economists, of the dominance and size of

_____

13. It is the view of radical economists that capitalism uses its resources irrationally and engages in wasteful production.

a. The primary cause of this is the capitalist's pursuit of _____

b. And some of the results are the deterioration of the _____, the creation of _____, unnecessary _____ spending, and _____ activities throughout the world.

14. The radical economists advocate the replacement of capitalism with some variety of _____; and agree that the new society should be _____, _____, and _____, and that there should be no private _____

15. The orthodox economists rebut the radical critique of capitalism by arguing that radical economics is non_____ and has an invalid perception of _____, that not all the problems of the American economy are the result of capitalism's _____ _____, and that the radical economists offer no viable or attainable _____ for the present economic system.

■ PROBLEMS AND PROJECTS

1. Suppose the subsistence wage for a worker is 4 units of output per day; and that the total daily output that can be produced by from 0 to 7 workers is as shown in the table below.

Number of workers	Output	Marginal product
0	0	—
1	8	_____
2	15	_____
3	21	_____
4	26	_____
5	30	_____
6	33	_____
7	35	_____

a. Compute the daily marginal product of each worker and enter them in the table.

b. If a capitalist can employ as many workers as he wishes at the subsistence wage, to maximize his profits he will employ _____ workers per day.

c. The total wages paid to workers each day will be _____

d. The daily output of the capitalist is _____ and his daily surplus value is _____

e. Were the capitalist to employ this number of workers, in order to obtain no surplus value he would have to pay each worker a daily wage of _____

f. The daily exploitation of each worker is, therefore, _____

2. In the table below is a Marxian picture of what happens in a capitalistic economy as it develops.

a. In addition to the economy's gross national product the table also shows its capital consumption allowances (CCA) in each of the three years. Compute and enter into the table the economy's net national product for each year.

b. Workers in this economy always receive a subsistence wage of 4 in each year. Find total employment in each year by dividing the wages paid in that year by the subsistence wage; and enter these employment figures into the table.

c. Marx defined surplus value as all of the NNP not paid to workers as wages. Compute the surplus value in the economy in each year; and enter these surplus values in the table.

d. Marx defined the rate of profit to be equal to surplus value divided by the sum of capital consumption allowances and wages.

(1) Compute capital consumption allowances plus wages in each year. Enter these into the table.

(2) Now compute the rate of profit in each year.

e. As the economy develops:

(1) Employment (increases, decreases, remains constant) _____; and, therefore, unemployment _____

(2) The rate of profit _____

Year	GNP	CCA	NNP	Wages	Employment	Surplus value	CCA plus wages	Rate of profit
1	500	100	_____	280	_____	_____	_____	_____
2	504	110	_____	276	_____	_____	_____	_____
3	509	120.4	_____	272	_____	_____	_____	_____

■ SELF-TEST

Circle the T if the statement is true, the F if it is false.

1. Among radical economists there is very little difference in their viewpoints.   **T   F**

2. Surplus value equals the value of the daily output of workers less their daily wage. **T   F**

3. Capitalists, according to Marx, are able to exploit workers because the capitalists have monopoly control of the machinery and equipment needed to produce goods in an industrial society.   **T   F**

4. In Marx's view the increasing degradation of the working class was the direct result of their tendency to have too many children.   **T   F**

5. Marx argued that in a capitalistic society the demand for consumer goods would increase more rapidly than the economy's capacity to produce them and that unemployment would result.   **T   F**

6. Marx's *Capital* contained a clear and detailed picture of the society that would emerge after the overthrow of capitalism by a revolution of the working class.   **T   F**

7. Radical economists contend that the solution to the problems of capitalistic societies requires an end to the private ownership of capital goods and the abolition of the market system as the decision-making device for society.   **T   F**

8. The modern and radical conception of capitalism is an extended and updated version of Marx's ideas.   **T   F**

9. Capitalism has reached a stage in the United States in which, according to radical economists, monopoly corporations dominate the economy.   **T   F**

10. Radical economists argue that because labor markets are not competitive workers receive a wage which is greater than their marginal revenue product.   **T   F**

11. Capitalistic institutions, in the opinion of radical economists, create and maintain most of the income inequality found in the United States.   **T   F**

12. Alienation refers to the increase in the proportion of the working class that is either foreign born or from a minority group.   **T   F**

13. The radical economists argue that capitalism uses its resources to produce little needed goods and services and fails to produce goods and services which are more needed.   **T   F**

14. From the radical viewpoint, two basic causes of the irrational use of resources in capitalistic societies are the pursuit of profits and pollution.   **T   F**

15. The radical economists agree on almost all the particulars of the socialism with which they would replace capitalism.   **T   F**

16. Most radical economists reject both the price-market system and government bureaucracy as a means of allocating scarce resources.   **T   F**

17. The orthodox economists concede that only capitalistic societies are monopolistic, militaristic, and imperialistic; but argue that the abolition of private property and the profit motive will not solve these problems.   **T   F**

18. In their rebuttal of the radical economists' critique of capitalism, orthodox economists argue that radical economists ignore any facts that do not support their conclusions.   **T   F**

Underscore the letter that corresponds to the best answer.

1. In the man-against-man struggle found in capitalistic societies, Marx envisioned the exploitation (a) of the bourgeois by capitalists; (b) of the proletariate by the bourgeois; (c) of workers by the proletariate; (d) of the bourgeois by the proletariate.

2. The institution which Marx believed made it possible for one class to exploit another in a capitalistic economy was (a) the use of money; (b) the use of capital goods; (c) the corporation; (d) private property.

3. Which of the following was *not* a consequence of capital accumulation in Marx's analysis of capitalism? (a) An increase in the profit rate; (b) an increase in unemployment; (c) an increase in national output; (d) an increase in the misery of the working class.

4. Marx argued that the development of capitalism would eventually result in (a) imperialism; (b) prolonged inflation; (c) a decline in the number of capitalists; (d) a rise in the real wages of workers.

5. Imperialism, according to Lenin, results from (a) the search of capitalists for cheap foreign labor; (b) the inability of capitalists to sell all of their output at home; (c) higher profit rates in less developed nations; (d) all of the above.

6. Which of the following is the process through which Marx predicted capitalism would be replaced by socialism? (a) Revolution; (b) evolution; (c) unionization; (d) liberalization.

7. The socialism which would replace capitalism would have all but one of the following characteristics. Which one? (a) The dictatorship of the proletariate; (b) the abolition of the capitalist class; (c) the sale of the capitalists' machinery and equipment to the proletariate; (d) the establishment of a classless society.

8. The radical economists contend that orthodox economics (a) is too broad a discipline to come to grips with real-world problems; (b) is overly concerned with the power of large corporations; (c) devotes too much of its attention to the study of conflict; (d) fails to recognize the political character of the modern corporation.

9. In the radical conception of American capitalism (a) the state dominates and controls the large corporations; (b) the presence in the economy of a large number of small businesses results in wasteful competition; (c) government employs progressive personal and corporate income taxes to subsidize greedy workers; (d) military spending by government provides markets for large corporations.

10. Which of the following, in the view of the radical economists, is *not* a consequence of capitalism in the United States? (a) Alienation; (b) anarchism; (c) inequality; (d) imperialism.

11. Capitalists, the radical economists contend, are able to exploit the working class because of (a) their monopsony position in labor markets; (b) their monopoly position in product markets; (c) the institution of private property; (d) all of the above.

12. Which of the following, in the view of radical economists, is *not* a major factor in producing inequality in the distribution of income and in the ownership of wealth in the United States? (a) Weak inheritance taxes; (b) tax loopholes; (c) foreign competition; (d) the system of higher education.

13. Of the following, which is neither a cause nor a result of alienation? (a) The large size of corporate employers; (b) the unionization of workers; (c) the inability of individuals to influence business decisions; (d) assembly-line production.

14. The new society advocated by all radical economists is (a) socialism; (b) anarchy; (c) communism; (d) a reformed price-market system.

15. The radical critique of capitalism is, in the opinion of orthodox economists, (a) scientific; (b) immoral; (c) valid; (d) ideological.

■ DISCUSSION QUESTIONS

1. Looking back into history Marx saw men engaged in two kinds of struggle. What were these two struggles?

2. Who, according to Marx, were the protagonists of the man-against-man struggle in a capitalistic society?

3. Why, in Marx's explanation of capitalism, are capitalists able to exploit workers? What does "exploit" mean?

4. What does capital accumulation mean? What forced Marx's capitalist to accumulate and what were the consequences of this accumulation?

5. Why did Marx believe that the working class would become increasingly more miserable?

6. What made Marx conclude that capitalistic development would lead to the monopolization of industry by a relatively few capitalists?

7. What is imperialism? Why did Lenin conclude that the development of capitalism would eventually lead to imperialism?

8. What did Marx envision as the causes and the results of the workers' revolution?

9. Explain the two methodological deficiencies which radical economists find in orthodox economics.

10. What evidence is there to suggest that a few large monopolistic corporations dominate the American economy? In what ways does the state allegedly cater to these corporations?

11. What, according to the radical economists, are the major problems that result from corporate capitalism?

12. Explain (a) the orthodox economists' theory of income distribution; and (b) the faults which the radical economists see in this theory.

13. In the view of the radical economists, how does the capitalistic system lead to inequality in the distribution of income and in the ownership of wealth? Why, in their view, are these causes "cumulative and self-reinforcing"?

14. What is alienation and what do the radical economists see as the causes of alienation in the United States?

15. Why do the radical economists argue that capitalistic production is irrational and its use of resources wasteful?

16. According to John G. Gurley (quoted in the text), what forms has American imperialism taken in the last thirty years and what has been the aim of these imperialistic activities?

17. "What kind of new society do the radicals envision or advocate?" What are the different economic systems they recommend as replacements for capitalism?

18. How do the orthodox economists rebut the radical economists' critique of American capitalism?

19. What evidence is there to suggest that radical economists (a) are not objective; (b) have invalid perceptions of reality; and (c) overemphasize the significance of ideology?

20. Now that you have examined the position of the radical economists, what are its greatest strengths and weaknesses? On balance, do you agree or disagree with their major contentions?

INTERNATIONAL TRADE
AND COMPARATIVE ADVANTAGE

This is the first of four chapters dealing with international trade and finance. International trade is a subject with which most students have little firsthand experience. For this reason many of the terms, concepts, and ideas encountered in these chapters will be unfamiliar and may not be readily grasped. However, most of this material is fairly simple if the student will take some pains to examine it. The ideas and concepts employed are new, but they are not especially complex or difficult.

At the beginning it is essential to recognize that international trade is important to the United States. Exports from and imports into the American economy are both close to $85 billion a year. The United States *absolutely* is the greatest exporting and importing nation in the world. In *relative* terms, other nations have exports and imports which are larger percentages of their GNPs. They may export and import more than 40% of GNP, while the United States exports and imports only about 4% of GNP. It is equally important for the student to understand from the beginning that international trade differs from the trade that goes on within nations. Different nations use different monies, not just one money; resources are less mobile internationally than they are *intra*nationally; and governments interfere more with foreign than they do with domestic trade.

But while foreign trade differs from domestic trade in these three ways, nations trade for the same basic reason that people within a nation trade: to take advantage of the benefits of specialization. The student has already examined the gains that result when there is specialization based on comparative advantage; he is urged to review pages 47 through 49 in Chapter 3. To supplement this review, the author of the text reexamines specialization and trade between two nations. The student should be sure he understands (1) what comparative advantage is, (2) why nations gain when they specialize in commodities for whose production they have a comparative advantage, meanwhile trading these commodities for the commodities in which other nations specialize, (3) what is meant by the terms of trade, and (4) how increasing costs limit but do not halt specialization and trade between nations.

The international specialization and trade in which the world engages have both microeconomic and macroeconomic effects. The microeconomic effect is a better allocation of the world's resources—a higher standard of living in all nations. And when there are no barriers to international trade there is also a tendency for the prices of products and of resources to be the same in every country.

But the total amount a nation exports and the total amount it imports also have important macroeconomic effects upon that nation's output and income and upon its level of employment. To understand these effects the student may have to return to Chapter 13 and review the explanation of what determines the equilibrium levels of income, output, and employment in a closed economy. Once this theory has been reviewed it is not really very difficult to add a new and fourth component —*net exports*—to aggregate demand and to find the equilibrium in an open economy. Then the student should be able to see that the more a nation exports (or the less it imports) the greater will be the levels of income, output, and employment in that nation; and that the less it exports (or the more it imports) the smaller these levels will be. The last things the student will learn in this chapter is that a change in net exports—like a change in investment or government expenditures—has a multiplier effect on the equilibrium NNP; and that the value of the multiplier in an open economy depends not only upon the marginal propensity to save but also upon the marginal propensity to import in that economy.

■ CHAPTER OUTLINE

1. Trade between nations is large enough and unique enough to warrant special attention.

a. While the relative importance of international trade to the United States is less than it is to other nations, this country's imports and exports are both about 4% of its GNP and $83 and $82 billion a year, respectively. This trade provides both important raw materials and markets for finished goods; and net exports have a multiplier effect.

b. International trade has three characteristics which distinguish it from domestic trade.

2. Specialization based on comparative advantage and trade between nations are advantageous because the world's resources are not equally distributed and the efficient production of different commodities necessitates different methods and combinations of resources.

3. A simple hypothetical example explains comparative advantage and the gains from trade.

a. Suppose the world is composed of only two nations, each of which is capable of producing two different commodities and in which the production possibilities curves are different straight lines (whose cost ratios are fixed and unequal).

b. With different cost ratios, each nation will have a comparative advantage in the production of one of the two products. And each nation finds that if it specializes entirely in that product, it can obtain the other product by trading at a cost lower than its own production cost.

c. The ratio at which one product is traded for another—the terms of trade—lies between the cost ratios of the two nations.

d. Each nation gains from this trade because specialization permits a greater total output from the same resources and a better allocation of the world's resources.

e. If costs ratios in the two nations are not constant, specialization may not be complete.

4. The microeconomic effects of international trade and specialization are:

a. A more efficient use of world resources.

b. A tendency toward equal prices for each product throughout the world.

c. A tendency toward equal prices for each resource throughout the world.

5. International trade and specialization have macroeconomic effects upon aggregate demand and, as a result, upon the total income, output, and employment of a nation.

a. In an open economy the equilibrium NNP is the NNP which is equal to consumption plus net investment plus government spending for goods and services plus net exports.

(1) Net exports equal exports minus imports; and a nation's exports depend directly upon the NNPs of foreign nations while its imports depend directly upon its own NNP.

(2) A change in its net exports has a multiplier effect upon a nation's NNP.

b. The value of the multiplier in a open economy is equal to one divided by the sum of the nation's marginal propensity to save and its marginal propensity to import.

■ IMPORTANT TERMS

Review

Comparative advantage

Net exports

Specialization

Terms of trade

Production possibilities curve

New

Closed economy

Open economy

Labor-(land-, capital-) intensive commodity

Cost ratio

Trading possibilities line

Open-economy multiplier

Marginal propensity to import

■ FILL-IN QUESTIONS

1. Special attention is devoted to international trade because resources are _____ between nations than within a nation, because every nation employs a different _____ and because international trade is subject to more _____ than domestic trade.

2. The imports and exports of the United States amount to about _____ % of the economy's GNP or between $_____ and $_____ billion.

3. Ranked in order of their importance the three principal exports of the United States are

_____ ,

_____ ,

and _____ ;

the three most important imports are _____

_____ ,

_____ ,

and _____

4. The nations of the world tend to specialize in those goods in the production of which they have a _____ , to export these goods, and to import those goods in the production of which they have a _____

5. Nations specialize and trade because it is more efficient: it enables each nation to obtain

_____

from the same quantity of _____ ; and because the distribution of _____ in the world is _____ and the efficient production of different products requires _____

6. If the cost ratio in country X is 4 Panama hats equal 1 pound of bananas, while in country Y, 3 Panama hats equal 1 pound of bananas:

a. Hats are relatively (expensive, inexpensive) _____ in country X and bananas relatively _____

b. Hats are relatively _____ in country Y and bananas relatively _____

c. X has a comparative advantage and should specialize in the production of _____ _____ and Y has a comparative advantage and should specialize in the production of _____

d. When X and Y specialize and trade, the terms of trade will be somewhere between _____ and _____ hats for each pound of bananas; and will depend upon _____

e. When the actual terms of trade turn out to be 3½ hats for 1 pound of bananas, the cost of obtaining:

(1) 1 Panama hat has been decreased from _____ to _____ pounds of bananas in Y

(2) 1 pound of bananas has been decreased from _____ to _____ Panama hats in X

7. International specialization is not complete because the _____ of producing a good _____ as a nation produces more of that good.

8. The microeconomic effects of international trade and specialization are:

a. The more _____ use of the world's resources.

b. A tendency for the _____ of a product to be the same in all nations.

c. A tendency for the price of a _____ to be the same in all nations.

9. When a nation is able to export and import goods and services:

a. Its net exports equal its _____ minus its _____

b. The volume of its total exports depends (directly, indirectly) _____ upon the level of _____ in foreign countries.

c. The volume of its total imports depends (directly, indirectly) _____

upon the level of _____

10. In an open economy:
a. Aggregate demand is equal to consumption plus net investment plus government

spending for goods and services plus _____
b. The equilibrium NNP is the NNP which is

equal to _____
c. The value of the multiplier is equal to one divided by the sum of the marginal pro-

pensities to _____ and to _____

11. An open economy's marginal propensity to import is equal to the fraction (or percent-

age) of an increase in its _____

which is spent on _____

12. What would be the effect—increase (+) or decrease (−)—of each of the following upon an open economy's equilibrium NNP?

a. An increase in its imports   _____

b. An increase in its exports   _____

c. A decrease in its imports   _____

d. A decrease in its exports   _____

■ PROBLEMS AND PROJECTS

1. Shown in next column are the production possibilities curves for two nations: the United States and Chile. Suppose these two nations do not currently engage in international trade and specialization, and suppose that points A and a show the combinations of wheat and copper they now produce and consume.
a. The straightness of the two curves indicates that the cost ratios in the two nations are

_____

b. Examination of the two curves reveals that the cost ratio in:

(1) The United States is _____ million

tons of wheat for _____ thousand pounds of copper.

(2) Chile is _____ million tons of wheat

for _____ thousand pounds of copper.

Copper (thousands of pounds)
c. If these two nations were to specialize and trade wheat for copper,
(1) The United States would specialize in the production of wheat because _____

_____

(2) Chile would specialize in the production

of copper because _____
d. The terms of trade, if specialization and trade occur, will be greater than 2 and less than 4 million tons of wheat for 1 thousand

pounds of copper because _____

_____

e. Assume the terms of trade turn out to be 3 million tons of wheat for 1 thousand pounds of copper. Draw in the trading possibilities curve for the United States and Chile.

f. With these trading possibilities curves, suppose the United States decides to consume 5 million tons of wheat and 1 thousand pounds of copper while Chile decides to consume 3 million tons of wheat and 1 thousand pounds of copper. The gains from trade to:

(1) The United States are _____ million tons of wheat and _____ thousand pounds of copper.

(2) Chile are _____ million tons of wheat and _____ thousand pounds of copper.

2. Imagine that France and the United States do not specialize or trade. Wine is relatively inexpensive in France and chicken is relatively expensive. In the United States, however, wine is relatively expensive and chicken is relatively inexpensive. This is the result of the relative scarcity and high price of resources used to produce chicken in France and of the relative scarcity and high price of wine-producing resources in the United States.

a. When these two nations begin to specialize and trade, the total demand for:

(1) French-produced wine will (increase, decrease) _____ and French-produced chicken will _____

(2) American-produced wine will _____ and American-produced chicken will _____

b. As a result of these changes in demand,

(1) The price of wine in France will (rise, fall) _____ and the price of wine in the United States will _____ until these two prices are _____

(2) The price of chicken in France will _____ and the price of chicken in the United States will _____ until these two prices are _____

c. Because the demand for resources is a derived demand,

(1) The demand for resources used in France to produce the wine will _____ and the demand for resources used to produce chicken in France will _____

(2) The demand for resources used in the United States to produce wine will _____ and the demand for resources used to produce chicken in the United States will _____

d. These changes in the demands for resources cause the prices paid:

(1) In France for wine-producing resources to _____ and for chicken-producing resources to _____ until they are _____

(2) In the United States for wine-producing resources to _____ and for chicken-producing resources to _____ until they are _____

e. The result is that:

(1) France will shift resources from the production of _____ to the production of _____

(2) The United States will shift resources from the production of _____ to the production of _____

3. On the next page is a schedule showing what aggregate demand (consumption plus net investment plus government spending for goods and services) would be at various levels of net national product in a closed economy.

a. Were this economy to become an open economy the volume of exports would be a constant $90 billion; and the volume of imports at the various levels of NNP would be the amount shown in the table. Compute net exports at each of the seven NNPs and enter them in the table.

b. Compute aggregate demand in this open economy at the seven NNP levels and enter them in the table.

c. The equilibrium NNP in this open economy would be $_____ billion.

d. In this open economy the marginal propensity to save is 0.20 and the marginal propensity to import is _____

e. The value of the multiplier in this open economy is equal to approximately _____

f. A $10 billion increase in:

(1) exports would (increase, decrease) _____ the equilibrium NNP by about $_____ billion.

Aggregate supply or NNP (billions)	Aggregate demand, closed economy (billions)	Exports (billions)	Imports (billions)	Net exports (billions)	Aggregate demand, open economy (billions)
$ 750	$ 776	$90	$74	$_____	$_____
800	816	90	78	_____	_____
850	856	90	82	_____	_____
900	896	90	86	_____	_____
950	936	90	90	_____	_____
1,000	976	90	94	_____	_____
1,050	1,016	90	98	_____	_____

(2) Imports would (increase, decrease) _____ the equilibrium NNP by about $_____ billion.

■ SELF-TEST

Circle the T if the statement is true, the F if it is false.

1. Nations tend to produce and export those goods in the production of which they have a comparative advantage.   **T   F**

2. The principal import of the United States is nonferrous metals.   **T   F**

3. The principal export of the United States is machinery.   **T   F**
Use the following production possibilities to answer questions 4, 5, and 6 in next column and to answer multiple-choice questions 4 and 5.

NEPAL PRODUCTION POSSIBILITIES TABLE

Product	Production alternatives					
	A	B	C	D	E	F
Yak fat	0	4	8	12	16	20
Camel hides	40	32	24	16	8	0

KASHMIR PRODUCTION POSSIBILITIES TABLE

Product	Production alternatives					
	A	B	C	D	E	F
Yak fat	0	3	6	9	12	15
Camel hides	60	48	36	24	12	0

4. In Kashmir the cost of 1 camel hide is 3 units of yak fat.   **T   F**

5. Nepal has a comparative advantage in producing camel hides.   **T   F**

6. With specialization and trade, the trading possibilities curves of both nations would move to the right of their production possibilities curves.   **T   F**

7. Increasing production costs tend to prevent specialization among trading nations from being complete.   **T   F**

8. Trade among nations tends to bring about a more efficient use of the world's resources and a greater world output of goods and services.   **T   F**

9. An increase in the volume of a nation's exports, other things being equal, will expand the nation's NNP.   **T   F**

10. The value of the multiplier in an open economy is equal to the reciprocal of the economy's marginal propensity to import.   **T   F**

Underscore the letter that corresponds to the best answer.

1. International trade is a special and separate area of economic study for several reasons. Which one of the following is not one of these reasons: (a) international trade is based on the principle of comparative advantage; (b) resources are less mobile internationally than domestically; (c) countries engaged in international trade use different monies; (d) international trade is subject to

a greater number of political restrictions than domestic trade.

2. In 1973 the imports of the United States amounted to approximately what percentage of the United States's GNP? (a) 2%; (b) 4%; (c) 6%; (d) 8%.

3. Nations would not need to engage in trade if: (a) all products were produced from the same combinations of resources; (b) world resources were evenly distributed among nations; (c) world resources were perfectly mobile; (d) all of the above.

Use the tables preceding true-false question 4 to answer the following two questions.

4. If Nepal and Kashmir engage in trade, the terms of trade will be: (a) between 2 and 4 camel hides for 1 unit of yak fat; (b) between ⅓ and ½ units of yak fat for 1 camel hide; (c) between 3 and 4 units of yak fat for 1 camel hide; (d) between 2 and 4 units of yak fat for 1 camel hide.

5. If Nepal and Kashmir, in the absence of trade between them, both produced combination C, the gains from trade would be: (a) 6 units of yak fat; (b) 8 units of yak fat; (c) 6 units of yak fat and 8 camel hides; (d) 8 units of yak fat and 6 camel hides.

6. Which of the following is *not* one of the effects when nations begin to specialize and trade? (a) a shift of resources away from the production of commodities in which nations have comparative advantages; (b) a fall in the prices of resources which were relatively expensive; (c) a rise in the prices of products which were relatively inexpensive; (d) an increased demand for relatively inexpensive products and resources.

Use the data in the table below to answer questions 7 and 8.

NNP	C + I + G	Net exports
$ 900	$ 913	$7
920	929	6
940	945	5
960	961	4
980	977	3
1,000	993	2
1,020	1,009	1

7. If exports in this economy are constant, its marginal propensity to import must be (a) .04; (b) .05; (c) .06; (d) .07.

8. The equilibrium NNP is (a) $960; (b) $980; (c) $1,000; (d) $1,020.

■ DISCUSSION QUESTIONS

1. Why do nations specialize in certain products and export their surplus production of these goods at the same time that they are importing other goods? Why do they not use the resources employed to produce the surpluses which they export to produce the goods which they import?

2. In what ways is international specialization and trade limited? In what ways is international trade different from the trade which takes place within a nation?

3. In relative and absolute terms, how important is international trade to the United States? What are the principal exports and imports of the American economy? What commodities used in the economy come almost entirely from abroad, and what American industries sell large percentages of their output abroad?

4. What two facts—one dealing with the distribution of the world's resources and the other related to the technology of producing different products—are the basis for trade among nations?

5. Explain (a) the theory or principle of comparative advantage; (b) what is meant by and what determines the terms of trade; and (c) the gains from trade.

6. What microeconomic effects does the commencement of specialization and trade among nations have upon (a) the allocation of the trading nations' resources, (b) resource prices in the trading nations, and (c) the prices of products in the nations that trade?

7. Explain how exports and how imports affect aggregate demand within a nation. What are the primary determinants of the volume of a nation's exports and imports? How does a change in the volume of exports and in the volume of imports affect income, output, and employment in a nation?

8. What determines the size or value of the multiplier in an open economy? Why is the multiplier larger in a closed than in an open economy?

THE ECONOMICS
OF FREE TRADE AND PROTECTION

For well over two hundred years people in America and throughout the world have debated whether free trade or protection was the better policy. Economists took part in this debate and, with few exceptions, argued for free trade and against protection. Those who favor free trade contend that free trade benefits both the nation and the world as a whole. Free trade allows nations to specialize in the production of those goods and services in which they have a comparative advantage; and it increases total production and the standard of living in all countries. "Free traders" argue that tariffs, import quotas, and other barriers to international trade prevent or reduce specialization and decrease both a nation's and the world's production and standard of living.

But nations have and continue to erect barriers to trade with other nations. The questions upon which this chapter focuses attention are (1) what motivates nations to impose tariffs and to limit by quotas the quantities of goods imported from abroad; (2) what effects do such tariffs and quotas have upon a nation's own prosperity and upon the prosperity of the world; and (3) what kinds of arguments do those who favor tariffs and quotas employ to support their position—on what grounds do they base their contention that their nation will benefit from the erection of barriers which reduce imports from foreign nations.

The chapter's final major section is a brief review of American policy toward trade barriers since 1934. That year began a series of gradual but substantial tariff-rate reductions which have continued almost up to the present year. Despite this progress in decreasing the barriers to trade with other nations, protectionism is not dead. Advocates of tariffs and quotas are alive—though not quite well—and living in the United States. These advocates of protectionism for the United States have dressed the old arguments for tariffs and quotas in modern clothes and hope that the new clothes will this time defeat the old argument that free trade benefits everyone.

Whether free trade or protection will be the policy of the United States in the years to come depends upon whether the American people understand that free trade helps everyone and that protection helps no one but the selfish. It is for this reason that Chapter 42 is important.

■ CHAPTER OUTLINE

1. The argument for free trade is that it leads to a better allocation of resources and a higher standard of living in the world.

2. Nations retard international trade by erecting artificial barriers.

a. Tariffs and import quotas are the principal barriers to trade.

b. Four motives induce nations to erect these barriers.

c. The economic impact of a protective tariff is a misallocation of the world's resources: the price of the good on which the tariff is levied is increased and its total production is reduced; and foreign producers of the good suffer while domestic producers benefit.

3. There are a number of different arguments in the case for protection. Most of these are fallacious or based on half-truths; but at least two of them warrant the protection of certain industries under certain conditions.

4. Until 1934 the United States steadily increased tariff rates to protect private-interest groups.

a. Since the passage of the Reciprocal Trade Agreements Act, tariff rates have been substantially reduced; many nations, including the United States, have signed the General Agreements on Tariffs and Trade in an attempt to eliminate trade barriers.

b. The European Common Market has sought the economic integration of Western Europe by the abolishment of internal tariffs and quotas, the establishment of common external tariffs, and the eventual free movement of labor and capital within the Common Market area. The Common Market nations have achieved considerable integration, have increased their growth rates, and have expanded trade; but their success has created problems for nonmember nations.

c. The Trade Expansion Act of 1962 permitted closer economic ties between the United States and the Common Market; and the "Kennedy Round" of tariff negotiations, despite some disappointments, did produce substantial tariff-rate reductions.

d. The United States and over 100 other nations began in 1973 a new round of negotiations to reduce still further the barriers to trade.

e. But the elimination of all tariffs would not result in free trade because the nontariff barriers would still impede trade among nations.

f. Since 1969 the United States has, for several good reasons, reduced the barriers to trade with communist nations; and while the potential for increased trade with these na-

tions is considerable, the problems involved in such trade are also considerable.

g. During the past few years the pressure to restrict American imports has increased.

h. Instead of trying to increase exports and reduce imports, many nations, including the United States, in the early 1970s restricted the exportation and encouraged the importation of certain foods and raw materials in order to relieve domestic shortages and prevent higher prices.

■ IMPORTANT TERMS

Tariff	**Economic integration**
Revenue tariff	**European Common**
Protective tariff	**Market (European Economic Community)**
Import quota	
Reciprocal Trade Agreements Act of 1934	**Trade Expansion Act of 1962**
Most favored nation clause	**Kennedy Round**
	Nontariff barriers (NTBs)
General Agreement on Tariffs and Trade	

■ FILL-IN QUESTIONS

1. The basic argument for free trade is that it results in _____

and _____

2. The two most widely employed barriers to international trade are _____

and _____,

which nations establish in order to _____

_____,

_____,

_____,

and _____

3. When the United States imposes a tariff on a good which is imported from abroad:

a. the price of that good in the United States will (increase, decrease) _____

b. the total purchases of the good in the United States will _____

c. the output of:

(1) American producers of the good will ____

(2) foreign producers of the good will _____
d. the ability of foreigners to buy goods and

services in the United States will _____
and, as a result, output and employment in
American industries that sell goods and ser-

vices abroad will _____

4. List the six arguments which protectionists
employ to justify trade barriers.

a. _____

b. _____

c. _____

d. _____

e. _____

f. _____

5. Until 1930 the trend of tariff rates in the

United States was _____,

but since the passage of the _____

Act in 1934 the trend has been _____.

This act empowered the President to _____

_____

and incorporated _____
in American trade agreements.

6. The three main principles set down in the
General Agreement on Tariffs and Trade are:

a. _____

b. _____

c. _____

7. The specific aims of the European Com-

mon Market were the abolishment of _____

_____,

the establishment of _____,

the free movement of _____,

and common policies with respect to _____

_____.

Its success, reflected in increased _____

_____

and _____
in the Common Market nations, can be attrib-

uted to a better _____

and to the _____
which have resulted from the creation of a
mass market.

8. The Trade Expansion Act of 1962 allowed

the President to _____

_____

and _____;

and resulted in the _____
of trade negotiations which ended in 1967.

9. The elimination of all tariff barriers to
trade would not bring about free trade in the

world because the _____
barriers would still exist.

10. Until recently the United States restricted

its trade with the _____
nations of the world; but in 1969 its policy
toward these nations began to change for
three reasons:

a. _____

b. _____

c. _____

11. The increasing pressures to restrict the
imports of the United States are the result of

greater _____ competition, discrimi-

nation against American _____ in

foreign markets, and the _____
problem in the United States.

12. In the early 1970s some nations began to
encourage importing and discourage exporting

of certain _____ and _____

in order to prevent _____ of and

higher _____ for these commodities.

■ PROBLEMS AND PROJECTS

1. The table on page 307 shows the quantities
of woolen gloves demanded (D) in the United
States at several different prices (P). Also

shown in the table are the quantities of woolen gloves that would be supplied by American producers (S_a) and the quantities that would be supplied by foreign producers (S_f) at the nine different prices.

P	D	S_a	S_f	S_t	S_f'	S_t'
$2.60	450	275	475	___	___	___
2.40	500	250	450	___	___	___
2.20	550	225	425	___	___	___
2.00	600	200	400	___	___	___
1.80	650	175	375	___	___	___
1.60	700	150	350	___	___	___
1.40	750	125	325	___	___	___
1.20	800	0	300	___	___	___
1.00	850	0	0	___	___	___

a. Compute and enter in the table the total quantities that would be supplied (S_t) by American and foreign producers at each of the prices.

b. If the market for woolen gloves in the United States is a competitive one the equilibrium prices for woolen gloves is $_____

and the equilibrium quantity is _____

c. Suppose now that the United States government imposes an 80 cents ($0.80) per pair of gloves tariff on all gloves imported into the United States from abroad. Compute and enter into the table the quantities that would be supplied (S_f') by foreign producers at the nine different prices. (*Hint:* If foreign producers were willing to supply 300 pairs at a price of $1.20 when there was no tariff they are now willing to supply 300 pairs at $2.00, the $0.80 per pair tariff plus the $1.20 they will receive for themselves. The quantities supplied at each of the other prices may be found in a similar fashion.)

d. Compute and enter into the table the total quantities that would now be supplied (S_t') by American and foreign producers at each of the nine prices.

e. As a result of the imposition of the tariff

the equilibrium price has risen to $_____ and the equilibrium quantity has fallen to

f. The number of pairs sold by:
(1) American producers has (increased, decreased) _____ by _____
(2) foreign producers has (increased, decreased) _____ by _____

g. The total revenues (after the payment of the tariff) of:
(1) American producers—who do *not* pay the tariff—have (increased, decreased) _____ by $_____
(2) foreign producers—who *do* pay the tariff—have (increased, decreased) _____ by $_____

h. The total amount spent by American buyers of woolen gloves has _____ by $_____

i. The tariff revenue of the United States government has _____ by $_____

j. The total number of dollars earned by foreigners has _____ by $_____; and, as a result, the total foreign demand for goods and services produced in the United States will _____ by $_____

■ SELF-TEST

Circle the T if the statement is true, the F if it is false.

1. The case for free trade is that it will result in the more efficient use of the world's resources and greater world output.　　**T　F**

2. A tariff on coffee in the United States is an example of a protective tariff.　　**T　F**

3. The imposition of a tariff on a good imported from abroad will raise the price of the good and lower the quantity of it bought and sold.　　**T　F**

4. One crop economies may be able to make themselves more stable and diversified by imposing tariffs on goods imported from abroad; but these tariffs are apt also to lower the standard of living in these economies.　**T　F**

5. Because the General Agreement on Tariffs and Trade committed its signers to eliminate their tariffs on imports, the U.S. Senate refused to ratify the agreement.　　**T　F**

6. Since the establishment of the European Common Market its members' share of world trade has increased.   **T   F**

7. Before a firm can enjoy economies of scale it must enjoy a mass market.   **T   F**

8. In order to offset the loss of export markets that will result from the growing strength of the European Common Market, the United States will find it necessary in the future to increase its tariff rates.   **T   F**

9. The Trade Expansion Act of 1962 reversed earlier American economic policy and attempted to expand GNP by restricting imports.   **T   F**

10. The Kennedy Round resulted in fairly substantial reciprocal tariff rate reductions. **T   F**

Underscore the letter that corresponds to the best answer.

1. Which one of the following is characteristic of tariffs? (a) they prevent the importation of goods from abroad; (b) they specify the maximum amounts of specific commodities which may be imported during a given period of time; (c) they often protect domestic producers from foreign competition; (d) they enable nations to reduce their exports and increase their imports during periods of depression.

2. Which one of the following arguments for protection is the least fallacious and most pertinent in the United States today? (a) the military self-sufficiency argument; (b) the increase-domestic-employment argument; (c) the protect-high-wages argument; (d) the infant-industry argument.

3. When a tariff is imposed on a good imported from abroad (a) the demand for the good increases; (b) the demand for the good decreases; (c) the supply of the good increases; (d) the supply of the good decreases.

4. Tariffs lead to (a) the contraction of relatively efficient industries; (b) an overallocation of resources to relatively efficient industries; (c) an increase in the foreign demand for domestically produced goods; (d) an underallocation of resources to relatively inefficient industries.

5. Which of the following is a likely result of imposing tariffs to increase domestic employment? (a) A short-run increase in domestic employment; (b) retaliatory increases in the tariff rates of foreign nations; (c) a long-run decline in exports; (d) all of the above.

6. Which of the following is the likely result of the United States employing tariffs to protect its high wages and standard of living? (a) An increase in U.S. exports; (b) a rise in the American real NNP; (c) a decrease in the average productivity of American workers; (d) a decrease in the quantities of resources employed by industries producing the goods on which tariffs have been levied.

7. The infant-industry argument for tariffs (a) is especially pertinent to the advanced industrial nations; (b) generally results in tariffs that are removed after the infant industry has matured; (c) makes it rather easy to determine which infant industries will become mature industries with comparative advantages in producing their goods; (d) might better be replaced by an argument for outright subsidies for infant industries.

8. Which one of the following specifically empowered the President of the United States to reduce its tariff rates up to 50% if other nations would reduce their tariffs on American goods? (a) the Underwood Act of 1913; (b) the Hawley-Smoot Act of 1930; (c) the Trade Agreements Act of 1934; (d) the General Agreement on Tariffs and Trade of 1947.

9. Which of the following is *not* characteristic of the General Agreement on Tariffs and Trade? Nations signing the agreement were committed to: (a) the elimination of import quotas; (b) the reciprocal reduction of tariffs by negotiation; (c) the nondiscriminatory treatment of all trading nations; (d) the establishment of a world customs union.

10. The European Common Market: (a) is designed to eliminate import quotas among its members; (b) includes Great Britain, Denmark, France, and Spain among others; (c) aims to abolish tariffs imposed on all goods which member nations import; (d) includes both East and West Germany.

■ DISCUSSION QUESTIONS

1. What is the "case for free trade"?

2. How are tariffs and import quotas used to restrict international trade? Why do nations wish to restrict trade?

3. Suppose the United States were to increase the tariff on automobiles imported from West Germany (and other foreign countries). What would be the effect of this tariff-rate increase on (a) the price of automobiles in the United States; (b) the total number of cars sold in the United States during a year; (c) the number of cars produced by and employment in the West German automobile industry; (d) production by and employment in the American automobile industry; (e) West German income obtained by selling cars in the United States; (f) the West German demand for goods produced in the U.S.; (g) the production of and employment in those American industries which now export goods to West Germany; (h) the standards of living in the U.S. and in West Germany; (i) the allocation of resources in the American economy; and (j) the allocation of the world's resources?

4. What is the "case for protection"? How valid and pertinent to the United States is each of the six basic arguments for protection?

5. What was the tariff policy of the United States: (a) between 1790 and 1930; (b) since 1934? Explain the basic provisions of the Reciprocal Trade Agreements Act. How has the United States cooperated with other nations since 1945 to reduce trade barriers?

6. What is meant by economic integration? What are the four main features of the European Common Market? How successful has it been in achieving its immediate goals and in increasing the economic well-being of its members? Why has it been successful?

7. What problems does the success of the Common Market create for the United States? How might the United States solve these problems?

8. What were the major provisions of the Trade Expansion Act of 1962? What were the accomplishments of the Kennedy Round?

9. What new effort to reduce the barriers to trade among nations was begun in 1973? Why was this new initiative particularly timely?

10. Why has the American attitude toward trading with the communist nations changed in recent years? Explain why the potential for trade with these nations is apt to be large. What are the problems that will be encountered in trading with the "communist bloc"?

11. Explain why pressures to restrict the importation of goods into the United States have revived in recent years.

12. Explain why the United States and many other nations began in the early 1970s to encourage the importation and to discourage the exportation of certain commodities. What were these "certain commodities"?

THE BALANCE OF PAYMENTS
AND EXCHANGE RATES

In the last two chapters the student learned *why* nations engage in international trade and *why* they may erect barriers to trade with other nations. In Chapter 43 he will learn *how* nations using different monies are able to trade among themselves. The means they employ to overcome the difficulties that result from the use of different monies is fairly simple. When a nation wishes to buy a good or service, make a loan, or present a gift in another nation, it *buys* some of the money used in the foreign nation. It pays for the foreign money with some of its own money. In other words, the nation exchanges its own money for foreign money. And when a nation sells a good or service abroad or receives a loan or a gift from abroad and obtains foreign money, it *sells* this foreign money—often called foreign exchange—in return for some of its own money. That is, it exchanges foreign money for its own money. The price a country pays for or is paid for foreign exchange is the foreign exchange rate. And like most prices, the foreign exchange rate is determined by the demand for and the supply of foreign money.

As the student knows from Chapter 42, nations buy and sell large quantities of goods and services across national boundaries. But nations also make and receive gifts and loans

abroad, buy and sell gold internationally, and own foreign bank accounts and foreign currency. At the end of a year, nations summarize their foreign sales and purchases of goods and services, their gifts and loans, and the changes in the amounts of gold and foreign money they own. This summary is a nation's international balance of payments: a record of how it obtained foreign exchange during the year and what it did with that money. Of course, all foreign money obtained was used for some purpose—it did not evaporate—and consequently the balance of payments *always* balances. The international balance of payments is an extremely important and useful device for understanding the amounts and kinds of international transactions in which a nation engages. But it also enables us to understand such things as international equilibrium and disequilibrium, balance of payments surpluses and deficits, and gold gains and losses, as well as the causes of these problems and how to deal with them.

Probably the most difficult sections of the chapter are concerned with what economists call international disequilibrium and the means by which international disequilibrium can be eliminated. Here the student should pay particular attention to: (1) exactly what is meant by international equilibrium and disequilibrium; (2) how foreign exchange rates which fluctuate will help to correct disequilibrium; (3) the disadvantages of freely fluctuating exchange rates; (4) how changing price and income levels help to eliminate disequilibrium; (5) the advantages and disadvantages of changing price and income levels as a device for correcting disequilibrium; (6) how nations may obtain international equilibrium through government regulation; and (7) the advantages and disadvantages of government controls.

One last word for the student. This chapter is filled with new terms. Some of these are just special words used in international economics to mean things with which the student is already familiar. Be very sure you learn what all of the new terms mean. It will simplify your comprehension of this chapter and enable you to understand more readily the international economic and financial problems and policies examined in the next chapter.

■ CHAPTER OUTLINE

1. Trade between two nations differs from domestic trade because the monies of both nations are used.

a. American exports create a demand for dollars and a supply of foreign money. They increase the number of dollars owned by Americans (or decrease the amount of foreign money owned by foreigners). American exports earn the monies to pay for American imports.

b. American imports create a supply of dollars and a demand for foreign money. They decrease the number of dollars owned by Americans (or increase the amount of foreign money owned by foreigners). American imports use up the monies obtained by exporting.

2. The international balance of payments for a nation is a record of its transactions with other nations in the world. It contains eight major sections.

a. The first three sections record a nation's exports of goods and services, its imports of these things, and the difference between exports and imports—its balance of trade.

b. The next three sections record net remittances (private gifts), net governmental transactions (loans and gifts), and net capital movements (loans and investments).

c. The seventh section records the amount

due to or from other nations as a result of the transactions in the first six sections.

d. The last section indicates how the amount due to or from other nations was financed or balanced: with gold and foreign monies or with a nation's money (international monetary reserves).

e. A nation may lose gold or money to other nations even if it has exported more goods and services than it has imported (that is, even if it has a balance of trade surplus). This occurs when the amounts it gives and invests abroad exceed the size of its balance of trade surplus.

3. A nation has a disequilibrium in its international balance of payments when the gold and international reserves it owns increase or decrease. An increase is a balance of payments surplus and a decrease is a deficit.

a. Just like an individual family, a nation has a surplus (or deficit) when it spends, gives, and invests less (or more) than its income.

b. The autonomous transactions are recorded in the first six sections of the international balance of payments and the accommodating transactions in the last section. The latter must make (or accommodate) themselves to the former.

4. When a nation has a payments surplus or deficit there is international disequilibrium and one of three kinds of adjustments may take place to bring about equilibrium.

a. If foreign exchange rates are free to rise and fall, a nation's outpayments will tend to increase (decrease) and its inpayments will tend to decrease (increase) if it began with a payments surplus (deficit).

(1) When a nation has a payments surplus (deficit) foreign exchange rates fall (rise). This makes foreign goods and services less (more) expensive to buy, increases (decreases) imports, makes a nation's goods and services more (less) expensive for foreigners to buy, and decreases (increases) exports.

(2) But freely fluctuating exchange rates increase the risks of exporters and importers (and reduce international trade), change the terms of trade, and destabilize economies (by creating unemployment or inflation).

b. Price and income levels in a nation with a payments surplus (deficit) tend to rise (fall), increase (decrease) outpayments, and decrease (increase) inpayments to restore equilibrium.

(1) Such adjustments affect price levels, the level and distribution of real income, and employment in the nations involved; and these effects may be unwanted by the nations.

(2) The international gold standard was one example of a system which worked in this way and kept exchange rates relatively stable.

c. Public controls are often employed by a nation to eliminate its payments deficit.

(1) The nation may reduce the price of its money to foreigners—devalue its money—and thus increase the price of foreign monies to its citizens in order to increase inpayments and decrease outpayments.

(2) It may also use tariffs, quotas, and subsidies to expand exports (inpayments) and reduce imports (outpayments) without changing exchange rates.

■ IMPORTANT TERMS

Rate of exchange (foreign exchange rate)	**International disequilibrium**
International balance of payments	**Autonomous transactions**
Balance of trade	**Accommodating transactions**
(Balance of) trade surplus	**Freely fluctuating exchange rate**
(Balance of) trade deficit	**Exchange rate depreciation**
Remittance	**Exchange rate appreciation**
Net capital movement	
Financing (balancing) transactions	**International gold standard**
(Balance of) payments deficit	**Gold export point**
(Balance of) payments surplus	**Gold import point**
International monetary reserves	**Foreign exchange control**
International equilibrium	**Currency devaluation**
	Currency depreciation
	Trade controls

■ FILL-IN QUESTIONS

1. The rate of exchange for the French franc is the number of _____ which an American must pay to obtain _____

_____

2. When the rate of exchange for the German mark is 40 cents, the rate of exchange for the dollar is _____ marks.

3. American _____ or foreign _____ create a demand for foreign money and a supply of dollars; American _____ or foreign _____ create a demand for dollars and a supply of foreign money.

4. American exports and foreign imports (increase, decrease) _____ the amount of foreign money owned by Americans or _____ the number of dollars owned by foreigners, and _____ the money supply in the United States while it _____ the money supply in foreign nations.

5. The eight principal sections in a nation's international balance of payments are:

a. _____

b. _____

c. _____

d. _____

e. _____

f. _____

g. _____

h. _____

6. The balance of trade is the difference between a nation's exports and imports of _____

_____,

_____,

and _____.

If a nation's exports of these items are greater than its imports of them, it has a balance of trade _____

7. Net capital movements record the _____ _____ and _____ which one nation makes in other nations. The financing (or balancing) transactions record the changes in a nation's holdings of _____

_____ and _____

and in the amount of its money owned by foreigners.

8. A nation has a balance of payments surplus (deficit) when its _____

(_____) exceeds its _____

(_____), and when it gains (loses)

_____ and/or _____

and the amount of its money owned by foreigners _____ (_____).

9. A nation is in international disequilibrium when it has either a payments _____

or payments _____ and is in equilibrium when it has neither.

10. A country can have a trade surplus *and* a payments deficit if it _____,

_____, and _____

more abroad than its trade surplus.

11. The accommodating transactions are gains and losses of _____,

_____, and _____.

Other transactions in the international balance of payments are _____ transactions.

12. The three mechanisms for eliminating international disequilibrium are _____,

_____,

and _____

13. If foreign exchange rates fluctuate freely and a nation has a balance of payments surplus, the price of that nation's money in the foreign exchange market will tend to _____

and the price of foreign exchange in that nation will tend to _____.

As these changes take place, the nation's inpayments will _____ and

its outpayments will _____

to reduce the surplus.

14. There are three problems which arise when foreign exchange rates fluctuate freely:

The _____

associated with flexible rates tend to _____

_____

trade, a nation's _____

can be worsened, and fluctuating exports and imports can affect _____

and _____ in an economy.

15. A nation is on the gold standard when

it _____

and _____

16. If the nations of the world are on the gold standard, rates of exchange will depend

upon _____

and _____;

and the rate will only fluctuate between the

_____

and the _____

17. Assuming exchange rates are stable and a nation has a balance of payments deficit:

a. The money supply and price level in that

nation will _____

b. This will make things bought at home

(more, less) _____ expensive and

things bought abroad _____ expensive.

c. As a result this country will _____

the amount it buys and _____

the amount it sells in the rest of the world.

d. This, in turn, _____ this

country's outpayments and _____

its inpayments, thereby reducing or eliminating its balance of payments deficit.

18. The principal advantage of using changing price and income levels to correct balance

of payments deficits or surpluses is _____

_____.

The chief disadvantage is that nations must

also accept changes in _____,

_____ ,

and _____

in order to have international equilibrium.

19. When a nation with a payments deficit employs exchange controls to obtain international equilibrium, the government of that nation _____

the rate of exchange in order to reduce the

_____

of that nation to the level of its _____

and the government will also have to _____

_____

foreign exchange; _____

and _____

tend to increase in those nations which employ exchange controls and to decrease in other nations.

20. Nations may also attempt to eliminate a

balance of payments deficit by placing _____

_____ and _____

on imports and by _____

exports.

■ PROBLEMS AND PROJECTS

1. Use the hypothetical international balance of payments data for the United States given in the table below.

	Dollars (in billions)
Net remittances	−1.5
Income from U.S. investments abroad	+7.3
Capital outflow	−10.2
Increase in liquid dollar balances held by foreigners	+3.9
Imports of goods	−31.1
Income from foreign investments in the United States	−1.8
Decrease in United States holdings of gold and foreign currencies	+0.7
Imports of services	−6.2
Capital inflow	+3.0
Exports of goods	+32.5
Exports of services	+8.1
Net government transactions	−4.7

a. Compute with the appropriate sign (+ or −):

(1) United States exports: $_____

(2) United States imports: $_____

(3) Net capital movements: $_____

(4) Financing transactions: $_____

b. Using the data and your computations in (a), complete the United States balance of international payments below. (Use Table 43–1 in the text as a model and assume that there are no errors or omissions.)

(1) _____ $_____

(1a) _____ _____

(1b) _____ _____

(1c) _____ _____

(2) _____ _____

(2a) _____ _____

(2b) _____ _____

(2c) _____ _____

(3) _____ _____

(4) _____ _____

(5) _____ _____

(6) _____ _____

(6a) _____ _____

(6b) _____ _____

(7) _____ _____

(8a) _____ _____

(8b) _____ _____

c. The United States had a balance of payments _____ of $_____

d. The autonomous transactions amounted to (use the proper sign) $_____ and the accommodating transactions to $_____

2. Below are a series of foreign exchange rates for the British pound. For each of these rates compute the rate of exchange for the American dollar:

$2.00: £ _____ $4.00: £ _____

$2.50: £ _____ $4.50: £ _____

$3.00: £ _____ $5.00: £ _____

$3.50: £ _____

It can be seen that the higher the rate of exchange for the pound, the _____ is the rate of exchange for the dollar.

3. Assume that both the United States and Great Britain are on the gold standard. The United States defines the dollar as being worth $\frac{1}{35}$ of an ounce of gold and Great Britain defines the pound as being worth $\frac{1}{7}$ of an ounce of gold. Assume that the cost of packing, insuring, and shipping *one ounce* of gold between the United States and Great Britain is $0.21.

   a. Ignoring the packing, insuring, and shiping charges, £1 is worth $_____

and $1.00 is worth £_____
   b. In the United States the gold export point

will be $_____ and the gold

import point will be $_____
   c. In Great Britain the gold export point will

be £_____ and the gold

import point will be £_____
(Carry your answers to three decimal places.)

4. Below are the demand and supply schedules for the British pound.

Quantity of pounds demanded	Price $	Quantity of pounds supplied
400	5.00	100
360	4.50	200
300	4.00	300
286	3.50	400
267	3.00	500
240	2.50	620
200	2.00	788

   a. What will be the rate of exchange for the

pound? $_____
   b. What will be the rate of exchange for the

dollar? £_____
   c. How many pounds will be purchased in

the market? _____
   d. How many dollars will be purchased in

the market? _____
   e. Suppose the British government regulates the exchange rate of the pound and declares

that the pound can only be sold at a price of $4.50:
   (1) People in Great Britain will be able to

buy one dollar at a price of £_____
   (2) The quantity of pounds supplied will exceed the quantity of pounds demanded at

this price by _____

■ SELF-TEST

Circle the T if the statement is true, the F if it is false.

1. The importation by Americans of goods from abroad creates a supply of dollars in the foreign exchange market.   **T   F**

2. If a nation's exports of goods and services are less than its imports of goods and services, the nation has a balance of trade surplus.   **T   F**

3. A nation is in international equilibrium when its exports equal its imports.   **T   F**

4. The financial or balancing transactions are remittances and capital movements.   **T   F**

5. A nation is in international disequilibrium when the accommodating transactions exceed the autonomous transactions.   **T   F**

6. If a nation has a balance of payments deficit and exchange rates are freely flexible, the price of that nation's money in the foreign exchange market will tend to fall, and this will reduce its imports and increase its exports.   **T   F**

7. If country A defines its money as worth 100 grains of gold and country B defines its money as worth 20 grains of gold, then, ignoring packing, insuring, and shipping charges, 5 units of country A's money will be worth 1 unit of country B's money.   **T   F**

8. When nations are on the gold standard, foreign exchange rates fluctuate only within limits determined by the cost of moving gold from one nation to another.   **T   F**

9. If exchange rates are stable and a nation has a payments surplus, prices and money incomes in that nation will tend to rise.   **T   F**

10. A nation using exchange controls to eliminate a payments surplus might devalue its currency.   **T   F**

Underscore the letter that corresponds to the best answer.

1. If an American can buy £25,000 for $100,000, the rate of exchange for the pound is: (*a*) $40; (*b*) $25; (*c*) $4; (*d*) $.25.

2. Which one of the following is a financial or balancing transaction? (*a*) gifts of Americans to foreign persons and countries; (*b*) the export of gold from the United States; (*c*) a loan by an American bank to a foreign firm; (*d*) the income from United States investments abroad.

3. If a nation's international balance of payments shows that it is losing gold and foreign monies and that foreigners are increasing the amount of dollars they own, that nation has: (*a*) a trade surplus; (*b*) a trade deficit; (*c*) a payments surplus; (*d*) a payments deficit.

4. When its balance of trade exceeds its net remittances to other nations, its governmental loans and grants, and its capital outflow to other nations, a nation has a: (*a*) trade surplus; (*b*) trade deficit; (*c*) payments surplus; (*d*) payments deficit.

5. Which of these is an accommodating transaction? (*a*) a gift from an American to his uncle in Scotland; (*b*) an increase in the size of American bank accounts in England; (*c*) a loan by the United States government to Turkey; (*d*) the purchase by an American of stock on the French stock exchange.

6. Which of the following would be one of the results associated with the use of freely fluctuating foreign exchange rates to correct a nation's balance of payments surplus? (*a*) the nation's terms of trade with other nations would be worsened; (*b*) importers in the nation who had made contracts for the future delivery of goods would find that they had to pay a higher price than expected for the goods; (*c*) if the nation were at full employment the decrease in exports and the increase in imports would be inflationary; (*d*) exporters in the nation would find their sales abroad had decreased.

7. If the nations of the world are on the gold standard and one nation has a balance of payments surplus: (*a*) foreign exchange rates in that nation will rise toward the gold import point; (*b*) gold will tend to be imported into

that country; (*c*) the level of prices in that country will tend to fall; (*d*) employment and output in that country will tend to fall.

8. When exchange rates are stable and a nation at full employment has a payments surplus, the result in that nation will be: (*a*) a declining price level; (*b*) falling money income; (*c*) inflation; (*d*) rising real income.

9. The use of exchange controls to eliminate a nation's balance of payments deficit results in: (*a*) decreasing the nation's imports; (*b*) decreasing the nation's exports; (*c*) decreasing the nation's price level; (*d*) decreasing the nation's income.

10. A nation with a balance of payments surplus might attempt to eliminate this surplus by employing: (*a*) import quotas; (*b*) higher tariffs; (*c*) subsidies on items which the nation exports; (*d*) none of the above.

■ DISCUSSION QUESTIONS

1. What is foreign exchange and the foreign exchange rate? Who are the demanders and suppliers of a particular foreign exchange, say, the French franc? Why is a buyer (demander) in the foreign exchange markets always a seller (supplier) also?

2. What is meant when it is said that "a nation's exports pay for its imports"? Do nations pay for all their imports with exports?

3. What is an international balance of payments? What are the principal sections of a nation's international balance of payments? What are the three kinds of exports and imports listed in it?

4. What are the two kinds of financial or balancing transactions in an international balance of payments? Why are they called balancing transactions?

5. What is meant by international equilibrium and disequilibrium? How does a balance of payments surplus (or deficit) differ from a balance of trade surplus (or deficit)?

6. How can a nation have both a trade surplus and a payments deficit?

7. Is it possible for a nation to have a trade deficit and an even larger payments deficit?

Or a trade deficit and a payments surplus? Explain how.

8. What is the difference between autonomous and accommodating transactions in a nation's international balance of payments? Which transactions are autonomous and which are accommodating?

9. How can freely fluctuating foreign exchange rates restore international equilibrium? What are the problems associated with this method of correcting international disequilibrium?

10. When is a nation on the gold standard? How does the international gold standard correct international disequilibrium? What are the disadvantages of this method of restoring international equilibrium?

11. Why does the operation of the international gold standard ensure relatively stable foreign exchange rates, that is, rates which fluctuate only within very narrow limits? What are the limits and what are the advantages of stable exchange rates?

12. How can foreign exchange controls be used to restore international equilibrium? Why do such exchange controls necessarily involve the rationing of foreign exchange? What effect do these controls have upon prices, output, and employment in nations that use them and in other nations?

13. What kinds of trade controls may nations with payments deficits employ to eliminate their deficits? Why do these controls often fail to achieve the desired result?

14. Why do nations devalue their currency during depressions or when faced with persistent balance of payments deficits? Why is devaluation seldom successful in solving these two problems?

INTERNATIONAL TRADE
AND FINANCE:
PROBLEMS AND POLICIES

The title of this chapter is a brief but clear summary of its contents. Chapter 44 looks at the major problems of the United States and of the world that have recently arisen because they engage in international trade. It also examines the policies that have been used or proposed to solve these problems.

After briefly outlining the history of international trade from the nineteenth century through the cold war and explaining how the problem of rebuilding the European economies following World War II was solved, the author turns his attention to two basic and interrelated problems: (1) how to organize the international monetary system so that foreign exchange rates are stable, international monetary reserves are sufficient to finance a large and expanding volume of international trade, and international equilibrium is achieved; and (2) how to eliminate the balance of payments deficits incurred by the United States over the past two and one-half decades.

To solve the first of these problems the Bretton Woods monetary system was introduced at the close of World War II. It replaced the gold standard as an international monetary system; relied upon adjustable pegs to stabilize exchange rates and to eliminate payments surpluses and deficits; and utilized gold, the dollar, and the British pound sterling

to finance international trade. More than a quarter of a century has elapsed since the Bretton Woods system was introduced. In that time it was immensely helpful in restoring world trade to its prewar level and in bringing about still further expansions in the volume of international trade. But in more recent years it became evident that the Bretton Woods system was unable to provide the increases in monetary reserves needed to finance continued expansion of imports and exports among nations and was unable to eliminate payments surpluses and deficits.

A particular instance of its inability to bring about a balance of payments equilibrium is the American economy's twenty-five year payments deficit which was matched in the rest of the world by a twenty-five year payments surplus. Professor McConnell examines the causes of this deficit; explains the basic measures that must be taken if it is to be eliminated; and considers (and rejects) the use of controls to solve the deficit problem. He also explains how the American payments deficits helped the Bretton Woods system to expand the world's monetary reserves and why the pegs employed by the International Monetary Fund to stabilize exchange rates were not adjusted to promote international equilibrium.

From a consideration of the recent short-comings of the Bretton Woods system it is but a short step to a consideration of three proposals for reforming the international monetary system. Each of these three proposals for reform resulted during the late 1960s and early 1970s in a number of significant changes in the international monetary system. But the reformed system appears to be only a temporary arrangement: the system itself is still changing. No one can be sure how it will change, how rapidly it will change, and what the new system will be like. The only thing that seems certain is that the new system will be very different from the Bretton Woods system because the Bretton Woods system was simply unable to provide the world with the necessary monetary reserves and to move the world toward international equilibrium.

The final brief section of Chapter 44 reaches a most important conclusion: the things a nation must do to promote full employment and stable prices are not always the things it has to do to achieve equilibrium in its balance of payments. The author explains when the policies that will eliminate unemployment and inflation are consistent and when they are inconsistent with the policies that will eliminate a payments surplus or deficit. The student must be sure to understand when domestic policies conflict with and when they reinforce a nation's international economic policies.

Again there are a number of new terms in the chapter. But there is really no new theory. The principles and basic notions necessary to understand these problems were developed in Chapters 41, 42 and 43; the same principles and notions should enable the student to see how policies have been developed to solve the problems. In fact, the men and governments who designed the policies first had to understand principles, just as the student first has to understand principles, in order to understand the problems and develop solutions for them.

■ CHAPTER OUTLINE

1. Prior to 1930 the volume of international trade was large and was based on the principle of comparative advantage, a philosophy of laissez faire, and the automatic operation of the gold standard.

a. The Depression of the 1930s drastically reduced the volume of international trade and lending, and most nations erected trade barriers in a futile attempt to solve their domestic unemployment problems.

b. World War II increased the warring nations' demands for imports, reduced their willingness to export, and resulted in inflation and in the destruction of productive capacity.

c. The cold war period was marked by restrictions upon trade between the communist and free worlds, the pursuit of stable prices and full employment at home, and the economic independence of the underdeveloped nations.

d. The world (and especially Europe) at the close of World War II faced the problem of rebuilding its economy. To solve this problem the productive capacity of Europe had to be restored, an international monetary system had to be provided to facilitate and increase trade, and artificial trade barriers had to be reduced.

2. The United Nations Relief and Rehabilitation Administration and the United States Marshall Plan provided the postwar aid to rebuild Europe.

3. To rebuild the international monetary system and stabilize exchange rates, the International Monetary Fund was formed at the end of World War II.

a. The IMF, using the Bretton Woods system (or adjustable-peg technique), stabilized exchange rates and provided for orderly changes in exchange rates to correct international disequilibria.

b. A well-functioning international monetary system required a sufficient amount of international monetary reserves. Gold and key currencies (the United States dollar and the British pound) provided these reserves.

c. By the early 1970s it had become evident that the Bretton Woods system was unable to bring about the needed expansion in the world's international monetary reserves and to correct balance of payments disequilibria.

4. Since 1949 the United States has had annual balance of payments deficits in all but two years and its gold reserves have decreased.

a. Because of productivity increases in many foreign nations and inflation in the United

States, the American balance of trade surplus has been less than its foreign aid and military expenditures and investments abroad, and the result has been a payments deficit.

b. Policies to reduce or eliminate the payments deficits would include having Western Europe assume a larger share of the costs of mutual defense and foreign aid; inducing nations with surpluses to lower their trade barriers and increase their investments in the United States; increasing productivity and limiting inflation in the United States; and devaluation of the dollar.

c. To control its payments deficit, the United States temporarily employed various measures or controls which limit and distort world trade.

d. The persistent American balance of payments deficits are related to the Bretton Woods system in two important ways.

(1) The deficits have been the major source of the increases in the world's international monetary reserves; but the elimination of these deficits will reduce the growth in reserves needed if world trade is to expand.

(2) The elimination of the payments deficits of the United States has been difficult because the exchange rate "pegs" were rarely adjusted and exchange rates were in fact rigid.

5. Three possible reforms have been suggested as a way of increasing international reserves and bringing about payments equilibrium.

a. If the United States raised the price of gold, reserves would increase; but several serious problems would be created.

b. It has been suggested by Professor Triffin that like nations' domestic monetary reserves, which are managed, international monetary reserves should also be managed.

c. It has also been suggested that the world return to freely fluctuating exchange rates. While this would solve the problem of insufficient reserves and would correct disequilibria, it would also result in several new problems.

6. A number of fairly recent events have brought about significant changes in the international monetary system.

a. The Rio de Janeiro conference of 1967 resulted in the creation of new international reserves called Special Drawing Rights (SDRs) which the IMF creates and lends to member nations.

b. In August of 1971 the United States (faced with continued balance of payments deficits and the prospects of a balance of trade deficit) suspended the convertibility of dollars into gold. Demand and supply caused the international value of the dollar to float downward; and the dollar was in effect devalued.

c. The Smithsonian Agreement in late 1971 realigned exchange rates to correct the overvaluation of the dollar and widened the limits within which exchange rates would be allowed to fluctuate. (As a part of the agreement the United States devalued the dollar by increasing the price of gold from $35 to $38 an ounce.)

d. Early in 1973 the United States abandoned the exchange rates of the Smithsonian Agreement when it again devalued the dollar (by raising the price of gold to $42.22 an ounce); and demand and supply became the major determinants of foreign exchange rates.

e. The old international monetary system is gradually changing into the system of the future and it is not clear what this future system will be. But it seems fairly certain that it will employ "crawling pegs" to determine foreign exchange rates and will reduce the importance of gold and dollars as international monetary reserves.

7. The domestic economic policies a nation employs to decrease unemployment or to reduce inflation may be either compatible or conflict with the international economic policies it would employ to achieve a balance of payments equilibrium.

a. The policies it would employ to eliminate unemployment conflict with (are compatible with) the policies it would utilize to reduce a payments deficit (surplus).

b. But the policies it would use to combat inflation are compatible with (conflict with) the policies it would invoke to reduce a payments deficit (surplus).

■ IMPORTANT TERMS

United Nations Relief and Rehabilitation Administration

European Recovery Program (Marshall Plan)

Bretton Woods system

Adjustable pegs

International Monetary Fund

International monetary reserves

Key currencies

Devaluation

Triffin Plan

Rio Plan

Special Drawing
Rights (SDRs)

"Floating" the
dollar

Smithsonian Agreement

Managed floating rate

Crawling-peg
system

a. _____

b. _____

c. _____

■ FILL-IN QUESTIONS

1. In the last half of the nineteenth century the volume of international trade in the world was _____ ; and this trade was primarily an exchange of the _____ of the _____ nations for the _____ of the _____ nations. Trade was based on the principle of _____ , the ideology of _____ , and the automatic operation of the _____ _____

2. In the years following 1929 the amount of international trade was substantially reduced by _____ , _____ , and _____ . The former event gave rise to reduced _____ , reduced long-term _____ , and _____

3. Nations at war usually want to increase their _____ and decrease their _____ and this creates a _____ problem for these nations. War also tends to result in _____ and the destruction of _____

4. The cold war environment has not been conducive to the reconstruction of international trade for at least three reasons:

5. The postwar programs and institutions to rebuild world trade had three related objectives: to _____ , to _____ , and to _____

6. The most pressing economic problem facing the world at the end of World War II was to _____ . The United States helped to solve this problem by contributing heavily to _____ and by instituting the _____ program.

7. The Bretton Woods system was established to bring about _____ exchange rates. To accomplish this, it employed an _____ system of exchange rates.

8. In the Bretton Woods system international monetary reserves included both _____ and the "_____" (which were the monies of two nations: _____ and _____)

9. The world has recently been short of _____ reserves because the demand for them has increased _____ rapidly than their supply and this shortage has made it difficult to expand _____

10. Reaching international equilibrium has been difficult because exchange rate pegs were _____

11. The recent balance of payments position of the United States reflects:
a. A smaller balance of trade surplus caused by increases in the _____ of

foreign producers and by _____ in the United States.

b. A payments deficit due to this smaller trade surplus, substantial American capital _____, and _____ _____ by the United States in foreign nations.

12. Without restricting imports; the United States might alter its payments position by:

a. _____

b. _____

c. _____

d. _____

e. _____

13. A nation with a balance of payments deficit might introduce controls to reduce its _____ _____ and to expand its _____. But these controls will reduce and distort _____ and are apt to induce other nations to _____

14. The American balance of payments deficits:

a. put dollars into the hands of foreign nations and, as a result, increased the world's _____

b. persisted because the Bretton Woods system did not in fact adjust the _____

15. To increase reserves and foster balance of payments equilibrium, the following three reforms have been suggested.

a. _____

b. _____

c. _____

16. Following the suggestions in the _____ _____ Plan, the Rio de Janeiro conference adopted a proposal to have the IMF create and lend a new international money called _____

17. Floating the dollar means that the dollar can no longer be converted into _____;

and that _____ now determine the international value of the dollar.

18. The Smithsonian Agreement:

a. corrected the (over-, under-) _____ valuation of the dollar;

b. (widened, narrowed) _____ the permissible limits of exchange rate fluctuations.

19. Following the Smithsonian Agreement the United States _____ the dollar for a second time by raising the dollar price of _____; and since then there has been a "_____ of exchange rates."

20. Any new international monetary system will probably include a _____ pegs system of exchange rates and the downgrading of _____ and _____ as international monetary reserves.

■ PROBLEMS AND PROJECTS

1. Below is a series of identifying phrases followed by a list of acts, programs, institutions, etc. Match the phrase with the act, program, institution, etc., by placing the appropriate letter in the space following each phrase. (*Note:* Not all the items in the list will have an identifying phrase.)

1. Makes short-term loans to member nations to stabilize foreign exchange rates and maintain exchange convertibility. _____

2. Agreement of 106 nations that authorized the IMF to create Special Drawing Rights. _____

3. Corrected the overvaluation of the dollar and widened the permissible limits of exchange rate fluctuation. _____

4. Provided food, clothing, and medical aid to European nations in the immediate postwar period. _____

5. The American dollar and the British pound. _____

6. Dollars could no longer be converted into gold and the exchange rate for the dollar depended upon demand and supply. _____

7. Relatively fixed foreign exchange rates managed by the International Monetary Fund.

8. Program that would allow nations with chronic balance of payments deficits to increase the par value of their currencies by a small percentage each month. _____

9. Program that would require all member nations to deposit their international monetary reserves with the International Monetary Fund and allow the IMF to create new reserves by making loans in excess of the amount of the deposits with it. _____

10. American program to aid European nations in rebuilding their productive capacities destroyed during World War II. _____

11. Allowing demand and supply to determine exchange rate trends and the smoothing out of day-to-day fluctuations in exchange rates. _____

A. United Nations Relief and Rehabilitation Administration
B. European Recovery Program (Marshall Plan)
C. Adjustment problem
D. Bretton Woods system
E. Tiffin Plan
F. International Monetary Fund
G. Managed floating of exchange rates
H. Key currencies
I. Floating the dollar
J. Smithsonian Agreement
K. Crawling-peg system
L. Rio de Janeiro conference

2. Assume:
a. the American economy has fully employed its labor force, is experiencing inflation, and has a balance of payments *deficit*.
(1) to reduce the inflationary pressures in the economy requires a(n) (expansionary, contractionary) _____ fiscal policy and a(n) (tight, easy) _____ monetary policy;
(2) if these measures are successful in curbing inflation without reducing employment, the economy's:
(a) exports will tend to (increase, decrease)

_____

(b) imports will tend to _____

(c) interest rates in the economy will (rise, fall) _____ and this will encourage the flow of capital (into, out of) _____ the United States
(d) the payments deficit of the American economy will tend to (increase, decrease)

(3) the measures undertaken to reduce inflation in the United States worked to (reduce, widen) _____ the payments deficit;
(4) but if the economy had begun with a payments *surplus* the fiscal and monetary measures taken to fight inflation would have:
(a) increased the economy's (exports, imports) _____
(b) reduced its _____
(c) driven _____ rates upward and encourage the flow of _____ in the United States
(d) and the payments surplus of the economy would have (widened, narrowed) _____
b. the American economy has a relatively large portion (8 to 10%) of its labor force unemployed, is experiencing a depression, and has a balance of payments *surplus*.
(1) to reduce unemployment and increase the economy's real output requires a(n) _____ _____ fiscal policy and a(n) _____ monetary policy;
(2) if these measures are successful in expanding employment and output in the economy:
(a) exports will tend to _____
(b) imports will tend to _____
(c) interest rates will tend to _____ and this will encourage the flow of capital (into, out of) _____ the United States;
(d) the payments surplus of the American economy will tend to _____
(3) the measures undertaken to reduce unemployment in the United States worked to (reduce, widen) _____ the payments surplus;
(4) but if the economy had begun with a payments *deficit* the fiscal and monetary poli-

cies employed to fight recession would have

(widened, narrowed) _____ the deficit.
  c. In summary, policies employed to
  (1) combat *inflation* (conflict, are compatible) _____

with the elimination of a payments deficit and

_____ with the reduction
of a payments surplus;

  (2) reduce *unemployment* _____
with the elimination of a payments deficit and

_____ with the reduction of
a payments surplus.

■ SELF-TEST

Circle the T if the statement is true, the F if it is false.

1. During the Depression of the 1930s most of the nations of the world lowered barriers to international trade in an attempt to increase domestic employment and output.   **T   F**

2. While the cold war left the Communist bloc and the Western nations ideologically divided, the volume of trade between them increased sharply in the twenty-year period following World War II.   **T   F**

3. The immediate postwar needs of Europe for food, clothing, and medical services were met by the United States through the establishment of the European Recovery Program (Marshall Plan).   **T   F**

4. Most experts agree that the European Recovery Program was highly successful in restoring the industrial and agricultural capacity of Western Europe.   **T   F**

5. In the Bretton Woods system a nation could not devalue its currency by more than 10% without the permission of the International Fund.   **T   F**

6. The "key currencies" in the Bretton Woods system were the American dollar and the British pound.   **T   F**

7. One of the basic shortcomings of the Bretton Woods system in recent years has been its inability to bring about the changes in exchange rates needed to correct persistent balance of payments deficits and surpluses.
        T   F

8. The world has become short of international monetary reserves because the demand for them has not increased as rapidly as the supply.   **T   F**

9. The smaller American balances of trade in the 1950s and 1960s can be attributed to the economic recovery of Japan and Western Europe and to unemployment in the United States.   **T   F**

10. When a nation devalues its currency the goods and services it produces become more expensive for foreigners to buy and goods and services produced abroad become more expensive for its citizens to buy.   **T   F**

11. One suggested solution for the current United States balance of payments problem is an increase in American foreign aid to underdeveloped nations.   **T   F**

12. The basic shortcomings of the adjustable-peg system was the failure to change exchange rates when permanent payments deficits existed.   **T   F**

13. Under the Bretton Woods system foreign exchange rates remained relatively stable, but the American dollar became overvalued. **T   F**

14. Advocates of the Triffin Plan proposed that the International Monetary Fund be allowed to create international monetary reserves by lending monies in excess of the amounts deposited with it.   **T   F**

15. The Rio de Janeiro conference of 1967 proposed that the world return to freely fluctuating foreign exchange rates.   **T   F**

16. The policies used by a country to eliminate unemployment are compatible with the elimination of that country's balance of payments deficit.   **T   F**

Underscore the letter that corresponds to the best answer.

1. Which one of the following was characteristic of international trade throughout most of the nineteenth century? (*a*) extensive barriers to trade; (*b*) the almost automatic operation of the gold standard; (*c*) a small volume of international trade; (*d*) government regulation of most foreign exchange rates.

2. Which one of the following was *not* characteristic of world trade during World War II?

(a) trade was based on military objectives rather than on comparative advantages; (b) shortages of foreign exchange existed in most countries at war; (c) inflation in the warring nations made the exports of these nations more attractive to foreign buyers; (d) inflation in the warring nations made foreign goods more attractive to buyers in the warring nations.

3. The *most urgent* of the world's economic problems immediately following World War II was: (a) the elimination of trade barriers; (b) the development of an international monetary system; (c) the economic development of the underdeveloped nations; (d) the reconstruction of the European economies.

4. Which of the following has had as its basic objective the restoration of the productive capacity of European industry and agriculture? (a) the Triffin Plan; (b) UNRRA; (c) the Marshall Plan; (d) the Bretton Woods Conference.

5. Which one of the following was *not* characteristic of the International Monetary Fund in the Bretton Woods system? (a) made short-term loans to member nations with balance of payments deficits; (b) tried to maintain relatively stable foreign exchange rates; (c) attempted to maintain foreign exchange convertibility; (d) extended long-term loans to underdeveloped nations for the purpose of increasing their productive capacities.

6. All but one of the following were elements in the adjustable-peg system of foreign exchange rates. Which one? (a) each nation defined its monetary unit in terms of gold or dollars; (b) nations maintained foreign exchange stabilization funds; (c) nations were allowed to devalue their currencies when faced with persistent payments deficits; (d) the deposit by all nations of their international reserves with the IMF.

7. Which of the following is the best definition of international monetary reserves in the Bretton Woods system? (a) gold; (b) gold and dollars; (c) gold, dollars, and British pounds; (d) gold, dollars, British pounds, and Russian rubles.

8. During most of the period since 1949 the United States position in world trade has been characterized by: (a) a balance of trade deficit; (b) the importation of gold into the United States; (c) a balance of payments surplus; (d) American military expenditures, economic aid, and investments abroad in excess of the world's balance of trade deficit with the United States.

9. Which of the following would be the *least* desirable method of reducing or eliminating the American balance of payments problem? (a) an increase in American tariff rates; (b) an expansion in the share of the costs of the North American Treaty Alliance borne by the Western European members of the alliance; (c) the restraint of inflation in the United States; (d) the relaxation of foreign restrictions on American goods.

10. Which one of the following was *not* one of the controls introduced by the United States to ease its balance of payments deficit? (a) the interest equalization tax; (b) the rejection of SDRs by Congress; (c) the executive order by the President limiting foreign investment; (d) the "tying" of foreign aid to American goods.

11. Which one of the following would *not* tend to reduce a nation's balance of payments deficit? (a) an increase in the productivity of the nation's resources; (b) an increase in the nation's price level; (c) an increase in the flow of private capital into the nation; (d) an increase in the nation's exports.

12. If the United States were to eliminate its annual balance of payments deficit (a) the world's international monetary reserves would decrease; (b) the annual increases in the world's international monetary reserves would decline; (c) the number of dollars owned by foreign nations would expand; (d) the amount of gold owned by the United States would increase.

13. An increase in the dollar price of gold (a) rewards those who have held dollars instead of gold; (b) penalizes those who have held gold instead of dollars; (c) decreases the dollar value of the world's stock of monetary gold; (d) devalues the dollar.

14. Freely fluctuating or floating exchange rates (a) would tend to correct balance of payments disequilibria quickly and automatically; (b) reduce the uncertainties and risks associated with international trade; (c) in-

crease the world's need for international monetary reserves; (d) tend to expand the volume of world trade.

15. Which of the following is *not* true of SDRs? (a) they serve as international reserves; (b) they have no gold backing; (c) they are issued by the United Nations; (d) they are acceptable in payment of international debts by the members of the IMF.

16. "Floating" the dollar means (a) the value of the dollar is determined by the demand for and the supply of the dollar; (b) the dollar price of gold has been increased; (c) the price of the dollar has been allowed to crawl upward at the rate of one-fourth of 1% a month; (d) the IMF decreased the value of the dollar by 10%.

17. The Smithsonian Agreement (a) increased the dollar price of gold to $42.22 per ounce; (b) devalued the French franc and the West German mark; (c) floated the dollar; (d) increased the limits within which exchange rates were allowed to fluctuate.

18. A year after the Smithsonian Agreement (a) the United States again devalued the dollar; (b) the system for determining exchange rates became one in which rates were managed and floating; (c) both of the above; (d) neither of the above.

19. The international monetary system of the future will probably (a) include a crawling peg system for determining exchange rates; (b) reduce the importance of gold and dollars as international monetary reserves; (c) both of the above; (d) neither of the above.

20. Which of the following policies are compatible? (a) those designed to eliminate inflation and a balance of payments deficit; (b) those utilized to eliminate unemployment and a payments surplus; (c) both of the above; (d) neither of the above.

■ DISCUSSION QUESTIONS

1. What were the extent and character of international trade in the nineteenth century?

2. Explain the effect of each of the following upon the volume and character of world trade and upon the international trade polices of

the nations of the world: (a) the Depression of the 1930s; (b) World War II; (c) the cold war.

3. What was the condition of world trade at the end of World War II? What were the three objectives of the postwar programs used to correct this condition?

4. Which of the economic problems faced by the world at the end of World War II was the most urgent? How did the United States help to solve this problem?

5. Explain (a) why the International Monetary Fund was established and what the objectives of the adjustable-pegs (or Bretton Woods) system were; (b) what the adjustable-pegs system was and the basic means it employed to stabilize exchange rates in the short run; and (c) when and how the system was to adjust exchange rates in the long run.

6. Why are international monetary reserves necessary? What is the effect of inadequate monetary reserves upon international trade? What did nations use for an international reserve during the twenty-five years following World War II?

7. Did the Bretton Woods system assist or impede the reconstruction and expansion of international trade between 1945 and 1970? What two problems lead to the breakdown of and a need for the reform of the system in the early 1970s?

8. In what way has the international trade position of the United States during the past twenty years differed from its position in the years immediately following World War II? What have been the main causes of this change?

9. What are the five basic measures which would help to correct the American balance of payments deficit?

10. What controls were employed temporarily to reduce the United States' payments deficit? Why are controls not generally an economically desirable means of eliminating payments deficits?

11. How was the American balance of payments deficit in the 1950s and 1960s linked to the international monetary reserves of the Bretton Woods system? What effect would the reduction or elimination of this payments deficit have upon the growth of these reserves?

12. How is the failure of the Bretton Woods system to adjust the exchange-rate pegs related to the persistent balance of payments deficits of the United States?

13. What two problems made the Bretton Woods system a less than satisfactory international monetary arrangement in the late 1960s and early 1970s; and what proposals for the reform of this system have been suggested? Explain the advantages and disadvantages of each of these proposals.

14. Explain the Rio Plan and Special Drawing Rights. How are SDRs created, what "backs" them, and how and for what purpose are they created?

15. In August of 1971 the United States suspended its thirty-seven year old policy of allowing foreign governments and central banks to convert their dollars into gold. Why did the United States do this? Why did this result in the "floating" of the dollar, in what amounted to a devaluation of the dollar, and in the end of the Bretton Woods system?

16. What were the two main provisions of the Smithsonian Agreement of December, 1971? Why did the United States again devalue the dollar and abandon the Smithsonian Agreement in early 1973? What is meant when it is said the present system for determining exchange rates is a "managed floating of exchange rates"?

17. What two predictions can be safely made about the international monetary system of the future?

18. Explain when and why the policies employed by a nation to reduce unemployment or inflation conflict with and when and why they are compatable with the elimination of a balance of payments disequilibrium.

THE ECONOMIC SYSTEM
OF SOVIET RUSSIA

In the past people in the United States were convinced that the economic system of the Soviet Union was totally unworkable and that it would sooner or later break down—proof that Marx, Lenin, and Stalin were unrealistic dreamers—and that the reconversion of their economy to a free enterprise, price-market system would follow. Slowly it dawned upon the American people that the breakdown would not occur and, on the contrary, the Soviet economy was becoming more workable and more productive, and that Soviet Russia was becoming a very strong nation. In part the early American belief that Soviet Russia would collapse was based on prejudice—they wanted it to collapse in order to prove to themselves that the system employed by American capitalism was both the only feasible system of economic organization and the most perfectly operated system—and in part it was based on ignorance of the institutions and methods employed by Russian communism.

The aim of Chapter 45 is to dispel some of the ignorance surrounding Soviet institutions and methods and by doing so eliminate the basis for much of the unwarranted prejudice against the Soviet *economic system*. (Chapter 45, of course, does not try to convince the reader that the United States should adopt the Soviet economic system, nor does it try

to persuade the reader that the Russian way of life *as a whole* is morally, politically, or socially preferable.) To accomplish its aim the chapter first examines the two institutions of the Soviet economy which are remarkably different from anything found in American capitalism and which are the framework of the Russian economy. Within this framework the Fundamental Economic Problems are solved through central economic planning. Central economic planning has no counterpart in the United States, and it is to further authoritarian central economic planning that the Soviet institutional framework is maintained. The better part of the chapter is devoted to explaining what central planning is and how it is employed in the U.S.S.R. to obtain answers to the Fundamental Economic Problems.

If the student learns anything from this chapter he ought to learn that the Soviet *economy* is the source of its political and military strength and that the performance and growth of the Soviet and American economic systems (and the social and political institutions that accompany them) are being watched by people throughout the world who will be inclined to adopt the economic *and* political *and* social system which promises them the best prospect of improving their own material well-being. In addition, the student should be aware that it is not a question of "Will the Soviet system work?" but of how well it works.

There is great strength in the Soviet Union because the government is able to compel the economy to do as it wishes. The large and almost continuous increases in Soviet output are mostly the result of authoritarian central economic planning and the direction of the economy toward the achievement of these plans by central authority. It is both the strength and weakness of the American economy that it lacks central direction. It was once assumed that central planning was too complex to be practical and that only the impersonal price-market system could coordinate the various parts of the economy, just as it was once imagined that only monetary self-interest and private property could provoke increased efficiency, effort, and output. The Soviet experiment suggests the contrary.

Of course, economic and political freedom is lacking in the Soviet Union, but for the underfed, the illiterate, the sick, and those without hope, this would be a small price to pay for even a slightly improved standard of living. Whether the Soviet system will be adopted by underdeveloped nations depends not only upon how successful the Soviet system is in the future, but also upon how well the American system functions in improving its own and others' standards of living, and upon the moral, political, and social costs of this improvement.

Although nondiscussion questions and problems are provided in this study guide, studying these questions is not sufficient to develop and test fully the student's understanding of the Soviet Union. The nature of the material is such that the student should spend considerable time and effort on the discussion questions.

■ CHAPTER OUTLINE

1. The major economic characteristics of the U.S.S.R. are:

a. The state ownership of most property resources (as opposed to private ownership).

b. Central and authoritarian economic planning or government direction (as opposed to the price-market system).

c. The limited freedom of choice of consumers and workers (as opposed to consumer sovereignty and freedom of occupation).

2. Central planning is used in the Soviet Union to answer the Five Fundamental Economic Questions.

a. Government in the U.S.S.R. sets forth the goals of the economy in its Five-Year and Annual Plans.

b. The basic problem encountered in planning for an entire economy is the difficulty of coordinating the many interdependent segments of the economy and the avoidance of the chain reaction that would result from a bottleneck in any one of these segments.

c. To coordinate the different sectors of the economy, *Gosplan* plans by negotiation, employs the priority principle, and uses inventories to offset bottlenecks.

d. To achieve the objectives of central planning the Soviet government relies upon control agencies such as *Gosplan* and other planning groups and especially upon *Gosbank*.

e. To motivate economic units to fulfill the plan the U.S.S.R. employs monetary and nonmonetary incentives and coercion.

f. Prices in the Soviet economy are established by the state and are used to promote the achievement of the plans.

3. Microeconomic problems troubled the Soviet economy in the late 1960s, and a number of reforms were instituted.

a. The three principal problems were the production of unsalable goods, distorted production and poor-quality goods, and resistance to innovation by producing enterprises.

b. At the suggestion of Liberman and others, the government introduced a modified profit motive, less central planning and more planning from below, and greater autonomy for the managers of individual enterprises.

4. The U.S.S.R. has sought the macroeconomic goal of rapid economic growth.

a. The GNP of the U.S.S.R. is about one-half that of the United States; but its growth rate has been greater than that of the United States.

b. The sources of this rapid growth in the Soviet Union were its large endowment of natural resources, its totalitarian government, its surplus farm labor, its adoption of the superior technologies developed in Western nations, and its virtual elimination of cyclical unemployment.

c. There are at least six factors which slowed Soviet growth in recent years.

d. But there are four reasons to believe that the U.S.S.R. may be able to continue to grow at the same rate.

e. On balance it is not possible to predict the Soviet growth rate in the future.

5. Any evaluation of the Soviet system requires an examination of its principal accomplishments and shortcomings.

a. Its major accomplishments are the great improvements in education and its complete system of social insurance.

b. The shortcomings are the small increases in the consumers' standard of living and the general absence of personal freedom.

6. The hypothesis that the capitalistic and communistic systems are converging and that the differences between the institutions and policies of the two systems are becoming smaller is supported by some evidence; but the differences between the two systems are still great and may not be narrowing at all.

■ IMPORTANT TERMS

State ownership

Central economic planning

Gosplan

Libermanism

Priority principle

Gosbank

Turnover tax

Forced economic growth

Convergence hypothesis

■ FILL-IN QUESTIONS

1. The two institutions of the U.S.S.R. which are in sharp contrast with private property and the price-market system of the United States are _____

and _____

2. In the U.S.S.R. the _____ determines the goals or objectives of the economy while in the United States it is the _____

_____

which sets goals or objectives.

3. The basic planning problem in the Soviet Union is the _____ of the various sectors of the economy. The failure of any one of these sectors to produce its planned output results in a _____ which causes a _____ throughout the remainder of the economy.

4. To coordinate the various segments of the economy the Soviet government plans by _____; and when bottlenecks appear it applies the _____ principle and draws upon _____

5. _____ is the agency primarily responsible for the construction of the economic plan in the Soviet Union, and _____ is the agency primarily responsible for ensuring that the provisions of the plan are enforced.

6. Production in the Soviet Union is motivated by _____,

_____,

and _____

7. In the U.S.S.R. prices perform two essential functions, namely, _____

and _____

8. Profits in the Soviet Union are essentially a means of determining _____ while in the United States profits serve to

_____

9. The Soviet economy in recent years has had serious microeconomic problems and has had to undertake reform to reduce these problems.

a. Three problems which plagued planners were:

(1) The production of _____ goods and the accumulation of _____ inventories.

(2) A distorted _____ of goods which were of poor _____

(3) The reluctance of enterprise managers

to _____

b. The reforms undertaken include:

(1) The introduction of a modified _____

_____

(2) More _____ in the

economy and more _____
for enterprise managers.

(3) More planning from _____

c. These reforms were suggested by _____

_____ and others.

10. The gross national product of the

U.S.S.R. is about _____ of the
GNP of the United States and grew during

the 1960s at a rate of about _____%
per year.

11. List five specific reasons why there has
been economic growth in the U.S.S.R.

a. _____

b. _____

c. _____

d. _____

e. _____

12. What six factors may retard future economic growth in the Soviet Union?

a. _____

b. _____

c. _____

d. _____

e. _____

f. _____

13. What considerations suggest that the Soviet economy may be able to sustain its rate
of economic growth?

a. _____

b. _____

c. _____

d. _____

14. What have been the two most significant
accomplishments of the U.S.S.R. since central
planning began?

a. _____

b. _____

15. The two chief shortcomings of the Soviet economy over the past years have been

_____

and _____

■ PROBLEMS AND PROJECTS

1. On the left side of the table on page 332 are
several of the major institutions or characteristics of American capitalism. In the spaces to
the right, name the institution or characteristic of the Soviet economy which compares
with the American institution or characteristic.

2. Below is a market demand schedule for
product X.

Price, rubles	Quantity demanded (million)
90	25
80	30
70	35
60	40
50	45
40	50
30	55

a. If Soviet planners decide to produce 50
million units of product X, the price of the
product *plus* the turnover tax will be set at

_____ rubles.

b. If the accounting cost of producing product X is 25 rubles, the turnover tax *rate* will

be set at _____%.

■ SELF-TEST

*Circle the T if the statement is true, the F if it
is false.*

1. The Soviet government sets the economic
objectives of the economy, directs the resources of the economy toward the achievement of these objectives, and uses the price
system as one of the means of achieving these
objectives.   **T   F**

American institution or characteristic	Russian institution or characteristic
Private ownership of economic resources	
Consumer freedom to spend income as he sees fit	
Consumer sovereignty	
Worker freedom to select occupation and place of work	
Profit motive	
Entrepreneurial freedom to select product, output, price, etc.	
System of prices and markets	
Self-interest	
Privately owned farms	
Privately owned industrial firms and retail stores	

2. Consumers in the U.S.S.R. are free to spend their incomes on any of the consumer goods provided by the economy's central plan. **T F**

3. *Gosplan* is the agency in the Soviet Union primarily responsible for preparing the economic plan. **T F**

4. In the U.S.S.R. individual plants and industries play no part in the formulation of the final economic plan. **T F**

5. The basic planning problem in the Soviet Union is the determination of the overall goals of the economy. **T F**

6. Application of the priority principle means that when production bottlenecks develop in the economy, inventories are used to prevent a chain reaction. **T F**

7. Most workers in the Soviet Union are paid on a piece-rate basis. **T F**

8. The turnover tax does not affect the price of consumer goods, but it does affect the consumer income available for the purchase of consumer goods. **T F**

9. The GNP of the U.S.S.R. is about one-half the size of GNP in the United States, and the rate of growth of the GNP in the Soviet Union has been greater than the rate of growth of GNP in the United States. **T F**

10. GNP in the U.S.S.R. will undoubtedly expand at a more rapid rate in the future than it has in the past. **T F**

Underscore the letter that corresponds to the best answer.

1. Which of the following is *not* true? (a) the standard of living in the U.S.S.R. is below the standard of living of the U.S.; (b) the output of the Russian economy exceeds the output of the American economy; (c) the output of the Russian economy is growing at a more rapid rate than the output of the American economy; (d) the Soviet economy devotes a larger percentage of its output to capital accumulation than does the American economy.

2. In the U.S.S.R.: (a) all property is owned by the state or by collective farms and cooperatives; (b) all property except urban housing and farms is owned either by the state or by cooperatives; (c) all property except retail and wholesale enterprises is owned either by the state or by collective farms and cooperatives; (d) all property except small tools, clothing, household furnishings, and rural homes is owned either by the state or by collective farms and cooperatives.

3. Which of the following is the most important agency in enforcing and carrying out the central economic plan in the Soviet Union?

(a) *Gosplan;* (b) *Gosbank;* (c) the Communist party; (d) the secret police.

4. Prices in the Soviet Union: (a) are used as a device for rationing consumer goods; (b) are determined by the demands for and the supplies of products and resources; (c) are used to allocate resources among different firms and industries; (d) perform a guiding function, but not a rationing function.

5. Profits and losses in the U.S.S.R. are used to determine whether: (a) the production of various consumer goods should be expanded or contracted; (b) various goods are being produced efficiently or inefficiently; (c) more or fewer resources should be devoted to the production of various goods; (d) a product should be taxed or subsidized.

6. Suppose the Soviet government determined that the annual output of a certain quality of wristwatch would be 100,000 and that the accounting cost of producing a watch is 300 rubles. If the demand schedule for these watches were as given in the table below, what turnover tax rate would be placed on watches? (a) 33⅓%; (b) 66⅔%; (c) 100%; (d) 133⅓%.

Price, rubles	Quantity demanded
700	85,000
600	90,000
500	100,000
400	120,000
300	150,000
200	190,000
100	240,000

7. In the late 1960s the Soviet government undertook a number of economic reforms. These include: (a) the abolition of central planning; (b) the introduction of a modified profit motive; (c) the return of public property to private ownership; (d) the reduction of the autonomy of the managers of individual enterprises.

8. In comparing the composition of GNP in the U.S.S.R. and the United States it can be said that: (a) over 25% of the GNP in the United States is devoted to capital goods while less than 20% is so devoted in the U.S.S.R.; (b) government in the U.S.S.R. ab-

sorbs over 20% and in the United States absorbs less than 10% of the GNP; (c) over 75% of the GNP in both nations is represented by consumer goods; (d) investment in the U.S.S.R. is over one-half again as large as it is in the United States.

9. Which of the following is *not* a significant factor in explaining the rapid rate of economic growth in the Soviet Union? (a) extensive investment by foreigners in the Soviet economy; (b) high levels of domestic investment in basic industries; (c) adoption of the advanced technological methods employed in Western nations; (d) the reallocation of labor from the agricultural to the industrial sector of the economy.

10. Which of the following is apt to make it possible for the Soviet Union to sustain or increase its rate of economic growth? (a) conditions in the agricultural sector of the economy; (b) the past efforts to improve education and technology; (c) the overall manpower situation; (d) increases in the level of replacement investment.

■ DISCUSSION QUESTIONS

1. What are the two principal economic institutions of the U.S.S.R.? How do these institutions compare with the economic institutions of the United Staes?

2. What is the basic planning problem in the U.S.S.R.? What techniques are used to overcome this problem and make central planning workable?

3. How is an economic plan drawn up in the Soviet Union? How is such a plan made "realistic and workable"? Why is the process of obtaining the final plan referred to as a "down-and-up evolution"?

4. What means and agencies are used in the Soviet Union to facilitate the achievement of the objectives of the economic plan? What types of incentives and inducements are offered to encourage the achievement of these objectives?

5. What is meant by the priority principle of resource allocation? What sectors of the Soviet economy have received high priorities in the past?

6. Explain the role *Gosbank* plays in the enforcement of the central economic plan in the U.S.S.R.

7. What functions do prices perform in the U.S.S.R.? How does the Russian government use the turnover tax to set the prices of consumer goods?

8. Plants and firms in the U.S.S.R. can earn profits or suffer losses just as plants and firms can in the United States. What role do profits and losses play in the U.S.S.R. and what role do they play in the United States?

9. How is the turnover tax used in the Soviet Union to match the quantities demanded of various consumer goods with the quantities of these goods which *Gosplan* has already decided to produce?

10. What microeconomic problems did the Soviet government encounter in the late 1960s, and what reforms did they introduce in an attempt to resolve these problems? What role did Professor Liberman play in these reforms?

11. Compare the GNP of the Soviet Union and the United States with respect to size, composition, and rate of growth.

12. Why has it been possible for the U.S.S.R. to achieve economic growth? Why is economic growth in the Soviet Union called "forced economic growth"?

13. What have been the major accomplishments of central planning in the U.S.S.R.? What are its chief shortcomings?

14. Explain the convergence hypothesis. What evidence is there in the U.S. and in the U.S.S.R. to support this hypothesis? Why may the tendency toward convergence be more apparent than real?

ANSWERS

CHAPTER 1

Fill-in questions

1. production, exchange, consumption

2. generalizations, abstraction

3. economics is not a laboratory science and economics deals with the behavior of human beings

4. control economic events

5. economic growth, full employment, price stability, economic freedom, equitable distribution of income, economic security

6. *a.* a clear statement of the objectives and goals of the policy; *b.* a statement and analysis of all possible alternative solutions to the problem; *c.* an evaluation of the results of the policy selected after it has been put into operation

7. *a.* failure to distinguish between relevant and irrelevant facts; *b.* failure to recognize economic models for what they are—useful first approximations; *c.* tendency to impute ethical or moral qualities to economic models

8. the economy may be in a different phase of the business cycle

9. employ two different terms to mean the same thing

10. total, general, individual industry, particular product

Problems and projects

1. An increase in the demand for an economic good will cause the price of that good to rise.

2. All the factors are relevant to *some degree.* However, the degree of relevance of the factors varies; and, depending upon the degree of abstraction and generality desired in the analysis of the production and the price of automobiles, the factors may be included or excluded from consideration. The noneconomic factors are *c* (political), *i* (sociological), *k* (ecological), *l* (psychological), and *m* (political).

5. *a.* The validity of the statement depends upon the phase of the business cycle; *b.* the fallacy of composition; *c.* dual terminology; *d.* the *post hoc, ergo propter hoc* fallacy.

6. *c.* direct, up; *d.* inverse, down.

Self-test

1. F; **2.** T; **3.** T; **4.** T; **5.** T; **6.** F; **7.** F; **8.** F; **9.** F; **10.** F

1. *b;* **2.** *c;* **3.** *a;* **4.** *a;* **5.** *d;* **6.** *b;* **7.** *a;* **8.** *d;* **9.** *a;* **10.** *b*

CHAPTER 2

Fill-in questions

1. *a.* society's material wants are unlimited; *b.* economic resources, which are the ultimate means of satisfying these wants, are scarce in relation to these wants

2. *a.* property resources; (1) land or raw materials, (2) capital; *b.* human resources; (1) labor, (2) entrepreneurial ability

3. rental income, interest income, wages, profits

4. the social science concerned with the problem of using or administering scarce resources to attain maximum fulfillment of our unlimited wants

5. *a.* the economy is operating at full employment and full production; *b.* the available supplies of the factors of production are fixed; *c.* technology does not change during the course of the analysis

6. directly, indirectly

7. *a.* fewer, more; *b.* unemployed, underemployed; *c.* more, more; *d.* increase resource supplies, improve its technology

8. less

9. economic resources are not completely adaptable between alternate uses

10. *a.* takes initiative of combining the other resources—land, labor, and capital; *b.* makes basic business policy decisions; *c.* takes position of innovator; *d.* takes position of risk bearer

11. *a.* determination of what is to be produced; *b.* determination of how the total output should be produced; *c.* determination of distribution of total output; *d.* determination of the extent of resource use; *e.* determination of provisions for flexibility and adaptability to change

12. opportunity cost

13. apparent, disguised

14. full employment, full production

15. willing, able

16. consumer tastes, supplies of resources, technology

17. values (or goals or priorities), nonscientific (or moral or subjective)

18. goals, institutions, organizations, pure (or laissez faire) capitalism, communism

Problems and projects

1. *a.* land; *b.* C; *c.* land; *d.* C; *e.* EA; *f.* land; *g.* C; *h.* C; *i.* labor; *j.* EA

2. *b.* 1, 2, 3, 4, 5, 6, 7

4. *a.* DEP; *b.* CAP; *c.* CAP; *d.* CAP; *e.* CAP; *f.* CAP; *g.* DEP; *h.* DEP; *i.* DEP; *j.* DEP; *k.* CAP; *l.* DEP

Self-test

1. T; **2.** T; **3.** F; **4.** F; **5.** T; **6.** T; **7.** F; **8.** T; **9.** T; **10.** F

1. *d;* **2.** *b;* **3.** *c;* **4.** *b;* **5.** *b;* **6.** *d;* **7.** *a;* **8.** *c;* **9.** *d;* **10.** *d*

CHAPTER 3

Fill-in questions

1. private property

2. enterprise, choice

3. attempts to do what is best for itself, competition

4. *a.* large numbers of independently acting buyers and sellers operating in the markets; *b.* freedom of those buyers and sellers to enter or leave these markets

5. control price

6. price, market

7. innovators, profit

8. the extensive use of capital, specialization, the use of money

9. interdependent, exchange

10. medium of exchange

11. coincidence of wants

12. product, resource

13. generally acceptable by buyers and sellers in exchange

14. the prices received for resources, the amount of resources sold, the prices received for products, the amounts sold

Problems and projects

1. *a.* (1) 4, (2) $\frac{1}{2}$; *b.* (1) 5, (2) $\frac{1}{3}$; *c.* (1) 8, (2) 2; *d.* (1) 15, (2) 3; *e.* Brobdingnag, Lilliput; *f.* bananas, apples; *g.* 2, 3, $\frac{1}{3}$, $\frac{1}{2}$; *h.* 69, 18, (1) 75, 20, (2) 6, 2

2. *a.* (1) $\frac{2}{3}$, (2) $1\frac{1}{2}$; *b.* (1) $\frac{1}{2}$, (2) 2; *c.* (1) Schaffner, $\frac{1}{2}$, $\frac{2}{3}$; (2) Hart, $1\frac{1}{2}$, 2; *d.* 60, 50, 10 pairs of trousers; *e.* $\frac{1}{2}$, $\frac{2}{3}$, $1\frac{1}{2}$, 2

3. *a.* goods and services; *b.* expenditures for goods and services; *c.* money income payments (wages, rent, interest, and profit) *d.* services of resources (land, labor, capital, and entrepreneurial ability)

Self-test

1. F; **2.** T; **3.** T; **4.** F; **5.** T; **6.** T; **7.** F; **8.** T; **9.** F; **10.** F

1. *c;* **2.** *c;* **3.** *c;* **4.** *a;* **5.** *a;* **6.** *d;* **7.** *c.*

CHAPTER 4

Fill-in questions

1. business firms, households; demand decisions of households, supply decisions of business firms

2. vertical, horizontal

3. indirect, direct

4. *a.* the tastes or preferences of consumers; *b.* the number of consumers in the market; *c.* the money income of consumers; *d.* the prices of related goods; *e.* consumer expectations with respect to future prices and incomes

5. smaller, less

6. inferior, normal (superior)

7. complementary, substitute

8. demand for, a change in the quantity demanded of the product

9. *a.* the technique of production; *b.* resource prices; *c.* prices of other goods; *d.* price expectations; *e.* the number of sellers in the market; *f.* taxes and subsidies

10. increase, decrease

11. quantity demanded and quantity supplied are equal

12. less

13. *a.* +, +; *b.* −, +; *c.* −, −; *d.* +, −; *e.* ?, +; *f.* +, ?; *g.* ?, −; *h.* −, ?

14. rationing

15. other things being equal

Problems and projects

2. Total: 5, 9, 17, 27, 39

3. Each quantity in column 3 is greater than in column 2, and each quantity in column 4 is less than in column 2.

4. *a.* 30, 4. *b.* (1) 20, 7; (2) inferior; (3) normal (superior)

5. *a.* complementary; *b.* substitute

6. *a.* 5.60; *b.* 25

7. 45,000; 33,000; 22,500; 13,500; 6,000; 0

8. 1.60, 1.55; 22,500, 31,000

9. *a.* decrease demand, decrease price; *b.* decrease supply, increase price; *c.* decrease supply, increase price; *d.* increase demand, increase price; *e.* decrease supply, increase price; *f.* increase demand, increase price; *g.* increase supply, decrease price; *h.* decrease demand, decrease price; *i.* increase demand, increase price; *j.* decrease supply, increase price

CHAPTER 5

Fill-in questions

1. communicating, coordinating

2. maximizes the satisfaction received from its income

3. resources are scarce, substitutes

4. it is payment which must be made to a businessman or entrepreneur to retain his services

5. enter, fall, larger, larger; fall, zero

6. *a.* determination of money incomes; *b.* determination of product prices

7. *a.* is the price system adaptable to change; *b.* is the price system conducive to change

8. artificial barriers

9. profits, borrowed funds

10. private, public (or social), invisible hand

11. it leads to an efficient allocation of resources; it emphasizes personal freedom

12. *a.* weaken, it is irksome to individual producers, technological advance contributes to its decline; *b.* (1) unequal; (2) costs, benefits; (3) immobile; (4) continuous full employment

10. Each price in column 3 is less than in column 1 and each price in column 4 is greater than in column 1.

Self-test

1. F; **2.** F; **3.** F; **4.** F; **5.** T; **6.** F; **7.** F; **8.** F

1. a; **2.** b; **3.** b; **4.** a; **5.** c; **6.** d; **7.** a; **8.** c

Problems and projects

1. $6, —$5; $10.00; *a.* C; *b.* produce A and have an economic profit of $14; *c.* it would increase

2. *a.* method 2; *b.* —$5, $5; *c.* (1) 13, 8; 3, 4; capital: 2, 4; (2) —5, $4

3. *a.* product B; *b.* (1) 40, (2) 9, (3) 10, (4) 1; *c.* $14; *d.* (1) product C; (2) increase to 90, increase to 12, increase to 12, remain constant at 1; (3) increase to $90

Self-test

1. T; **2.** T; **3.** T; **4.** T; **5.** T; **6.** T; **7.** T; **8.** F; **9.** T; **10.** T

1. b; **2.** b; **3.** c; **4.** d; **5.** d; **6.** c; **7.** a; **8.** a; **9.** c; **10.** b

CHAPTER 6

Fill-in questions

1. market, planned

2. *a.* provide legal foundation and social environment; *b.* maintain competition; *c.* redistribute income and wealth; *d.* reallocate resources; *e.* stabilize the economy

3. *a.* regulate, natural; *b.* ownership of; *c.* antitrust (antimonopoly)

4. inequality; *a.* public assistance; *b.* direct market; *c.* income

5. *a.* demand; *b.* supply; *c.* benefit, cost

6. spillover costs, spillover benefits

7. people other than the buyers and sellers

8. *a.* over, cost, benefit; *b.* under, benefit, cost

9. *a.* (1) enact legislation, (2) pass special taxes; *b.* (1) subsidize production, (2) take over the production of the product

10. exclusion, spillover

11. taxing, spends the revenue to buy

12. *a.* increases, increasing, decreasing; *b.* decreases, decreasing, increasing

13. stabilizing the economy

14. public goods, private goods

15. *a.* estimate; *b.* output and price level, distribution

16. private sector

17. private goods, public (social) goods

18. demand, supply; *a.* Wagner's Law; *b.* (1) the remoteness of the benefits of social goods; (2) the burden of proving to citizens that more social goods are needed is upon government; (3) the advertising of private goods and the absence of advertising of public goods; (4) inflation; (5) the frequent inability of the economy to decide how the new taxes needed to finance more social goods should be apportioned

19. output, national output, overallocation, public (government)

20. limited decisions

Problems and projects

1. *a.* reallocates resources; *b.* redistributes income; *c.* provides a legal foundation and social environment *and* stabilizes the economy; *d.* reallocates resources; *e.* maintains competition; *f.* provides a legal foundation and social environment *and* maintains competition; *g.* reallocates income; *h.* reallocates resources; *i.* provides a legal foundation and social environment; *j.* reallocates income

2. *a.* p_2, p_1; *b.* p_2, p_1; *c.* optimum, p_e

3. *a.* a supply curve to the left of the one shown should be drawn in, (1) decreases, increases, (2) greater; *b.* a demand curve to the right of the one shown should be drawn in, (1) increases, increases, (2) less

4. *a.* marginal cost: $500, $180, $80, $100; marginal benefit: $650, $100, $50, $25; *b.* yes; *c.* (1) 2, (2) $500, (3) $650, (4) $150

Self-test

1. F; **2.** F; **3.** F; **4.** F; **5.** T; **6.** T; **7.** F; **8.** T; **9.** T; **10.** T; **11.** F; **12.** T; **13.** F; **14.** F; **15.** F; **16.** F; **17.** T; **18.** T; **19.** T; **20.** F.

1. *a;* **2.** *a;* **3.** *b;* **4.** *a;* **5.** *d;* **6.** *c;* **7.** *b;* **8.** *c;* **9.** *a;* **10.** *d;* **11.** *b;* **12.** *a*

CHAPTER 7

Fill-in questions

1. 62, furnish resources, buy the bulk of the total output of the economy

2. 75

3. composition of national output, level

4. contribution of resources

5. personal consumption, personal saving, personal taxes

6. 15, Federal, income

7. services, nondurable goods, durable goods

8. security, speculation

9. 11.6 million

10. unlimited, limited

11. *a.* CORP; *b.* PRO and PART; *c.* PRO; *d.* CORP; *e.* CORP; *f.* CORP; *g.* PART; *h.* PART; *i.* CORP

12. *a.* desire to achieve greater productive efficiency; *b.* seeking of power and prestige; *c.* security and insurance of long-run survival; *d.* seeking of greater financial rewards

13. internal growth, combination, combination

14. producing goods and services, hiring the bulk of the economic resources

15. the sources of a firm's receipts, how these receipts were dispersed

16. the amount of capital equipment worn out in the process of producing goods during a year

17. consumers, government, businesses

18. the product sold is the final good or service; the output of the business sector, the value of the intermediate transactions are included in the value of the final product

Problems and projects

1. 75.1%, 7.9%, 9.7%, 4.8%, 2.6%

3.

Allocations			Receipts	
(1) Wages and salaries		$ 42,000	(8) Sales of output	$128,000
(2) Materials		37,000		
(3) Interest		2,000		
(4) Rents		5,000		
(5) Depreciation		6,000		
(6) Taxes		21,000		
(a) Payroll	$ 4,000			
(b) Indirect Business	1,000			
(c) Corporate profits	16,000			
(7) Corporate profits (after taxes)		15,000		
(a) Dividends	7,000			
(b) Undistributed profits	8,000			
Total allocations		$128,000	Total receipts	$128,000

4.

Allocations			Receipts		
(1) Wages and salaries		$186	(8) Sales of output		$375
(2) Interest		6	(a) To consumers	$270	
(3) Rents		11	(b) To other		
(4) Depreciation		37	businesses	58	
(5) Taxes		64	(c) To government	47	
(a) Payroll	$ 5				
(b) Indirect business	35				
(c) Corporate income	24				
(6) Corporate profits after taxes		19			
(a) Dividends	11				
(b) Undistributed profits	8				
(7) Proprietors' income		52			
Total allocations		$375	Total receipts		$375

Self-test

1. F; **2.** T; **3.** T; **4.** T; **5.** T; **6.** T; **7.** T; **8.** F; **9.** T; **10.** F; **11.** T; **12.** F; **13.** T; **14.** F; **15.** T; **16.** F

1. c; **2.** d; **3.** b; **4.** b; **5.** a; **6.** a; **7.** c; **8.** b; **9.** d; **10.** a; **11.** a; **12.** b; **13.** b; **14.** d; **15.** c; **16.** a

CHAPTER 8

Fill-in questions

1. taxation, expenditures

2. voluntary, compulsory

3. money expenditures for which government currently receives no products or services in return

4. personal income, payroll, war and defense

5. corporate profits are taxed and then the dividends paid out of these profits are taxed as personal income

6. value-added

7. sales, excise, education, highways

8. property, education

9. a. tax exempt securities; b. the capital gains tax; c. depletion allowances

10. revenue sharing

11. benefits-received, ability-to-pay

12. constant, increasing, decreasing

13. a. P; b. R; c. R; d. R; e. P

14. a. the persons upon whom it is levied; b. those who buy the taxed product; c. either the firm or its customers; d. owners when they occupy their own residences, tenants who rent residences from the owners, consumers who buy the products produced on business property

15. a. regressive; b. progressive; c. proportional; d. progressive

Problems and projects

1. tax: $520, $770, $1,060, $1,400, $1,800, $2,270; average tax rate: 20.8%, 22%, 23.6%, 25.5%, 27.7%, 30.3%

2. Tax A: average tax rate: 3, 3, 3, 3, 3, 3, 3; type of tax: proportional. Tax B: average tax rate: 1, 2, 3, 3, 2.5, 2, 2; type of tax: combination. Tax C: average tax rate: 10, 9, 8, 7, 6, 5, 4; type of tax: regressive

3. a. $200, $232, $264, $296, $328, $360; b. 4%, 3.87%, 3.77%, 3.70%, 3.66%, 3.6%; c. regressive

4. a.—400, 400, 2400, 4200, 7500; b. —20, 10, 24, 28, 30; c. progressive, increases

Self-test

1. T; **2.** F; **3,** F; **4.** F; **5.** F; **6.** F; **7.** F; **8.** T; **9.** F; **10.** T

1. d; **2.** a; **3.** a; **4.** a; **5.** d; **6.** b; **7.** c; **8.** a; **9.** a; **10.** c

CHAPTER 9

Fill-in questions

1. level of production in the economy at some point in time and to plot the long-run course the economy has been following, public policies to improve the performance of the economy

2. market prices

3. the value of money (i.e., the price level) changes

4. double counting

5. value added

6. the market value of the final product

7. purely financial

8. nonincome

9. all final purchases of machinery, tools, and equipment by business firms; all construction; changes in inventories; depreciation

10. expanding, stationary

11. supplements; social insurance programs; private pension, health and welfare funds

12. corporation income taxes, dividends, undistributed corporate profits

13. make allowance for that part of this year's output which is necessary to replace the capital goods consumed in the year's production

14. depreciation

15. indirect business taxes; earned

16. *a.* old age and survivors' insurance and unemployment compensation insurance payments; *b.* relief payments; *c.* veterans' payments; *d.* private pension and welfare payments; *e.* interest payments made by government and consumers

17. transfer payments, social security contributions, undistributed corporate profits, corporation income taxes; personal consumption expenditures, interest paid by consumers, personal saving, personal taxes

18. personal taxes; personal consumption expenditures, interest paid by consumers, personal saving

19. personal consumption expenditures, interest paid by consumers

20. depreciation

Problems and projects

1. *a.* (1) price index (1927 = 100): 100, 122, 67, 78, 89; (2) price index (1935 = 100): 113, 138, 75, 88, 100. *b.* (1) adjusted GNP in 1927 dollars (billions): 90, 98.4, 89.6, 83.3, 78.7; (2) adjusted GNP in 1935 dollars (billions): 79.6, 87, 80, 73.9, 70

2. *a.* 445 billion; *b.* 426 billion; *c.* 361 billion; *d.* 324 billion; *e.* 6 billion

3. All figures are in billions of dollars.

Income (allocations) method		Output (expenditures) method	
Gross National Product			
(1) Compensation to employees	$238	(1) Personal consumption expenditures	$217
(2) Rents	9	(2) Government expenditures for goods and services	71
(3) Interest	6	(3) Gross private domestic investment	56
(4) Proprietors' income	21	(4) Net exports	5
(5) Dividends	13		$349
(6) Corporate income taxes	15		
(7) Undistributed corporate profits	14		
(8) Indirect business taxes	11		
(9) Depreciation	22		
	$349		
Net National Product			
(1) Compensation to employees	$238	(1) Personal consumption expenditures	$217
(2) Rents	9	(2) Government expenditures for goods and services	71
(3) Interest	6	(3) Net private domestic investment	34
(4) Proprietors' income	21	(4) Net exports	5
(5) Dividends	13		$327
(6) Corporate income taxes	15		
(7) Undistributed corporate profits	14		
(8) Indirect business taxes	11		
	$327		
National Income			
(1) Compensation to employees	$238	(1) Net national product	$327
(2) Rents	9	(2) Less: indirect business taxes	11
(3) Interest	6		$316
(4) Proprietors' income	21		
(5) Dividends	13		
(6) Corporate income taxes	15		
(7) Undistributed corporate profits	14		
	$316		

Personal Income

(1) National income $316
(2) Plus: transfer payments   26
(3) Less: social security contributions   7
(4) Less: Corporate income taxes   15
(5) Less: Undistributed corporate
profits   14
$306

(1) Personal consumption
expenditures $217
(2) Personal saving   29
(3) Personal taxes   55
(4) Interest paid by consumers   5
$306

Disposable Income

(1) Personal income $306
(2) Less: personal taxes   55
$251

(1) Personal consumption
expenditures $217
(2) Personal saving   29
(3) Interest paid by consumers   5
$251

4. *a.* peronal income and disposable income, a public transfer payment; *b.* none; a second-hand sale; *c.* all, represents investment (additions to inventories); *d.* all; *e.* none, a purely financial transaction; *f.* all; *g.* none, a nonmarket transaction; *h.* all; *i.* none, a private transfer payment; *j.* all; *k.* none, a nonmarket transaction; *l.* all; *m.* all, represents additions to the inventory of the retailer; *n.* personal income and disposable income, a public transfer payment; *o.* all; estimate of rental value of owner-occupied homes is included in rents

Self-test

1. F; 2. F; 3. T; 4. T; 5. F; 6. T; 7. F; 8. F; 9. T; 10. T

1. *b;* 2. *d;* 3. *d;* 4. *b;* 5. *a;* 6. *c;* 7. *c;* 8. *a;* 9. *a;* 10. *d*

CHAPTER 10

Fill-in questions

1. total spending

2. larger, more, increases, increase

3. premature, pure

4. 96, cyclical, frictional, structural

5. potential, actual

6. rising general level of prices, falling general level of prices

7. money income, the prices which he must pay for the goods and services he purchases

8. The following is a partial answer. Inflation: hurt—savers, creditors, fixed-income groups; benefit—debtors, some profit receivers. Deflation: hurt—debtors, some profit receivers; benefit—savers, creditors, fixed-income groups

9. 2, 4

10. prosperity, recession, depression, recovery; expansion, contraction, upswing, downswing

11. seasonal variations, secular trends

12. capital and durable, nondurable, low

13. expand, low, stable; high and prolonged, capital equipment, construction

14. *a.* strong demand for capital goods; *b.* development of new products and industries; *c.* declining labor costs and general business optimism

15. excess industrial capacity, decline in residential construction

16. increased, decreased

17. a backlog of demand, the means to finance expenditures, rising

18. *a.* a backlog of demand for capital goods; *b.* confidence that the Federal government would prevent unemployment; *c.* a high level of foreign demand for American goods as a result of Marshall Plan aid; *d.* inflation created an expectation of rising prices

19. 1954, 1958, economic growth, rising

20. *a.* a change in economic policy; *b.* expansion of the Vietnam war; *c.* increased spending by state and local governments; *d.* suburban growth and an increase in the number of people driving automobiles; *e.* rapid rate of technological progress

21. increased, declined, fairly stable, the worst inflation in two decades

22. *a.* inflation, unemployment; *b.* stagflation; *c.* New Economic, decrease, controls; *d.* full employment, price stability

23. investment, money, cumulative

24. *a.* the institutional and structural changes which have occurred in the economy; *b.* the expansion of the public sector of the economy; *c.* more knowledge about the business cycle and how to use fiscal and monetary policy

Problems and projects

1. The following figures complete the table: 1971: 84,113, 58.9, 4,993, 94.1, 5.9; 1972: 86,542, 59.3, 4,840, 94.4, 5.6; 1973: 88,714, 59.8, 4,305, 95.1, 4.9; *a.* the labor force increased more than employment increased; *b.* because unemployment and employment in relative terms are percentages of the labor force and *always* add to 100%; if one increases the other must decrease; *c.* no, because unemployment was greater than the 4% considered

CHAPTER 11

1. closed economy, personal, neither taxes nor spends, net national product, national income, personal income, disposable income

2. demand for these goods and services

3. the rate of interest

4. decrease, increase; stabilize

5. Say's Law, price-wage flexibility

6. decrease; unemployment; down, increase; all who are willing to work at the going wage rate are employed, and total output equals total spending

7. it does not exist in the degree necessary for ensuring the restoration of full employment in the face of a decline in total spending, lower money incomes, reductions in total spending, lower prices

8. the fallacy of composition

9. different groups, different reasons

10. income, increase

11. consumption

12. increase, decrease

13. *a.* stocks of liquid assets which households have on hand; *b.* the stocks of durable goods consumers have on hand; *c.* expectations with respect to incomes, prices, and the availability of goods; *d.* the current volume of consumer credit outstanding; *e.* attitudes toward thrift; *f.* taxation of consumer income

14. the amount consumers will consume (save) will be different at every level of income, the level of income has changed and that consumers

CHAPTER 12
Fill-in questions

1. aggregate demand–aggregate supply, leakages-injections

2. aggregate demand

normal; *d.* because the number of people looking for jobs expands

2. *a.* B, B, B, A; *b.* B. B. B. B. B.; *c.* C, A, A, C

3. Prices: % decline—34, 7; output; % decline—22, 38. *a.* A; *b.* B; *c.* B; *d.* B

4. *a.* D, B; *b.* I, I; *c.* B, D; *d.* D, B; *e.* D, B; *f.* D, B; *g.* I, I; *h.* D. B

5. *a.* $1,260, $1,323; *b.* $24, $37

6. *a.* 7.2; *b.* 10; *c.* 14.4

Self-test

1. T; **2.** T; **3.** F; **4.** F; **5.** T; **6.** F; **7.** T; **8.** F; **9.** F; **10.** F; **11.** F; **12.** T; **13.** F; **14.** F; **15.** T

1. *d;* **2.** *c;* **3.** *b;* **4.** *b;* **5.** *d;* **6.** *b;* **7.** *c;* **8.** *a;* **9.** *d;* **10.** *b;* **11.** *a;* **12.** *a;* **13.** *c;* **14.** *a;* **15.** *d*

will change their consumption (saving) as a result

15. capital goods; *a.* expected, profit; *b.* interest

16. *a.* technological change; *b.* the cost of acquiring, maintaining, and operating the capital goods; *c.* the stock of capital on hand; *d.* expectations; *e.* government policies

17. greater

18. inverse; *a.* decrease; *b.* increase

19. stable, unstable

20. durability, irregularity, variability

Problems and projects

1. saving: −1, 0, 1, 3, 5, 8, 11, 15; APC: 100.3%, 100%, 99.7%, 99.2%, 98.7%, 98%, 97.3%, 96.4%; APS: −0.3%, 0, 0.3%, 0.8%, 1.3%, 2%, 2.7%, 3.6%; MPC: 90%, 90%, 80%, 80%, 70%, 70%, 60%; MPS: 10%, 10%, 20%, 20%, 30%, 30%, 40%

2. *a.* −; *b.* −; *c.* +; *d.* +; *e.* +; *f.* none; *g.* −; *h.* −

3. *a.* 0, 1; *b.* 2, 3; *c.* 3, 6; *d.* 10, 15, 21, 28, 36, 45; *f.* inverse, (1) decrease, (2) increase; *g.* (1) lower, (2) raise

4. *a.* +; *b.* −; *c.* +; *d.* +; *e.* −; *f.* −; *g.* −; *h.* +; *i.* −

Self-test

1. F; **2.** F; **3.** T; **4.** T; **5.** F; **6.** F; **7.** T; **8.** T; **9.** F; **10.** T

1. *c;* **2.** *a;* **3.** *a;* **4.** *b;* **5.** *b;* **6.** *c;* **7.** *d;* **8.** *d;* **9.** *d;* **10.** *b*

3. consumption, net investment

4. *a.* saving, net investment; *b.* (1) taxes, imports; (2) government expenditures, exports

5. *a.* less than, increase; *b.* greater than, decrease; *c.* equal to, remain unchanged

6. actual, actual, increase, equal to 1/MPS times; decrease, an amount equal to 1/MPS times $5

7. greater than, increase, remain constant, increase, remain constant, inflation

8. 1/MPS, 1/(1-MPC); the economy is characterized by repetitive, continuous flows of expenditures and income; any change in income will cause changes in both consumption and saving to vary in the same direction as, and by a fraction of, the change in income

9. decrease, decrease, remain constant, paradox of thrift

10. less, increase, the multiplier

11. inflationary, aggregate demand, the amount by which equilibrium NNP exceeds the full-employment noninflationary NNP

12. a. demand-pull; b. premature

Problems and projects

1. a. S: 10, 12, 14, 16, 18, 20, 22, 24, 26, 28, 30; I: 22, 22, 22, 22, 22, 22, 22, 22, 22, 22; 22; C + I: 312, 320, 328, 336, 344, 352, 360, 368, 376, 384, 392. b. 360. c. 0.80, 0.20. d. 5. e. 15. f. 20

2. change in income: $8.00, $6.40, $5.12, $4.10, $16.38, $50.00; change in consumption: $8.00, $6.40, $5.12, $4.10, $3.28, $13.10, $40.00; change in saving: $2.00, $1.60, $1.28, $1.02, $0.82, $3.28, $10.00

3. a. 350, 15; b. 0.20, 5; c. 10, 20; d. 10; e. (1) decrease, 340, 15; (2) decrease, 330, 13; (3) decrease, decrease, leave unchanged the amount of, paradox of thrift; (4) multiplier

4. a. 2½; b. 620, 30, inflationary, 12; c. 570, 20, 8

Self-test

1. T; 2. T; 3. T; 4. F; 5. F; 6. F; 7. T; 8. T
1. c; 2. d; 3. a; 4. b; 5. b; 6. c; 7. c; 8. a

CHAPTER 13

Fill-in questions

1. it intensifies both inflation and contraction (tax receipts tend to decrease and expenditures to increase during inflation while taxes tend to increase and expenditures to decrease during depression)

2. recession, inflation, the upswing and downswing of the cycle may not be of equal magnitude and duration

3. full employment without inflation, deficits, public debt

4. Employment, 1946; Council of Economic Advisors, Joint Economic Committee

5. marginal propensity to consume, marginal propensity to save

6. a. consumption, investment, government expenditures for goods and services; b. saving, taxes, investment, government expenditures. for goods and services

7. decrease, the decrease in taxes or in government spending

8. decreased, increased, increased, decreased

9. deficit, surplus

10. a. taxes, transfer payments; b. increase, decrease

11. built-in; a. increase, increase, decrease; b. decrease, increase, decrease

12. a. assuring full employment without inflation; b. fiscal drag; c. countercyclical

13. employment, full employment

14. a. budget surplus or deficit, full employment; b. expansionary, contractionary

15. borrowing from the public, creating new

money; latter, financing in this manner will avoid the depressing effects upon consumption and investment which borrowing from the public may have

16. 5, 4

17. regressive

18. recognition, administrative, operational

19. internally

20. 40, 1.9

21. the goods and services that could not be produced because of the production of war goods

22. increases, borrowed, spent

23. government; a. decrease; b. increase

24. investment, income inequality, monetary policy

25. highly liquid and virtually riskless securities for small and conservative investors, cyclical downswings, monetary

Problems and projects

1. a. C': 316, 325, 334, 343, 352, 361, 370, 379, 388, 397, 406, 415, 424; S': 24, 25, 26, 27, 28, 29, 30, 31, 32, 33, 34, 35, 36; S' + T: 34, 35, 36, 37, 38, 39, 40, 41, 42, 43, 44, 45, 46. b. I + G: 35, 35, 35, 35, 35, 35, 35, 35, 35, 35, 35, 35, 35; C' + I + G: 351, 360, 369, 378, 387, 396, 405, 414, 423, 432, 441, 450, 459. d. 360. e. 100. f. 90. g. increase, $10

2. a. (1) increase, $10, (2) decrease, $20, (3) direct; b. (1) $100, (2) increase, (3) less, (4) lessened; c. (1) $5, (2) decrease, (3) less, (4) lessened, more; d. (1) government expenditures are $200 at all NNPs, government surplus: −40, −30, −20, −10, 0, 10, 20, 30, 40, (2) $30,

(3) deficit, $20, (4) expansionary, recession, (5) deficit, $40, (6) deficit, $50

3. *a.* (1) −, −, −; (2) +, +, +; (3) +, +, +; (4) −, −, −; (5) +, +, +. *b.* (1) +, 0, 0; (2) +, 0, 0; (3) +, 0, 0; (4) −, −, −; (5) −, −, −

Self-test

1. T; 2. T; 3. T; 4. T; 5. F; 6. T; 7. F; 8. T; 9. F; 10. F; 11. T; 12. F; 13. T; 14. F; 15. T; 16. F; 17. T; 18. T

1. *a*; 2. *c*; 3. *b*; 4. *b*; 5. *a*; 6. *b*; 7. *a*; 8. *b*; 9. *c*; 10. *d*; 11. *d*; 12. *d*; 13. *b*; 14. *a*; 15. *b*; 16. *c*; 17. *d*; 18. *b*

CHAPTER 14

Fill-in questions

1. *a.* medium of exchange; *b.* standard of value; *c.* store of value

2. coins, paper money, bank money (or demand deposits), banks, government

3. banks, the Federal government

4. savings accounts (or time deposits), government bonds

5. it can be exchanged for goods and services which people desire; inversely, price level

6. demand deposits, currency

7. Federal Open Market Committee, Federal Advisory Council

8. *a.* set the discount rate; *b.* set the reserve ratio; *c.* open-market operations

9. *a.* they are central banks; *b.* they are quasi-public banks; *c.* they are bankers' banks

10. it accepts deposits of banks, makes loans to banks

11. *a.* holding the deposits of member banks; *b.* providing for the collection of checks; *c.* supplying the economy with paper currency; *d.* act-

ing as fiscal agent for the government; *e.* supervising member banks; *f.* regulating the supply of money

12. accept demand deposits, make loans, create money

13. create money, destroy money

14. hold most of the treasury's checking accounts, aid the government in collecting taxes, administer sale and redemption of government bonds

15. regulating the supply of money

Problems and projects

1. *a.* 263.2 = (64.3 + 7.2 + 0.8 + 203.2) − (7.1 + 4.4 + 0.8); *b.* 519.3 = 345.8 + 173.5

2. remained unchanged, changed to include $500 less in currency and $500 more in bank money (demanded deposits)

3. *a.* rise, 25; *b.* fall, 9.1

Self-test

1. F; 2. F; 3. T; 4. T; 5. F; 6. T; 7. T; 8. T
1. *d*; 2. *c*; 3. *b*; 4. *d*; 5. *a*; 6. *b*; 7. *d*; 8. *b*

CHAPTER 15

Fill-in questions

1. assets, liabilities

2. vault cash, till money

3. demand deposit; time deposit

4. Federal Reserve Bank in its district, deposit liabilities, reserve ratio

5. actual reserves, required reserves

6. fractional

7. not changed

8. decreased, increased; decreased, increased

9. excess reserves

10. increases, 10,000

11. decreases, 2,000

12. profits, liquidity

13. reciprocal of the reserve ratio (deposit multiplier)

14. smaller

15. decrease, 36 million

Problems and projects

1.

	(1)	(2)	(3)	(4)
Assets:				
Cash	$100	$100	$100	$100
Reserves	150	150	260	300
Loans	500	500	500	500
Securities	200	200	200	100
Liabilities:				
Demand deposits	850	850	960	900
Capital stock	100	100	100	100

2. column 2: 8, 6, 5, 4, 3⅓, 3; column 3: 1, 1, 1, 1, 1, 1; column 4: 8, 6, 5, 4, 3⅓, 3

3.

	(1a)	(2a)	(3a)	(4a)	(5a)
A. Required reserve	$35	$40	$30	$36	$44
B. Excess reserve	5	0	−5	4	1
C. New loans— single bank	5	0	*	4	1
D. New loans— monopoly bank	25	0	*	20	5

* If an individual bank or a monopoly bank is $5 short of reserves it must either obtain additional reserves of $5 by selling loans, securities, or its own IOUs to the reserve bank or contract its loans by $25.

	(1b)	(1c)	(2b)	(2c)	(3b)	(3c)	(4b)	(4c)	(5b)	(5c)
Assets:										
Cash	$ 10	$ 10	$ 20	$ 20	$20	$20	$ 20	$ 20	$ 15	$ 15
Reserves	40	40	40	40	25	25	40	40	45	45
Loans	105	125	100	100	*	*	104	120	151	155
Securities	50	50	60	60	30	30	70	70	60	60
Liabilities:										
Demand deposits	180	200	200	200	*	*	184	200	221	225
Capital stock	25	25	20	20	25	25	50	50	50	50

* If an individual bank or a monopoly bank is $5 short of reserves it must either obtain additional reserves of $5 by selling loans, securities, or its own IOUs to the reserve bank or contract its loans by $25.

4.

	(1)	(2)	(3)	(4)	(5)	(6)
Assets:						
Cash	$ 50	$ 50	$ 50	$ 50	$ 50	$ 50
Reserves	105	105	108	108	110	110
Loans	200	220	200	240	200	250
Securities	200	200	192	192	200	200
Liabilities:						
Demand deposits	505	525	500	540	500	550
Capital stock	50	50	50	50	50	50
Loans from Federal Reserve	0	0	0	0	10	10
Excess reserves	4	0	8	0	10	0
Maximum possible expansion of the money supply	20	0	40	0	50	0

Self-test

1. F; 2. T; 3. F; 4. F; 5. T; 6. T; 7. F; 8. F; 9. F; 10. F; 11. T; 12. T; 13. T; 14. T; 15. F

1. c; 2. d; 3. b; 4. a; 5. b; 6. b; 7. d; 8. b; 9. b; 10. b

CHAPTER 16

Fill-in questions

1. a full-employment noninflationary level of total output; Board of Governors of the Federal Reserve, the Federal Reserve Banks

2. decrease, contract, rise, decline

3. securities, gold certificates, Federal Reserve Notes, reserves of member banks

4. influence the ability of commercial banks to create money by lending, influence the rate of interest

5. securities held by the Federal Reserve Banks, loans to commercial banks by the Federal Reserve Banks

6. the reserve ratio, the discount rate, open market operations

7. excess reserves, the multiple by which the banking system can lend

8. decrease, decrease, buy; increase, increase, sell

9. 10 million, 10 million, 7.5 million; 0, 10 million, 10 million

10. *a.* —; *b.* +; *c.* +

11. *a.* margin requirements; *b.* consumer credit regulations; *c.* the maximum interest rate commercial banks may pay on time deposits

12. *M:* the supply of money; *V:* the income (circuit) velocity of money; *P:* the price level; *Q:* the physical volume of output

13. *a.* +, 0; *b.* 0, +; *c.* +, +; *d.* 0, +; *e.* +, 0

14. *a.* one month; *b.* 6

15. *a.* the resting time of money (the demand for money) in the private sector of the economy; *b.* rise; *c.* may be

16. $34.39

17. refuse to make loans, refuses to borrow from commercial banks

18. speed and flexibility

Problems and Projects

1. Assets: securities, gold certificates, loans to member banks, cash; liabilities: Federal Reserve Notes, member bank reserves, Treasury deposits

2. *a.* (1) reduce, 20; (2) buy, 25; (3) decrease, 1; *b.* (1) increase, 28$\frac{4}{7}$; (2) sell, 12$\frac{1}{2}$; (3) increase, 2$\frac{1}{2}$

3.

	(2)	(3)	(4)	(5)	(6)
Federal Reserve Banks					
Assets:					
Gold certificates	$ 25	$ 25	$ 25	$ 25	$ 25
Securities	27	34	30	30	30
Loans to commercial banks	10	10	10	10	4
Liabilities:					
Reserve of commercial banks	47	54	50	55	44
Treasury deposits	5	5	5	0	5
Federal Reserve Notes	10	10	10	10	10
Commercial Banks					
Assets:					
Reserves	$ 47	$ 54	$ 50	$ 55	$ 44
Securities	70	66	70	70	70
Loans	90	90	90	90	90
Liabilities:					
Demand deposits	197	200	200	205	200
Loans from Federal Reserve	10	10	10	10	4
A. Required reserves	49.25	50	40	51.25	50
B. Excess reserves	−2.25	4	10	3.75	−6
C. Initial change in the money supply	−3	0	0	+5	0
D. Total potential change in money supply	−12	+16	+50	+20	−24

4. *a.* year 1: 450; year 2: $2; year 3: 4; year 4: $450; year 5: $4; year 6; 750. *b.* (1) *Q*, 33$\frac{1}{3}$; (2) *P*, 14$\frac{1}{7}$, *Q*, 16$\frac{2}{3}$; (3) 31$\frac{1}{4}$, 7$\frac{1}{7}$; (4) *P*, 33$\frac{1}{3}$; (5) *P*, 20

Self-test

1. F; **2.** T; **3.** T; **4.** F; **5.** F; **6.** T; **7.** F; **8.** F; **9.** F; **10.** F

1. *b*; **2.** *a*; **3.** *c*; **4.** *b*; **5.** *d*; **6.** *c*; **7.** *d*; **8.** *d*; **9.** *d*; **10.** *c*

CHAPTER 17

Fill-in questions

1. aggregate demand, consumption, investment, government expenditures for goods and services

2. *a.* net national product (or disposable income), consumption schedule; *b.* expected, profit, interest; *c.* public policy

3. fiscal, monetary

4. *a.* government, aggregate demand; *b.* net tax, consumption, investment

5. money, rate of interest, investment

6. complex, quantify, noneconomic

7. fiscal

8. *a.* demand, velocity, supply; *b.* real GNP, 3, 5

9. composition (allocation), output (resources), distribution, income

10. coordinated

Problems and projects

1. *a.* C': $150, 190, 230, 270, 310, 350, 390, 430, 470; S': $0, 10, 20, 30, 40, 50, 60, 70, 80; *b.* $200; *c.* $250, 300, 350, 400, 450, 500, 550, 600; *e.* (1) −, +; (2) +, −; (3) +, −; (4) +, −; *f.* (1) −, +; (2) +, −; (3) +, −; (4) +, −; *g.* increase in net taxes, decrease in government expenditures, decrease in investment demand, decrease in consumption schedule; decrease in net taxes, increase in government expenditures, increase in investment demand, increase in consumption schedule

CHAPTER 18

Fill-in questions

1. *a.* full employment; *b.* aggregate demand, demand-pull

2. *a.* before full employment is reached; *b.* business firms, labor unions, labor

3. *a.* price level, unemployment; *b.* negative; *c.* premature

4. training, time consuming and costly, aware, restrictions

5. market power, market power, less than full employment, something extra, higher prices

6. *a.* unit labor cost; *b.* the wage rate; *c.* the productivity of labor; *d.* (1) increase, (2) decrease, (3) remain constant

7. inflation, unemployment

8. market, wage-price, left

9. *a.* manpower, bottlenecks; *b.* pro-competition, market power

10. *a.* vocationally oriented education and training programs; *b.* improvement of the flow of information between unemployed workers and potential employers and of geographic mobility; *c.* reduction of artificial obstacles to employment

11. *a.* antitrust (antimonopoly), tariffs; *b.* antitrust (antimonopoly), bargaining on a centralized nationwide level

12. *a.* incomes, the wages received and the

CHAPTER 19

Fill-in questions

1. fixed, changes (increases)

2. total real output, per capita real output

3. increases, decreases

2. *a.* greater; *b.* smaller; *c.* (1) $20; (2) $80, 1.0%; *d.* 1.5, 2.0, 2.5, 3.0, 3.5, 4.0, 4.5, 5.0; *f.* (1) decrease, 0.5%; (2) increase, 0.5%; *g.* (1) a curve to the right of LM_2; (2) a curve to the left of LM_2

3. *a.* (1) 400; (2) 3.0; *b.* (1) 400; (2) 3.0; *c.* (1) +, +, +, −; (2) −, −, −, +; (3) +, −, +, +; (4) −, −, −, ?; (5) +, +, +, −; *d.* increase the supply of money, increase government expenditures for goods and services, decrease net taxes; *e.* decrease the supply of money, decrease government expenditures, increase net taxes

Self-test

1. T; 2. F; 3. T; 4. T; 5. T; 6. T; 7. F; 8. T; 9. F; 10. T

1. c; 2. b; 3. c; 4. c; 5. b; 6. a; 7. d; 8. c; 9. a; 10. a

prices paid determine real incomes; *b.* (1) guideposts, voluntary, (2) controls, law

13. productivity, unit labor cost

14. *a.* employment, output, inflation; *b.* wages, salaries, prices, rents

15. unworkable, enforce, allocation, freedom, inequities

16. *a.* shortage, black, ration; *b.* will not, under-

17. *a.* (1) 825, 75, 275, 25, (2) will not; *b.* (1) 68, 32, (2) decreased

18. *a.* excess wage settlement; *b.* stop, go, fiscal, monetary, inflation, unemployment

Problems and projects

1. *a.* 7; *b.* 6; *c.* (it's your choice)

2. *a.* 4; *b.* (1) increase, increase, (2), decrease, decrease, (3) remain constant, remain constant; *c.* (1) remain constant, (2) increase, decrease, remain constant

3. *a.* 11.00, 4,500; *b.* (1) 5,500, 3,500, (2) shortage, 2,000; *c.* 13.00; *d.* 11.00, 1,000, 1,000; *e.* more

Self-test

1. F; 2. T; 3. T; 4. T; 5. T; 6. F; 7. T; 8. F; 9. T; 10. T; 11. F; 12. F

1. a; 2. d; 3. a; 4. c; 5. b; 6. a; 7. a; 8. a; 9. b; 10. d; 11. d; 12. d

4. $30, $18, $12

5. quantity and quality of natural resources, quantity and quality of human resources, the supply or stock of capital goods, technology, demand, allocative

6. 8

7. increase, decreasing

8. 10

9. average, decrease

10. optimum population

11. population, decrease

12. productivity

13. aggregate demand (or investment)

14. aggregate demand, productive capacity, capital-output ratio

15. reallocate, speed, completeness

Problems and Projects

1. *a.* 80, 120, 130, 70, 50, 30, 10, −10; *b.* third, fourth; *c.* positive, negative; *d.* 80, 100, 110, 100, 90, 80, 70, 60; *e.* increasing, decreasing; *f.* 3, average product, a maximum

2. *a.* 100; *b.* 100, 110, 120, 125, 120, 110,

CHAPTER 20

Fill-in questions

1. *a.* 6; *b.* 2½

2. 3.6%, 1.9%

3. quality, leisure, environment, life

4. natural resources

5. size of the population, health, education, training

6. production; investment

7. 30,000, three

8. GNP, slower

9. it must encourage those changes in products, productive techniques, and capital facilities vital to economic growth; it must provide a mechanism which will efficiently reallocate resources in a way appropriate to these changes; price system

10. 43; improved training and education, improved technology, resource reallocation, the economies of scale

11. spillovers, domestic problems, anxiety, insecurity, good life

12. benefits, costs, quality of life, equitable, income

13. *a.* population, natural resources, pollution, food output per capita, industrial output per capita; *b.* 100, population, industrial output (or capacity)

CHAPTER 21

Fill-in questions

1. poverty (i.e., a low standard of living)

2. Asia, South America, Africa, southeastern Europe, ⅔

100, 90; *c.* 25; *d.* capital, technology, labor; *e.* increased, 4; *f.* (1) increased, 120; (2) remained constant; (3) decreased to 90

3. *a.* (1) 1,100, 1,210; (2) consumption: 880, 968; saving: 220, 242; (3) investment: 220, 242; aggregate demand: 1,100, 1,210; *b.* (1) 10; (2) 10; *c.* (1) 0.8, constant; (2) 0.2, constant; (3) 5; *d.* 1,050; (1) 5; (2) less than; (3) unemployment; *e.* 1,150; (1) greater than, cannot; (2) inflation; *f.* increases.

4. *a.* 270, 270; *b.* 90; *c.* 990, 297, 297, 99; *d.* 1,089, 326.7, 326.7, 108.9; *e.* (1) investment; (2) average propensity to save, capital-output ratio; *f.* 2.5

Self-test

1. T; **2.** F; **3.** T; **4.** F; **5.** T; **6.** T; **7.** F; **8.** F; **9.** T; **10.** F; **11.** F; **12.** T

1. *a*; **2.** *d*; **3.** *b*; **4.** *a*; **5.** *b*; **6.** *c*; **7.** *b*; **8.** *c*; **9.** *b*; **10.** *b*

14. zero population growth, zero economic growth

15. unrealistic, technological progress, feedback

16. shortage, prices; *a.* increased, fixed; *b.* technological, price; *c.* conspiracy, profits

Problems and projects

1. *a.* $300, 400, 500, 550, 600, 550, 500; *b.* 150 million; *c.* (1) $15 billion; (2) $100; *d.* (1) 46⅔%; (2) 9.1%

2. *a.* $200.0, 210.0, 242.0, 266.2; *b.* 5%, less, aggregate demand did not increase by enough to induce the economy to produce at capacity; *c.* (1) $10; (2) 4.5%; *d.* (1) $22; (2) $55; (3) more; (4) 15.2%; (5) rise, aggregate demand in constant dollars was greater than the constant dollar productive capacity; (6) by having idle productive capacity in year 2; *e.* (1) greater, equal to; (2) fall; (3) would

3. *a.* (1) increased, increasing; (2) decreased, increasing; *b.* (1) decrease; (2) pollution, decrease; (3) natural resources; *c.* population, industrial output

Self-test

1. T; **2.** F; **3.** T; **4.** F; **5.** T; **6.** F; **7.** F; **8.** F; **9.** F; **10.** F; **11.** T; **12.** F

1. *c*; **2.** *c*; **3.** *b*; **4.** *a*; **5.** *c*; **6.** *d*; **7.** *b*; **8.** *a*; **9.** *c*; **10.** *d*; **11.** *b*; **12.** *b*

3. supplies of natural resources, human resources, capital goods; technology

4. natural resources

5. *a.* overpopulation; *b.* widespread disguised

unemployment; *c.* the poor quality of the labor force

6. consumer goods (food) production ÷ population, aspirations, standard of living

7. zero or less than zero

8. capital accumulation increases output and increased output allows a greater volume of saving and more capital accumulation

9. save, invest; low saving potential, investors, incentives to invest

10. agriculture, the improvement of agricultural facilities, the construction of basic social capital

11. the underdeveloped nations may adopt and apply the superior technologies of the advanced nations

12. capital saving

13. institutions and social arrangements

14. income; investment; productivity, output (income)

15. *a.* the existence of widespread banditry and intertribal warfare in many underdeveloped nations; *b.* the absence of a sizable and vigorous entrepreneurial class; *c.* the great need for social goods and services; *d.* government action may be the only means of promoting saving and investment; *e.* government can more effectively

deal with the social-institutional obstacles to growth; *f.* government may be the only mechanism for speeding up the rate of growth

16. by expanding trade with the underdeveloped nations (lowering the barriers to trade), private flows of capital, foreign aid (public loans and grants)

17. GNP

18. 5.2, 2.7

Problems and projects

1. *a.* low; *b.* short; *c.* widespread; *d.* poor; *e.* primitive; *f.* large; *g.* large; *h.* high; *i.* poor; *j.* small; *k.* low; *l.* absent; *m.* small; *n.* small; *o.* small and poor

2. *a.* food supply: 400, 600, 800, 1,000, 1,200, 1,400; population: 40, 80, 160, 320, 640, 1,280. *b.* the food supply is just able to support the population. *c.* the inability of the food supply to support a population growing at this rate. *d.* (1) 200, (2) 240, (3) 280. *e.* the population increased as rapidly as the food supply.

Self-test

1. T; **2.** F; **3.** F; **4.** F; **5.** T; **6.** F; **7.** F; **8.** T; **9.** F; **10.** T; **11.** F; **12.** T

1. *d;* **2.** *a;* **3.** *b;* **4.** *b;* **5.** *c;* **6.** *d;* **7.** *b;* **8.** *d;* **9.** *b;* **10.** *a;* **11.** *c;* **12.** *d*

CHAPTER 22

Fill-in questions

1. *a.* a large number of independent sellers in a highly organized market; *b.* the firms produce a standardized or virtually standardized product; *c.* individual firms exert no significant control over product price; *d.* new firms are free to enter and existing firms are free to leave the industry; *e.* there is virtually no room for nonprice competition

2. sellers', buyers'

3. fully employed, allocated among alternative uses in the most efficient way; latter

4. standardized, differentiated; close substitutes

5. there are barriers to entry into the industry

6. public relations, good-will

7. there are large numbers of sellers, entry into the industry is fairly easy, the firm has some control over the price of its product

8. there is only one firm in the industry; *b.* the firm produces a product for which there are no close substitutes; *c.* the firm exercises considerable control over the price of its product; *d.* there are barriers to entry into the industry; *e.* advertising is limited and of a good-will or public relations nature

9. each firm produces a fairly small share of the total industry output

10. *a.* a large number of independent sellers; *b.* the product is differentiated; *c.* the firm has a limited amount of control over the price of its product; *d.* entry into the industry is relatively easy; *e.* there is extensive and vigorous nonprice competition

11. the product is standardized in pure competition and differentiated in monopolistic competition

12. standardized, differentiated

13. raw materials, semifinished goods

14. few, a significant percentage

15. the number of rivals the firm has, the extent to which the products of rival firms are substitutes for the product of the oligopolistic firm.

16. (1) pure competition, monopsony, monopsonistic competition, oligopsony; (2) large number of buyers, one buyer, fairly large number of buyers, a few buyers

17. the geographic size of the market, the extent of interindustry competition, the extent of nonprice competition, the rate of technological advance

18. *a.* the legislation and policies of government; *b.* business policies and practices; *c.* technological development and the role of research in industry; *d.* the permissive characteristic of American capitalism

Problems and projects

1. number of firms: d, a, c, b; type of product: e, e, f, e or f; control over price: m, h, g, g; entry: i, j, k, l; nonprice competition: m, g, h, g or h

2. *a.* oligopoly or monopolistic competition; standardized product, number of firms is fairly large, easy entry; *b.* oligopoly or monopolistic competition; differentiated product, number of firms is fairly large, entry is moderately difficult; *c.* pure competition; large number of firms, standardized product, easy entry; *d.* oligopoly; small number of firms, difficult entry; *e.* oligopoly or monopolistic competition; differentiated product, number of firms is fairly large, easy entry; *f.* oligopoly; small number of firms, entry is fairly difficult

3. *a.* yes; railroads, buses, automobiles; *b.* yes; synthetic fibers (nylon, rayon); *c.* yes; aluminum, steel, wood, copper, glass; *d.* yes; radios, movies, books, records, all forms of entertainment; *e.* yes; aluminum, steel, wood, glass, plastics

Self-test

1. F; **2.** F; **3.** T; **4.** T; **5.** T; **6.** F; **7.** T; **8.** F; **9.** T; **10.** F; **11.** T; **12.** T; **13.** F; **14.** F; **15.** F

1. d; **2.** c; **3.** b; **4.** b; **5.** a; **6.** a; **7.** b; **8.** b; **9.** d; **10.** a; **11.** b; **12.** b

CHAPTER 23

Fill-in questions

1. inelastic, elastic

2. sensitive, insensitive

3. negatively (inversely), positively (directly)

4. elastic: greater than 1, decrease, increase; inelastic: less than 1, increase, decrease; of unitary elasticity: equal to 1, remain constant, remain constant

5. perfectly inelastic, perfectly elastic, parallel to the vertical axis, parallel to the horizontal axis

6. *a.* greater than; *b.* less than; *c.* equal to

7. *a.* the number of good substitutes for the product which are available; *b.* the relative importance of the product in the total budget of the buyer; *c.* whether the good is a necessity or a luxury; *d.* the period of time in which demand is being considered; *e.* the durability of the good

8. the amount of time which a producer has to respond to a price change

9. *a.* 7.00, 15,000; *b.* shortage, 4,000; *c.* surplus, 2,000

10. war, shortages, rationing

11. rationing

12. minimum wages, agricultural price supports

13. surplus, attempt to reduce supply or increase demand, purchase the surplus and store or dispose of it

14. the amount the price of the commodity rises as a result of the tax; *a.* less, more; *b.* more, less

15. remains constant, decreases, equal to, less than

16. elastic, inelastic

Problems and projects

1. *a.* 0.70, 0.80, 0.75; *b.* 500, 600, 550; *c.* total revenue: $300, 360, 400, 420, 420, 400, 360; elasticity coefficient: $2\frac{5}{7}$ (2.72), $1\frac{8}{9}$ (1.89), $1\frac{4}{11}$ (1.36), 1, $\frac{11}{15}$ (0.73), $\frac{9}{17}$ (0.53); character of demand: elastic, elastic, elastic, unitary elasticity, inelastic, inelastic; *d.* elasticity coefficient; $1\frac{4}{15}$ (1.27), $1\frac{4}{13}$ (1.31), $1\frac{4}{11}$ (1.36), $1\frac{4}{9}$ (1.44), $1\frac{4}{7}$ (1.57), $1\frac{4}{5}$ (1.8); character of supply: elastic, elastic, elastic, elastic, elastic, elastic; *e.* (1) shortage, 300; (2) surplus, 500

2. *a.* (1) S_3; (2) S_2; (3) S_1; *b.* p_1, q_1; *c.* (1) p_4, remain at q_1; (2) p_3, q_2; (3) p_2, q_3; *d.* more; *e.* less, greater

3. *a.* $3.60; *b.* (reading down) 600, 500, 400, 300, 200, 100; *c.* $4.00; *d.* (1) $.40, $66\frac{2}{3}$; (2) $.20, $33\frac{1}{3}$

4. *a.* (2) has not changed; (3) none, all; (4) smaller, larger; (5) larger, smaller; *b.* (2) increased by the amount of the tax; (3) all, none; (4) larger, smaller; (5) smaller, larger

5. *a.* average revenue: $11.00, 10.00, 9.00, 8.00, 7.00, 6.00, 5.00, 4.00, 3.00, 2.00; total revenue: $0, 10.00, 18.00, 24.00, 28.00, 30.00, 30.00, 28.00, 24.00, 18.00; marginal revenue: $10.00, 8.00, 6.00, 4.00, 2.00, 0, −2.00, −4.00, −6.00; elasticity coefficient: 21.0, 6.33, 3.4, 2.14, 1.44, 1.0, 0.7, 0.47, 0.29; *b.* imperfectly competitive; price (average revenue) decreases as the output of the firm increases and is greater than marginal revenue; *d.* (1) elastic, positive; (2) inelastic, negative; (3) of unitary elasticity, equal to 0; *e.* in order to sell a larger quantity, it is necessary for the firm to lower its price not only on the additional units but also on the units which it could have sold at the higher price

6. *a.* average revenue: all are $10.00; total revenue: $0, 10.00, 20.00, 30.00, 40.00, 50.00, 60.00; marginal revenue: all are $10.00; *b.* purely competitive, because price (average revenue) is constant and equal to marginal revenue; *d.* infinity; *e.* they are equal

Self-test

1. F; **2.** T; **3.** F; **4.** T; **5.** T; **6.** F; **7.** F; **8.** T; **9.** F; **10.** T; **11.** T; **12.** T

1. c; **2.** b; **3.** a; **4.** a; **5.** c; **6.** b; **7.** c; **8.** c; **9.** a; **10.** b; **11.** a; **12.** b

CHAPTER 24

Fill-in questions

1. increase, decrease, income

2. more, lower, less, more, substitution

3. rational, tastes

4. limited, prices, budget restraint

5. ratio of the marginal utility of the last unit purchased of a product to its price

6. *a.* the income of the consumer; *b.* the prices of other products

7. increase, decrease

8. marginal utility, decrease

Problems and projects

1. *a.* (1) increase, 1½; (2) inelastic; *b.* (1) decrease, 1; (2) elastic

2. marginal utility of good A: 21, 20, 18, 15, 11, 6, 0; marginal utility of good B: 7, 6, 5, 4, 3, 2, 1.2; marginal utility of good C: 23, 17, 12, 8, 5, 3, 2

3. *a.* marginal utility per dollar of good A: 4⅕, 4, 3⅗, 3, 2⅕, 1⅕, 0; marginal utility per dollar

of good B: 7, 6, 5, 4, 3, 2, 1⅕; marginal utility per dollar of good C: 5¾, 4¼, 3, 2, 1¼, ¾, ½; *b.* the marginal utility per dollar spent on good B (7) is greater than the marginal utility per dollar spent on good A (3), and the latter is greater than the marginal utility per dollar spent on good C (2); he would not be maximizing his utility; *c.* he would be spending more than his $37 income; *d.* (1) 4; (2) 5; (3) 3; 151; 3. e. A, he would obtain the greatest marginal utility for his dollar (2⅕)

4. *a.* MU/$ of good A: 15, 10, 6⅔, 5, 4, 3⅓, 3, 2½; MU/$ of good B: 6, 5½, 5, 4½, 4, 3½, 3, 2½; MU/$ of good C: 10, 9, 8, 7, 6, 5, 4, 3; MU/$ of good D: 8, 6⅘, 6, 5⅖, 5, 4⅗, 4, 3; MU/$ of saving: 6, 5, 4, 3, 2, 1, ½, ¼; *b.* (1) 4; (2) 3; (3) 6; (4) 5, 2, 490; *c.* (1) 2; (2) 3; (3) 6; (4) 8; *d.* price of A: 6.00, 4.00, 3.00, 2.00, 1.50; quantity of A demanded: 2, 3, 4, 6, 8. The relationship between price and quantity is the demand schedule

Self-test

1. F; 2. T; 3. T; 4. F; 5. F; 6. T

1. *c;* 2. *b;* 3. *a;* 4. *b;* 5. *c;* 6. *c*

CHAPTER 25

Fill-in questions

1. other products, opportunity, alternative

2. attract the resources, explicit, implicit

3. implicit, the services of entrepreneurs, total, explicit, implicit

4. amounts of variable resources (labor, raw materials, etc.), the fixed resources (the size of the plant) it employs

5. enter, leave, fixed (constant)

6. variable resource, fixed resource, extra or marginal product, variable resource, decline

7. fixed, variable, variable

8. increase, decreasing, increase, increasing

10. average variable, average total, marginal

11. total variable, total cost

12. decreasing, increasing

13. had time to make all appropriate adjustments in its plant size

14. *a.* increased specialization in the use of labor; *b.* better utilization of and increased specialization in management; *c.* more efficient productive equipment; *d.* greater utilization of by-products

15. managerial inefficiency

Problems and projects

1. *a.* 15 units of good Y; *b.* 1½ units of good Y; *c.* 7 units of good Y

2. *a.* 5, 6, 7, 6, 5, 4, 3, 2, 1, ½; *b.* $0, 10, 20, 30, 40, 50, 60, 70, 80, 90, 100; *c.* $2.00, 1.67, 1.43, 1.67, 2.00, 2.50, 3.33, 5.00, 10.00, 20.00; *d.* (1) decreases; (2) increases

3. *a.*

Total cost	Average fixed cost	Average variable cost	Average total cost	Marginal cost
$ 200	—	—	—	—
250	$200.00	$50.00	$250.00	$ 50
290	100.00	45.00	145.00	40
320	66.67	40.00	106.67	30
360	50.00	40.00	90.00	40
420	40.00	44.00	84.00	60
500	33.33	50.00	83.33	80
600	28.57	57.14	85.71	100
720	25.00	65.00	90.00	120
870	22.22	74.44	96.67	150
1,100	20.00	90.00	110.00	230

4. *a.* $7.00, 6.00, 5.00, 4.00, 4.00, 3.00, 4.00, 5.00, 6.00, 5.00, 7.00, 10.00; *b.* (1) 10, 40; (2) 50, 80; (3) 90, 120

Self-test

1. F; 2. T; 3. T; 4. F; 5. F; 6. T; 7. T; 8. T; 9. F; 10. F

1. *a;* 2. *b;* 3. *d;* 4. *a;* 5. *d;* 6. *c;* 7. *d;* 8. *b;* 9. *b;* 10. *a*

CHAPTER 26

Fill-in questions

1. *a.* a large number of independent sellers; *b.* a standardized product; *c.* no single firm supplies enough to influence market price; *d.* no obstacles to the entry of new firms or the exodus of old firms

2. total revenue minus total cost

3. total-receipts—total-cost, marginal-revenue—marginal-cost

4. it can realize a profit or a loss which is less than its fixed costs; its profit is the greatest or its loss the least, marginal revenue equals marginal cost

5. the minimum average variable cost

6. that portion of the firm's marginal-cost curve which lies above the average-variable-cost curve, the sum of the short-run supply curves of all firms in the industry

7. total quantity demanded, total quantity supplied, the quantity demanded and supplied at the equilibrium price

8. fixed (constant), variable

9. price (average revenue), marginal revenue, long-run marginal cost, a minimum

10. the firms in the industry are realizing profits in the short run, the firms in the industry are realizing losses in the short run

11. increasing cost

12. the industry's demand for resources is small relative to the total demand for these resources, the industry is using unspecialized resources which are used by other industries

13. total satisfaction of consumers; consumers most want, the most efficient way

14. *a.* the best available (least-cost); *b.* price, cost; *c.* are essential to produce the product; *d.* minimum

15. marginal cost, price

16. *a.* the competitive price system does not necessarily result in an ideal distribution of money income in the economy; *b.* the competitive price system does not accurately measure costs and benefits where spillover costs and benefits are significant; *c.* the competitive price system does not entail the use of the most efficient productive techniques; *d.* the competitive price system may not provide for a sufficient range of consumer choice or for the development of new products

Problems and projects

1. *a.* (see table below); *b.* (1) 0, −$300; (2) 5, −$100; (3) 7, $380;

Market price = $55		Market price = $120		Market price = $200	
Revenue	Profit	Revenue	Profit	Revenue	Profit
$ 0	$ −300	$ 0	$ −300	$ 0	$ −300
55	−345	120	−280	200	−200
110	−340	240	−210	400	−50
165	−345	360	−150	600	90
220	−370	480	−110	800	210
275	−425	600	−100	1,000	300
330	−510	720	−120	1,200	360
385	−635	840	−180	1,400	380
440	−810	960	−290	1,600	350
495	−1,045	1,080	−460	1,800	260
550	−1,350	1,200	−700	2,000	100

c.

Price	Quantity supplied	Profit
$360	10	$1,700
290	9	1,070
230	8	590
180	7	240
140	6	0
110	5	−150
80	4	−270
60	0	−300

d. (1) quantity supplied: 1,000, 900, 800, 700, 600, 500, 400; (2) (a) 180; (b) 7; (c) 240; (d) enter, profits in the industry will attract them into the industry

2. *a.* 140; *b.* 6; *c.* 133 = 800 (the total quantity demanded at $140) ÷ 6 (the output of each firm); *d.* 150 = 900 ÷ 6

Self-test

1. F; **2.** T; **3.** T; **4.** T; **5.** F; **6.** F; **7.** T; **8.** T; **9.** F; **10.** T; **11.** T; **12.** T

1. c; **2.** a; **3.** d; **4.** b; **5.** b; **6.** b; **7.** c; **8.** c; **9.** b; **10.** a; **11.** b; **12.** d

CHAPTER 27

Fill-in questions

1. reasonable approximations, monopolistic competition, oligopoly

2. *a.* nonexistent; *b.* strongest; *c.* weak; *d.* strong

3. *a.* the economies of scale; *b.* natural monopolies; *c.* ownership of essential raw materials; *d.* patents and research; *e.* unfair competition; *f.* the economies of being established

4. their costs of production will be greater than those of the large-scale firms, they will find it difficult to obtain the money capital necessary to acquire a large-scale plant

5. natural, regulated

6. tying agreement

7. product disparagement, pressure on resource suppliers and banks to withhold materials and credit, hiring away of strategic personnel, aggressive price cutting designed to bankrupt competitors

8. advantages over potential new firms, easier access to the capital market; an efficient administrative framework staffed by competent and experienced personnel; past profits from which to finance expansion; a product which is highly advertised, which is sold through well-established marketing channels, and for which customers have a preference

9. less than, less than, will decrease

10. marginal revenue, marginal cost, greater than

11. *a.* highest possible; *b.* a maximum; *c.* profit

12. public criticism or pressure, the entry of new firms into the industry

13. entry of new firms

14. a minimum, price (or average revenue), marginal cost

15. costs (or cost schedule), economies of scale

16. the amount by which price exceeds average cost becomes the income of stockholders who are largely in the upper income groups

17. past profits, the profits, automatic impetus

18. less evident than in a static economy

19. marginal cost, average (total) cost

20. average (total) cost, the misallocation of resources caused by monopoly

Problems and projects

1. *a.* total revenue: $0, 650, 1,200, 1,650, 2,000, 2,250, 2,400, 2,450, 2,400, 2,250, 2,000; marginal revenue: $650, 550, 450, 350, 250, 150, 50, −50, −150, −250; *b.* (1) 6; (2) 400; (3) 1,560; (4) 260; *c.* $250, 750, 1,140, 1,410, 1,550, 1,560, 1,430, 1,150, 710, 100

2. output of the firm: 3, 0; price it will charge: $150, −; total profit: $−60, $−300; average profit: $−20, −

3. *a.* 4, 11.50, 4.00; *b.* 6, 8.50, −7.50, bankrupt, subsidize; *c.* 5, 10.00, zero; *d.* b, a, c

Self-test

1. F; **2.** T; **3.** T; **4.** F; **5.** T; **6.** F; **7.** F; **8.** T; **9.** T; **10.** T

1. *b*; **2.** *c*; **3.** *a*; **4.** *d*; **5.** *a*; **6.** *c*; **7.** *b*; **8.** *c*; **9.** *a*; **10.** *d*

CHAPTER 28

Fill-in questions

1. relatively large, differentiated, collude, price, nonprice, fairly easy

2. limited, rivalry

3. *a.* more, less; *b.* number of rivals the firm has, the degree of product differentiation; *c.* marginal cost, marginal revenue

4. reduce, increase

5. equal average cost, equal zero, greater

6. average cost is greater than minimum average cost, price is greater than marginal cost

7. product differentiation, product promotion

8. a wider variety of goods, an improved quality of goods

9. informative, competitive

10. (a) information; (b) newspapers, magazines, radio, and television; (c) new products; (d) costs; (e) spending in the economy

11. (a) informative; (b) wastes; (c) social costs; (d) costs; (e) spending; (f) barrier to entry

12. product, promotion

Problems and projects

2. *a.* marginal cost: $30, 10, 20, 30, 40, 50, 60, 70, 80, 90; marginal revenue: $110, 90, 70, 50, 30, 10, −10, −30, −50, −70; *b.* (1) 4; (2) $80; (3) $180; *c.* (1) decrease; (2) average cost; (3) equal to zero

Self-test

1. F; **2.** F; **3.** T; **4.** F; **5.** T; **6.** T; **7.** F; **8.** F

1. *c*; **2.** *b*; **3.** *c*; **4.** *d*; **5.** *b*; **6.** *c*; **7.** *a*; **8.** *b*

CHAPTER 29

Fill-in questions

1. few, standardized, differentiated, difficult

2. mutually interdependent, the reactions of rivals, no, so many

3. the economies of scale, the advantages of merger

4. oligopoly encompasses many specific market situations, the element of mutual interdependence which fewness adds complicates analysis

5. inflexible, simultaneously

6. price, nonprice

7. elastic, elastic, inelastic

8. not raise their prices, lower their prices

9. gap, price the oligopolist will charge in order to maximize his profits

10. would be set by a pure monopolist

11. a. legal obstacles (the antitrust laws); b. a large number of firms in the industry; c. differentiated products; d. price breaks

12. set price or output, divide the market

13. informal, prices, the ingenuity of each seller (i.e., nonprice competition), price leader

14. prices one firm might charge, prices the other firm might charge, profits of the two firms

15. a. the price charged by the other firm; b. decrease, not raise its price, also lower its price; c. collusion, merger

16. price cuts can be quickly and easily met by a firm's rivals, oligopolists are typically blessed with substantial financial resources which allow them to support such measures as advertising and product development

17. substantial profits; a. technological advance provides an alternative means for enlarging total profits; b. technological superiority is a basic

means by which survival is ensured; c. the presence of strong rivals places the oligopolist under severe pressure to seek maximum productive efficiency; d. existence of barriers to entry give the progressive oligopolist some assurance that he will realize some of the profit rewards of research

18. have not, modest, financed from public funds.

19. resource suppliers, customers, abuses of original power, share in the profits of original power

20. costs, better, countervailing power, smaller, higher

Problems and projects

1. a. total revenue: 290, 560, 810, 1,040, 1,250, 1,260, 1,265, 1,265, 1,260; b. marginal revenue: 2.70, 2.50, 2.30, 2.10, 0.40, 0.20, 0, −0.20; elasticity of demand: 19, 11, 7.57, 5.67, 1.2, 1.1, 1.0, 0.9; c. 2.50, 500; e. (1) 2.50, 500; (2) 2.50, 500, they have decreased; (3) 2.50, 500, they have increased

2. a. marginal cost: $30, 20, 30, 40, 50, 60, 70, 80; marginal revenue: $130, 110, 90, 70, 50, 30, 10, −10; b. $90; c. (1) 5; (2) $280; d. (1) 15; (2) $840; e. no; f. $90

3. a. $3, $2, $2; b. (1) would not, its profits would decrease; (2) would not, its profits would decrease; (3) would, this would prevent an even larger decrease in its profits; (4) would not, its profits would decrease; c. (1) $4, $49; (2) $4, $50; (3) $99

Self-test

1. T; 2. F; 3. F; 4. T; 5. F; 6. F; 7. T; 8. T; 9. F; 10. T

1. c; 2. d; 3. c; 4. c; 5. d; 6. a; 7. b; 8. c; 9. d; 10. d

CHAPTER 30

Fill-in questions

1. resources, incomes, costs

2. derived, productivity of the resource, value of the product produced from the resource

3. marginal revenue product, marginal resource cost; price, marginal resource cost

4. marginal revenue product, quantities, prices

5. lower, less

6. 15.00, 27, 5.00, 20, 6.00

7. adding up the demand curves for the resource of all the firms hiring the resource

8. product, productivity, prices

9. a. +; b. −; c. +; d. +; e. +

10. more, less, substitution, more, output

11. marginal physical product, substituted, elasticity of demand, portion of total production costs accounted for by the resource

12. marginal revenue product, price

13. marginal physical product, price

14. one

15. a. marginal revenue product, marginal resource cost, marginal revenue product, marginal resource cost, one; b. marginal physical product, marginal resource cost

Problems and projects

1. a. marginal physical product of A: 12, 10, 8,

6, 4, 2, 1; *b.* total revenue: 0, 18.00, 33.00, 45.00, 54.00, 60.00, 63.00, 64.50; marginal revenue product of A: 18.00, 15.00, 12.00, 9.00, 6.00, 3.00, 1.50; *c.* 0, 1, 2, 3, 4, 5, 6, 7

2. *a.* total product: 0, 22, 43, 62, 78, 90, 97, 98; *b.* (1) total revenue: 0, 22.00, 38.70, 49.60, 54.60, 54.00, 48.50, 39.20; (2) marginal revenue product of B: 22.00, 16.70, 10.90, 5.00, −0.60, −5.50, −9.30; *c.* 0, 1, 2, 3, 4, 4

CHAPTER 31

Fill-in questions

1. unit of time, the wage rate multiplied by the amount of time worked; the goods and services money wages will purchase

2. capital equipment, natural resources, technological, work

3. it is necessary for employers to pay higher wages to attract workers from alternative employment; total quantity of labor demanded, total quantity of labor supplied; marginal-revenue-product schedules for labor

4. perfectly, an individual employer is unable to affect the market wage rate

5. marginal revenue product, wage rate, marginal labor cost

6. marginal revenue product, marginal labor cost; marginal labor cost, the wage rate, the marginal revenue product of labor, marginal labor cost

7. lower, less

8. increase wages, increasing the demand for labor, restricting the supply of labor, imposing above-equilibrium wage rates on employers

9. restricting the supply of labor, imposing above-equilibrium wage rates, decreased

10. marginal revenue product of labor, competitive and monopsonistic equilibrium wage, the relative bargaining strength of the union and monopsonist

11. *a.* increase, decrease; *b.* increase, increase; *c.* increase, decrease

12. increase, decrease, leave uneffected

3. *a.* (1) 1, 3; (2) 3, 5; *b.* 5, 6; *c.* the marginal physical product of C divided by its price, the marginal physical product of D divided by its price; *d.* purely, $.50; *e.* (1) 114; (2) $57; (3) $28; (4) $29

Self-test

1. T; **2.** F; **3.** T; **4.** T; **5.** T; **6.** F; **7.** F; **8.** T

1. *c*; **2.** *c*; **3.** *a*; **4.** *c*; **5.** *c*; **6.** *c*; **7.** *d*; **8.** *a*

13. homogeneous, attractiveness, imperfect

14. noncompeting, equalizing differences, they must be paid to compensate workers for the nonmonetary differences or unattractive aspects of various jobs

15. immobilities, geographical, sociological, artificial-institutional

16. *a.* education, health, mobility; *b.* productivity, wage rates (income); *c.* real wages; *d.* groups

Problems and projects

1. *a.* quantity of labor demanded: 100, 200, 300, 400, 500, 600, 700, 800; *b.* (1) 10.00; (2) 600; *c.* (1) 10.00; (2) 6; (3) 10.00; *f.* 400

2. *a.* total labor cost: 0, 4.00, 12.00, 24.00, 40.00, 60.00, 84.00, 112.00, 144.00; marginal labor cost: 4.00, 8.00, 12.00, 16.00, 20.00, 24.00, 28.00, 32.00; *b.* (1) 5; (2) 12.00; (3) 20.00; *d.* 6, 14.00

3. *a.* wage rate: 16.00, 16.00, 16.00, 16.00, 16.00, 16.00, 16.00, 18.00; *b.* total labor cost: 16.00, 32.00, 48.00, 64.00, 80.00, 96.00, 112.00, 144.00; marginal labor cost: 16.00, 16.00, 16.00, 16.00, 16.00, 16.00, 16.00, 32.00; *c.* (1) 6; (2) 16.00; (3) 96.00; *d.* increased, increased, increased

Self-test

1. F; **2.** T; **3.** T; **4.** F; **5.** T; **6.** F; **7.** T; **8.** T; **9.** T; **10.** T

1. *a*; **2.** *c*; **3.** *d*; **4.** *d*; **5.** *d*; **6.** *a*; **7.** *a*; **8.** *a*; **9.** *b*; **10** *d*

CHAPTER 32

Fill-in questions

1. land, natural resources, fixed (perfectly inelastic)

2. demand, supply, incentive, surplus

3. unearned, confiscated, the single tax

4. land differs in productivity (quality), individual, alternative uses

5. money, loanable funds, they can use them to purchase capital goods

6. risk, the length of loan, the amount of the loan, market imperfections

7. business firms, the expected net return from the purchase of capital

8. negative, inelastic

9. current, past, households, business firms, newly created, commercial banks, government

10. transactions, precautionary, speculative

11. administered, investment, rations

12. entrepreneurial ability, resources, non-routine decisions, innovating, uncertain

13. uncertain, insurable, uninsurable, economy as a whole, innovation

14. *a.* investment, employment, output; *b.* allocation, monopoly

15. *a.* 80; *b.* rent, interest, corporate profit, 20; *c.* (1) remained constant, (2) remained constant

16. *a.* profits; *b.* productivity, the prices of the products they produce; *c.* labor's share of the national income

Problems and projects

1. *a.* 250.00; *b.* 300,000; *d.* 0, 300,000

2. *a.* −; *b.* ?; *c.* ?; *d.* −; *e.* +; *f.* +; *g.* +; *h.* +

Self-test

1. F; **2.** T; **3.** T; **4.** T; **5.** T; **6.** F; **7.** T; **8.** T; **9.** F; **10.** F

1. *a;* **2.** *d;* **3.** *b;* **4.** *c;* **5.** *d;* **6.** *b;* **7.** *c;* **8.** *d*

CHAPTER 33

Fill-in questions

1. particular, interrelationships

2. *a.* the resources used to produce Z; *b.* other products which use these same resources; *c.* products which are substitutes for or complements to product Z; *d.* resources which are substitutes for the resources used to produce Z and other products

3. equilibrium, product, resource

4. tastes, availability of resources, technology

5. downward, upward; *a.* (1) diminishing marginal utility, (2) diminishing marginal productivity; *b.* (1) increasing marginal cost, (2) work-leisure preferences and increasing marginal cost

6. *a.* increase, decrease; *b.* P, Q; *c.* increase, decrease; *d.* C, D

7. *a.* P, Q; *b.* increase, decrease; *c.* increase, decrease; *d.* C, D; *e.* increase, decrease

8. *a.* substitutes, complements; *b.* increase, decrease; *c.* Q, P

9. maximizes the satisfaction of the wants; *a.* price, marginal cost; *b.* minimum; *c.* the same

10. imperfectly, less than ideal, incomplete, slow

11. technological progress, product variety

12. *a.* spillover costs, spillover benefits, social goods; *b.* distribution, income

13. producing, consuming (using), output, input

14. 7.5

15. performance of the economy, economic problems, economic policies

Problems and projects

2. *a.* From left to right: 75, 0, 75, 10, 400; *b.* 25; *c.* (1) $37\frac{1}{2}$; (2) 15; (3) $8\frac{3}{4}$; (4) 35; *d.* (1) 8.8; (2) 13.6; (3) 2.9; (4) 8.97; *e.* each sector will have to increase its inputs in order to increase its output, and this will require still further increases in the outputs of the various sectors

Self-test

1. F; **2.** T; **3.** T; **4.** F; **5.** T; **6.** T; **7.** T; **8.** F; **9.** F; **10.** T

1. *c;* **2.** *b;* **3.** *c;* **4.** *a;* **5.** *d;* **6.** *d;* **7.** *c;* **8.** *a;* **9.** *c;* **10.** *c;* **11.** *d;* **12.** *a*

CHAPTER 34

Fill-in questions

1. small number of, all or a large portion, major, relative, absolute

2. workable, economies of mass production, high rate, investment, pricing, social responsibility

3. *a.* pervasive competition; *b.* interproduct competition; *c.* innovative competition; *d.* countervailing power; *e.* potential competition

4. *a.* technological imperatives, capital, technology, planning; *b.* security, stability, vertically, internally, advertising, salesmanship, government

5. restrict, charge higher, misallocate, greater inequality, slow rate, instability, political

6. competition, monopoly

7. natural, agencies, commissions

8. monopoly, restraint of trade

9. price discrimination, tying contracts, acquisition of stock of competing corporations to lessen competition, interlocking directorates

10. investigate unfair competitive practices, public hearing on such complaints, "cease and desist" orders, the courts, interpret the meaning of antitrust laws

11. Celler-Kefauver Antimerger, Clayton

12. Wheeler-Lea, Robinson-Patman, price discounts

13. conglomerate, other industries

14. exempts, patients, protective tariffs

15. Webb-Pomerene, Miller-Tydings; labor unions, agricultural cooperatives

16. patent laws, protective tariffs

17. *a.* maintenance of the status quo; *b.* move toward public regulation and ownership; *c.* restore vigorous competition

18. no individual firm possess considerable market power, collusion, entry into markets is relatively unrestricted.

Problems and projects

CHAPTER 35

Fill-in questions

1. *a.* prosperity; *b.* prosperity; *c.* depression; *d.* prosperity; *e.* depression

2. less, highly unequal

3. falling farm prices and incomes over the years, extreme year-to-year fluctuations in farm prices and incomes

4. inelastic demand for agricultural products, the fact that the supply of agricultural products has tended to increase more rapidly than the demand for these products, the relative immobility of agricultural resources

5. farm products have few good substitutes

6. technological advances in the production of agricultural products

7. the increase in the size of the American population has not been rapid enough; as the income of Americans has increased, their expenditures for farm products have not increased proportionately

8. immobile

9. inelastic, small, large, small, large

10. resources, agriculture, the nonagricultural sectors of the economy

11. *a.* cost, economic growth; *b.* purely competitive, price

12. *a.* prices, incomes, output; *b.* soil conservation; *c.* agricultural research; *d.* farm credit; *e.* crop insurance; raise farm incomes by raising the prices of farm products

1. G; 2. C; 3. I; 4. A; 5. E; 6. F; 7. D; 8. B; 9. H

Self-test

1. F; 2. F; 3. T; 4. F; 5. F; 6. T; 7. F; 8. F; 9. T; 10. F

1. *d*; 2. *b*; 3. *c*; 4. *a*; 5. *a*; 6. *b*; 7. *b*; 8. *d*; 9. *c*; 10. *b*

13. given, a fixed amount of goods and services

14. surpluses, purchase

15. increase, decrease

16. acreage-allotment, acreage-reserve; new uses, domestic consumption, export

17. reallocated, already have high incomes

18. *a.* increased foreign demand; *b.* poor harvests abroad; *c.* devaluation of the dollar; *d.* the opening of markets in Communist countries; *e.* increases in incomes in the United States

19. prices, capacity, reserves (stockpiles), income

20. decrease, Agriculture and Consumer Protection, target, 20,000

Problems and projects

1. .42, .70

2. *a.* inelastic; *b.* decrease, 1,200.00, 700.00, 16⅔, decrease, 41⅔; *c.* fall, 1.00, 0.80, fall, 700.00, 560.00; *d.* 100, 180.00; *e.* (1) 0.80, 1.00; (2) 720.00; (3) greater, disposing of a surplus; (4) inelastic

3. *a.* increase, 153,750.00, 200,000.00; *b.* increase, 153,750.00, 205,000.00

Self-test

1. T; 2. T; 3. F; 4. T; 5. F; 6. T; 7. F; 8. F; 9. T; 10. T

1. *c*; 2. *d*; 3. *a*; 4. *c*; 5. *d*; 6. *c*; 7. *b*; 8. *c*; 9. *a*; 10. *b*

CHAPTER 36

Fill-in questions

1. 150, 75, increase

2. where, transport, resources, buyers

3. surplus, labor

4. near each other and their markets; *a.* internal economies of scale; *b.* locational (transport) economics; *c.* urban economies

5. higher, internal, external, society, spillover

6. the advantages and opportunities of a metropolitan area, the disadvantages, fragmentation, imbalance

7. *a.* property, base, rates; *b.* large, welfare, densely, high

8. *a.* jobs; *b.* transportation; *c.* highways, congestion, pollution; *d.* highways, suburbs, automobiles, highways; *e.* public mass transit

9. *a.* user charge, peak-pricing; *b.* public mass-transit systems

10. weight, wastes, nature (the ecological system), absorb (reabsorb or recycle), population, per capita income, technology, incentives

11. *a.* prosperous, trained and educated, suburbs, buildings; *b.* educated, low, South; *c.* central city, suburbs, mass transit, discrimination

12. jobs, education, training, maintenance

13. public mass-transit system, Black capitalism

14. consolidation, revenues

15. decision, needs, means

16. sharing, the Federal government, property, land, buildings

Problems and projects

1. 300, 15, 30, 10, 510, 30, 5; *a.* 1,800, 900; *b.* $.50; *c.* $.50; *d.* (1) 810, (2) Total revenue:

CHAPTER 37

Fill-in questions

1. considerable

2. native abilities; education, training, and opportunity; market power; property resources; misfortune

3. decreased, significant, has not changed significantly

4. *a.* after-tax, before-tax; *b.* mobility

5. consumer satisfaction, occupational opportunities, productivity, social and political

6. a high volume of saving; incentives to work, produce, and innovate; the incomes necessary to bring forth improved products and cultural advances

7. *a.* $4,275; $2,207; *b.* 12, 25

8. *a.* the aged; *b.* farmers; *c.* children; *d.* families headed by women; *e.* the unhealthy; *f.* the unemployed; *g.* the poorly educated and trained; *h.* nonwhites

9. 62, racial discrimination; *a.* wage discrimination; *b.* employment discrimination; *c.* occupational discrimination; *d.* human-capital discrimination

10. *a.* much of it is isolated and unseen in the hearts of large cities; *b.* the sick and old seldom venture onto the streets; *c.* rural poverty is away from the main highways; *d.* the poor have no political voice

CHAPTER 38

Fill-in questions

1. 19, 25

2. of the attitude of the courts, the resistance of employers to recognizing and bargaining with unions

3. criminal conspiracy, injunctions

4. discriminatory discharge, blacklisting, lockout, strikebreakers, yellow-dog contracts, paternalism, company unions

225, 67.50, 90, 45, 270, 90, 22.50; 810, (3) 7am–9am, 4pm–6pm; *e.* (1) 55, (2) 64

2. *a.* 4,000, 2,500; *b.* 5,000; *c.* 7,500,000; *d.* 1,000, 1,500,000

3. *a.* grossly inadequate; *b.* high; *c.* low; *d.* inadequate; *e.* old, deteriorated, crowded; *f.* high; *g.* deplorable; *h.* high

Self-test

1. T; **2.** T; **3.** T; **4.** F; **5.** F; **6.** F; **7.** F; **8.** T; **9.** T; **10.** F

1. *b*; **2.** *c*; **3.** *a*; **4.** *a*; **5.** *d*; **6.** *d*; **7.** *a*; **8.** *c*; **9.** *b*; **10.** *c*

11. the fault of the individual, social forces

12. old age, survivors, disability and health; unemployment; public assistance

13. least, most

14. opportunities, education (training), skills

15. minimum income, negative income

Problems and projects

1. *a.* (1) column 4: 18, 30, 44, 61, 80, 91, 100; (2) column 5: 4, 10, 22, 36, 51, 71, 100; *b.* (1) 30, 10; (2) 20, 49

2. *a.* 5,000, 4,000, 3,000, 2,000, 1,000, 0; *b.* Income subsidy: 3,000, 2,400, 1,800, 1,200, 600, 0; Total income: 3,000, 3,400, 3,800, 4,200, 4,600, 5,000; *c.* 600, 400; *d.* 5,000; *e.* Income subsidy: 5,000, 4,000 3,000, 2,000, 1,000, 0; 1,000, 0; *f.* (1) 8,333⅓, 7,333⅓, 6,333⅓, 5,333⅓, 4,333⅓, 3,333⅓; (2) Income subsidy: 5,000, 4,400, 3,800, 3,200, 2,600, 2,000; Total income: 5,000, 5,400, 5,800, 6,200, 6,600, 7,000; (3) 600, 400; (4) 5,000, 0

Self-test

1. T; **2.** T; **3.** T; **4.** F; **5.** T; **6.** T; **7.** T; **8.** F; **9.** T; **10.** F

1. *d*; **2.** *b*; **3.** *c*; **4.** *d*; **5.** *c*; **6.** *a*; **7.** *b*; **8.** *d*; **9.** *c*; **10.** *d*

5. business unionism, political neutrality, craft unionism

6. Norris-La Guardia, Wagner; CIO, industrial, unskilled mass-production

7. organize, bargain collectively; National Labor Relations Board, unfair labor practices of management

8. Taft-Hartley, Landrum-Griffin, merger of the AFL and the CIO, static (constant), stagnation, public

9. *a.* provisions which designate and outlaw certain "unfair union practices"; *b.* provisions which regulate the internal administration of unions; *c.* provisions which specify collective bargaining procedures and regulate the actual contents of bargaining agreements; *d.* provisions for the handling of strikes which threaten to imperil the health and safety of the nation

10. elections, finances, union members, union officers

11. *a.* the degree of recognition and status accorded the union and the prerogatives of management; *b.* wages and hours; *c.* seniority and job opportunities; *d.* a procedure for settling grievances

12. what are others getting, productivity, ability to pay, cost of living

13. status, security, administering, interpreting

14. increased; *a.* greater opportunities; *b.* increased education; *c.* smaller family size; *d.* increased working life; *e.* the substitution of capital for labor at home.

15. 60, discrimination, justifiable disparities

Problems and projects

1. 1. K; 2. D; 3. Q; 4. E; 5. O; 6. G; 7. A; 8. C; 9. F; 10. J

2. *a.* C; *b.* B; *c.* B; *d.* A; *e.* D; *f.* C; *g.* C; *h.* B

Self-test

1. F; 2. F; 3. F; 4. T; 5. F; 6. F; 7. T; 8. T; 9. T; 10. T

1. *b*; 2. *b*; 3. *d*; 4. *a*; 5. *a*; 6. *d*; 7. *b*; 8. *b*; 9. *c*; 10. *b*

CHAPTER 39

Fill-in questions

1. 76, 6

2. civilian goods and services

3. *a.* the Federal government budget, the sale of products in the market; *b.* nonprofit, profit; *c.* rival military establishments in other nations

4. *a.* defense budget; *b.* central-management, subsidiaries, expand its size; *c.* cost, progress payments, patent

5. distributes, less, occupational choice

6. monetary cost, professional mercenaries

7. taxes, demand-pull, borrowing, money

8. instability

9. civilian goods and services, military goods and services

10. decrease, increase, easy

11. *a.* military, civilian; *b.* spillover; *c.* private, inevitable; *d.* fiscal, monetary; *e.* conflict, development

12. national priorities, civilian, military

Problems and projects

1. *a.* 8, 0; *b.* 7, 100; *c.* 300; *d.* 200

Self-test

1. F; 2. F; 3. F; 4. T; 5. F; 6. T; 7. T; 8. F; 9. T; 10. F

1. *a*; 2. *a*; 3. *a*; 4. *c*; 5. *a*; 6. *d*; 7. *d*; 8. *b*; 9. *a*; 10. *c*

CHAPTER 40

Fill-in questions

1. nature; *a.* other men; *b.* capitalists, bourgeois, workers, proletariat

2. private property, machinery, equipment, employment (a livelihood), profit, surplus value, exploit, wage

3. competition, profits (surplus value) machinery, equipment, national output, capital, labor, profits

4. exploitation

5. *a.* monopolization; *b.* imperialism

6. revolution, proletariate, capital, capitalistic, socialist

7. *a.* harmony, conflict; *b.* narrow, problems, political power

8. *a.* large, monopolistic, state (government), markets, workers, consumers; *b.* inequality, alienation, irrational, imperialism; *c.* socialism

9. *a.* It fails to control monopolies; *b.* It uses revenues from regressive taxes to subsidize them; *c.* It provides markets for them

10. marginal product, national income; *a.* competitive; *b.* labor; *c.* unearned

11. institutions, private property, power, power

12. *a.* lives, decision, making; *b.* large corporations

13. *a.* profit; *b.* environment, wants, military, imperialistic

14. socialism, democratic, decent, human, profit

15. objective, reality, ideology, option

Problems and projects

1. *a.* 8, 7, 6, 5, 4, 3, 2; *b.* 5; *c.* 20; *d.* 30, 10; *e.* 6; *f.* 2

2. *a.* 400; 394, 388.6; *b.* 70, 69, 68; *c.* 120,

118, 116.6; *d.* (1) 380, 386, 392.4, (2) .316, .306, .297; *e.* (1) decreases, increases, (2) decreases

Self-test

CHAPTER 41

Fill-in questions

1. less mobile, money, restrictions

2. 4, 82, 83

3. machinery, automobiles and tractors, chemicals; autos and parts; petroleum and products, electrical machinery

4. comparative advantage, comparative disadvantage

5. more output, inputs (resources); resources, uneven, different combination of resources

6. *a.* inexpensive, expensive; *b.* expensive, inexpensive; *c.* hats, bananas; *d.* 3, 4, world demand and supply for hats and bananas; *e.* (1) ⅓, ⅔, (2) 4, 3½

7. cost, increases

8. *a.* efficient; *b.* prices; *c.* resource

9. *a.* exports, imports; *b.* directly, total income; *c.* directly, its own total income (or net national product)

10. *a.* net exports; *b.* aggregate demand; *c.* save, import

11. national income (or net national product), imports

12. *a.* −; *b.* +; *c.* +; *d.* −

CHAPTER 42

Fill-in questions

1. a better allocation of resources, a higher standard of living

2. tariffs, import quotas, protect special interest groups, attemp to increase net exports, protect domestic producers of essential war goods, industrialize and diversify their economies

3. *a.* increase; *b.* decrease; *c.* (1) increase, (2) decrease; *d.* decrease, decrease

4. *a.* military self-sufficiency; *b.* infant industry; *c.* increase domestic employment; *d.* diversification for stability; *e.* protect high wages and the high standard of living; *f.* slow down the diffusion of technology

5. upward, Reciprocal Trade Agreements, downward; lower tariff rates up to 50 % in return for a reduction of foreign restrictions on American goods, most-favored-nation clauses

6. *a* equal, nondiscriminatory treatment of all trading nations; *b.* reduction of tariffs by negotiation; *c.* elimination of import quotas

1. F; **2.** T; **3.** T; **4.** F; **5.** F; **6.** F; **7.** T; **8.** T; **9.** T; **10.** F; **11.** T; **12.** F; **13.** T; **14.** F; **15.** F; **16.** T; **17.** F; **18.** T

1. *b;* **2.** *d;* **3.** *a;* **4.** *c;* **5.** *d;* **6.** *a;* **7.** *c;* **8.** *d;* **9.** *d;* **10.** *b;* **11.** *d;* **12.** *c;* **13.** *b;* **14.** *a;* **15.** *d*

Problems and projects

1. *a.* constant; *b.* (1) 8, 2, (2) 4, 2; *c.* (1) it has a comparative advantage in producing wheat (its cost of producing wheat is less than Chile's), (2) it has a comparative advantage in producing copper (its cost of producing copper is less than the United States); *d.* one of the two nations would be unwilling to trade if the terms of trade are outside this range; *f.* (1) 1, 0, (2) 1, 0

2. *a.* (1) increase, decrease, (2) decrease, increase; *b.* (1) rise, fall, equal, (2) fall, rise, equal; *c.* (1) increase, decrease, (2) decrease, increase; *d.* (1) rise, fall, they are the same as the prices for these resources in the United States, (2) fall, rise, they are the same as the prices for these resources in France; *e.* (1) chicken, wine, (2) wine, chicken

3. *a.* $16, 12, 8, 4, 0, −4, −8; *b.* $792, 828, 864, 900, 936, 972, 1,008; *c.* $900; *d.* 0.08; *e.* 3.57; *f.* (1) increase, $35.7, (2) decrease, $35.7

Self-test

1. T; **2.** F; **3.** T; **4.** F; **5.** F; **6.** T; **7.** T; **8.** T; **9.** T; **10.** F

1. *a;* **2.** *b;* **3.** *d;* **4.** *a;* **5.** *a;* **6.** *a;* **7.** *b;* **8.** *b*

7. tariffs and import quotas among members, common tariffs on goods imported from nonmembers, capital and labor among member nations, other matters, growth, trade, allocation of resources, economies of scale

8. lower or eliminate tariffs on products where the United States and the Common Market have 80% or more of the world's trade, lower tariffs on other goods up to 50 % over five years; Kennedy Round

9. nontariff

10. communist; *a.* the easing of the political climate; *b.* the growing interest of the USSR in American products; *c.* recognition that the restrictionist American policy was unrealistic and a failure

11. foreign, exports, unemployment

12. foods, raw materials, shortages, prices

Problems and projects

a. 750, 700, 650, 600, 550, 500, 450, 300, 0;

b. $2.00, 600; *c.* 375, 350, 325, 300, 0, 0, 0, 0, 0; *d.* 650, 600, 550, 500, 175, 150, 125, 0, 0; *e.* $2.20, 550; *f.* (1) increased, 25, (2) decreased, 75; *g.* (1) increased, $95, (2) decreased, $345; *h.* increased, $10; *i.* increased, $260; *j.* decreased, $345, decrease, $345

Self-test

1. T; **2.** F; **3.** T; **4.** T; **5.** F; **6.** T; **7.** T; **8.** F; **9.** F; **10.** T

1. c; **2.** a; **3.** d; **4.** a; **5.** d; **6.** c; **7.** d; **8.** c; **9.** d. **10.** a

CHAPTER 43

Fill-in questions

1. dollars, one French franc

2. 2½

3. imports, exports, exports, imports

4. increase, decrease, increase, decreases

5. *a.* exports of goods and services *b.* imports of goods and services; *c.* net balance due on exports and imports; *d.* net remittances; *e.* net government transactions; *f.* net capital movements; *g.* balance due to or from rest of world; *h.* financing (balancing) transactions

6. goods, services, and the services of money capital; surplus

7. loans, investments, gold, foreign money

8. inpayments (outpayments), outpayments (inpayments), gold, foreign money, decreases (increases)

9. surplus, deficit

10. gives, loans, invests

11. gold, foreign money, its own money owned by foreigners, autonomous

12. freely fluctuating foreign exchange rates, changing price and income levels, public controls

13. increase, decrease, decrease, increase

14. risks, reduce, terms of trade, prices, output

15. defines its monetary unit in terms of gold and will buy and sell gold at the rate set down

in its definition of the monetary unit, allows gold to be exported and imported freely

16. the gold equivalent of monetary units, the cost of transporting gold; gold export point, gold import point

17. *a.* decrease; *b.* less, more; *c.* decrease, increase; *d.* decreases, increases

18. stable exchange rates, price levels, outputs, levels of employment

19. legally establishes, imports, exports, ration, prices, national output (or employment)

20. tariffs, quotas, subsidizing

Problems and projects

1. *a.* (1) +47.9, (2) −39.1, (3) −7.2, (4) +4.6; *b.* (reading down) +47.9, +32.5, +8.1, +7.3, −39.1, −31.1, −6.2, −1.8, +8.8, −1.5, −4.7, −7.2, −10.2, +3.0, −4.6, +0.7, +3.9; *c.* deficit, 4.6; *d.* +4.6, −4.6

2. ½, ⅖, ⅓, 2/7, ¼, 2/9, ⅕, lower

3. *a.* 5.00, ⅕; *b.* 5.03, 4.97; *c.* 0.201, 0.199

4. *a.* 4.00; *b.* ¼; *c.* 300; *d.* 1,200; *e.* (1) 2/9, (2) 160

Self-test

1. T; **2.** F; **3.** F; **4.** F; **5.** F; **6.** T; **7.** F; **8.** T; **9.** T; **10.** F

1. c; **2.** b; **3.** d; **4.** c; **5.** b; **6.** d; **7.** b; **8.** c; **9.** a; **10.** d

CHAPTER 44

Fill-in questions

1. large, raw materials, underdeveloped, manufactured goods, manufacturing nations, comparative advantage, laissez faire, gold standard

2. depression, war, cold war; exports, capital flows, trade barriers

3. imports, exports, balance of payments; inflation, productive capacities

4. *a.* political objectives have been placed above economic objectives; *b.* nationalistic tendencies and the pursuit of domestic stability often conflict with the rebuilding of international trade; *c.* the underdeveloped countries have restricted trade in order to industrialize and diversify their economies

5. assist European recovery, create an international monetary system, reduce trade barriers

6. rebuild the European economies; the United Nations Relief and Rehabilitation Administration, European Recovery

7. stable, adjustable peg

8. gold, key currencies, the American dollar, the British pound

9. international monetary reserves, more, international trade

10. seldom changed

11. *a.* productivity, inflation; *b.* outflows, military and economic aid expenditures

12. *a.* increasing the productivity of American firms; *b.* using monetary and fiscal policies to restrain domestic inflation; *c.* getting Western Europe to assume a larger share of the costs of mutual defense and economic aid to underdeveloped nations; *d.* obtaining the reduction or elimination of the foreign restrictions on the import of American goods; *e.* devaluing the dollar

13. imports, exports, international trade, retaliate

14. *a.* international monetary reserves; *b.* exchange-rate pegs

15. *a.* increase the dollar price of gold (devalue the dollar); *b.* have nations manage international reserves, return to freely fluctuating foreign exchange rates

16. Triffin, Special Drawing Rights (SDRs)

17. gold, demand and supply

18. *a.* over-; *b.* widened

19. devalued, gold, managed floating

20. crawling, gold, dollars

Problems and projects

1. 1. F; 2. L; 3. J; 4. A; 5. H; 6. I; 7. D; 8. K; 9. E; 10. B; 11. G

2. *a.* (1) contractionary, tight, (2) (*a*) increase, (*b*) decrease, (*c*) rise, into, (*d*) decrease, (3) reduce, (4) (*a*)exports, (*b*) imports, (*c*) interest, capital, (*d*) widened; *b.* (1) expansionary, easy, (2) (*a*) decrease, (*b*) increase, (*c*) fall, out of, (*d*) increase, (3) widen, (4) narrowed; *c.* (1) are compatible, conflict, (2) conflict, are compatible

Self-test

1. F; **2.** F; **3.** F; **4.** T; **5.** T; **6.** T; **7.** T; **8.** F; **9.** F; **10.** T; **11.** F; **12.** T; **13.** T; **14.** T; **15.** F; **16.** F

1. *b*; **2.** *c*; **3.** *d*; **4.** *c*; **5.** *d*; **6.** *d*; **7.** *c*; **8.** *d*; **9.** *a*; **10.** *b*; **11.** *b*; **12.** *b*; **13.** *d*; **14.** *a*; **15.** *c*; **16.** *a*; **17.** *d*; **18.** *c*; **19.** *c*; **20.** *d*

CHAPTER 45

Fill-in questions

1. state ownership of property resources, central economic planning

2. Soviet government, many small economic units

3. coordination, bottleneck, chain reaction

4. negotiation, priority, reserve stocks

5. Gosplan, Gosbank

6. monetary incentives, nonmonetary incentives, coercive techniques

7. as an accounting device for checking productive efficiency, as a means of rationing products among consumers

8. the efficiency of production, affect the allocation of resources

9. *a.* (1) unsalable, unwanted, (2) production, quality, (3) innovate; *b.* (1) profit motive, (2) decentralized planning, autonomy, (3) below; *c.* Professor E. Liberman

10. one-half, 5

11. *a.* the large natural resource base; *b.* the totalitarian government has allocated resources to promote growth; *c.* the surplus of farm labor; *d.* the employment of the superior technologies developed in Western nations; *e.* the absence of cyclical unemployment

12. *a.* the diversion of resources to consumer goods, foreign aid, and military goods; *b.* increasing replacement investment; *c.* the closing of the technological gap between Soviet and Western methods of production; *d.* a manpower shortage; *e.* the backwardness of Soviet agricul-

ture; *f.* the increasing complexity of economic planning as the economy grows

13. *a.* the large annual increases in GNP available for consumer goods, foreign aid, and military goods; *b.* improvements in education and technology promise to make the economy more productive; *c.* possible improvements in planning techniques; *d.* the ability of the Soviet Union to force economic growth

14. *a.* the increased quantity and quality of education; *b.* the development of a complete system of social insurance

15. the failure of the consumer's standard of living to increase by as much as is possible; the limited freedom of Soviet citizens

Problems and projects

1. state ownership of property resources; relative consumer freedom to spend income as he sees fit; central economic planning; workers are generally free to choose occupation and place of work; central economic planning and various forms of incentives; central economic planning; central economic planning with prices playing an implemental role; central economic planning and various forms of inventives which appeal to self-interest; state and collective farms; state-owned and cooperative firms and retail stores

2. *a.* 40; *b.* 60

Self-test

1. T; **2.** T; **3.** T; **4.** F; **5.** F; **6.** F; **7.** T; **8.** F; **9.** T; **10.** F

1. *b*; **2.** *d*; **3.** *b*; **4.** *a*; **5.** *b*; **6.** *b*; **7.** *b*; **8.** *d*; **9.** *a*; **10.** *b*